D1570022

Advance Praise for

DISSIDENT KNOWLEDGE IN HIGHER EDUCATION

"The space for dissent and real democratic debate is quickly shrinking both in public life and academic institutions in western democracies. Today, the cries of 'fake news' make the loudest (though rarely the best informed) voices the site of authority and truth. This volume helps readers in higher education ask critical and conscious questions about what it means to contend for truth. It is an important and significant read for those who want the intellectual space to remain a terrain for thinkers."

—Gloria Ladson-Billings, author of *The Dreamkeepers*

"This deep and layered book maps the path toward a university based on ethics and justice rather than corporate needs and military standards. It reaches anyone who wants to understand the social, political, and economic trends that define our times. It is an outstanding contribution to the scholarship on higher education."

—William Ayers, author of *Teaching with Conscience in an Imperfect World*

"*Dissident Knowledge in Higher Education* is a rich and multi-layered examination of the impact of corporatization on our universities, as well as how they can be reclaimed. Highly recommended."

—James Turk, editor of *Academic Freedom in Conflict*

DISSIDENT KNOWLEDGE IN HIGHER EDUCATION

EDITED WITH AN INTRODUCTION BY
MARC SPOONER
& JAMES McNINCH

University of Regina Press

Printed and bound in Canada at Marquis. The text of this book is printed on 100% post-consumer recycled paper with earth-friendly vegetable-based inks.

Cover design: Duncan Campbell, University of Regina Press
Text design: John van der Woude, JVDW Designs
Copy editor: Kirsten Craven
Proofreader: Nadine Coderre
Indexer: Sergey Lobachev, Brookfield Indexing Services
Cover art: "Apple Core" by Barcin / iStockphoto.

Library and Archives Canada Cataloguing in Publication

Dissident knowledge in higher education / edited with an introduction by Marc Spooner & James McNinch.

Includes bibliographical references and index. Issued in print and electronic formats.
ISBN 978-0-88977-536-7 (softcover).—ISBN 978-0-88977-537-4 (PDF).—ISBN 978-0-88977-538-1 (HTML)

1. Education, Higher. 2. Educational change. 3. Neoliberalism. I. Spooner, Marc, 1969-, editor II. McNinch, James, 1947-, editor

LB2322.2.D57 2018   378   C2017-907936-0   C2017-907937-9

10 9 8 7 6 5 4 3 2 1

University of Regina Press, University of Regina
Regina, Saskatchewan, Canada, S4S 0A2
tel: (306) 585-4758 fax: (306) 585-4699
U OF R PRESS web: www.uofrpress.ca

We acknowledge the support of the Canada Council for the Arts for our publishing program. We acknowledge the financial support of the Government of Canada. / Nous reconnaissons l'appui financier du gouvernement du Canada. This publication was made possible with support from Creative Saskatchewan's Creative Industries Production Grant Program.

We dedicate this collection to, in the words of Martin Luther King Jr., all the "creatively maladjusted" who are working toward justice within and beyond the academy. This collection is devoted to all your efforts in resisting colonialism, neoliberalism, and audit culture locally and globally.

Truly, I live in dark times!
The guileless word is folly. A smooth forehead
Suggests insensitivity. The man who laughs
Has simply not yet had
The terrible news.

—Bertolt Brecht, from "To Those Born Later"

CONTENTS

THE TRUMP CARD: RACIALIZED SPEECH IN THE ERA OF DESPERATE WHITE SUPREMACY

Zeus Leonardo

I submitted this foreword to Marc Spooner and James McNinch on January 20, 2017, or "J20" to some, as President-Elect Trump was sworn in as the forty-fifth president of the United States amid nationwide protests. The world is in a state of crisis and the United States is no exception. If it is a leading nation of the world, it has not always earned that title for the right reasons. That is, many of the country's citizens question whether the United States is leading the world in the wrong direction. With the election of Donald Trump, the United States finds itself in a maelstrom of debates, deep insecurities, and divisions it was by and large surprised by and for which it was unprepared. Trump's election to "make America great again" reinvigorates the old Right found in white, working-class resentment and energizes an apparently new and alternative Right dressed in Banana Republic metrowear. The interesting word here is "again," a nostalgia or return to a past that can only be accomplished with naïveté, a time that harkens back to Jim Crow, Manifest Destiny, and when whites ruled this earth with an iron fist rather than a soft touch. Yet this is not the Klan, as satirized by popular comedian Dave Chappelle in the first episode of his celebrated *Chappelle's Show*. It is an alternative Right resulting in the confluence of new technologies, a newfound confidence, and a newbie politician-president it considers a card-carrying member of the club even if Trump disavows it. Kristen Buras's (2008, 2010) and Michael Apple's (Apple and Oliver 1998; Apple 2006) studies of the hegemonic process (applicable to the Right or Left) have never been more useful. This critical moment represents at once the conservative movement's triumphalist cry, as well as the Right's desperate move to recapture the "greatness" of that endangered empire known as the United States. It is indeed a dangerous moment in American history as part of overall global development, a new era trumpeted by United States conservatives whose discourse divides at the same time they profess to heal said divisions. To anyone observing, it is quite a trick or deception to throw both water and gas at the fire.

The American Right is not alone, of course. It is joined by Russian President Vladimir Putin, who would also like to make his nation great again, spurring a second Cold War fought in the trenches of the computer-hacking business. It also includes Philippines President Rodrigo Duterte, whose masculine bluster and death squad tactics against known and suspected drug dealers speak of secret desires to re-establish the archipelago's former economic status as one of Asia's best, that is, before Marcos stepped in. Although Trump has called the Philippines a terrorist nation and shows some caution in his dealings with Putin, all three leaders' Marlboro Man personae, albeit from radically different social contexts, are eerily compatible, cut from the same cloth, one might say. Of course, we should recall Margaret Thatcher, who, with Ronald Reagan's help, wanted to make Britain great again (see Hall 1996). But, just as a *New York Times* article states that oppositional books are more relevant in this antagonistic predicament (which would apply equally had Hillary Clinton won), this edited book's timing is impeccable and provides a resounding voice of dissent in a neoliberal, neomacho, and, to some, a neofascist condition. To Foucault's (1980) pleasure, power begets resistance (itself an expression of power), and it is comforting to see the Left organize against a strident and emboldened yet desperate Right.

The gender dynamics and consequences of the 2016 elections are clear. They make Jackson Katz's (2010) unrelenting study of masculinity more relevant than ever. Presidential masculinity is never not at play, which may go a long way to explain Hillary Clinton's twice-failed bid for the presidency. In 2008, the naturalized entitlement and perceived superiority of white masculinity suffered a devastating blow from the election of Barack Obama. The return of the literary conceit of "cuck," at once a reference to the cuckoo bird's habit of laying eggs in another bird's nest and a man cuckolded by his woman partner's infidelity, speaks to the felt emasculation of a conservative understanding of white masculinity that must now reclaim its proper place if the United States is to grow some hair on its global chest. Even new conservatism, under the likes of Mitt Romney or Marco Rubio, may be perceived as emasculating. As "cuckservatives," establishment Republicans are derided as effeminate politicians who do not possess the appropriate endowment to stem the tide of complaining Americans: those immigrants, feminists, and identitarians in general. To these true blue (red?) conservatives, it is time for the Right to "man up" and assert its manhood against what it considers the sorry Other, from Democrats to those without documents, to NATO and the New Left, and Muslims and Marxists. Enter Donald Trump, who succeeds in grabbing the Right's imagination and prides himself for not pussyfooting around.

The threats to education in President Trump's use of flagrant misogyny, racism, and xenophobia are already clear to some educational scholars. The Politics of Learning Writing Collective states,

> Trump's victory did not emerge in a social vacuum. These political and powered contestations have always been with us, but have been obscured by the dominant discourse that the nation was making adequate progress toward equity and justice. The mandate for Trump, which is inextricably tied into his rhetoric of hate and bigotry, shatters the illusion of incremental progress and the accompanying narratives of American exceptionalism. It has made visible the contemporary tensions and fissures in our nation, in unprecedented ways, to those outside of non-dominant communities. The hostility that characterized Trump's successful campaign did not require an electorate that was *actively* and *overtly* committed to hate and bigotry. It succeeded, in part, through indifference to contemporary inequities and injustices that were glaring if we looked below the surface. But indifference itself is a political stance—an action that in this election enabled racism, xenophobia, and misogyny to flourish. (Politics of Learning Writing Collective 2017)

Amid this threat to retreat from civil rights and democratic institutions, the university sits in the uncomfortable position of promoting cherished notions of academic freedom, freedom of speech, indeed freedom of thought within what I might call "desperate white supremacy." Trump's ascension represents, on one hand, a re-instalment of Rightist politics, a certain Reaganism on steroids (even the Ol' Gipper would not have been man enough), evidenced by the alliance among the white working class, libertarian nationalism, and populist authoritarianism. On the other hand, it is a sign of desperation on the Right that its best option invites such popular resistance not witnessed since the likes of former and stained President Nixon. The American Right found its inspiration in the "Dangerous Faggot Tour" of the inimitable Milo Yiannopoulos, whose national university campus tour of 2016–17 was filled with legally protected hate speech and threw into a frenzy his college Republican supporters, including my own campus of UC Berkeley. It is almost as if he wanted a public brawl in the campus square. And who can blame him when he courts the media in this day and age of conspicuous journalism that Herman and Chomsky (1993) describe so well in *Manufacturing Consent*? In other words, it is not without some sense of irony that "making America great again" has spawned such lowbrow, racialized, and macho speech that it would have made the comedian Andrew Dice Clay blush. Had Trump chosen Howard Stern as his secretary of state, it may not have surprised anyone that the shock-prez paired with the shock-jock.

Meanwhile, multiple defences of Yiannopoulos and media company Breitbart in the name of "free speech" have flooded blogs, emails, and social media. In tandem, critiques of liberal contradictions regarding playing both sides of the free speech fence (i.e., censoring speech that does not fall in line with its own values) follow predictably. This tactic does not come without difficulties for the progressive and radical Left, which pushes the limits of our understanding with respect to free speech that extend well beyond the lawlessness of yelling "fire" in a theatre. I will not speak overly about legal discourse on this issue but am interested in the thorny thicket of contradictions in which academics are now ensnared. It is striking that an in/resurgent Right relies on at the same time that it disavows what some have called neofascist tactics, in the technical and historical sense witnessed in the middle of twentieth-century regimes. For his own part, Yiannopoulos seems to rely on his "bad boy" intentions (at this point we can refer to intentions since he repeats them at different venues), reasonably captured as harassment and violence toward transgender people and women, to name a few of his target groups. After all, university settings are promoted as places where ideas are engaged and where free speech is valued, which makes them different from your run-of-the mill public square, such as Sproul Plaza and Sather Gate at UC Berkeley, where one can expect evangelical Christians to sermon passersby on any given day. On the other hand, course instructors' speech is protected even when provocative, justified as part of pedagogical process and encouraging students to deal with ideas opposing their own.

The limits of speech are not clear, even more so for invited guest speakers like Yiannopoulos. We also take into consideration that Title IX federal legislation protects women from harassment in the university and workplace. Yiannopoulos has been cited by multiple sources as involved in what amounts to a premeditated attack not only on groups but on an individual in the case of his visit to the University of Wisconsin, Milwaukee, where he mocked and ridiculed a transgender woman, flashed her/their photo on his PowerPoint presentation, and announced her/their name. If it were comedy, then we would at least have the luxury of knowing that it was all an act. But stakes are high, which is not funny. It seems Yiannopoulos and the Right want it both ways, acting like a spade and resenting being called one. It is like setting down roots in someone else's land, uprooting its people, and then objecting when it is characterized as the tragedy called colonialism. These are not trumped-up charges but theatre of another kind.

Trump supporters and dissenters agree on at least one thing: free speech is precious and not to be taken lightly. The university is one of the last places where open debate still takes place, so polarized the political sphere has become in the last couple decades. Although I have no desire to romanticize the images of Ronald Reagan sharing a drink with his Democratic opponents in the 1980s, the overall impression is that the two parties have become recalcitrant, fulfilling Reagan's own trickle-down theory whereby social division is palpable in the public's dialogue (or lack thereof). Obama attempted to mend those fences, amid criticisms that he could not stand up to opposition when it counted, by focusing on rational dialogue guided by a baseline understanding of certain facts, such as climate change, from where discussion could begin. This Herculean attempt was frustrated at every turn by a Republican Congress, as well as an anti-Black, bifurcated citizenry (young vs. old). As a result, it becomes increasingly harder to discern Obama's "legacy" as the first Black leader in the White House, other than the most obvious. That said, his ability to take the higher road and consistently dignified ways is admirable and will be missed. It is not a coincidence that his public presidentiality is replaced by an inexperienced, gruff, and, by many accounts, unpresidential president, the former's sense of class trumped by the latter's race. After eight years of an ambiguous veer to the Left lane under Obama, Trump and the nation take a hard Right. It lends support to the notion that Blacks have to be twice as good to get half as much. Equally, it is prima facie evidence that whites can be half as good and get twice as much.

To the new or alt-Right (in some respects, an "old" Right), free speech becomes the freedom to offend, harass, and threaten already targeted groups, such as Muslim and Mexican Americans. This overt or "traditional" racist language is quite different from, if not opposite to, what several social scientists from Bonilla-Silva (2006) to Bobo and Smith (1998) have called "colour-blind" or "laissez-faire" racism, whereby race is coded in apparently race-neutral, yet knowing-wink, rhetoric. It is adjacent to, but not the same as, "racialism" (Goldberg and Essed 2002) or raciology (Gilroy 2000), whereby previously biological notions of race give way to its cultural logic, such that Blacks are not biologically inferior to whites but make consistently bad choices as part of the former's cultural makeup. In fact, the shift from biological racism to cultural racism may be more recent for Blacks, but the re-education of Indigenous people was already a favoured cultural method of white supremacy dating back centuries in the "kill the Indian, save the human" project.

With respect to a reinvigorated attack on Muslim (i.e., the "registry") and Mexican Americans (i.e., the "wall"), this front-stage racism, to appropriate Goffman (1959, 22), is deemed acceptable in *public* places in a way that offends a general mood for Americans regarding narratives about Blacks since the Civil Rights Movement. This is the moral victory of the Civil Rights Movement to make it generally unacceptable to frame Blacks in such light in the public sphere. But not so for Muslims and Mexicans. The new xenophobia evidenced in Trump's campaign and inaugural speech is a particular form of racism that hearkens back to either the early-twentieth-century Americanization project (see Leonardo and Vafai 2016), or its more recent, hysterical version and alarmist treatment in Huntington's (1997) "clash of civilization" thesis, or a variety of nationalism more common in European contexts where populist politicians incite fear of immigrants and other non-European groups.

Racialized speech is going through another transformation in the Trump era, something that dates back at least to the Tea Party's insurgence. It would be overreaching to say that the United States is experiencing a shift from neoliberalism to neofascism, since the Trump administration clings onto central aspects of neoliberalism, such as encouraging the privatization of schools. We are witnessing the whitelash against eight years of Obama, twenty-five years of multiculturalism, forty years of affirmative action, and fifty years of civil rights legislation. Trump's appointment of Secretary of Education Betsy DeVos, a vocal proponent of educational vouchers and part of the billionaire family that owns Amway, gestures as much in this direction. And for the first time in several administrations, the presidential Cabinet will not consist of any Latinos. But neither does that matter since racial and ethnic diversity is a ploy of complaining people, a sign of their weakness. This follows on the heels of racial resentment signalled by the Michigan affirmative action case that questioned the use of race considerations in admissions, the Fisher case of Texas where the plaintiff claims that her whiteness was used against her admission to UT Austin, and a general trend verified by survey after survey that whites perceive that the United States has witnessed much progress when compared with Blacks' lower perceptions of the same phenomenon.

One senses that white America has had enough of the only several decades-old minority identity politics. But unable to hide behind the previously opaque veil of whiteness, the Trump election was clearly about the assertion of and possessive investment in white identity politics (Lipsitz 1998). Whites not only spoke up by voting, particularly the rural and white working-class voters, but they spoke up as an *interest group*. This is even different from the earlier images of "Joe the Plumber" from Ohio during Obama's first bid for the presidency. There is a universal appeal for Joe as the common, hardworking, family man, and that is precisely its power and effectiveness. Now Joe's whiteness is surely an issue, indeed a weapon for the Right. For this reason, the shift in race discourse is not simply a return to a previous white chauvinism disguised as universal humanism. The Trump, alt-Right, and Breitbart triumvirate is precisely the appropriation of Leftist identity politics and deployment of its very logic for the purposes of white nationalism *as a white project*.

Ingenious on several fronts for its populist appeal, *new whiteness* also speaks to its desperation, as a last measure, to resort making itself finally visible. Whites perform this apostasy not necessarily to expose themselves to people of colour, whose survival has always located whiteness, but to *whites themselves and to each other*. They publicly acknowledge the interpellation known as whiteness (see Althusser 1971; Leonardo 2010; Chideya 2016). Once established, it will be difficult for whites henceforth to disappear into the brightness of the cave out of which they have been forced. The new race predicament suggests the rejuvenation of whiteness, but it may also be evidence of its last gasp, the prelude to the preconditions of its own demise. Its irrationality is becoming more noticeable, its desperation transforming whites into anxious or nervous subjects. If Trump proves unable to lift the lives of the vast majority of whites who toil in unlivable conditions under late capitalism, the desperation could turn into rock bottom, which, like a cornered rat, turns toward violence but could also turn inward into relief and release.

New whiteness's spokespeople resort to ever more complicated schemes to win over whites' hearts, ever more hateful speech to diminish the Other, and ever more authoritarianism in attempts to return whiteness to its previous greatness at the head of the table. It leads to that familiar abuse that Thandeka (2000) describes as part of every "white" child's process of becoming white. Denying uniqueness, restricting intrinsic curiosity in the Other, and exchanging self-love for white-love (tantamount to self-loathing), the child is now bullied into becoming white. As part of their loyalty to whiteness (Ignatiev and Garvey 1996), whites visit abuse on non-white Others in order to avoid further abuse from their caretakers (e.g., family, government, and nation) or to assuage the unresolved guilt they carry about having become white (see Leonardo 2016). This *troubled consciousness* (cf. Du Bois's "double consciousness" 1989) is ultimately unlivable, even if it is sustainable for longer than anyone thought; its days are numbered and whites' human freedom awaits them. Trumpalism may be one of the last and empty sounds they hear.

References

Althusser, L. 1971. *Lenin and Philosophy*. Translated by B. Brewster. New York: Monthly Review Press.

Apple, M. 2006. *Educating the "Right" Way*. 2nd ed. New York: Routledge.

Apple, M., and A. Oliver. 1998. "Becoming Right: Education and the Formation of Conservative Movements." In *Sociology of Education: Emerging Perspectives*, edited by C. Torres and T. Mitchell, 91–119. Albany, NY: SUNY Press.

Bobo, L., and R. Smith. 1998. "From Jim Crow Racism to Laissez-Faire Racism: The Transformation of Racial Attitudes." In *Beyond Pluralism: The Conception of Groups and Group Identities in America*, edited by W. Katkin, N. Landsman, and A. Tyree, 182–220. Urbana: University of Illinois Press.

Bonilla-Silva, E. 2006. *Racism without Racists: Color-Blind Racism and the Persistence of Racial Inequality in the United States*. 2nd ed. Lanham, MD: Rowman & Littlefield.

Buras, K. 2010. "Education, Cultural Politics, and the New Hegemony." In *Handbook of Cultural Politics and Education*, edited by Z. Leonardo, 341–71. Rotterdam, the Netherlands: SensePublishers.

———. 2008. *Rightist Multiculturalism*. New York: Routledge.

Chideya, F. 2016. "The Call-to-Whiteness: The Rise of the New White Nationalism and Inadequate Establishment Whiteness Response." http://farai.com/the-call-to-whiteness/.

Du Bois, W. E. B. 1989. *The Souls of Black Folk*. New York: Penguin Books. First published 1903.

Foucault, M. 1980. *Power/Knowledge*. Edited by C. Gordon. New York: Pantheon Books.

Gilroy, P. 2000. *Against Race*. Cambridge, MA: Belknap Press of Harvard University.

Goffman, E. 1959. *The Presentation of Self in Everyday Life*. Garden City, NY: Doubleday.

Goldberg, D. T., and P. Essed. 2002. "Introduction: From Racial Demarcations to Multiple Identifications." In *Race Critical Theories*, edited by P. Essed and D. T. Goldberg, 1–11. Malden, MA: Blackwell.

Hall, S. 1996. "What Is This 'Black' in Black Popular Culture?" In *Stuart Hall*, edited by D. Morley and K. Chen, 465–75. London: Routledge.

Herman, E., and N. Chomsky. 1993. *Manufacturing Consent*. New York: Pantheon Books.

Huntington, S. P. 1997. *The Clash of Civilizations and the Remaking of World Order*. New York: Touchstone.

Ignatiev, N., and J. Garvey. 1996. "Editorial: When Does the Unreasonable Act Make Sense?" In *Race Traitor*, edited by N. Ignatiev and J. Garvey, 35–37. New York: Routledge.

Katz, J. 2010. "It's the Masculinity, Stupid: A Cultural Studies Analysis of Media, the Presidency and Pedagogy." In *Handbook of Cultural Politics and Education*, edited by Z. Leonardo, 477–507. Rotterdam, the Netherlands: SensePublishers.

Leonardo, Z. 2010. "Ideology and Its Modes of Existence: Toward an Althusserian Theory of Race and Racism." In *Handbook of Cultural Politics and Education*, edited by Z. Leonardo, 195–217. Rotterdam, the Netherlands: SensePublishers.

———. 2016. "Tropics of Whiteness: Metaphor and the Literary Turn in White Studies." *Whiteness and Education* 1(1): 3–14. doi:10.1080/23793406.2016.11 67111.

Leonardo, Z., and M. Vafai. 2016. "Citizenship Education and the Colonial Contract: The Elusive Search for Social Justice in U.S. Education." In *The Palgrave International Handbook of Education for Citizenship and Social Justice*, edited by A. Peterson, R. Hattam, M. Zembylas, and J. Arthur, 613–34. New York: Palgrave.

Lipsitz, G. 1998. *The Possessive Investment in Whiteness*. Philadelphia: Temple University Press.

The Politics of Learning Writing Collective. 2017. "The Learning Sciences in a New Era of U.S. Nationalism." *Cognition and Instruction* 35(2), 91–102. doi:10.1080/07370008.2017.1282486.

Thandeka. 2000. *Learning to Be White: Money, Race, and God in America*. New York: Bloomsbury Academic.

PREFACE

Marc Spooner and James McNinch

Dissident Knowledge in Higher Education is the result of the symposium, "Public Engagement and the Politics of Evidence in an Age of Neoliberalism and Audit Culture," held on July 23–25, 2015, at the University of Regina.[1]

Guiding questions for the symposium interrogated the politics of evidence: What counts as scholarship and why? How do we measure research impact? Impact for whom? Who determines and how do we determine whose evidence and what research is legitimate? What can be done and how do we effect change to university practices?

For three intense days in 2015, two hundred concerned and committed scholars[2]—together with a field of internationally renowned presenters from Canada, New Zealand, the United Kingdom, and the United States— responded to a pressing call and convened at the University of Regina, a mid-sized institution nested in the northern reaches of the Great Plains, in what is now the Province of Saskatchewan, Canada. The city of Regina, as a gathering location for discussions of colonialism, neoliberalism, audit culture, and the politics of evidence, is at once paradoxically ironic and ideal. Ironic in that only faint hauntings remain of the collaborative spirit that once demarcated this provincial capital as the birthplace of both socialized medicine and the first publicly funded arts board in North America. And yet ideal for it is on these very Treaty 4 Lands[3] that thriving herds of buffalo (bison) rise again to roam wild; where distant Indigenous ceremonies echo in consonance with present-day determination and a future guided, yet not bound, by history and the promise of the "new buffalo"—higher education (Stonechild 2006).

We envisioned the "Regina Gathering" to be one in a series of organized, as well as spontaneous and theoretically informed collective resistances to the market logics that worm ever closer to the modern academy's core, itself contaminated by an intertwined, and often unacknowledged, religious, imperial, and colonial root system. To help further this defiant and collaboratively imagined goal, the present collection is intended to serve as a tool for new and seasoned scholars alike who are seeking to navigate, critically resist, and collectively reclaim and reimagine the academy. You, the reader, are now an integral part of this gathering and will help shape the future as you engage with these and other texts and groups. The future is on all of us. Time to resist, organize, and act in concert with initiatives, collaborations, affinity groups, and movements within and well-beyond the academy at both local and global levels—it is incumbent on us to expose, provoke, and tear down these systems of illegitimate authority and power.

Notes

1   For the complete video archive of the symposium, see http://www. politicsofevidence.ca.
2   Many others watched the simultaneously webcasted proceedings via the Internet.
3   The numbered treaties, or post-Confederation treaties, are
    a series of eleven treaties signed between the Aboriginal peoples
    in Canada (or First Nations) and the reigning monarch of Canada
    (Victoria, Edward VII, or George V) from 1871 to 1921. These
    agreements were created to allow the Canadian Government to
    pursue settlement and resource extraction in the affected regions,
    which include modern-day Alberta, British Columbia, Manitoba,
    Ontario, Saskatchewan, and the Northwest Territories. These treaties
    provided the Dominion of Canada large tracts of land in exchange for
    promises made to the Aboriginal people of the area. These terms were
    dependent on individual negotiations and so specific terms differed
    with each treaty. ("Numbered Treaties")

References

"Numbered Treaties." *Wikipedia*. https://en.wikipedia.org/wiki/Numbered_Treaties.
Stonechild, B. 2006. *The New Buffalo: The Struggle for Aboriginal Post-Secondary Education in Canada*. Winnipeg: University of Manitoba Press.

INTRODUCTION

Marc Spooner and James McNinch

> What we are witnessing is an attack on universities not because they are failing, but because they are public. This is not just an attack on political liberty but also an attack on dissent, critical education, and any public institution that might exercise a democratizing influence on the nation. In this case the autonomy of institutions such as higher education, particularly public institutions are threatened as much by state politics as by corporate interests. How else to explain in neoliberal societies such as the U.S., U.K. and India the massive defunding of public institutions of higher education, the raising of tuition for students, and the closing of areas of study that do not translate immediately into profits for the corporate sector? (Giroux 2016)

If you are experiencing a reflexive unease, sensing that something is awry in the academy, then this book is for you. Perhaps you are growing increasingly alarmed with the negative changes you are witnessing at your university. Is a rise in managerialism and punitive accountability limiting or coercing your research program, your academic freedom, or impacting your relationships and your personal and organizational health? Or perhaps you have been experimenting with, or thinking about, expanding the forms and formats your scholarship may take. Have you been seeking to disrupt hegemonic knowledge systems, including the manner in which knowledge is conceptualized, legitimized, represented, and disseminated? Are you working to expand your methodological imagination? Looking for resources to justify, or to learn more about, engaging in critical, qualitative, and participatory research designs, publicly engaged scholarship, or Indigenous and decolonized epistemologies? Are you curious or concerned with the ethics, exploitation, significance, or gaming of past and ongoing academic research endeavours, practices, and outcomes?

If any of the above applies, the good news is: *you are not alone.*

The bad news: As educational institutions and entire societies shift toward neoliberalism, New Public Management, and accountability frameworks (Spooner 2018), "the university is in crisis, almost everywhere" (Burawoy 2011, 27); the specific mechanisms and implementation levels may vary, but in large part their effect is similar. As Edwards and Roy (2016) recently observed,

> Academics are human and readily respond to incentives. The need to achieve tenure has influenced faculty decisions, priorities, and activities since the concept first became popular (Wolverton, 1998). Recently, however, an emphasis on quantitative performance metrics (Van Noorden, 2010), increased competition for static or reduced federal research funding (e.g., NIH, NSF, and EPA), and a steady shift toward operating public universities on a private business model (Plerou, et al., 1999; Brownlee, 2014; Kasperkevic, 2014) are creating an increasingly perverse Academic culture. (1–2)

Even the harshest critics and most prominent scholars cannot easily escape our de-funded, highly individualized, hyper-competitive, and perversely incentivized moment. We live in an age in which value is often equated with accountancy, in which we are increasingly governed by and through numbers, incentives, de-incentives and competitive benchmarking (Shore and Wright 2015). Examples include official and unofficial funding and impact metric targets, journal impact factors, *h*-indexes, and even the very reporting systems used to provide these data, all of which have the power to guide and coerce our behaviours in subtle and not so subtle ways. As Shore and Wright explain,

> What is distinctive about performance indicators and audits today is the scale of their diffusion....indicators become targets as institutions are reshaped according to the criteria and

methods used to measure them; and organizations and people are transformed into "auditable" entities that focus their energies on doing "what counts." (2015, 423)

As managerialism creeps into every facet of the academy, we risk conceding what little autonomy remains to collaboratively and collegially manage ourselves, and to freely research, critique, act, and organize with the wider communities and movements that characterize our location. The seductive and insidious nature of management is such that it holds the potential to disorient people, causing them to lose sight of universities' more laudable missions—as typically encapsulated in their mottos—and to focus rather on depersonalized spreadsheets and the false idol of a narrowly defined accountability. Audit culture's tentacles diminish disciplinary autonomy and local authority, bypassing criteria documents and performance review bodies. Ultimately at stake is the very notion of what can be considered knowledge itself.

Managerialism strips the academy of its moral purpose and concern for the public good in favour of accountancy, control, and efficiency for their own sake. Managerialism is "the organizational form of neo-liberalism" (Lynch 2014). As a dean of a faculty of education, co-editor James McNinch experienced the reality of being a member of middle management, expected to "sell" to his faculty the increasing bureaucratization and centralization of the organization promoted by the "senior leadership team," that is, the associate vice-presidents of various operations, including human resources, facilities management, and research services, as well as the vice-presidents of administration and academics. Inherent in the move away from teaching and research for their own sake, was a serious attempt to market a "brand" of the university and woo "student-customers" with the promise of a rich social experience and assurances of employability upon graduation. The continual decline experienced this decade in public funding for post-secondary education, the ongoing rise in tuition rates, and an emphasis on "public-private" partnerships and business models for the entrepreneurial sale of programs to individuals and third-party institutions all have the effect of positioning faculty members as mere knowledge workers who need to be managed so the fruits of their labour can be sold for a profit. In this context, "teacher education" (or "training," as it is reductively dismissed) is a relatively easy sell in the marketplace because of the steady demand for a supply of teachers and because of continuing opportunities to deliver professional development at the graduate and in-service levels (McNinch 2014). Professional faculties and MBA programs claim successes and increase tuitions according to what the market can bear. Contrast that with liberal arts and sciences departments that provide large introductory service courses to such students but are starved for senior undergraduate majors and graduate students. The irony is that managerialism is articulated as apolitical and simply a "common sense" necessity in tough times, rather than the ideological enterprise it is. Managerialism can masquerade as many things: team spirit, leadership opportunities, enthusiastic allegiance to the institution, and an all round kind of "rah-rah" boosterism—*"Good job! Thank you for choosing this faculty"*—that caters to and privileges, and at the same time isolates, individuals who are ultimately on their own as students, adjuncts, sessionals, or faculty. Of course, a check and counterbalance to this individualism is the power of the collective found in organized student and labour unions, where members are empowered and protected by their existence.

The ideology that everything and everybody can be and must be managed is dangerous (Klikauer 2013). Universities have now had to take it upon themselves to manage a wide spectrum of risks and liabilities based on fear: fear of audits, fear of backlash or apathy from the public, fear of not being politically correct, fear of not attracting students or not accommodating their learning needs or of having too many of them drop out, fear of being sued, fear of litigation, fear of indemnity, fear of collusion, fear of corruption, or fear of reprisal from antagonistic governments or funders. A climate of fear does not promote collegiality, innovation, experimentation, critical thinking, or creativity in students or faculty. Yvonna Lincoln put it succinctly: "the academy I am leaving is not the one I entered" (personal communication, n.d.).

However, as several chapters in this book foreground, this is not to suggest or to leave the impression that the liberal academy of old was ever a golden time for everyone, or even always benevolent for that matter. In fact, let there be no misunderstanding: "Empires of knowledge rest on the foundation of racial statecraft, militarized science, and enduring notions of civilizational superiority....[and] these processes must also be understood within the epistemologies of 'othering' being constructed by disciplines" (Chatterjee and Maira 2014, 14). On the (more hopeful) other hand,

> the modern university has always contained the contradictory tensions of both servicing power as well as providing the tools necessary to critique power (Brownlee, 2015). Giroux (2014) points out that "higher education increasingly stands alone, even in its attenuated state, as a public arena where ideas can

be debated, critical knowledge produced, and learning linked to important social issues" (p. 18). If universities are to live up to their potential in helping to bring about a more just future, they must endeavor to be a "liberating force that fosters the challenging of conventional thinking and of systems of illegitimate authority" (Brownlee, 2015, p. 13). (Spooner 2018, 897)

That is, universities must strive to live up to their aspirational ideal by encouraging "the *potential* to disrupt existing hierarchies and inequitable power structures and the *possibility* to create spaces that welcome and foster alternative ways of knowing and being" (Spooner 2018, 897). It is hoped that this book will serve as both a guide and tool, joining wider efforts to resist colonialism, neoliberalism, and audit culture in all their context-specific manifestations.

This book imagines a post-managerial academy where teaching and research embody new forms of possibility and resistance, rather than compliance to management standards and predetermined outcomes. This imagined space exists where collegial governance respects the tensions and ambiguities inherent in working in an institution that has, as one of its prime mandates, the critique of the social and cultural milieu that created and funds it. We call on scholars to go beyond the audited confines of the academy and to be teacher-researcher-advocates, to assume the responsible long view, to face head-on our own domestication and query the purposes and consequences of knowledge production, consumption, and engagement.

The book is organized into four parts; however, naturally these chapters overlap and move in spaces beyond the part in which they have been placed and contribute to the overall impact we hope this collection will provide.

Part I: Historical Perspectives and Overview

This first part provides a historical and contemporary overview of neoliberalism, audit culture, and the politics of evidence from several different standpoints. In "A Dangerous Accountability: Neoliberalism's Veer toward Accountancy in Higher Education, " Yvonna Lincoln begins with an examination of the "neoliberal-cum-managerialistic" rituals imposed upon public higher education faculties in the name of accountability. She then provides examples of both burdensome reporting requirements and how these slide into simplistic accountancy. Linda Tuhiwai Smith's chapter, "The Art of the Impossible—Defining and Measuring Indigenous Research?" then sets the context for the twenty-first-century neoliberal university against the historical development of the liberal university while discussing the structural obstacles and challenges inherent in performance-based research funding models. She concludes with a discussion of how the impact of Indigenous research must be assessed as part of an "intergenerational long game of decolonization" leading to positive transformational change for Indigenous peoples.

These two chapters are followed by two interviews. The first, with Norman K. Denzin, provides a comprehensive overview of recent and historic definitions and understandings of what we call research, science, and evidence. Following Denzin, Noam Chomsky provides us with an important historical perspective, describing the continued dangers of corporatized campuses and the difficult responsibilities of intellectuals and dissidents. Both Denzin and Chomsky contextualize current critiques of the academy by calling into question the neutrality of science and the corrupting nature of state and corporate power.

Part II: Activism, Science, and Global and Local Knowledge

In Part II, the reader is invited to consider scholarly activism, science, and global and local knowledge from a variety of spaces, including the repercussions of presenting evidence contrary to state and corporate agendas, as well as how notions of legitimate science are distorted by power at local and global levels. In "Accumulation and Its Dis'(sed) Contents: The Politics of Evidence in the Struggle for Public Education," Michelle Fine begins with a powerful testimony highlighting the neoliberal agenda masquerading as school reform. She reveals how, even in light of sound evidence, such evidence is often ignored, and those who dare speak it are bullied. Next, in "Beyond Epistemicide: Knowledge Democracy and Higher Education," Budd Hall provides a global perspective of colonial dispossession and its concomitant "epistemicide, linguicide, and cultural genocide." He further illustrates several examples of community-based knowledge reclamation initiatives that counter the Western hegemony of knowledge. This part concludes with a critical review, as well as contemporary observations, from Patti Lather. In "Within and Beyond Neoliberalism: Doing Qualitative Research in the Afterward," Lather outlines the progression of qualitative research methods from conventional interpretive inquiry to post-qualitative approaches. She then offers a synthesis of these trajectories vis-à-vis the struggle against neoliberal governmentality and standards-based science.

Part III: Theorizing the Colonial Academy and Indigenous Knowledge

This part critiques higher education's colonial project while reasserting the inherent legitimacy of Indigenous Knowledge from three distinct, but complementary, positions. Marie Battiste's chapter, "Reconciling Indigenous Knowledge in Education: Promises, Possibilities, and Imperatives," positions Indigenous Knowledge in the Canadian context, specifically from an educational, constitutional, and legal perspective. Battiste uses the Canadian Truth and Reconciliation Commission's report, *Honouring the Truth, Reconciling for the Future*, as the most recent call to assert the educational rights of Canadian Indigenous peoples, while highlighting the growing recognition of the constitutional rights and global human rights of Indigenous peoples everywhere. Eve Tuck's chapter, "Biting the University That Feeds Us," links settler colonialism to the roots of neoliberalism, and implicates the modern and historic university in this ongoing agenda. She concludes by inviting readers to reconsider and reimagine implicit theories of change by moving beyond "raising awareness" and "documenting damage" toward alternative Indigenous theories of change. Next, Sandy Grande, in "Refusing the University," reminds us that the university cannot escape its own culpability. She outlines the differentiated yet parallel manner in which Black and Native bodies have been racialized to serve, and continue to serve, the interests of the settler state, a process only accelerated under neoliberalism. She then leaves us with several specific strategies for "refusing the university."

Part IV: From Counting Out, to Counting On, the Scholars

With its title giving a nod to William Bruneau and Donald C. Savage's book, *Counting Out the Scholars* (2002), this last part raises critical questions about current practices in the academy while inviting readers to reimagine the possible as we collectively map alternative trajectories for higher education. In "Beyond Individualism: The Psychosocial Life of the Neoliberal University," Rosalind Gill shares an intimate analysis of the toll neoliberalism takes on the body and the body politic. By bringing the affective dimension of academic life to the fore, she calls upon us to resist the alienation and personal injury that is produced, and often overlooked, as the inevitable collateral damage that results from the enforced individualism of the neoliberal project. Next, Joel Westheimer, in "Fatal Distraction: Audit Culture and Accountability in the Corporate University," reminds us of the mission and aspirational ideals of the university, as well as how these are increasingly compromised under neo-liberalism. He warns of the danger when we as academics are either coerced, or complicit, in becoming obedient conformists under corporate-styled governance. Subsequently, Christopher Meyers, in "Public Scholarship and Faculty Agency: Rethinking 'Teaching, Scholarship, and Service,'" provides a cogent examination of how faculty are evaluated against arbitrary lines that divide research, teaching, and service. Drawing on his own experience as an ethicist in a public hospital, he is able to offer a rational argument for why the present system needs to be rethought, and he strongly advocates for a reaffirmation of the academy's mission of working toward the public good.

Afterword

Peter McLaren, in his Afterword, leaves us with the haunting prospect that under the corporatized university academics have largely "withdrawn their submission to search for the meaning of truth and justice in favour of set-tling for the demands of the corporate bottom line." He calls upon us as cit-izens and academics to live up to our responsibility, recognizing that the struggle within the university mirrors the larger struggle for a democratic and just society and, ultimately, a definition of our humanity.

Call to Action

The present collection is a challenge to the colonial, corporate, and manage-rial university in all its iterations; it is concerned with reclaiming, or, perhaps more appropriately, reimagining knowledge, scholarship, and the academy. It recognizes the academy's sordid past, perilous present, and what we envi-sion as its defiantly hopeful future. With Deepa Kumar, various scholars have been in our thoughts of late, including

Edward Said, Karl Marx, W. E. B. Du Bois, Steven Salaita and Sara Ahmed. Each of them in their own ways were or are on the margins, in exile, or have been outsiders of one sort or another, but have fought from those places because they saw or see marginality—the position of being an outsider—as having given them, as Du Bois put it "second sight," or intellectual freedom for Said, or the capacity to be a "feminist killjoy" for Ahmed, or for Salaita to be "uncivil" as a way to challenge the establishment....Marx was a political refugee in the heart of empire, and thus obviously marginal, but he was also marginal to the broader Western intellectual tradition....The second reason I chose the word margin is because of the high degree of alienation in the academic world. Being involved in my union, I am aware on a daily basis of the struggles that people encounter: adjunct professors who do the bulk of teaching but who are paid throwaway wages and live on the margins of the university; women and people of color who are still fighting to be taken seriously and treated equitably at the university; and tenured professors who work around the clock and are forced to "do more with less,"...and who are increasingly alienated from the corporate university and its values. (Kumar 2017, 2–3)

From within the academy, we need to invoke the courage to defend intellectual freedom, to embrace feminism, Indigenous epistemologies, critical approaches, and activist and unorthodox scholarship. We must oppose the marginalization of legitimate scholarly discourses via the simplistic labelling mechanisms of incivility, unprofessionalism, and political correctness. However, as each of our academies is nested within a larger polity, sadly, the aforementioned is not enough. As George Orwell's *1984* continues to warn,

the road to tyranny often begins with a misplaced trust in a managerial elite promising simple solutions to hard problems....With our own fondness for think tanks and government bodies bearing Orwellian names and dubious claims of competence, we are always in danger of waking up to find a Ministry of Truth feeding us "alternative facts." (Shelden 2017)

In this vicious Trump age, with its contempt for justice, equity, evidence, science, art, intellectual life, and critical examination, it is time for the privileged to join with the many *already aware*, *already in* the struggle for freedom, dignity, and survival. We must redouble our energies toward linking with, learning from, and joining movements and efforts well underway that seek to expose, denounce, and collectivize resistance/s.

Make no mistake, this book is a clarion call.

References

Bruneau, W., and D. C. Savage. 2002. *Counting Out the Scholars: The Case against Performance Indicators in Higher Education*. Toronto: James Lorimer.

Burawoy, M. 2011. "Redefining the Public University: Global and National Contexts." In *A Manifesto for the Public University*, edited by J. Holmwood, 27–41. New York: Bloomsbury.

Chatterjee, P., and S. Maira, eds. 2014. *The Imperial University: Academic Repression and Scholarly Dissent*. Minneapolis: University of Minnesota Press.

Edwards, M. A., and S. Roy. 2016. "Academic Research in the 21st Century: Maintaining Scientific Integrity in a Climate of Perverse Incentives and Hypercompetition." *Environmental Engineering Science* 34(1): 1–11.

Giroux, H. 2016. "Neoliberal Savagery and the Assault on Higher Education as a Democratic Public Sphere." *Café Dissensus*, September 15. https://cafedissensus.com/2016/09/15/neoliberal-savagery-and-the-assault-on-higher-education-as-a-democratic-public-sphere/.

Klikauer, T. 2013. *Managerialism: A Critique of an Ideology*. London: Palgrave Macmillan.

Kumar, D. 2017. "Fighting from the Margins: Neoliberalism, Imperialism, and the Struggle to Democratize the University." Dallas Smythe Award Keynote Lecture. Democratic Communiqué. http://www.democraticcommunications.org/wp-content/uploads/2017/03/Dallas-Smythe-Lecture-for-DC-2.pdf.

Lynch, K. 2014. "'New Managerialism' in Education: The Organisational Form of Neoliberalism." *Open Democracy*, September 16. https://www.opendemocracy.net/kathleen-lynch/'new-managerialism'-in-education-organisational-form-of-neoliberalism.

McNinch, J. 2014. "Working against the Grain." In *Leadership for Change in Teacher Education: Voices of Canadian Deans of Education*, edited by S. E. Elliott-Johns, 73–79. Amsterdam: Sense Publishers.

Shelden, M. 2017. "Big Brother Is Still Watching." *The Globe and Mail*, January 26. http://www.theglobeandmail.com/arts/books-and-media/george-orwells-nineteen-eighty-four-in-the-age-oftrump/article33776339/.

Shore, C., and S. Wright. 2015. "Audit Culture Revisited: Rankings, Ratings, and the Reassembling of Society." *Current Anthropology* 56(3): 421–44.

Spooner, M. 2018. "Qualitative Research and Global Audit Culture: The Politics of Productivity, Accountability, & Possibility." In *The SAGE Handbook of Qualitative Research*, 5th ed., edited by N. K. Denzin and Y. S. Lincoln, 894–914. Thousand Oaks, CA: Sage Publications.

PART I

HISTORICAL PERSPECTIVES AND OVERVIEW

CHAPTER 1

A DANGEROUS ACCOUNTABILITY: NEOLIBERALISM'S VEER TOWARD ACCOUNTANCY IN HIGHER EDUCATION

Yvonna S. Lincoln

Ultimately, I sincerely believe that…much of how we attempt to assess higher education programs actually devalues rather than adds value to the educational experience for students and professors alike.

—Robert Engvall, *Corporatization of Higher Education*

The primary problem with "greater accountability" through greater assessment lies in who determines who is doing that assessing, what standards should be used, and what judgments should be rendered after the assessment has been completed.

—Robert Engvall, *Corporatization of Higher Education*

The issue now is not whether higher education needs to be made accountable, but whether the accountability movement itself can be made accountable.

—Earl F. Cheit, "What Price Accountability?"

> Only recently has there been some concern expressed that an insistence on ever-stricter accountability must not be allowed to trump other cherished values, including trust, innovation and productivity.
>
> —Paul G. Thomas, "Accountability"

Introduction

When Edward Snowden described the National Security Agency's bulk collection of telephone and email information from private citizens as the most dangerous weapon ever invented, he might as well have been talking about the neoliberal-cum-managerialistic rituals imposed upon public higher education faculties in the name of accountability. In their introduction to *Evil Paradises*, Davis and Monk (2007, ix) ask the most direct question we might ask about the future of higher education: "Toward what kind of future are we being led by savage, fanatical capitalism?" Another way of asking the question is "What will the neoliberal, fully 'transformed' university look like, and what will we have lost in the democratic societies around the world?" To answer this question is to lead inevitably to the question "What is this neoliberalism of which we speak?" Neoliberalism has become a buzzword, a handy circumlocution around which are gathered multiple grievances and discontents. But what does it signify, and for what has it become a meme?

Neoliberalism is a set of political, social, and economic theories and ideologies loosely rooted in the eighteenth-century liberal economic theory of Adam Smith. Its basic premises include lip service to the free market economy, although Anderson argues that "the free-market doctrine has never guided the policies and practices of neoliberal supporters" but rather that "state intervention in favor of capital has been the driving force" (2007, 1022); limited or little public expenditure on social services "such as welfare and healthcare" (Dolhinow 2006, 350); a focus on individual initiative and a distaste for collective action (such as unions); a workforce that is mobile and "flexible," as well as often being part-time, inexpensive, and largely without traditional benefits; few, if any, regulatory interventions from the state; the mobility of production and manufacturing operations, chasing the least expensive workforce; a high tolerance for unemployment; and a tendency to blame individuals for their own poverty, unemployment, and ill health. Little examination of social structures and infrastructures is done to account for such social and civic decrements as structural issues.

On the even darker side, neoliberalism has been credited with widening the "gap between the rich and the poor and increasingly high levels of global poverty" (Dolhinow 2006, 331); with "the gutting of civic values" (Porfilio and Malott 2007, 1025); with the increasing corporatization of both public (Saltman and Gabbard 2003) and university education; with the concentration of wealth in the hands of fewer and fewer corporations, individuals, and families; with the assault on academic freedom and tenure at the university level; and with the attacks on the liberal arts at tertiary levels. Davis and Monk (2007, ix) describe this globalized neoliberalism as a place where the "winner-take-all ethos is unfettered by any remnant of social contract and undisturbed by any ghost of the labor movement, where the rich can walk like gods in the nightmare gardens of their deepest and most secret desires."

Burrows (2012, 356), drawing from Foucault's analyses, points out that, traditionally, neoliberalism is characterized by viewing "the role of the state [as]...largely restricted to supervising the market." But Foucault himself rather "suggests that this relation between state and market under neoliberalism is, in fact, the converse: 'a state under the supervision of the market rather than a market supervised by the state'" (quoted in Burrows 2012, 356). The point here, of course, is that just as the state, for Foucault, has come under the supervision (if not the domination) of the market, so has the university, with its deep ties to the states and the federal government.[1] And how does this shape, reinvent, and construct life for faculty? Shore and Wright are very clear about this:

> Why does something as seemingly mundane as a "technology transfer" merit the grand term "epochal cultural change"? The French philosopher Foucault provides ample evidence of ways in which seemingly dull, routine and bureaucratic practices often have profound effects on social life. Our analysis underlines the fact that audit technologies being introduced into higher education and elsewhere are not simply innocuously neutral, legal-rational practices; rather, they are instruments for new forms of governance and power. They embody a new rationality and morality and are designed to engender amongst academic staff new norms of conduct and professional behavior. In short, they are agents for the creation of new kinds of subjectivity: self-managing individuals who render themselves auditable. (2000, 57)

Indeed, examining Tom Schwandt's definition of "audit culture/society" in *The* SAGE *Dictionary of Qualitative Inquiry*, he posits,

> Some scholars argue that auditing (and associated practices...) is not simply a set of techniques but a system of values and goals that becomes inscribed in social practices thereby influencing the self-understanding of a practice and its role in society. To be audited, an organization (or practice like teaching or providing mental health care) must transform itself into an auditable commodity—auditing thus reshapes in its own image those organizations and practices which are monitored for performance. (2015, 9–10)

It is no far leap from these definitions and critical analyses to argue that the values of the traditional university are being replaced by a second set of values, namely those that characterize the marketplace and corporate culture. Schwandt goes on to note that "others contend that the growing influence of an audit culture contributes to the disappearance of the idea of publicness as traditional public service norms of citizenship, representation, equality, accountability, impartiality, openness, responsiveness, and justice are being marginalized or replaced by business norms like competitiveness, efficiency, productivity, profitability, and consumer satisfaction" (2015, 10). Indeed, in the global desire to produce "competitive" faculty, the value of collegial life, of colleagues teaching and sometimes researching in concert, sharing and constructively criticizing the ideas of others, collegiality, along with its norms of academic community, is slowly withering away. As competition for external funding becomes fiercer, colleagues view colleagues as competitors for the same slice of the pie, with the consequence that the deep, amiable, conversational friendships between and among colleagues are likewise disappearing.

What does neoliberalism look like on campus, and how do faculty experience this free market doctrine in their everyday lives? As faculty twist and gyrate around this vortex of political doctrines and fiscal policies, how is neoliberalism translated into higher education's social ecology? What are the specific expressions of free market ideologies in academic life? While readers could no doubt add many of their own, a foundational laundry list would include the quasi-privatization of the great public and land-grant universities as a result of the diminution of state and federal funding; the increasing influence of corporate monies on building programs, on academic curricula, and on the research programs of faculty; the commodification of intellectual property, including publication (Lincoln 1998, 2011, 2012; Schiffrin 1996; Spooner 2015, 2018); the rise of top-down managerialism, including a sharp increase in administrative staff versus teaching and research faculty; the pressing emphasis on entrepreneurialism as a criterion for faculty promotion, tenure, and merit pay (Steck 2003); a shift in thinking of students as consumers and purchasers, rather than as junior partners in citizenship and critical-thinking learning journeys; a focus on metrics and rankings as a measure of quality (Burrows 2012; Tuck 2003); the strange, perverse, and utterly ridiculous idea that universities need a "brand," a twisted—indeed demented—distortion of academic values in favour of Lock and Martins's "quantitative, economic criterion" (quoted in Burrows 2012, 355); a view of faculty that demands ever more "accountability" measures, to assure that faculty are doing what they have been hired to do; an emphasis on external funding for faculty, even when external fund priorities do not match faculty interests or research programs; and the increasing use of contingent, part-time, and nontenure track labour (Levin, Shaker, and Wagoner 2012).

There are, of course, other signals. For instance, there is the ever-widening gap between administrative salaries and faculty salaries; the moves to outsource nontechnical core campus services (maintenance, housekeeping, grounds services, food service, and the like), with concomitant ripple effects throughout the surrounding community, where most of the traditional workers in these services areas live, which is quite similar to globalization's move to seek cheaper labour on foreign soil, rather than pay workers a living wage here in North America. All of these signs signal the *assemblage* of neoliberal doctrine-corporatization-and-managerialistic metrics (Burrows 2012). Burrows refers to this assemblage as "metrics, markets and affect," but it might well be more alliteratively termed metrics, markets, managers, and morale (2012, 355).

Three Examples: A "Common Core" of Accountability Measures

It might be useful at this point to describe briefly three innovations in accountability in my own institution that have become almost routinized and institutionalized, all as a consequence of one or more extra-institutional agency's call for additional accountability from faculty. These three examples represent what Shore and Wright (2000) term "coercive accountability," and what Michelle Fine has termed, in this volume, "punitive accountability" (see also Tuck 2003). These forms are both punishing and manipulative.

WEAVE Online

WEAVE Online is an extended "accounting" system for faculty work and productivity vis-à-vis students and teaching. At our institution, it was mandated by SACS (Southern Association of Colleges and Schools), the regional accrediting body. In this system, every program area or department must enter "goals"—for admission, for what constitutes adequate progress through program areas (or departments), for curricular content. Then the program must create or enter criteria that speak to the achievement of those goals. Then each department or program area must collect massive amounts of data to address the criteria to demonstrate whether or not goals are being met, students are moving through coursework, certain elements are included in every course structure (multiculturalism, diversity, critical thinking, etc.), and original goals are being met.

Try to imagine a university with fifty-five thousand students and three thousand faculty, eleven colleges and 180 departments, plus another number of separate program areas (my own department, for instance, has three program areas). In any given year, I estimate that roughly ten million units of data are collected and entered for the entire university. Who is analyzing those data? Who is processing them? Who can cope with ten million data points from such disparate departments as rural public health and geology? As English and poultry science? What could such data possibly mean? And how does it demonstrate in any meaningful way that faculty are doing their jobs? Most of the data are quantitative, which many of you will intuitively understand gives us no context for interpretation or assigning meaning. And so WEAVE Online, with its endless data collection and entry requirements, strangles faculty and steals their time for other truly meaningful activities.

Faculty Syllabi and Salaries

As of two years ago, by State of Texas legislative fiat, all faculty who teach undergraduates (and, now, all faculty at my institution) must have their complete curricula vitae, as well as syllabi for every course they teach online by department, and, by law, the faculty curricula vitae must be no further than three clicks away from the salary figure the faculty member is paid in the current year. By "faculty" it is meant all tenured and tenure-track faculty, all lecturers, clinicals, and research associates, as well as teaching assistants, who teach. This means somewhat over six thousand people. The argument was made in the legislature that "the public"—that amorphous, anonymous gaggle of unspecified people—had a "right to know" what the state was paying professors, and the right to see whether or not the syllabi covered "relevant material," as if Mr. and Mrs. Jones, who sent their boy Charlie to my institution, would know relevant material from irrelevant (whatever that means).

Computer Information Services, the major technical service unit on campus, estimates that in the two years we have had this system, there have been—in a state of over seventeen million people—fewer than one hundred "searches" for these data. So much for the public's curiosity. The hidden meaning behind this legislative mandate, of course, is the right-wing claim, emanating from a variety of sources, that faculty are simply a waste of public resources, that they are "parasites" on the body politic, that they spend their time, not in teaching undergraduates but rather in research and especially consulting (Sykes 1990). A further hidden or latent meaning behind this demand for accountancy is the argument fostered on the political right that professors promulgate ultraliberal, left-wing ideas in the impressionable young—ideas such as democracy, tolerance, welcoming diversity, freedom from racial and ethnic prejudice, and the rights of a citizenry to criticize and demand change in government.

Forms, Forms, Forms
The most recent intrusion into faculty time came in the guise of a new form to fill out. The A&M College of Education faculty are awarded merit pay points on, among other things, the extent to which they mentor their advanced doctoral students to publish, or present at national and refereed conferences. We must indicate on our vitas which publications and/or presentations we have completed with our students, which is not onerous. But we also fill out a form mandated by the state (termed an "A-1"). On the A-1, we provide information on teaching, research, and service, including indicating where we have published or presented with students. Last year, a new form came down for everyone to fill out. The form asked for the names of journal articles and/or refereed conference papers presented with students: venue, dates, etc. This form was due at the same time as the curricula vitae of faculty and their state-mandated A-1 forms. This is where accountability becomes accountancy, and it is foolishly, blindly, lazily punitive.

Although normally I am a very compliant employee, I simply sent it back to the dean with the observation that all faculty supplied these data on the two other forms in two different formats (electronic and print), and, clearly, someone in the administrative suite was simply too lazy to turn the page to get it. Further, I demurred, I simply was not going to fill out one more redundant form, and was going to encourage the faculty in my department not to do it either. Two days later, the form was withdrawn.

I lay out these examples—they are not necessarily the best, but they come quickly to hand—in order to make a larger point: the ongoing "auditing" of faculty life has become a kind of bean-counting accountancy,[2] and the necessity of faculty to self-surveil or to risk running afoul of some administrative or legislative dictum is an ever-present danger, a point to which I will return later, briefly. First, I would like to engage in a short "deconstruction," if I may, of what these requirements mean for faculty. A bit of context would help here.

Gallarotti (2010) argues there are two forms of influence operating in international relations: soft empowerment and hard empowerment. Hard empowerment could be considered roughly comparable to hard diplomacy, or war, and soft empowerment could be roughly compared to diplomacy, or diplomatic negotiations. I would argue, following his logic, that there are two faces to neoliberalism's influence felt in the academy: hard diplomacy, or accountability and surveillance systems, coupled with threats of dismissal, or failure to honour proffered contracts (as in the case of Steven Salaita);[3] and soft systems, frequently felt as an ongoing sense of fear and terror, referenced by Di Leo et al. (2013). The terrorism of these accountability regimes may be directly related to the very real threats of program discontinuation, contract nonrenewal, failure to tenure and promote (a threat felt especially keenly by new, young, and as-yet-untenured faculty), failure to provide merit pay, or the removal of courses from the course catalogue, with its implication that certain topics would no longer be covered in the curriculum. Especially vulnerable are program areas that are not yet departments; examples would be race and ethnic studies programs, language programs not residing in departments (e.g., Arabic, Urdu, Pashto, Russian, and the like), gender studies, women's studies, and other specialized units that have never been more than certification programs, and which have never been assigned departmental status.

In the first example, that of WEAVE Online, we are looking at what I think of as hard influence, or hard diplomacy. It is hard influence because it forces professors to self-surveil. In order to provide the data that feeds the maw of the system, professors must keep track of every meeting with every student (which actually must be reported on yet another form, along with evaluations of whether or not the student is making adequate progress toward graduation, a dissertation proposal, or a completed dissertation), and must log somewhere every student who graduates, his/her degree, and the faculty member's role in the student's completion. Failure to input data from one's program area into WEAVE Online will earn one a series of ever more threatening emails from the central bureaucracy set up to monitor the input from every single program area on campus. There are more than a dozen full-time people, under a director, who do nothing but monitor when data go in and who is not compliant with data inputting. This is a part of the "punitive accountability" of which Michelle Fine speaks. I have no idea what the punishment is if I fail to complete the assignments, but I can speak for the endless nagging from a department head and the full-time clinical faculty member we have hired to do nothing but oversee the department's collection. This is accountancy run amok.

The second example, of putting one's curriculum vitae and syllabi online, by legislative fiat, is what is termed by Shore and Wright (2000) as "coercive accountability" or "coercive accountancy." Rather than signify what an instructor thinks are basic concepts and ideas that should go into this course or that, the syllabus becomes a kind of advertisement. When coupled with the professor's vita and her salary, it announces what kind of expertise the student will be purchasing, and how well that expertise is paid. Moreover, like some "truth in advertising" regulation, this requirement is now a part of state law, such that professors not in compliance are subject to some kind of penalty or unpleasant consequences (such penalties are not specified in the legislation).

The third example—from the "Department of Redundancy Department"—is a good example of what happens when the audit culture so thoroughly replaces both academic values and common sense that the same material is asked for again and again, although on different forms, and is said to be used for different purposes. It is what I would term the soft diplomacy, and is the most readily resisted. Because it is so clearly superfluous, redundant, duplicative, and wasteful, it is easy to call out the perpetrators. All of these forms, however, speak to an institution accountable not to itself or its faculty, students, and parents but rather an institution increasingly making itself accountable to political interests abiding in the states, to market forces (particularly in the commodification of knowledge [see Lincoln 1998, 2011, 2012; Slaughter and Leslie 1997), and to corporate and business interests.

There is one more example, that of promotion, tenure, and merit pay policies, but I shall deal with that in a moment. First, I would like to review some concepts for clarity, and to set the context for what I believe are the implications for faculty, students, and, occasionally, staff. *Neoliberalism* represents the politico-economic-social theory from which many of the assumptions regarding the market's power and its presumed ability to determine appropriate arrays of labour, capital, education, and social services emerge. *Ordoliberalism* is neoliberalism on steroids, wherein the market also governs governmentality and the roles of government in providing services and creating the conditions for the market to operate freely, as it wishes, with a minimum of regulation. I would argue that we are rapidly headed toward ordoliberalism, as Foucault warned against, if we are not already there. *Corporatization* references a major premise of neoliberalism, to wit, that institutions behaving as corporations will exhibit successful competition within their institutional ecology, with those failing to introduce corporate practices (and perhaps retaining classical academic values) moved to the margins of professional practice, teaching, and learning. Ultimately, such institutions as the latter, which focus on classical liberal arts educations and critical thinking, might well be considered "dangerous" institutions, since they might promulgate a serious critique of the dominant social system and the very real social injustices it perpetrates.

The Slide from Stewardship to Accountancy

It is possible to review the effects of the arterial connection between neoliberalism and the creeping corporatization of the research university (Steck 2003; Engvall 2010; Tuchman 2009; Considine and Painter 1997; Turk 2008; Woodhouse 2009; Chan and Fisher 2008), but perhaps it is more useful to signal the ways in which faculty and student life are being "McDonald-ized" in service to creating the conditions for "total quality management," "re-engineering," auditability/accountability, and other standardizing metrics.

Promotion and Tenure

Two years ago, the large and well-respected University of Southern California announced a new promotion and tenure policy. To even be considered for the first promotion and tenure decision, a young assistant professor must have a book out—but not just any book; the book has to be from an academic/university press—and at least a half-million in grants and contracts under her belt. Without these accomplishments on her vita, she is not even eligible to be considered. This conforms quite tightly to Steck's (2003) notion that scholars have now become "researchers," and it likewise demonstrates why the National Research Council (2002) was able to claim that qualitative researchers might produce "scholarship" but were not producing "research" for sure, and, consequently, were not researchers (thereby not having to be taken seriously).

I speak first of promotion and tenure because it is on everyone's mind at some point or another; or, if you mentor new, young faculty in the academy, it is on even the minds of senior faculty. One example is from my own history. When I went up for promotion to associate, what I submitted was not only the candidate's statement, which is de rigueur today, but also every single thing I had written, published, and presented: every journal article, every conference paper, every book. While I am certain most of my departmental colleagues did not read my book, they certainly read enough of my articles and conference papers that they were able to converse quite explicitly about the various pieces some weeks after the initial vote. Just this year, we sent up a young assistant professor with three articles, a vita, a candidate's statement, and six external letters of review. In reviewing her dossier, the promotion and tenure committee looked at the *number* of articles, and the overall ISI ranking of the journals in which she published; the number of refereed conference papers; perhaps read the three pieces sent with the dossier; and ran a tally of the actual number of dollars she had brought in, and a tally of the dollar amounts of grant proposals still pending. The committee examined her teaching evaluation "scores," and, where included, cursorily read the student comments on those evaluations. They counted the number of doctoral dissertation advisorships and committee memberships, and tallied those, finding her in compliance with coordinating board recommended numbers, and voted unanimously "yes." I sincerely doubt a single member of the department could talk in a sophisticated way about her publications, having likely not read them. Most of the discussion was an exercise in counting and productivity measures. Quality and originality were absent from the discussion; journal ISI ratings having become a proxy for those criteria.

This year, again, I will serve as external reviewer for several young scholars going up for either promotion and tenure or promotion to full professor. And, once again, the implied metric goes something like this: "Does this level of productivity appear appropriate for an individual achieving this rank?" Nowhere are there instructions that call for analyzing the research portion of the dossier for its quality, its contribution to some discourse in my field, its originality, its novel approach, its new and fresh insights. The competition aspect of corporatization comes out as a question, such as "How would you rank this individual alongside other individuals at the same rank in your discipline?" I suspect that is why senior scholars as renowned as Laurel Richardson can openly admit they begin books with great excitement, only to set them down soon after because they are boring. In the corporatized university, it is the amount of productivity that is audited, rather than the power or creativity or insight of that productivity. This is a counting function. The discourse of accounting, or accountancy, unable to account for ideas or critical approaches to problems, or even to audit meaningful problems, resorts to quantifying academic labour by bottom-line numbers.

Merit Pay
The very idea of "merit" pay signifies that some members of the academy are perhaps not very meritorious, while others—whose contributions might well be significant to and for the enterprise—appear to be extremely meritorious. Merit pay, as a form of compensation, was largely borrowed from the corporate world, where specific forms of productivity were valued by the organization, while other forms were not. What merit pay signifies is that the total enterprise of higher education is not valued, or, at least, is not as highly valued as refereed journal articles, external funding, and patents and technological inventions that can be commercialized. When we ceased giving credit for institutional governance labour, such as serving on the faculty senate, or working with university committees, we inadvertently began to abdicate our responsibilities for self-governance and self-evaluation. When teaching is found to be less rewarded and rewarding on the merit pay scale, we have given up much of the moral authority of the professoriate that we traditionally held for enculturating the next generation to sound citizenship and critical thinking.

Publication and the Professor
One of the more insidious ways in which universities are corporatizing their goals and aims under a neoliberal or ordoliberal regime lies in the publication industry. Searching for new products to commodify, the corporate lens focused on research and publication. The past fifty years—and especially the past thirty—have seen a veritable explosion in journal and book publications. Both books and journals have undergone a massive increase in cost, effectively making them prohibitive in many places where they might prove useful, principally developing and underdeveloped countries and regions (Lincoln 2012).

There is a move abroad in the land, of course, toward open access. In the United States, the federal government has ruled that certain kinds of research funded with federal dollars must be open access within a year or so (principally medical research)—a move that has the journals protesting loudly. In other fields, however, the open-access movement is somewhat balked and beleaguered. A very prominent social science publisher, for example, has created an open-access journal. I have not been published in it, but I looked over the requirements, and while the published articles are open access, to submit a piece for review and possible publication is $600. That is a fairly stout amount for any but the most senior faculty, and, of course, virtually impossible for those at the bottom end of the pay scale. At the same time, the democratic desire of many librarians to create what is called a "knowledge commons" appears to be partly stalled by powerful commercial interests in the publishing world. To the extent that universities rely on commercial academic journal publication as a criterion for promotion and tenure, and look with disdain, if not disfavour, on electronic or open-access publication, this situation will continue to obtain, and commercial presses will continue to commodify, the products of faculty scholarly labour, and strive to maintain such publication in the capital-value stream.

Some universities are undermining this knowledge monopoly—or what I term the "knowledge-opoly"—by requesting that faculty help create a knowledge commons on their own universities' campuses. They do this by contributing every paper, lecture, and journal article they prepare to a campus archive, which may be accessed by anyone with access to the Internet. Some campuses, however, have gotten into a bit of hot water from scholarly presses over posting materials prior to their printing. The jury is out on whether or not this strategy will work to open up the gates to knowledge for all comers, or whether the publishing houses will manage to kill these archival experiments aborning.

Academic Freedom on the Block?
A fourth and final consequence of the corporatizing of higher education is the possibility of an eroding sense of academic freedom. The intrusion of social media into the educational environment and personal lives of faculty and students alike has made academic freedom appear more fragile, more arguable, more tenuous than in previous decades, although it has always been a somewhat slippery legal-theoretic concept (Menand 1993, 1996; O'Neil 2008). Faculty, however, feel a sense of "heightened scrutiny" of their work, the hours they are on campus, their syllabi and coverage of the course material, their grading practices, and other normal and routine practices of university faculty. As Di Leo et al. (2013) point out, this intense and pervasive surveillance, as well as the implied mandate to self-surveil (Argyrou 2000; Amit 2000), creates a climate of fear among those surveilled, with a corresponding loss of confidence, a loss of academic freedom, and a withdrawal away from commitment. What this "heightened scrutiny" adds up to is something that Inglis and Aers describe in the following way:

> There are the key concepts of accountability, and they lock together in a powerful structure of surveillance...[but] the new accountability officers are well-armed, punitive and everywhere...The result is much less a vindication of public trust than an intensification of mistrust, and a steady diminution of personal commitment in the activity under audit. (2008, ix)

What this failure of trust, and a growing mistrust, of public officials also leads to is something that Di Leo et al. (2013) term "academic terrorism."

How do we cope with this ongoing sense of fear, mistrust, terror over our own tenure, insecurity, coercive surveillance, meaningless counting of nonimportant characteristics of our work? For scholars, Shore and Wright suggest

> three ways of identifying and analyzing the character and direction of the new cultural epoch of managerialism and its impact on higher education. The first is through tracking key changes in language, including the emergence of new discourses and the "semantic clusters" from which they are constituted. The second is by identifying the new kinds of practices associated with these discourses, and the new institutions, norms and areas of expertise that they hail into existence, and through which they are implemented. The third is the effect of these norms and practices—embedded in mundane routines and duties—on conditions of work and through and, more importantly, on the way in which individuals construct themselves as professional subjects. (2000, 58)

They go on to ask, "How do individuals confront the new cultural logic, with its implicit morality and its reworked notions of professionalism, when they are 'inside'—and therefore subject to the disciplines of—the new regime itself?" (58)

Garrett Broad (2011) asks, what would a post-neoliberal university look like, and what would be the actions needed to take us there? Until we can agree on a set of actions and plans, I believe there are two strategies we can employ to resist the massive transformation of higher education into something it should never be. First, we need to take on "managerialist assumptions and language" in order to "denaturalize and challenge them" (Broad 2011, E25) every chance we get. This may mean we transition from formal scholarly writing solely to addressing broader audiences, including the public, through letters to the editor, op-ed pieces in newspapers, available blogs, Web newsletters, and any available social media that come to hand. We might address groups to whom we have not spoken before: the Lions Club, the Kiwanis Club, our chambers of commerce.

Second, we can denaturalize the language of accountancy by renaturalizing the language of citizenship, social responsibility, community, service, and other liberal and progressive values to everyone with whom we speak, or to whom we write. The discourse of higher education as a private good needs to be countered calmly but strongly with a discourse of higher education as a public good, enlarging democratic and communitarian norms and values. We need to speak of what is important in higher education, not what is counted, and why the core values add both practical and symbolic value to the entire country. And, within our own institutions, we need to defend and protect both tenure and academic freedom (Amit 2000; Csorba 1988; De George 1997; Eliot 1907; Kahn and Pavlich 2000; O'Neil 2008; Woodhouse 2009), as they are core values to a free and unfettered faculty. We can also stand up for what is meaningful accountability, and what is mindless dross. We can urge our colleagues to be concerned about these matters. We can invent other forms of resistance and strategic challenge (Bargh 2007), and draw on our Indigenous colleagues for help in this. As Thomas Paine, the great American patriot, observed, "If we do not hang together, we shall surely all hang separately."

Notes

1   Just as we have unfortunately seen virtually the entire political process in the United States come under the influence of the market, with elections being bought by millionaires and billionaires out to purchase candidates believed to be willing to pander to their patrons' corporate, social, and religious aims.
2   Terry Eagleton (2015) calls the troubles with the university a problem attributable to "bean counters, bureaucrats and barbarians."
3   Steven Salaita, a Native American studies scholar, had his signed contract revoked by the board of trustees at the University of Illinois at Urbana-Champaign when it objected to a tweet (Twitter) it considered to be anti-Israel, in which Salaita criticized a recent decision made by the Israeli Knesset (parliament).

References

Amit, V. 2000. "The University as Panopticon: Moral Claims and Attacks on Academic Freedom." In *Audit Cultures: Anthropological Studies in Accountability, Ethics and the Academy*, edited by M. Strathern, 215–35. London: Routledge.

Anderson, G. L. 2007. "Neoliberalism." In *Encyclopedia of Activism and Social Justice*, edited by G. L. Anderson and K. G. Herr, 1022–24. Thousand Oaks, CA: Sage.

Argyrou, V. 2000. "Self-Accountability, Ethics and the Problem of Meaning." In *Audit Cultures: Anthropological Studies in Accountability, Ethics and the Academy*, edited by M. Strathern, 196–212. London: Routledge.

Bargh, M., ed. 2007. *Resistance: An Indigenous Response to Neoliberalism*. Auckland, New Zealand: Huia Publishers.

Broad, G. M. 2011. "Why Voice Matters—Culture and Politics after Neoliberalism" [book review]. *Journal of Communication* 61: E24–E27.

Burrows, R. 2012. "Living with the H-Index? Metric Assemblages in the Contemporary Academy." *The Sociological Review* 60(2): 355–72.

Chan, A. S., and D. Fisher, eds. 2008. *The Exchange University: Corporatization of Academic Culture*. Vancouver: UBC Press.

Cheit, E. F. 1994. "What Price Accountability?" *Change* 26(3) (May–June): 71.

Considine, M., and M. Painter, eds. 1997. *Managerialism: The Great Debate*. Melbourne, Australia: Melbourne University Press.

Csorba, L., ed. 1988. *Academic License: The War on Academic Freedom*. Evanston, IL: UCA Books.

Davis, M., and D. B. Monk, eds. 2007. *Evil Paradises: Dreamworlds of Neoliberalism*. New York: The New Press.

De George, R. T. 1997. *Academic Freedom and Tenure: Ethical Issues*. Lanham, MD: Rowman & Littlefield.

Di Leo, J. R., H. A. Giroux, S. A. McClennen, and K. J. Saltman. 2013. *Neoliberalism, Education and Terrorism: Contemporary Dialogues*. Boulder, CO: Paradigm Publishers.

Dolhinow, R. 2006. "Mexican Women's Activism in New Mexico Colonias." In *Women and Change at the U.S./Mexico Border: Mobility, Labor, and Activism*, edited by D. J. Mattingly and E. R. Hansen, Chapter 8. Tucson: The University of Arizona Press.

Eagleton, T. 2015. "The Slow Death of the University." *The Chronicle of Higher Education*, April 6. http://www.chronicle.com/article/The-Slow-Death-of-the/228991.

Eliot, C. W. 1907. "Academic Freedom." Harvard University President's Address before the Cornell Phi Beta Kappa induction. *Science* 26 (July 5): 1–12.

Engvall, R. 2010. *Corporatization of Higher Education: The Move for Greater Standardized Assessment Programs*. Cresskill, NJ: Hampton Press, Inc.

Gallarotti, G. M. 2010. *Cosmopolitan Power in International Relations: A Synthesis of Realism, Neoliberalism and Constructivism*. Cambridge, UK: Cambridge University Press.

Inglis, F., and L. Aers. 2008. *Key Concepts in Education*. London: Sage.

Kahn, S. E., and D. Pavlich, eds. 2000. *Academic Freedom and the Inclusive University*. Vancouver: UBC Press.

Levin, J. S., G. Shaker, and R. Wagoner. 2012. "Post-Neoliberalism: The Professional Identity of Faculty off the Tenure Track." In *Universities and the Public Sphere: Knowledge Creation and State Building in the Era of Globalization*, edited by B. Pusser, K. Kempner, S. Marginson, and I. Ordorika, 197–218. New York: Routledge.

Lincoln, Y. S. 1998. "Commodification and Contradiction in Academic Research." *Studies in Cultures, Organizations, and Societies* 5(1): 1–16.

———. 2012. "The Political Economy of Publication: Marketing, Commodification, and Qualitative Scholarly Work." *Qualitative Health Research* 22(11) (November): 1451–59. doi:10.1177/1049732312457713.

———. 2011. "'A Well-Regulated *Faculty* . . .': The Coerciveness of Accountability and Other Measures That Abridge Faculties' Right to Teach and Research." *Cultural Studies ↔ Critical Methodologies* 11(4) (August): 369–72.

Menand, L. 1993. "The Future of Academic Freedom." *Academe* 79(3) (May–June): 11–17.

Menand, L., ed. 1996. *The Future of Academic Freedom*. Chicago: University of Chicago Press.

National Research Council. 2002. *Scientific Research in Education*. Edited by R. J. Shavelson and L. Towne. Committee on Scientific Principles for Education Research, Center for Education, Division of Behavioral and Social Sciences and Education. Washington, DC: National Academy Press.

O'Neil, R. M. 2008. *Academic Freedom in the Wired World: Political Extremism, Corporate Power and the University*. Cambridge, MA: Harvard University Press.

Porfilio, B. J., and C. Malott. 2007. "Neoliberalism." In *Encyclopedia of Activism and Social Justice*, edited by G. L. Anderson and K. G. Herr. New York: Sage.

Saltman, K. J., and D. A. Gabbard, eds. 2003. *Education as Enforcement: The Militarization and Corporatization of Schools*. New York: Routledge.

Schiffrin, A. 1996. "The Corporatization of Publishing: Books Are Becoming Like Everything Else the Mass Media Turn Out." *The Nation*, June 3, 29–32.

Schwandt, T. A. 2015. *The SAGE Dictionary of Qualitative Inquiry*, 4th ed. Thousand Oaks, CA: Sage Publications.

Shore, C., and S. Wright. 2000. "Coercive Accountability: The Rise of Audit Culture in Higher Education." In *Audit Culture: Anthropological Studies in Accountability, Ethics and the Academy*, edited by M. Strathern, 57–89. London: Routledge.

Slaughter, S., and L. Leslie. 1997. *Academic Capitalism*. Baltimore, MD: Johns Hopkins University Press.

Spooner, M. 2015. "The Deleterious Personal and Societal Effects of the 'Audit Culture' and a Domesticated Academy: Another Way Is Possible." *International Review of Qualitative Research* 8: 212–28.

———. 2018. "Qualitative Research and Global Audit Culture: The Politics of Productivity, Accountability, & Possibility." In *The SAGE Handbook of Qualitative Research*, 5th ed., edited by N. K. Denzin and Y. S. Lincoln, 894–914. Thousand Oaks, CA: Sage Publications.

Steck, H. 2003. "Corporatization of the University: Seeking Conceptual Clarity." *Annals of the American Academy of Political and Social Science* 585 (January): 66–83.

Sykes, C. J. 1990. *Prof Scam: Professors and the Demise of Higher Education*. New York: St. Martin's Griffin.

Thomas, P. G. 2012. "Accountability." In *The SAGE Handbook of Public Administration*, edited by B. G. Peters, 593–600. Thousand Oaks, CA: Sage Publications.

Tuchman, G. 2009. *Wannabe U.: Inside the Corporate University*. Chicago: University of Chicago Press.

Tuck, A. 2003. "Impact Factors: A Tool of the Sterile Audit Culture" [letter to the editor]. *Nature* 424 (July): 14.

Turk, J. L., ed. 2008. *Universities at Risk: How Politics, Special Interests, and Corporatization Threaten Academic Integrity*. Toronto: James Lorimer and Company, Ltd.

Woodhouse, H. 2009. *Selling Out: Academic Freedom and the Corporate Market*. Montreal: McGill-Queen's University Press.

CHAPTER 2

THE ART OF THE IMPOSSIBLE— DEFINING AND MEASURING INDIGENOUS RESEARCH?

Linda Tuhiwai Smith

Introduction

This chapter discusses the measurement of research impact as it relates to Indigenous research, particularly research that draws on Indigenous Knowledge, uses Indigenous methodologies, and seeks to improve the lives of Indigenous peoples. Increasingly, research impact is being used to shape broader decisions about the kind of research being supported by governments, philanthropic foundations, and institutions. It can be argued that this "turn" to impact measurement legitimates certain kinds of research either deemed to have greater impact than other kinds of research or to be simply more easily "measured." It has also led to a growth of other practices, such as the use of "impact factors" for journals, for individual researchers, and for the status and prestige of research institutions.

There are different ways for understanding research impact and providing evidence for making informed policies and translating research findings into outcomes that make a positive contribution to society. Normative ideologies about research and evidence play a significant role in defining impact and creating research metrics and performance measures. More importantly, such normative ideologies play a key role in determining the rules of the game, choosing the referees and champions, and identifying what really counts and how it counts.

For Indigenous research, arguably one of the newest research fields on the block, albeit with ancient veins, the concept of impact is interesting, to say the least. Researchers who work in the field of "Indigenous research," which has diverse international and national strands, are mostly motivated by making a positive difference and actively work toward having an impact that overturns the hundreds of years of colonization and institutional hostility to Indigenous Knowledge and practices. In many ways, impact is exactly what Indigenous research is designed to achieve, but perhaps the social transformations being sought by many Indigenous approaches are not quite what research measurement is trying to capture. This chapter addresses some of the issues of impact at the level of a new field of knowledge, such as Indigenous studies and its national and regional variations, rather than specifically at individual researcher impact.

The Twenty-First-Century Neoliberal University Context

A number of critiques of research performance contextualize the turn to measurement as an aspect of the neoliberal university and its implication in free market globalization, the commodification of knowledge, and the new academic performativity requirements on staff (Thornton 2009). It is important not to romanticize the pre-neoliberal university as one that did not measure research performance or was disinterested in society and the economy. From an Indigenous perspective, the pre-neoliberal university and the current neoliberal university can both be viewed as part of an unbroken line of cultural imperialism that characterizes the academy as a set of teaching and research institutions deeply rooted in European intellectual traditions, even when recently established in other parts of the non-Western world.

In many contexts, including Canada, Australia, the United States, New Zealand, large parts of Africa, Asia, and Latin America, the British colonial influence on universities has been profound, even after countries have become independent nation-states. Institutions, that is individual universities, are only a part of the much more pervasive "Institution of Knowledge"; the hegemonic power of academic knowledge used to shape the common sense of society, to train and socialize high-status professions, to set the "standards" and model the "values" of an educated society, and to influence and regulate relations of power.

Indigenous peoples, and the Other, more broadly identified by Said (1977) in terms of Orientalism, were not only systematically excluded from the Institution of Knowledge but were the focus of hostile, racist, and unethical research. What was deemed "attractive" was appropriated and the rest condemned. The genealogy of terms that defined Indigenous peoples, their knowledge, culture, and languages was forged and entrenched in Western consciousness and discourses. The old liberal university actively excluded difference, carefully rationing the rare appearance of social diversity, including students from the working class, women, and anyone racially different. Elitism was a characteristic of the old liberal university, and the fostering of research and teaching programs, many based on eugenics, supported these elitist structures of privilege. There were also very old debates at play about the best pathway to progress and assimilation for Native and Black peoples, some advocating vocational options that led to working-class jobs, and others advocating a strong liberal and academic education that led to professional work. This structure changed in the 1970s with the "massification" of universities, which greatly increased the numbers of students, qualifications, and new areas of study (Englund 2002; Guri-Rosenblit, Sebkova, and Teichler 2007). By most accounts, the changes toward increasing access to university and widening the curriculum were to meet economic, demographic, and "democratic" and social-inclusion challenges of the generations born after the end of the Second World War. At this time, more active equality of opportunity programs were introduced, which, while mostly benefitting white women, wedged the doors open in some of the professions, such as teaching, law, and medicine, for Indigenous students and minorities.

The neoliberal institution has opened up some possibilities for Indigenous peoples, with programs and research that were not available in the old liberal institution. Why? One reason is the development of what has been referred to as a new kind of neoliberal multiculturalism that "accepted" more categories of difference, in terms of access to universities, but still expected students to attain the standards they set and maintained (Hale 2005; Kymlicka 2015). Neoliberal multiculturalism coincided with and contributed to the massification of universities from the 1980s and the widening of curricula that were generated in newer, younger, and more open public universities that have arisen in the last fifty years. Another reason was that, in contexts such as New Zealand, Māori people, who already had a tenuous foothold in universities that began in the early twentieth century with the teaching of

Māori language, were able to expand the teaching of Māori studies beyond anthropology, which was its disciplinary "home" across and into other disciplines and professional qualifications. The expansion of non-anthropological versions of Māori studies that drew on Indigenous theories and methodologies, such as Kaupapa Māori, opened up more opportunities for teaching and research for Indigenous scholars (Pihama 2011; Smith 2012).

In the last twenty-five years, there has been a significant increase in the numbers of Māori entering tertiary education including universities. There are more institutions teaching Māori-related curricula, and there has been a systematic program of capacity building in supporting more Māori to complete doctoral qualifications and more Māori to participate in research. The MAI doctoral program has played a significant part in graduating more than five hundred Māori with PhD qualifications across many disciplines. Three distinctive Māori tertiary institutions called Wānanga, which offer programs from foundation studies to doctoral qualifications, have been officially established and accredited by the government. The academic programs are mandated to teach and reflect "*ahuatanga and tikanga Māori*" or Māori knowledge, values, and practices. There are a number of Māori-focused research institutes and a National Centre of Research Excellence, Ngā Pae o Te Māramatanga, that are situated within universities. There is also an increase in the number of Māori researchers working across a wide range of disciplines (Tertiary Education Commission 2013). This growth of Māori Indigenous research capacity has occurred in the twenty-first-century neoliberal university, most of it since the 1990s.

For Māori researchers working within universities, the realities of being assessed for research performance have been in place since 2002, when New Zealand's Performance-Based Research Fund, known as the PBRF, was established. The PBRF is an assessment of individual portfolios of research submitted by every academic staff member teaching on a degree qualification or working in a research position. The major part of the assessment is a quality score for research outputs—publications, performances, and exhibitions. Research impact is one of a number of other factors that are assessed at an individual level. One of the assessment panels within this system of assessment is the Māori Knowledge and Development Panel, which is a multidisciplinary panel that reviews proposals from Māori and non-Māori academic staff who do research in the field of Māori knowledge. In 2003, the first panel reported its finding that 481 Māori researchers had submitted portfolios, representing 5.9 per cent of all researchers. In 2006, the number had grown to 517 Māori researchers. Unfortunately, the number then dropped to 299 in the 2012 PBRF round, due most likely to a reassignment of staff, seen by their own institutions as being "non-research active," to either full-time teaching loads or to redundancy. This represents only part of the Māori research workforce, as it does not include researchers working for Crown research institutes, community organizations, government agencies, or private research businesses, nor those who are based overseas. Measuring research performance, and what counts as "performance" at an individual, group, and system level, is part of the issue this chapter examines, namely the issue of measuring impact for research that is explicitly self-defined as Indigenous research, uses Indigenous methodologies, and draws on Indigenous Knowledges and languages.

Public Accountability, Performance Measurement,
and the Metrics of Research Impact

New Zealand's PBRF is one of a number of national research measurement exercises. These measures are attached to public funding mostly for universities and have been seized upon by institutions as measures of status and of that elusive notion of "excellence." The public policy framework for such measures is sometimes referred to as New Public Management and Public Accountability, informed by public choice theory, a paradigm for the public sector that started in the 1980s and an underpinning framework for operationalizing neoliberal ideology in higher education. In this paradigm, measuring impact is about trying to demonstrate a clear line between public investment in research and economic returns in society. Knowledge production as research is simply a mode of production expected to produce a return on investment that is measurable.

Measures of research performance are part of a package of measures that have mapped onto traditional forms of research assessment and definitions of what counts as quality research. Some of the traditional forms of research quality used notions of "merit," as measured by both quantity and presumed quality of peer-reviewed publications; track record, as measured by consistency of performance by publications; and peer esteem, as measured by scholarly reviews and citations. Newer additions to measurement have included the amount of funding that a researcher gains, the impact quality and ranking of journals, and then the individual "impact" factor based on the quantity and quality of publications. New performance measures ask not only what research has been produced but also what impact has that research made or what is the return on investment? Teams of researchers, themselves, rather than distant policy analysts, have designed many of the new performance "measures." The exercise of having researchers design their own benchmarks and measures is somewhat akin to having them make their own noose. It brings out the best and often the worst of human motivations and inclinations under the guise of fairness, consultation, and inclusion. There has also been some deep belief in the fiction that the best research is produced by a heroic individual researcher, who, without the help of others, and indeed in competition with others, "discovers" the breakthrough that will save the human race. This all leads to an ideal that one can measure in an instrumental way the impact of an individual piece of research undertaken by an individual researcher working alone. The default norm in this exercise is often the biomedical sciences, or, more precisely, the disciplines of knowledge that have long held internal-unit-based measures of status and prestige. In fact, the journal impact factor was developed in the medical sciences in the 1950s as a way to broaden the range of journals that were available at the time and as part of the Science Citation Index (Garfield 2005). The h-index was developed as an alternative to the journal impact factor and is more a measure of an individual's research impact factor (Hirsch 2005).

In New Zealand, assessment processes for the likely impact of research have introduced new players into standard research assessment exercises, including private sector and business interests, end-users or stakeholders, and, in some government-funded research, Māori representatives. In other words, research is assessed for both its "science" excellence, often through one process, and then its likely "impact" through a second-tier process. The meaning of "impact" in the assessment context is complicated, as end-users might well rank "relevance" to their needs as one criterion for impact, while scientists might still see the h-index as the "more scientific" way to assess impact. It is a term that can mean the research is simply relevant or fills a gap; that it can be translated into policy, and social and economic outcomes; that it addresses funding priorities; and that it is likely to have an impact in terms of innovation and technology translation. The role of Māori in this level of assessment is important and is one part of a series of arguments for inclusion and engagement that have been hard-won by Māori researchers, *iwi* (tribes), and as an expression of the Treaty of Waitangi partnership between the Crown and Māori.

Of course, research impact measurement has developed over time, and it has become its own field of study, known as scientometrics, with another related field called journalology. Those whose concern it is to measure impact across all dimensions of research have broadened and refined the approach to include a wider range of quantitative and qualitative measurements. In brief, the measurement models have gone through at least four stages of metric design (Donovan 2011). *Bibliometrics* measures numbers of journals, citations, and impact factors, such as the *h*-index, but has proven difficult to apply in disciplines other than the sciences. *Technometrics* measures economic returns and patents but has had limited application. *Sociometrics* has attempted to use big data sets and macro social statistics but is seen as problematic (Donovan 2011). *Altmetrics* is the current advanced form of impact measurement incorporating narratives, case studies, impact stories alongside peer and end-user judgments, as well as standard quantitative measures of publications and citations. This model explores social media sites and includes Twitter and other modes of research engagement. The more a measure such as the *h*-index takes on some form of meaning or truth, the higher the stakes escalate in terms of individual and institutional behaviour and esteem. High-ranking scholars bring prestige and value to institutions. Whereas once no such factor appeared on academic vitas, now some scholars provide full details of their science impact rating alongside numbers of citations and peer reviews of their work.

It can be argued that, in response to demonstrating impact, new forms of research are emerging, such as co-production of knowledge where researchers, stakeholders, end-users, and other collaborators join forces to work on research in a way that is likely to have high impact in terms of transformation, faster take-up of ideas, and embedding research, policy, and change in the single co-production framework. Interestingly, co-production has emerged from a different trajectory than the social justice, participatory action research model. For example, it has come from the technology, science, and society fields but shares some similar research practices in terms of the roles of the "participants" and "actors" in research (Jasanoff 2004). Co-production may not work for researchers who are motivated more by exploring new knowledge and who work alone over a much longer time frame, although even some of those scholars have been put into research groups or research clusters as a means to show the capacity of institutional research "teams."

Indigenous Knowledge and Research Approaches as Disruptive Practices

The emergence of Indigenous research in the academy as an old/new field converges with the rise of the managerial and measurement culture of the corporate neoliberal institution and has its own history of development grounded in the anti-colonial pursuit of the rights of Indigenous peoples. Most Indigenous research methodologies are designed to translate into impact through their very approaches to ethics, community inclusion, and participation, and their adherence to principles of respect, relationships, and reciprocity. Indigenous research is also a form of co-production of knowledge. Indigenous research aims to make positive transformations for Indigenous nations and communities that overturn colonial paradigms of thinking and working and that create new spaces for Indigenous Knowledges, cultures, and peoples to thrive. Indigenous researchers are quite explicit about the impacts they seek (Deloria 1988; Brayboy 2005; Hokowhitu 2010; Pidgeon and Hardy Cox 2002; Pihama 2011; Rigney 2001). It is what motivates their research and their practice as scholars, teachers, researchers, and members of a community.

With these broad aims, the question of impact and what research impact might look like for Indigenous research is not a threatening idea. The challenge is in how impact is understood between those who seek to measure it through a set of normative assumptions and metrics and the kind of impact being valued. Communicating to government agencies and the institutions the different approaches and motivations for research held by Indigenous researchers is a fraught endeavour. One example of how difficult it sometimes appears to have Indigenous research understood is when, in 2014, the Māori Centre of Research Excellence, Ngā Pae o Te Māramatanga, was not awarded further funding by New Zealand's Tertiary Education Commission. Along with many other Māori scholars, leaders, and a wider public, we felt a sense of disappointment and outrage that the process was flawed by a lack of genuine peer review by Indigenous scholars, and a sense that our work was completely negated by the criteria used to assess excellence and innovation. The minister of Māori development, the Honourable Dr. Pita Sharples (2014), called it a "slap in the face to Māori research and researchers and is a clear sign that Government agencies are marginalizing Māori development and communities." Associate Professor Leonie Pihama (2014) called it an "issue of 'white-streaming' (to borrow a word from Dr. Anne Milne) of research and research funds.... and as an entrenched fundamental structural and systemic act of racism." Writing in the *Wanganui Chronicle*, Tariana Turia (2014), the associate minister of social development and health, and co-leader of the Māori Party with Pita Sharples, which was in the coalition government, emphasized that the decision to not fund the centre would only have "resulted in marginalization of Māori research and the mainstreaming of Māori-led research. I believe we are seeing a focus on pure economic research investment at the expense of Māori research priorities." What is of genuine significance in the public defence of Ngā Pae o Te Māramatanga is that Māori people were publicly supporting research, research by Māori, research for Māori, and research about matters important to Māori. For our communities to defend the work of researchers is a story of "impact," a turn from skepticism and antagonism to one of public support.

As a former and founding co-director of Ngā Pae o Te Māramatanga, I also responded through a series of blogs that were sent around the world, as well as actively soliciting letters of support from Indigenous and non-Indigenous scholars. The blogs were published by Te Wharepora Hou, a collective of Māori women. Some of the points made in the first blog, reprinted here, speak to the idea of impact when considering Indigenous research, and the work that needs to be done to achieve a platform for making an impact.

It takes years to develop a research infrastructure. It takes years to develop centres of research excellence. It takes an excellent education system as researchers must succeed to the highest qualifications in their fields and new researchers need to be trained continuously. It takes the right synergies of knowledge as excellent researchers are trained and supported in diverse knowledge cultures. It takes discipline, perseverance and tolerance as researchers learn as much through failure and elimination as they do from success. It takes insight to understand the implications of serendipity. It takes difference and determination to carve out new areas of knowledge that challenge current thinking. It takes a wide community and network of similar minds as researchers learn from each other. It takes vision and stamina to build novel programmes of research that can address complex and inter-related problems. It takes a dose of sheer doggedness to forge a research direction when others want to set out to someplace different or to stay put. It takes an alliance of related systems that review, fund and publish research, that translate it into public knowledge like curriculum, that apply research into other contexts, that produce new or improved practices and products. It takes collaborations across disciplinary, institutional, national and international boundaries to get the best minds and skills available to advance the research. It takes institutional support to provide the best working environment for researchers. It takes institutional and public patience to wait for the next chapter of life changing research. It takes massive investment by the public through education and by the public and others through the funding of research. It takes a certain kind of ambition to persist in the pursuit of knowledge that may not yield quick fixes, widgets and gadgets, or social transformation in this generation and it takes a certain kind of society that believes it important to invest in the continuous development of knowledge for its longer term well-being.

In my area of Māori research, it took decades to develop the foundations of a single national research infrastructure. It took decades upon decades for Māori to make their way, one by one, through an education system that was not excellent to gain the highest qualifications. It took persistence to survive in knowledge cultures that did not value diversity let alone Māori knowledge. It took vision to focus on producing a critical mass of Māori with the highest academic qualifications from New Zealand and international institutions. It took the largest and possibly the most novel and challenging of collaborations to build a strong network of researchers who would focus their minds and efforts on Māori development. It rounded up all the "ones" and the "twos" of Māori researchers scattered across institutions to create a critical community of researchers who could support new research. It established journals, created avenues of engagement with the most suspicious of communities, and stimulated intellectual engagements across disciplines, communities, and languages. It supported research that was explicitly focussed on creating change, on improving outcomes and on developing communities. It had to win institutional support by winning funding. It created novel approaches that other centres of excellence borrowed and adapted. It created new methodologies for exploring social and cultural interfaces that are cited in international journals and applied in many other contexts. Its capacity development programme for PhDs is replicated in parts of Canada and the U.S. at top institutions.

So what tumbles down when Ngā Pae o Te Māramatanga is informed it will no longer be funded? A centre? Some funding? Yes of course, but much more. What tumbles down will cut more deeply into the capacity, momentum, community, system of knowledge, networks, relationships, intellectual excitement that was emerging from this Centre of Research Excellence. What tumbles down is an infrastructure that was built from scratch, from ones and twos, that had no previous models to borrow from, that was truly internationally innovative, multi-multidisciplinary, that was producing exciting young scholars footing it internationally and in our own communities. What tumbles down is a national infrastructure that could support Māori development across a range of dimensions that simply cannot be provided for by existing institutions. More importantly what tumbles down is a set of beliefs that the research system is genuinely interested in innovation, has a capacity to recognise or know how to support innovation outside its cultural frame, believes in its own rhetoric or actually understands the short term nature of its investments in research. (Smith 2014)

Most other traditional academic research is supported by major infrastructure and investment by governments over hundreds of years. New university institutions inherit most of the infrastructure and privileges accrued by old institutions. The academic power of research is reflected not only in libraries but in society and in the knowledge of social elites. Our colleagues will sigh and suggest that building infrastructure is not research, except that every time they get funded they are enhancing the infrastructure they have inherited. They may scratch their foreheads and say that graduating PhD graduates is what every good scientist does, but reproducing yourself is simply reproducing existing systems of power. They may also suggest that having only "one" researcher is insufficient, but the common story of scientific discovery is always the story of a heroic individual scientist. Indigenous researchers can also be heroic but value their collective community and have established strong international collaborations and networks.

Research excellence is often framed as being about innovation, introducing new knowledge, and showing new possibilities. One of our non-Indigenous colleagues, Professor Tove Skutnabb-Kangas, responded to an online Facebook petition started by Vanessa Kupenga with these comments:

I have just heard the shocking news that your Centre of Research Excellence Nga Pae o Te Maramatanga has not been shortlisted for funding after 2015. The Centre and its staff have been role models for all of us worldwide who have worked with Indigenous issues, regardless of whether we are Indigenous ourselves or not (I am not). We have all been inspired by and referred to its

long-term work in developing a completely new type of intellectual thinking, decolonising the minds of academics and communities alike. Not only have they lovingly fostered a new generation
of researchers, but they have also been patiently teaching non-
Indigenous (and even Indigenous) politicians, administrators,
and educators about how to develop and implement Indigenous
world views in research and in relations between research(ers)
and surrounding communities. The work of the Centre has given
confidence, inspiration, and hope to thousands of Indigenous
youth all over the world, inside and outside the academia.

As a result of the activism of scholars and Māori public figures, and pressure coming from other eminent scholars associated with other centres that
had missed out, the Tertiary Education Commission was instructed to run a
second-round process, but with less money to be gained. In the process, a
revised application from Ngā Pae o Te Māramatanga was eventually refunded.

Decolonizing knowledge and the academy is probably not considered
the desired focus or outcome of dominant mainstream academic research,
although transformation for the betterment of society is desired (Tuck and
Yang 2012; also Tuck this volume). What is the difference? One idea, decolonizing research, is clearly more disruptive of current relations of power than
the other idea, transformation. Furthermore, the betterment of society
depends very much on how society is understood. Discourse in the world of
research is as important as it is in the world.

The Impacts That Indigenous Research Seeks: What Do "You" People Want?

Firstly, "Indigenous research" tends to be the current preferred term for
research carried out by Indigenous researchers, for Indigenous researchers,
and with Indigenous communities. There are other terms that may or may
not imply the same thing (e.g., Kaupapa Māori research). Non-Indigenous
allies may work alongside and with Indigenous researchers, as allies and as
specialists, but are not generally considered the research leaders. Indigenous
researchers belong to diverse nations and communities of Indigenous peoples around the world. There is no singular agenda for Indigenous research
as determined by Indigenous nations at the international level, and probably none at the national jurisdiction level either. In New Zealand, there are
research agendas that have been developed for Māori health research, and

there are priorities that groups of researchers have agreed upon. What is held in common is a set of aspirations and political drivers that helped support the United Nations Declaration on the Rights of Indigenous Peoples and a range of declarations, charters, and ethical guidelines that aim to prevent the further exploitation by researchers of Indigenous people, their knowledges, their cultures, their remaining environments, and their bodies. The exploitative, destructive, and unethical history of research on Indigenous peoples that justified colonial practices and ideologies is a significant shared story across all Indigenous peoples. That one narrative frames the moral intention of Indigenous research, as an intention that halts further exploitation, addresses the damage that has been hurled upon generations of our communities, and respects Indigenous sovereignty and restores Indigenous principles of well-being. This intention can be contrasted by research that is motivated purely by "discovery," research motivated by a desire to "save" lives, and research motivated by a desire to create wealth. Governments have strategies that drive and resource the kinds of research intentions of discovery, application, and wealth creation. While individual Indigenous researchers also seek "discovery," it is probably more accurately framed in Māori knowledge terms as the "recovery" of knowledge that human beings were granted in the first place.

Indigenous research is attempting to put right a great wrong, to turn something "dirty" into an act of re-empowerment and self-determination. This makes Indigenous research an act of great hopefulness, an investment in engagement with the academy and with settler society, both of which excluded us, and an engagement in drawing knowledges together. The big political agenda of Indigenous research is for the paradigm shifts and transformations that overturn colonialism and create new relations of power with the nation-state so that Indigenous well-being and ability to be self-determining is achieved. At the level of many researchers, however, the agenda is perhaps more modest: to make a positive difference in the lives of Indigenous peoples; to improve health, social, and economic outcomes; to regenerate languages and cultures; to remove institutional barriers to Indigenous participation; to restore Indigenous Knowledge and values as a way of living and being. What Indigenous researchers have learned is that to achieve these outcomes requires diverse research approaches, including specifically "Indigenist" methodologies, a term used by Rigney (1999), and critical methodologies that deploy a range of disciplinary lenses. Considerable effort in the last two decades has been invested in developing compelling methodologies, Indigenous theories and practices of research, conceptual frameworks, and the ethical principles of engagement with Indigenous nations and communities. These approaches have all called upon, and worked with, Indigenous conceptions of knowledge, values, and practices.

Indigenous research has also been concerned with developing capacity and the infrastructure needed to sustain research. In the absence of secure and stable institutional and financial support, either from public or private funding, Indigenous researchers have developed very powerful networks of support and collaboration. These networks are across disciplines, are with Indigenous nations and communities, and are highly internationalized. Networks are a form of resistance to marginalization, they join people up across borders, they broaden participation, they enable and strengthen collaborations, and they are inherently dynamic and can accommodate diversity. Indigenous networks helped develop and bring to fruition the Declaration on the Rights of Indigenous Peoples. Within Indigenous discourse, the network idea is simply referred to as "relationships," one of the key ethical principles of Indigenous Knowledge and practice. Indigenous networks have developed research capacity, despite the limitations of many universities and research institutions. Where centres and institutes, or even clusters of vibrant Indigenous research groups, are important, it is that they provide a vital connection point of a network, the moment of synergy for networks to form, to cross-fertilize, or to re-form. Centres introduce a more stable leadership structure, a structure for mentoring younger researchers, and an intellectual hub for stimulating new ideas.

In New Zealand, Māori leaders and researchers have attempted over decades, and mostly with limited success, to participate in the full range of publicly funded research, including governance and decision-making participation. Having greater capacity has meant researchers have seen the sheer scale of research from which Māori have been excluded. The Waitangi Tribunal has provided a mechanism for Māori to argue a grievance that breaches the articles and principles of the Treaty of Waitangi. One of the relevant cases for research is known variously as the WAI-262 Claim for Flora and Fauna and the WAI-262 Taonga Claim, which broadly asked, "Who 'owns' and controls Māori culture?" The claim that was lodged in 1991 by six *iwi* was hugely complex and contentious, and the report from the tribunal was not produced until 2011. The report is called *Ko Aotearoa Tēnei* or *This Is Aotearoa* (Waitangi Tribunal 2011). The claim covered intellectual property, control over our genetic and biological resources, Māori relationship with the environment, *taonga* or legacies from the ancestors, and Crown engagement with *mātauranga* or Māori knowledge. While the claim was being heard, there were government policy changes and other engagements with Māori that included the introduction in 2005 of a Vision Mātauranga Policy for Science, Research and Technology. That policy still stands as a government policy for "unlocking the innovation potential of Māori knowledge, resources and people." The policy covers all the major research funding streams (Ministry of Research, Science and Technology 2005). In health research, the statutory Māori Health Committee was included in the legislation that established the Health Research Council in 1990. Early Māori health leaders, Dr. Eru Pōmare and Dr. Mason Durie, were skilful in creating opportunities for Māori researchers working across a range of Māori health areas other than biomedical and public health and in establishing a committee and assessment structure alongside scholarships, as well as a specific funding stream for Māori health. In many ways, the government policy context is encouraging Māori research, albeit in a limited way. The scientific research community, however, is struggling to come to terms with that context. This is the community that designs the rules, leads most assessment and peer review processes, sets research priorities, decides scholarships and allocation of post-doctoral fellowships, supervises PhDs and the early careers of researchers, makes appointments, determines promotions, provides departmental leadership, and allocates resources. This is the community that defines "excellence." Suffice to say that this community is currently led by a generation dominated by a specific demographic group.

What Impacts Can Be Seen?

In the last three decades there has been enormous growth in scholarship that is about Indigenous Knowledge. There are four terms commonly used in the literature. "Traditional Knowledge" and "Traditional Ecological Knowledge" have been in published scholarly use for the longest time and remain the domain still dominated by non-Indigenous scholarship. "Indigenous Knowledge" and "Mātauranga Māori," the latter of which refers to Māori knowledge, are more recent terms, appearing more in the 1980s. The following Table 2.1 (Smith et al. 2016) shows this emergence just by using a Google Scholar search of these key terms. "Traditional Knowledge" also brings up articles and citations for "Traditional Ecological Knowledge," and so only "Traditional Knowledge" has been used. Similarly, "Māori knowledge" brings up Māori culture, Māori dancing, and Māori games, and so the search has been restricted to "Mātauranga Māori." Mātauranga Māori publications are

likely to also use the term "Indigenous Knowledge" when publishing internationally, and so some of these references will be included in the entries for
Indigenous Knowledge. Nevertheless, even with this crude count, the sheer
number of references in Google Scholar attests to a growth of published and
cited scholarly works, covering a diverse array of subject matter and disciplinary interfaces.

Table 2.1. *Number of Entries in Google Scholar When Searching for*
Mātauranga Māori, Indigenous Knowledge, and Traditional Knowledge

Google Scholar Search Terms	Entries 1980–90	Entries 1990–2000	Entries 2000–15	Total
Mātauranga Māori/ Matauranga Maori	18	214	2,818	3,050
Indigenous Knowledge	41,500	187,500	1,401,000	1,630,000
Traditional Knowledge, including Traditional Ecological Knowledge	352,000	778,000	2,260,000	3,390,000

Google search August 11, 2015, 2:30 p.m. Table first published in Smith et al. (2016).

There is also a growth in the number of publications, books, and international peer-reviewed journals about Indigenous research, Indigenous theory, and Indigenous philosophy, and also by Indigenous authors that cover
topics from politics and archaeology to Indigenous science and engineering,
education, and health. In some cases, these publications are supported by
Indigenous publishing houses, for example, Huia Publishers in New Zealand,
and Indigenous-owned bookstores, such as Native Books in Honolulu, as well as
by university presses such as University of British Columbia Press, University
of Arizona Press, and the University of Hawaii Press, to name a few. There are
scholarly networks, special interest groups, and organizations that support
the work of Māori and Indigenous researchers, such as the Native American
and Indigenous Studies Association (NAISA), the Alaska Native Knowledge
Network, and the Māori Association of Social Science group (MASS).

In New Zealand, there are an increasing number of Māori research centres and institutes within universities and in communities, as well as large
research institutes having substantial Māori research programs. In the town
of Whanangui, in the lower North Island of New Zealand, two community
and *iwi*-based research organizations have been successful in gaining large

infrastructure and program grants. Te Atawhai o Te Ao established an independent research organization that focuses on environment and health, and Whakauae Research for Māori Health and Development also specializes in Māori health. Some *iwi* have also established research entities. For example, Nga Tahu in the South Island has established a joint research centre with Canterbury University, and Waikato-Tainui has established the Waikato Tainui College for Research and Development. These centres are all indicators of Indigenous engagement with research and Indigenous research capacity. They did not exist twenty years ago. These centres are also an indicator of research capacity and the number of Indigenous researchers who are qualified and experienced and working as researchers with their communities. In the context of Indigenous education, this level of capacity is a significant achievement. There are examples of Indigenous research informing the practice of organizations, especially those that deliver services to Indigenous communities. In New Zealand, the current government Whānau Ora policy is an outcome of years of Māori intellectual ideas, the establishment of Māori frameworks, Māori research, and active support from Māori communities being communicated to government. It may not just be the result of the impact of Indigenous research, but the contribution of Indigenous research on health and social service policy would be hard to deny.

Impact as the Long Game back to Indigenous
Knowing and Being in Relation to the World

The translation of research back into Indigenous contexts to make a positive difference to the lives of Indigenous peoples is an aim of many Indigenous research approaches. It is a goal often embedded in the methodology and the critical questions Indigenous researchers are asked (and often challenged on by communities) in relation to the formulation of their research. Who is this research for? Who is asking the question? Who will own this research? Who will benefit from this research? It is reinforced by the ethical questions around the practice of research and the protection of data. What does it mean to give consent? How is collective consent negotiated? How will data be stored and protected? It is further reinforced by issues surrounding intellectual and cultural property. Whose knowledge is this? How is Indigenous Knowledge, which has been developed over millennia by our ancestors, to be acknowledged and protected? Who owns copyright of Indigenous Knowledge and cultural artifacts? The Indigenous paradigm is deeply sensitive to the ways in which knowledge, knowing, and coming to know are balanced in relation to the being and coming to be of Indigenous identity. Indigenous research seeks to recover a peoples' path to well-being, to find the new/old solutions that restore Indigenous being in the world. The impacts are part of an intergenerational long game of decolonization, societal transformation, healing and reconciliation, and the recovery of a world where all is well.

This chapter has outlined some tensions for the field of Indigenous research as it strives for legitimacy across Indigenous and academic worlds. Defining what matters as an impact is significant for Indigenous research, which developed to make a transformational difference for the situation and condition of Indigenous peoples. Measuring research impact is a more complicated beast, in that definitions, and then measures, of research impact are designed within academic normative, as well as performative, expectations. It is easy to see the "turn" to the measurement of research impact as an invention of the neoliberal and corporate university. However, in this chapter, it has been argued that the old liberal university also defined and measured "performance" and tended to privilege definitions and measures of what matters and what counts that rest on old traditions located in the imperial and colonial foundations of the academy.

Author's Note

The author wishes to acknowledge and thank the University of Melbourne for its support in the preparation of this chapter. Thanks also to the Australian National Indigenous Research and Knowledge Network (NIRAKN) for its support in helping to develop these ideas.

References

Brayboy, B. A. 2005. "Toward a Critical Race Theory in Education." *The Urban Indian Review* 37(5): 425–46.

Deloria, V. 1988. *Custer Died for Your Sins: An Indian Manifesto*. Norman: University of Oklahoma Press.

Donovan, C. 2011. "State of the Art in Assessing Research Impact: Introduction to a Special Issue." *Research Evaluation* 3: 175–79.

Englund, T. 2002. "Higher Education, Democracy and Citizenship—The Democratic Potential of the University?" *Studies in Philosophy and Education* 21: 281.

doi:10.1023/A:1019840006193.

Garfield, E. 2005. *The Agony and the Ecstasy—The History and Meaning of the Journal Impact Factor*. Chicago: International Congress on Peer Review and Biomedical Publication.

Guri-Rosenblit, S., H. Sebkova, and U. Teichler. 2007. *Massification and Diversity of Higher Education Systems: Interplay of Complex Dimensions*. Paris: UNESCO.

Hale, C. R. 2005. "Neoliberal Multiculturalism." *PoLAR: Political and Legal Anthropology Review* 28: 10–19. doi:10.1525/pol.2005.28.1.10.

Hirsch, J. 2005. "An Index to Quantify an Individual's Scientific Research Output." *Proceedings of the National Academy of Sciences* 102(46): 16569–72.

Hokowhitu, B., ed. 2010. *Indigenous Identity and Resistance: Researching the Diversity of Knowledge*. Dunedin, New Zealand: Otago University Press.

Jasanoff, S. 2004. *States of Knowledge: The Co-Production of Science and the Social Order*. London: Routledge.

Kymlicka, W. 2015. "The Essentialist Critique of Multiculturalism: Theory, Policies and Ethos." In *Multiculturalism Rethought: Interpretations, Dilemmas and New Directions*, edited by V. Uberoi and T. Modood, 209–49. Edinburgh, Scotland: Edinburgh University Press.

Ministry of Research, Science and Technology. 2005. *Vision Mātauranga: Unlocking the Innovation Potential of Māori Knowledge, People and Resources*. Wellington: New Zealand Government.

Pidgeon, M., and D. G. Hardy Cox. 2002. "Researching with Aboriginal Peoples: Practices and Principles." *Canadian Journal of Native Education* 26(2): 96–106.

Pihama, L. 2011. "Kaupapa Māori Theory: Transforming Theory in Aotearoa." *He Pukenga Kōrero* 9(2): 5–14.

———. 2014. "The Denial of Maori Research Development." *Te Wharepora Hou* [blog], March 6. http://tewhareporahou.wordpress.com/2014/03/06/the-denial-of-maori-research-development/.

Rigney, L-I. 2001. *A First Perspective of Indigenous Australian Participation in Science: Framing Indigenous Research towards Indigenous Australian Intellectual Sovereignty*. https://ncis.anu.edu.au/_lib/doc/LI_Rigney_First_perspective.pdf.

———. 1999. "Internationalization of an Indigenous Anticolonial Cultural Critique of Research Methodologies: A Guide to Indigenist Research Methodology and Its Principles." *Wicazo SA Review* 14(2): 109–21.

Said, E. 1978. *Orientalism*. New York: Pantheon Books.

Sharples, P. 2014. "Stop Marginalising Māori Research." *Whānau Ora Research*, March 7. http://whanauoraresearch.co.nz/news/stop-marginalising-maori-research/.

Smith, L. T. 2012. *Decolonising Methodologies: Research and Indigenous Peoples*. London: Zed Books.

———. 2014. "An Open Statement on the True Impact of the Non-Funding of Ngā Pae o Te Māramatanga." *Te Wharepora Hou* [blog], March 10. https://tewhareporahou.wordpress.com/2014/03/10/an-open-statement-on-the-true-impact-of-the-non-funding-of-nga-pae-o-te-maramatanga/.

Smith, L. T., et al. 2016. "Indigenous Knowledge, Methodology and Mayhem: What Is the Role of Methodology in Producing Indigenous Insights? A Discussion from Mātauranga Māori." *Knowledge Cultures* 4(3): 131–56.

Tertiary Education Commission. 2013. *2013 Tertiary Education Performance Report.* Government of New Zealand. http://pr2013.publications.tec.govt.nz/uploads/TEC-Tertiary-Education-Performance-Report-2013.pdf.

Thornton, M. 2009. "Academic Un-Freedom in the New Knowledge Economy." In *Academic Research and Researchers*, edited by A. Brew and L. Lucas, 2–13. Berkshire, UK: Open University Press.

Tuck, E., and W. Yang. 2012. "Decolonization Is Not a Metaphor." *Decolonization: Indigeneity, Education & Society* 1(1): 1–40.

Turia, T. 2014. "Refusal to Fund Maori Research Centre Detrimental to Country." *Wanganui Chronicle*, March 13. http://www.nzherald.co.nz/wanganui-chronicle/opinion/news/article.cfm?c_id=1503423&objectid=11218838.

Waitangi Tribunal. 2011. *Ko Aotearoa Tenei*. Wellington: New Zealand Government.

CHAPTER 3

AN INTERVIEW WITH DR. NORMAN K. DENZIN ON THE POLITICS OF EVIDENCE, SCIENCE, AND RESEARCH

Marc Spooner: We are pleased to have the participation of Dr. Norman Denzin from the University of Illinois at Urbana-Champaign. Thanks for participating in our symposium, "Public Engagement and the Politics of Evidence in an Age of Neoliberalism and Audit Culture." As many of you know, Norman Denzin has written extensively on qualitative methodologies and is famously one of the co-editors, with Yvonna Lincoln, of the Handbook of Qualitative Research, *most recently the fifth edition out in 2017.*

Norman K. Denzin: It's a privilege and a pleasure to be here. Thank you.

MS: Could you unpack the term "politics of evidence" and what that means? I know you've written about that in the past.

ND: Yes, I think that is a good place to start. I think this term is critical to the phase that qualitative inquiry is currently in. Taking the notion of evidence and prefacing it with the word "politics" is like saying that evidence itself is a contested term. This is a pushback against the notion of science having its own evidentiary base as a criteria or a standpoint for evaluating what we do. When we speak of the politics of evidence, then, we talk about the structures of power and discourse that put in place a particular set of regulatory practices and criteria that will judge what evidence is, and how evidence can be used then for particular purposes.

The politics of evidence then contests that notion by saying that science is no longer just a neutral apparatus, but it is a structure integrated into a larger system of discourse connected to the three crises that the symposium and this book are addressing: the crises concerning managerialism, marketing, and measurement. Those three terms are at the core of the crisis that now confronts the qualitative interpretive community but also the larger global scholarly and university communities. Previously, we were addressing crises that came primarily from within our own paradigms and our own scholarship and discourse. There are some qualifications here because science has always been a product of a larger, global, colonial apparatus that was folded into the structures of capitalism as it connected to the colonial projects of Europe, Asia, and North America.

Science has always been part of a larger governmental initiative, but up until now—primarily, at least, in the post–paradigm wars of the '60s and the '70s, wars over quantitative/qualitative inquiry—we were struggling internally to resolve those issues. But, since 2000, and turning into this new century—in the United States at least, science-based research, No Child Left Behind legislation, the federal government mandating what will count as science and what will count as evidence—all of that has pushed its way into our research communities. Meanwhile, the universities themselves have capitulated, so to speak, to the pressures of state and federal governments to provide a set of criteria that would warrant or validate the activities they engage in, that they reward, and that they fund.

We are now fighting a war on two sides. On one side is the pressure down from the neoliberal audit-based university, and then internally within our own interpretative, qualitative communities, we are fighting against pressures from science-based research, randomized clinical trial protocols, and mixed-methods initiatives. Then, on the other side, but again within our own community, we are asking, "Well, what is science-based research? What is a qualitative inquiry? Whose voice should be heard? How should we hear that voice?" So the pressures are coming from two directions at the same time, internally and externally, and to fight the battle on one front is to fight it on the other. But I think the symposium, and this book based on it, will bring to the fore the centrality of these external, outside-the-academy pressures that are coming down upon what our qualitative project has always been about.

MS: Norman, you are at the cutting edge of a lot of advances in methods and methodology and approaches to viewing and understanding the world. What scholarship is exciting you the most right now?

ND: Well, I think we are moving in several directions at the same time from within what I would call the qualitative interpretive community, which I connect to the International Congress of Qualitative Inquiry, which is a global project, and your initiative, which is a global project, international. So I will just list some of the new developments that I think are pushing us forward. But first I want to backtrack for a moment and revisit the paradigm wars of the '60s and then the '80s. I was trained in the '60s as a sociologist; we had no training as qualitative researchers. The fact is qualitative researchers did not exist as a category within sociology.

There was something called the Chicago School of Sociology, and they supposedly did something like case studies and they borrowed from anthropologists who were doing participant observation. But we were not trained in those methods, at least at the University of Iowa where I graduated. We were trained in quantitative methodology only. Well, that breaks in the '60s, and in the '70s there was the discovery of grounded theory, which is the Glaser and Strauss breakthrough text, *The Discovery of Grounded Theory: Strategies for Qualitative Research* (1967), which was really—if you read it today—a positivistic account of how to do research that would satisfy the criteria of an audit culture. In a pre-audit culture, it was a tool kit, a road map.

In the '80s, the big paradigm war happens between "the quants and the quals," so to speak; Egon Guba is a major voice and Yvonna Lincoln is a major voice. In that moment, the discourse coalesces around the notion that we have two incompatible, incommensurate discourses: one is quantitative and one is qualitative. And they cannot be measured against each other; they have to be allowed to speak with each other and to have their own autonomy. That was a breakthrough. That opened up a space for qualitative inquiry, and for twenty years that is what reigns. As qualitative researchers, we can write books, we can talk about our methodologies, we can train people how to do this kind of work or that kind of work, and we are in a new space, a free space. And that is when the field explodes; Sage Press becomes a small industry publishing qualitative research textbooks.

At this point, with the first edition of the *Handbook of Qualitative Research* in 1994, we are thinking that the war between the quants and the quals is over. What is this qualitative field all about? It is a separate, complicated discourse and we can celebrate it. It has all these paradigms and points of view and methodologies and the war was over; we had really won the battle. Well, that holds for a little less than ten years, because we turn the corner into the next century and, suddenly, on the horizon, there is this science-based research movement that is then co-opted by the mixed-methods movement. These people come out of nowhere, or they were there and we were not listening to them. Suddenly, the mixed-methods people are saying, "Well, there's really no difference between quantitative and qualitative, they're just different approaches to the same project."

But they are profoundly different. Quantitative and qualitative methods have different methodological, epistemological, and ontological assumptions and they can't be folded together. We tried to fight this in the 2000 and 2005 editions of the *Handbook* and say we have to push back against this attempt to fold us into this larger community of mixed methods, which then becomes a handmaiden to the science-based research (SBR) movement. The two come together and, suddenly, this is the elephant in the room. So what are we going to do? How are we going to respond to this? And that is where we were ethically by 2005. Suddenly, we were on the defensive again, caught off guard, so to speak.

It has taken almost a decade to get back on our feet again and determine what battle has to be fought. One of the most exciting new developments is what I call the "third moment" of pushing back and critiquing in sophisticated ways the mixed-methods SBR movement. We adopted the stance that we need no longer be on the defensive; we should no longer be stumbling around trying to write articles saying, "Well, of course you can't do randomized clinical trials on human beings. I mean, really, you can't do that. It doesn't work, the model doesn't work; it's never worked."

We have wasted a lot of ink and a lot of pages critiquing SBR initiatives and what Patti Lather called the alphabet soup of different institutional approaches and apparatuses from the Institute of Educational Studies to the Cochrane Initiative, to the Campbell Initiative, and so forth. We were poking holes in all those approaches, but we should not have taken this on as our major fight.

Along the side, then, what emerges parallel to this anti-SBR conversation is Indigenization and the decolonization project that is sweeping the globe as Indigenous communities mobilize themselves, through their own critical discourse and educational structures, to push back against the colonial apparatus of sites that we were all a part of. So the Indigenization of the academy and the articulation of Indigenous methodologies is a major breakthrough. There are many fine Indigenous scholars, such as Maggie Kovach, Sandy Grande, Linda

Smith, Graham Smith, and so on; there's a long list now. With the *Handbook of Critical and Indigenous Methodologies* (2008), we tried to bring many of those voices together into a kind of overlapping, compatible framework.

This is one major move that in the next decade will become even stronger. What is so critical is that Indigenization interrogates from within the very notions of evidence, of science, of methodology, and of community. As deeply and importantly, Indigenous methodologies remind us that science is a moral discourse; it is not a clinical discourse and it is not a discourse based just on evidence, but it is a moral and political discourse. If that is the case, then we need to discuss the implications of any kind of scientific practice—morally, ethically—for a particular community and its welfare, and in the relationships between that community, its land, its sacred rituals, its history, its culture, its community leaders, and its kinship systems. In this approach science now is embedded directly into a moral community. Science never was folded into morality under the colonial apparatus, or under the post-positivist apparatus, because it always came in from the outside and made visible only those things that scientists wanted, that the ethnographer, the interviewer, the travelling scholar would make visible. Indigenous methodologies and ways of knowing are a major intervention now.

There is a second growing discourse, and I'm going to call it post-humanist, post-materialist, post-science; it's informed by Deleuze, by Guattari, by Barad, by Rancière, and a number of different philosophers of science. Donna Haraway, Bruno Latour, and science technology studies provide some of the background to this work. It is a rhizomatic movement that draws on several strands, including feminism and queer theory. This discourse questions the whole post-qualitative project, as it was formulated under the umbrella of traditional positivism—that's Elizabeth St. Pierre's questioning—and then it is asking, "What would post-humanist, post-qualitative inquiry look like?" Here there's a plugging in of the use of terms from Barad and Deleuze and others, such as "science without humans," "materialism," and "the materiality of inquiry." We have a long chapter on it in the new *Handbook* (SAGE *Handbook of Qualitative Research*, 5th Edition, 2017) by Maggie MacLure and Mirka Koro-Ljungberg, which provides a comprehensive layout of that landscape. This is a major fresh new space: it is drawing on a new set of philosophical arguments and refurbishing a set of philosophical arguments and trying to open up a new way of looking at things like data, like analysis, like coding, like interviewing, like observing. Key terms in the tradition of the qualitative project are being questioned by this group as they try to move us forward into a rearticulated space of inquiry and what inquiry means.

I don't follow all of it, and I don't agree with all of it. I did a little piece in *Cultural Studies* ↔ *Critical Methodologies*, questioning some of it when I talked about the death of data, because these people are still talking about data and what they want to do with the data. My argument is that we should draw a line of erasure through the word "data." I don't allow my students to use the word, and, if they do use the word in my class, we give them the D-hat, a data hat—and they have to sit in the corner with their back to the class, because the word "data" carries the lingering effects of positivism and of positivistic science and of the politics of evidence. Why would we keep that word alive? We need to draw a line of erasure through that. So this is the second major move, the post-humanist, post-materialist approach to inquiry.

MS: What did you replace "data" with?

ND: "Ergo Empirical." I'm a pragmatist, so I take it from doing John Dewey and William James. I use the phrase "empirical material."

MS: Empirical material.

ND: I am comfortable with that. The word "empirical" lodges me in the world of experience, and "material," because it suggests it could be any trace or any form of representation. I really like the word "representation" more than "data," and I talk about the politics of representation. I think that's what we should be using, the word "representation" and the phrase, "the politics of representation."

MS: I interrupted you there, you were about to go to the third…

ND: Well, the third would be the proliferation of paradigms. It is a proliferation along several lines of the politics of identity: queer, race, class, ableness, Indigenous, gender, all sorts. The intertwining of multiple forms of which the human, the inquirer, is implicated in the world in terms of their situated identity and their biography and their gender and their class and their race. Not only do we study the configurations of those identities within the world but we see that there are separate discourses themselves connected to those identities. So we have a feminist science; we have an Indigenous science; and we have queer theory, which queers the concept of science.

We didn't have this conversation twenty years ago. This is a major development move and it cannot be squashed, and there are journals connected to each of those discourses, which, in itself, is phenomenal and important. When we come back to the audit culture and the managerialism that operates in the university, and the measurement of scholarly productivity, one of the things we must do is to figure into that set of equations the work that goes on in these kinds of journals, work that represents this kind of discourse, which is not, up until the present, considered mainstream discourse. But it is extraordinarily important interventionist discourse, which has to be part of the conversation and part of the way in which we measure—if we're going to use that horrible word—a person's productivity or contributions to the scientific community.

This paradigm proliferation opens up the space along situated identities or the politics of identity. Within the qualitative space itself we have—I've just jotted down a few of the discourses that come across our desk with the journals—arts-based research, which is getting more complicated and more and more politicized. The innovative discourse of critical ethnography is getting much more sophisticated. We now have a special division within the Congress [ICQI] that deals with autoethnography, which was initiated by Carolyn Ellis and Art Bochner, and the new *Handbook of Autoethnography* (2016). There is a rethinking of traditional qualitative methods. In a journal like *Qualitative Research*, you will find articles in every issue rethinking and critiquing things like interviewing, reflexivity, coding, and analysis. But this is not rethinking the traditional in terms of some positivistic set of terms but, rather, say in the hands of Hammersley or Atkinson or Delamont, or their students, critically interrogating how we do the practices that produce these phenomena. That situated approach to the doing of these more traditional forms of inquiry is also occurring, and that is really an important discourse.

So rather than just having journals that report results of qualitative study, we now have journals committed to interrogating the apparatus of doing qualitative inquiry. That is major, and that is why we founded the journal, *Qualitative Inquiry*. We were less concerned with what people were revealing but more with how they interrogated the work of doing the inquiry. That is going to continue, I think, and, done in its very best way, the interrogation of the apparatus also makes the world visible in a different way, so content has folded into the politics and strategies of representing something. We are pushing for works that push the envelope in terms of the representation of the world out there.

So under this third development of multiple paradigms, there are new criteria operating implicitly in terms of what counts as scholarly work of these particular situated interpretive practices, as those practices make the world visible to us. In the old days, we published research that reported on interviews and people quoted their interviews and recorded from the interviews, and that was the way we did qualitative research. Now I'm not doing that. Other journals are doing that, but my attempt was always to determine how we articulate this critical approach in the deployment of the apparatus. The biggest influence on me in this particular argument has been the notion from Stuart Hall that we are always engaged in the politics of representation and making the world visible to a set of situated practices. That is the bar that we work from always, and, if that is the case, how do we move that bar forward in terms of these particular inquiries? It doesn't matter what you are studying, that is how you move the bar forward.

There is another set of movements occurring that involve the ethics of inquiry and institutional review boards. They are called different things in different countries, but regulation of the ethics of inquiry occurs where the government says so suddenly, "We're not going to fund this research unless it's ethically acceptable." As a researcher, you had to be using methodologies that produce research that is regarded as acceptable. So funded research now becomes ethically accepted research using methodologies that are appropriated to the managerial ethic of the larger apparatus. Coming in under the tent of ethics was a regulatory apparatus for deregulating positivist research and repressing qualitative research. On our campus, students doing qualitative research had enormous difficulties for a number of years getting approval from the Institutional Review Board (IRB) for group or campus research initiatives because it wasn't deemed scientific. Yvonna Lincoln and Gaile Cannella show powerfully how these three things tie together: ethics, inquiry, and science.

In a recent report on the protection of human subjects at the federal level in the States, the government has responded to this pushback and they are now creating a new category of research that does not have to be pre-reviewed. If it fits, it is serious qualitative inquiry, whatever that is—qualitative inquiry, it could be excused from research. Well, that is huge. That is the recommendation, and I think it will probably be approved, so that means the fight that the historians fought for history, which was to get exempted from the IRB review, that fight has now carried over to the rest of us who are doing qualitative research. What I find most depressing about this particular initiative is that we have to legitimate our inquiry in terms of some outside, external board made up of—on my campus—psychologists and economists and biologists.

MS: And lawyers as well?

ND: And lawyers, right. Lawyers debating what science is and what should be done. It has become such a part of the graduate student culture here that people could spend a semester doing their IRB forms, which is just ridiculous. So this is another pushback, I think, and it is connected to the pushback that, in a sense, comes out of the Indigenous initiative saying, "We have our own set of ethical protocols and criteria to adhere to from within our culture. Don't impose your ethics on us, and don't think you can come into our culture, take blood samples, study our kinship systems, and make judgments about how we train and educate our students." So these two pushbacks go together, I think, although they are not necessarily tied together directly.

MS: I think another place where that might enter is in participatory and community-engaged scholarship, where the outcomes may not even lead to a journal article. The community may decide that it's not a journal article it needs, but says we need a report on how best to do this local practice, or whatever it is that they've decided is important to them. That is another arena that we need to fight in: this is legitimate scholarship, even though it doesn't lead to a journal article.

ND: Right, it is a form of action, or activism or community involvement.

MS: Sure, and I think here too of the Indigenous movement, where it is about a relationship with community. What do we bring to the community that might lead to better practices but not a journal article?

ND: Right, I think that is foundational, and assessing impact should become part of the review process for any given scholar as they reach out and become involved with this kind of community work. That leads to what I think is another development, which is on policy and government regulation of inquiry and federal boards and federal standards that are evaluating what is acceptable research. How can our work, our qualitative inquiry, become an integral part of the policy process and move into the policy space? What would that look like, and what would that mean? Harry Torrance has written well on this, and his chapter in the last *Handbook* (2011) took up many of the issues surrounding qualitative inquiry and how it gets diminished within the policy arena. So how can we push into the policy arena and have our voices heard at the congress? Scholars from Latin and South America, from Asia, from New Zealand, and from Australia are all talking about how in their local university qualitative research has been diminished as a presence at the policy level.

This is not just in the U.S. or Canada; this is global. We need to demand a place at the table and insist that we have that. Indigenous scholars have been very good at this, demanding a space at the table, I think. It has taken five hundred years to get to the table and to get the space, but, by God, they have got it now and I don't think they are going to lose it. We can learn from that; we can become part of that. I don't mean for a second to co-opt anything, but there needs to be a commonly accepted position that critical qualitative inquiry needs to be a part of every conversation at the level of policy. Period.

In the West, politicians make judgments all the time on single cases and on flimsy evidence, and massive changes occur because the politics of evidence folds itself into a particular rhetorical and ideological program that the government wants to fund. That is no different from what we're talking about here, but, yes, we should be part of that conversation as a matter of course. And we need university leaders, we need university presidents, we need deans, we need provosts, we need chancellors committed to this kind of position, and they need to be educated.

Our trouble here in the States is our university administrators all come out of the hard sciences, almost without exception. The chemists, the physicists, the biologists, the engineers, maybe psychologists now and then, you know, they are not English professors, they are not sociologists, they are not people from communications or from history or from educational policy; they're from the hard sciences because science has always been the integral part of governmentality in the government apparatus. So I think this is not just a utopian dream. Well, it is a utopian dream, but until that power structure is filled with people who have a broader understanding of what science and policy is, this goal is not going to be achievable with any degree of success. I think it may be different in Canada than it is here.

MS: Well, I'd probably say that at least our university president is from the Faculty of Education.

ND: That's terrific.

MS: Andrea Smith talks about how we are so good at applying our critical lens outward, but when we go to apply it inward we seem to shy away from that. Why have we as a body of scholars allowed this audit culture to take such prominence on our campuses? Were we caught sleeping or what happened? How did the mechanisms work that they were able to...?

ND: That is a good question. I think we were caught sleeping. I think the tenure promotion apparatus, which is the lifeblood of the whole project, drives everybody into a narrow set of initiatives and projects so they themselves can get tenure. I think the larger picture is never brought forward on a continuous basis because all sorts of other things have to be taken into account. I think it has been pushed to the side largely because of that.

The idea that science is a moral discourse and that inquiry is a moral discourse and that nothing is neutral, that it is always political and it is always moral—that is not part of the conversation in the audit managerial university, and it is not that conversation that happens at the level of the department or a division within a department or a college. It gets folded into the academic concerns of a particular discipline and its history, and then into the politics of that unit. So those other issues push it to the side, and then it is only the occasional scholar who speaks out, the one who has tenure, to bring it to the fore. Your question is very important, and it sounds like your university is taking some important steps in this direction. That, I think, is encouraging.

MS: We have good guidance from qualitative inquiry conferences and other places.

ND: Another major initiative is the social justice initiative; the legacy of the protest movements two, three, or four decades ago are alive still and they're alive now within the movements from the situated identity spheres and the Indigenous spheres. Putting the social justice initiative, the inquiry for social justice, and equity to the forefront is something that everybody can support and it cuts across all of these other developments, but it can get pushed to the side too. So to privilege the social justice initiative is a way of pushing back against a top-down market managerial measurement apparatus and is absolutely pivotal.

We could always say, how does this impact the lives of real people in the real world suffering from structures of oppression and inequity? That is the mantra, the byword, and if we keep that in front of us, then we can continue to push forward in that direction as well. And that's happening, I think, at the level of conferences and congresses and events like the one you're having this summer [July 2015]. Now to work that into the day-to-day funding apparatus of the campus and the college is another issue, and how that happens is up to each particular department in part. But then it is also where can you get funding that supports social justice initiatives, and what does that inquiry look like, and how is that inquiry going to be judged and evaluated, and by whose terms? And here there are huge battles to be fought and to be pushed forward, I would say.

MS: Sure.

ND: You know, we've gone from quantitating versus qualitating to an enormously complicated role for what qualitative inquiry is as a complex moral discourse. We need to always hold onto that notion, and then we need to recommit ourselves to fighting back against these very terms that the symposium and this book are about. And we need to re-engage the paradigm wars of the '80s, perhaps not as wars but to bring forward the very terms that we've been talking about this morning into the proliferation of paradigms, the post-humanist critique, multiple interpretative communities, the influence of qualitative inquiry in the policy arena, the moral leadership from Indigenous scholars. So it is not now just a war between the quantitative and the qualitative, or between the science-based research and the mixed-methods people and the qualitative people and the feminists and the queer theorists. That is just part of the skirmish that is going on; it is the larger project, which is what we are doing in this space. What are our principles and commitments, and where do we want this discourse to take us? What is the utopian vision we have for critical qualitative inquiry?

How can these old battles inform our struggles today, and how can we escape from those old battles and not repeat them, not get tangled but create a new conversation with a new set of utopian hopes and dreams now that we have really weathered a series of attacks—if I can use that word—and we are on the other side of the SBR project, on the other side of the mixed-methods project, I think, and so let's take stock. The Congress [ICQI] theme this year is reimagining or constructing a new critical qualitative inquiry. We are eleven years into the Congress; we are thirty or forty years past the original paradigm dialogue, and so where do we go now? What can we do? That's the challenge that the conference is giving us.

MS: I am hoping we reinvigorate a reclamation of our collective collegial autonomy. I think as a body of scholars we need to fight back against new management technologies and externally imposed audits that are narrow in their framework and measure outputs in such a limiting and positivist way. As a body of collective scholars, we need to take back our own governances. I am hoping that at the Qualitative Inquiry Congress and the symposium this summer we are able to act as a support for each other and organize together and say, you know, enough, we have to push back.

ND: Collaborate and co-operate and mutually empower and have an ongoing global conversation.

MS: And stop looking at each other with skepticism about who is worthy and who is not and start working together to make each other stronger. Obviously, a healthy skepticism is good.

ND: Exactly.

MS: I always liken it to a bully in the playground that we have to stand up to and say that each of us gets to play with the ball.

ND: Right, it's a big tent and nobody is going to control the ball, that's right, that's a nice model.

MS: If I asked you to identify the three greatest threats and the three greatest areas of hope for the academy, would you be able to answer that, or would you not like to be limited to three?

ND: Well, I would like to see greater commitment to this notion that science is a moral discourse, period. We accept it, or we push it aside. And, secondly, a renewed commitment to the politics of representation; how do we make things visible? And, thirdly, then a commitment to a social justice agenda. The moral discourse revolves around politics and representation that makes the world visible and allows us to address issues of social inequity and social justice.

And if those three things can become a rallying point for us, I think this global community would then have the principles that it could take to any site and implement so it is not tied to a specific set of demands, but rather that these are principles before personalities or specific issues, and they would give us guideposts to move forward. Those would be my three wishes, and your conference is moving and taking significant steps in that direction.

MS: I want to thank you so much for agreeing to participate and contributing to the symposium and to the discourses and conversations we need to have about the way forward. And, also, Dr. Norman Denzin, I want to thank you for all your work over the years; you've been a great mentor and generous with your time, and we thank you so much.

ND: Thank you, Marc. I'm honoured by this opportunity to speak to you and to your colleagues, and I wish everybody well at this wonderful conference this summer. Thank you.[1]

Notes

1 This chapter is based on a pre-symposium interview that took place on December 9, 2014. It has been lightly edited for readability and accuracy.

CHAPTER 4

AN INTERVIEW WITH DR. NOAM CHOMSKY ON NEOLIBERALISM, SOCIETY, AND HIGHER EDUCATION

Marc Spooner: Dr. Chomsky, thank you very much for agreeing to participate in our symposium, "Public Engagement and the Politics of Evidence in an Age of Neoliberalism and Audit Culture." It is often said about people that they need no introduction, and there is no question that is the case here, so thank you Dr. Chomsky. It has been nearly fifty years since you famously wrote in the New York Review of Books *about the responsibility of intellectuals. Has your view changed on the importance to society of the public intellectual and the publicly engaged scholar?*

Noam Chomsky: I did write an update for the *Boston Review* a couple of years ago, but basically it is the same, and has been true for many years. If you ask about the phrase "responsibility of intellectuals," it actually has two meanings. There is one responsibility that is based on ethical, moral principles. There is another kind of responsibility that is demanded by authoritarian structures such as state and corporate power. But it is only different kinds of responsibility and two different roles of intellectuals, and that has been proven through history. We understand that very clearly in the case of enemies. For example, in the case of, say, Iran, Russia, and China, we have only contempt for intellectuals who follow the responsibility of serving state policy and defending state doctrine; we dismiss them with contempt. On the other hand, we honour and respect those who carry out critical analysis of state crimes and often endanger themselves in doing so. When we look at ourselves, we reverse the values completely. In our own society, we honour and respect those who support and serve the prevailing doctrinal systems reflecting state and corporate powers, and we condemn and dismiss the critics who raise questions about the exercise of power and critique its crimes and excesses. It is interesting that the honorary word "dissident" is restricted to foreigners and enemy societies. We don't call critics in the United States dissidents. I mean, I may, but it is not generally done. And those whom we massacre in our dependencies, like the Jesuit lecturers who were murdered in 1989 in El Salvador by the U.S.-trained and armed forces, we don't call them dissidents. If they are mentioned at all, they are referred to as some kind of Marxists. We see how the values are reversed. And that's typical. If you go through history—back to classical Greece and the Biblical era, the term "intellectual" wasn't used, but there were those who, by asking questions, criticized the crimes of the kings and who corrupted the youth of Athens. They may be honoured today, but at the time they were condemned and killed or driven into the desert or exiled. It's a pattern that persists to the present. The term "intellectual" in its modern sense came into Western usage in connection with the Dreyfus trials in France at the end of the nineteenth century. Today, we honour the Dreyfusards as those who oppose state crimes and state power, but it was not true at the time. They were harshly condemned and had to flee the country. And the grand intellectuals, the "immortals" of the Académie Française, denounced these writers and playwrights, saying they had no right to criticize the august institutions of the army and the state and its institutions. This is very similar to what we see today. There is a regular pattern through history of the two concepts of intellectual responsibility.

MS: Turning that critical gaze toward higher education, over your career, have you noticed changes in how scholarship is measured and valued within the academy? I think of audit cultures and impact factors and journal rankings, and that sort of thing.

NC: There are technical changes like that, but I think there are more important changes, frankly. I can see it very clearly at the institution [MIT] where I work, but it is happening everywhere. This happens to be a science-based university, and I've been here sixty years. There have been changes reflecting political changes in the country. In the pre-neoliberal period—the great growth period of the '50s and '60s—MIT was mostly funded by the Pentagon. I was actually working in a laboratory that was 100 per cent Pentagon-funded and most of the academic program was funded this way. It was quite an open and free culture, the work was done as you wanted, and there was no classified or secret work on campus.

Over the years, the Pentagon funding has declined, and the reason has little to do with the military. The United States has a kind of industrial policy; it is hidden because we are supposed to be a market society. But the reality is that a substantial part of the advanced economy in the age of computers and the Internet has been developed for decades within the dynamic state sector and mostly at public expense. Later it's handed over to private companies and corporations. Corporate funding has a much bigger effect on influencing scholarly work than the kinds of technical measures like impact factors and journal rankings.

Corporate funding, for example, tends to be short-term and applied. The corporation is not interested in producing something that will be useful for the public in twenty years; they want something that is useful for them, and not their competitors, tomorrow. And it also introduces a measure of secrecy. Corporations can't impose it formally, but they can make it clear that renewed funding requires secrecy. The effect on the institutions is notable. For departments that are more immediately involved in applied research, like the computer science department, it has changed the culture a lot. And, in general, this is part of the whole neoliberal assault on the public, and on universities in particular. Attempts to drive the higher education system toward service to the private sector sometimes take extreme forms. In the state of Wisconsin, Governor Scott Walker and other reactionaries are attempting to undermine what was once the great University of Wisconsin. One of the measures is to try to turn the institution toward producing an "output"—as they say in market terms—that is, students who will serve the needs of the business community of Wisconsin. In addition to cutting the budget and reducing tenured appointments, one of the initiatives was so outrageous that it hit the newspapers. The state government wanted to change the traditional mission of the university, which included the mission of "seeking truth." They wanted to delete that—because "who needs that kind of thing?"—and turn the university directly to producing people who will be good for the Wisconsin workforce and businesses. That was so outrageous they had to claim it was a clerical error and withdraw it.

But it is illustrative of what is happening, not only in the United States but throughout the world. Stefan Collini,[1] a critical analyst of the university, has concluded correctly in several articles in the *London Review of Books* that the Tory government of David Cameron (now Theresa May) is attempting to turn first-class universities into third-class commercial institutions. So the Classics department at Oxford will have to prove that it can sell itself on the market if people want to study Greek literature or classical philology, say. That's the ultimate vulgarization that results from imposing the state capitalist principles of the business classes on the whole of society. This imposition is happening in much harsher ways, as you can see in Greece and elsewhere. But, in the university system, it is very destructive.

MS: Do you see a change in the manner in which professors are engaging with the public? Are we less engaged as public intellectuals as a result of neoliberalism and the way in which we are ranked and ordered and valued or not?

NC: There are effects. One effect is simply the decline of the autonomy of the faculty, outlined in *The Fall of the Faculty* (2011) by the American sociologist Benjamin Ginsberg. He discusses the changes during the neoliberal period within the university systems as the role and the number of administrators has increased sharply through massive levels of bureaucratization, including layers of deans, sub-deans, and assistants to sub-deans. It is very inefficient, but that is typical of the way the corporate system works. But then there is a system of control and management, and the faculty role [in decision making] has declined accordingly.

The neoliberal system, remember, is an attempt to impose business models. Business models focus on the bottom line; they want what economists call "flexibility of labour," which is a euphemism for beating working people over the head. The way this is done in universities is by reducing the possibilities for secure positions in which you can function effectively as a teacher and researcher. So cut back on tenure appointments and turn to temporary employees like adjuncts and graduate students [and sessional instructors]. They are much more easily controlled and they don't have rights. Let them do the work and the teaching and meet the students, and cut back on the possibilities of doing authentic research and serious teaching, which [from a business perspective] is an expensive waste of time.

One of the aspects of the corporate model is simply reducing the role of faculty in running the university. In many of the better universities, the faculty basically ran them, but that has sharply declined. One of the effects is there are more restrictions on the faculties. For junior faculty and temporary adjuncts, who are not on the academic ladder, it is much harder for them to act as public intellectuals until they have more security or opportunity. Corporatization restricts the possibilities of acting freely and independently; that requires security. Overall, I think the general pattern through history remains: intellectuals and academics want to work within the system and gain the benefits that come from obedience and passivity, and not rock the boat and not take on the role of what we call, in other societies, "dissidents," a term we are not allowed to use for ourselves.

MS: What are some of the other greatest threats or challenges to the academy and higher learning, as you see them?

NC: One major problem is the sharp rise in the cost of tuition, which is associated with a significant cutback in public support for the university system. The contribution of the states to the college and university system has significantly declined overall. All of this, again, is part of the general imposition of business models on institutions of higher education, which is detrimental, of course, and part of the general neoliberal agenda. Neoliberalism should be understood as a form of class war, which as we can see from experience and is obvious by design, that tends to assign power and authority to narrow sectors of concentrated capital and to political leadership that is closely linked and which by now capitalists virtually buy. This shows up in all institutions, including universities. It includes the deterioration of all public services. What economists call "economic efficiency" is, in reality, often economic *inefficiency*, in which costs, like tuition, are transferred to individuals, costs that economists don't measure.

Here is a simple example: You call your bank because there was an error in your last statement they sent and you want to correct the error. What happens? You call the number and get a recorded message, and it gives you a menu that doesn't include what you are interested in, and then you push a couple of buttons and you finally get something and another recorded message comes along, and then you get something that says, "Thank you for your business, we love you," and some music plays and goes on for half an hour. Finally, if you hang on long enough, you may get a human being and you can say what you want and they will send you in some wrong direction. From an economic point of view, that is highly efficient; it is reducing the cost to the bank. If the bank simply had a person answering the phone, who could fix what you wanted in thirty seconds, that would be costly for the bank, so it is inefficient. Here it is very costly, but because the cost [in terms of time] is transferred to the individual, there appears to be no economic costs to be counted. The same is true with other institutions such as public transport and hospitals. An automated call menu is an example of an ideological decision in the economy and reflects the needs of big business. The same is true of the bureaucratization of the universities. Instead of the faculty saying let's fix this, you have to go through a dean, a provost, an assistant provost, committees, and finally maybe you can get somebody to listen to what you are talking about.

The use of temporary labour is efficient from an economic point of view. By ideological measures of economic efficiency, that means that most of the people who are actually doing the teaching and the research can't even participate; they are not part of the system, they are temporary workers who can be thrown out at any time and have no role. Along with this comes the disciplinary technique of imposing high tuitions. If you take a look at other countries, say, Mexico, a poor country that has a very good higher education system. They don't pay the faculty much because it is a poor country, but the universities are quite good and they are free. Look at one of the most successful economies in the world: in Germany, a rich country, higher education is free there too. Finland repeatedly sets the highest standards, and it is free there as well. In the United States, during the period of great growth and development—the '50s and the '60s—education was mostly free. The GI Bill gave free education to a vast number of people who never would have gone to college. It was very good for them, and it was very good for the country. Even at private colleges, the costs were so low that by today's standards it was almost free. I went to a private Ivy League school—the University of Pennsylvania. It cost $100 a year and you could get a scholarship easily, so a working student like me could get by. It is radically different today, and it imposes tremendous burdens on students. A student can't even declare bankruptcy, so they will take your social security and you're essentially trapped for life. It's a very effective disciplinary technique related to the bureaucratization of the universities. The whole university system is being undermined worldwide by the imposition of corporate business models that are highly inefficient, and designed for control and management and the undermining of independence, freedom, and creativity. This makes perfect sense from a business point of view. You don't want your workers to be free and independent; you want them to do what they are told.

MS: This interview was part of a collective call to action as it is. What actions would you suggest would be the most effective?

NC: There are important moves taking place to unionize adjuncts and graduate students to give them the kind of support that comes from solidarity and acting together, especially if the faculty will join in supporting them. At some level, these are governmental decisions; the defunding of state colleges, for example, is a matter of action at a legislative level, and that means trying to reverse policies that are harmful, and, indeed, opposed by most of the population. We have to bear in mind that, in our current sharp deterioration of democracy, the public attitudes don't really matter very much. For another example, look at taxes. For decades there have been polls on what people think about taxes, and there are good studies about this in the political science literature. Overwhelmingly, people want higher taxes on the rich. That is rarely reported. A poll will ask: "Do you think you pay too much tax?" And the person replies, "Yeah, for sure." Next question: "So do you want higher taxes on the rich?" Answer: "Sure, we should have higher taxes on the rich." But what gets reported is that people are opposed to taxes, not let us have higher taxes on the rich. That gives the impression to those who read the polls that I must be kind of a weirdo because everybody else just wants taxes reduced. That's even true of people who call themselves fiscal conservatives and who want less government.

Look at the health system; it is a huge drain on the economy. It is an international scandal: in the U.S., we pay twice the costs per capita of comparable countries and have relatively poor outcomes. For decades, a large part of the population wanted national health care. In the late '80s, for example, during the Reagan years, about 70 per cent of the public thought there should be a constitutional guarantee for public health care. In fact, 40 per cent of the population thought there already was such a guarantee in place. But it never became policy. When the Obama program was instituted, there was discussion of at least a public option: Do you want something like Medicare? A considerable majority of the population favoured that, but it wasn't even considered. I mean, business control of the political system and the undermining of democracy is so extreme that what the public wants isn't considered. The result is the Obama program has been an improvement and better than the awful system there was, but it is still very complex and very costly. Again, many of the costs are transferred to individuals. If you have taken the trouble to try to register in the system, you will find out quickly how the costs are transferred to you. In most countries, if you are sick, you go to the hospital and they take care of you, period. But this health system is a huge cost to the economy and the infrastructure to support it is ludicrous.

Another example is the U.S. is one of the few countries where you cannot take a high-speed train. You can ride high-speed rail from China to Kazakhstan, but you can't from New York to Boston. In fact, the fastest train today, when it runs and doesn't have an accident, is not much faster than one I took about seventy years ago. All of these examples are understandable consequences of business domination of the economy, and it shows up in very destructive ways that rarely get reported.

As a final illustration: the International Monetary Fund published an important study of public subsidies to the fossil fuel industry. It is not a secret to people who don't live under a rock that, unless we leave most of the fossil fuels in the ground, we're essentially doomed. How do governments react to this? According to the IMF, by providing over $5 trillion a year in public subsidies to the industries that are dedicated to destroying human existence. You'd think that might make it to the newspapers somewhere. But all of these things are linked, and universities are but one example.

MS: Thank you so much for your participation in our symposium and for your sage advice and for your lifetime of work. It's been a real pleasure.

NC: Thanks, good to talk to you.

MS: Thank you.[2]

Notes

1   Stefan Collini is a professor of English literature at Cambridge University and is the author of the book *What Are Universities For?* (2012).
2   This chapter is based on a pre-symposium interview that took place on May 26, 2015. It has been lightly edited for readability and accuracy.

PART II

ACTIVISM, SCIENCE, AND GLOBAL AND LOCAL KNOWLEDGE

CHAPTER 5

ACCUMULATION AND ITS DIS'(SED) CONTENTS: THE POLITICS OF EVIDENCE IN THE STRUGGLE FOR PUBLIC EDUCATION

Michelle Fine

> Man has, as it were, become a kind of prosthetic God. When he puts on all his auxiliary organs he is truly magnificent; but those organs have not grown on to him and they still give him much trouble at times.
>
> —Sigmund Freud, *Civilization and Its Discontents*

Chicago's Mayor Rahm Emanuel, perhaps imagining himself a prosthetic God, oversaw a massive neoliberal education reform plan in 2011: closing fifty neighbourhood schools and opening dozens of privately operated charter schools in communities that were 88 per cent Black and 94 per cent low income. Dyett High School, one of the fifty, was accused of low performance and graduation rates. Plastered with evidence, shamed and exiled, Dyett was locked in the "failing school" stockade in Bronzeville, Chicago, an early-twentieth-century destination community for African Americans migrating from the rural South, seeking freedom and opportunity, home to Louis Armstrong, Richard Wright, and Ida B. Wells.

The community around Dyett had long argued that disinvestment of the school would feed poor performance. Their protests were ignored until neoliberal "designs" for the Renaissance of Chicago took hold. Then the critique harmonized well with a sea of allied interests intended to lure whites and elites back to the core of urban America: gentrification, corporate penetration of public education, profits from testing and technology, union busting, and the demonization of teachers. All of this could be accomplished easily in an "evidence-based" policy to close "failing schools." Community organizer Jitu Brown, director of the Journey for Justice Alliance, and eleven other community members in the Bronzeville neighbourhood of Chicago launched a hunger strike to fight the closing of Dyett High School. With signs that read "HUNGRY FOR DYETT," demonstrators supported the Coalition to Revitalize Dyett High School's plan to reopen the school as a community-based, green technology school. A competing bid proposed a city-wide, open admissions, arts school. On September 3, 2015, in Washington, DC, hunger strikers explained that if Dyett reopened as a school of "choice," open by lottery or application to all children in the city of Chicago, neighbourhood children would have no school to call their own.

If Freud understood the fate of men who believe themselves to be god in *Civilization and Its Discontents*, Rosa Luxemburg and community organizer Jitu Brown understand the voracious appetite of capital: *accumulation and its dis'(sed) contents*. The (racial/class) cleansing of school buildings, the extraction of children of colour and need, to make room for the new urban gentry is the über-exemplar of neoliberal transformation. Disposable bodies are the excrement, or dis'(sed) contents of corporate education reform, and audit culture is the very clean apparatus of accumulation.

On September 4, 2015, the Chicago CEO announced the school would be reopened next fall—a victory—but as an open-enrolment, arts-focused high school: "We hope that they will recognize that this is a win for everybody," district CEO Forrest Claypool said. "It may not be the green technology global leadership academy that they supported and that they were going to run, but it is, I think, something that really represents the will of the community" (Perez 2015, B2).

One might ask: Whose will?

It was 1913 when Rosa Luxemburg published *The Accumulation of Capital* and described capital's insatiable thirst for expansion:

Capitalist methods of production do more than awaken in the capitalist this thirst for surplus value...Expansion becomes in truth a coercive law, an economic condition of existence...A growing tendency towards reproduction at a progressively increasing scale thus, ensues, which spreads automatically like a tidal wave over ever larger surfaces of reproduction. (2015, 12)

A century later, David Harvey articulated the varied tactics of *accumulation by dispossession* that facilitate accumulation for the wealthy and corporate interests:

The main substantive achievement of neoliberalization, however, has been to redistribute, rather than to generate, wealth and income....This was achieved under the rubric of "accumulation by dispossession." By this I mean the continuation and proliferation of accumulation practices which Marx had treated of as "primitive" or "original" during the rise of capitalism. These include the commodification and privatization of land and the forceful expulsion of peasant populations, compare the cases, described above, of Mexico and of China, where 70 million peasants are thought to have been displaced in recent times; conversion of various forms of property rights (common, collective, state, etc.) into exclusive private property rights (most spectacularly represented by China); suppression of rights to the commons; commodification of labour power and the suppression of alternative (indigenous) forms of production and consumption; colonial, neocolonial, and imperial processes of appropriation of assets (including natural resources); monetization of exchange and taxation, particularly of land; the slave trade (which continues particularly in the sex industry); and usury, the national debt and, most devastating of all, the use of the credit system as a radical means of accumulation by dispossession. (Harvey 2007, 22)

We witness today, as in the past, these tactics of accumulation in the aggressive corporate takeover of K–12 schools and higher education, provoked and legitimated by the promiscuous politics of evidence. This chapter is designed to track the discourses, tactics, and aggressive adventures of accumulation enacted by elites and financial and corporate interests on the body and soul of public education and to interrogate how "evidence" has been deployed to legitimate land grab, labour disruption, and the hollowing and colonizing of public institutions.

I have spent three decades gathering stories of educational wounds and desires, narrated by young people who have been betrayed by public institutions and still yearn to be educated, recognized, respected, and to engage. In this chapter I hold those stories as a conscience but seek to interrogate the (usually) invisible hand of elite and corporate privilege shaming and closing schools in poor communities of colour to consolidate power and control, accumulate profit and land, seduce a small segment of Black and Latin@ educational desire out of community into charter schools or boarding schools, mute critical curriculum, pedagogy, and, therefore, consciousness, and to soil the soul of public education.

A slightly obnoxious preface to my university friends who have failed to pay attention to the ravaging of K–12: Most of us ignored the cries of "Testing!" "Evaluation!" "School closings!" and "Privatization!" voiced by K–12 educators for the past three decades. Typically, colleges of education have been complicit or passive, at least in the United States...But as, Luxemburg predicted, the thirst for expansion did not stop at Grade 12. Now it is our turn. As other chapters in this book remind us, today, we in higher education are also being eaten by the corporate logic and metrics that constitute punitive accountability.

The Complicit Role of "Evidence" in Activating
Circuits of Dispossession and Privilege

Drawing on Luxemburg and Harvey, Jessica Ruglis and I (Fine and Ruglis 2009) advocated that educational researchers should track accumulation through the entangled circuits of dispossession and privilege if we were to understand the racialized and classed dismantling of *public* education for the poor, and the fortification of public education for middle- and upper-middle-class students, enacted through land grabs of largely Black schools in pre-gentrifying neighbourhoods; the assault on labour, particularly teachers and principals of colour lost to school closings and test-based teacher evaluations; the narrowing of curriculum and attack on critical inquiry and race consciousness unleashed by high-stakes testing and the shuttering of ethnic studies courses throughout high school and university; and then the carceral penetration of schooling advanced by zero tolerance and policing within schools. At the time, we wrote,

[By introducing the language of] "circuits and consequences of dispossession," we problematize how educational policies laminate credentials of merit onto most White and Asian elite youth, while tattooing the material and psychic scars of "lack" onto most Black, Latin@, immigrant, and/or poor students...we seek to make visible the sturdy neo-liberal policy matrix that reliably produces cumulative disadvantage for youth of color and academic water wings for most young people who are White, especially if they are wealthy. We are interested in how these policies simultaneously install in public institutions mechanisms for corporate and carceral profit while accelerating the disparagement of the public sphere; how they simultaneously inject in youth of color a deep sense of structural outrage and a shadow discourse of personal responsibility. We're interested in the breadth of consequence, that is, how educational public policies move across sectors of economics, education, health, and criminal justice, carving a racialized geography of youth development and dispossession that appears to be so natural. The facade of "naturalness," itself an expression of white privilege, anchors these circuits of dispossession. (Fine and Ruglis 2009, 20)

The twinning of accumulation and dispossession, as well as the reproduction of privilege, are difficult to document. As discourses and material evidence of decay and fear circulate, calls to intervene and innovate are mobilized, animating, appropriately, the desperate fears, disappointments, and desires of communities long betrayed by public institutions. Desperate parents may be suspect of the newest "reform," but they also fear for their children attending vastly disinvested and potentially unsafe buildings. The state, emboldened by corporate resources and logic, dismantled and intervened with the "will of the community."

Education "reform" is carried on tongues coated in a language of good intentions and "better than" what was. Privilege multiplies and metastasizes in ways that seem inevitable, and advertises itself as good for the commons, even as it eats away at our collective humanity. And yet, truly, it is hard to defend what was, and the corporate machine keeps us from seeing "forgotten alternatives."

Feminist philosopher Linda Alcoff has called for an examination of "the social-structural context for the production of historical modes of perception that result in ignorance" (Sullivan and Tuana 2007, 54). I draw upon

Alcoff's epistemologies of ignorance to think about how we study both accumulation and the dis(posable) consequences and how we can see, with intention, that which we have been structured to not see and conditioned to not imagine. Studying privilege and accumulation is like tracing invisible ink; tracking the predatory relationship of accumulation to the promiscuous politics of evidence makes slightly more visible the unquenchable thirst for expansion, the strategic use of data, and the complicity of us all.

Scenarios of Ethnographic Ruptures

In his book *Two Cheers for Anarchism* (2012) James Scott advances what he calls the "anarchist squint," whereby critical scholars should attend to what he called "infrapolitics"—the small and large, verbal and embodied, active and passive practices not quite legible as political activism, engaged by non-elites. I take inspiration from Scott but turn my attention away from infrapolitics and toward what might be called *uberpolitics*: the equally unseen and unnoticed—naturalized—elite discourses, behaviours, back-room meetings, real estate and financial deals, media campaigns, violations of democratic practices, appropriation of social media, tokenistic displays of marginalized faces speaking the benefits of the neoliberal takeover. Most relevant, for our purposes, I am interested in the insidious (mis)uses of "evidence" to facilitate and justify accumulation and dispossession. This I call *punitive accountability*.

I offer this analysis to cut deeply through the language and "evidence" that shield, protect, and justify a whitening of urban space and the privatization of all things public, and to consider how researchers might pierce the ideologies, science, enactments, and embodiments of privilege as innocence. It seems important to consider how "evidence" has become the scientific ink of racialized and classed dispossession and accumulation, and how audit culture and punitive accountability have penetrated spaces of public educational practice.

The two scenes sketched below are cropped at what I call *ethnographic ruptures*: fracture points in an ethnography where the laminated discourses of privilege are pierced delicately—and then maybe more aggressively—by democratically posed questions about evidence. In the language of liberation psychologist Ignacio Martín-Baró, these are moments when the people contest "the Official Lie" (1994, 10). In each case, community members challenged the evidence offered by the state. In both cases we can see how the state repairs the torn fabric of the dominant lie by invalidating the critique, defending a posture of neutrality, innocence, and a commitment to justice. These moments of evidence, when the public contests the state, and the state demurs behind the skirts of neutrality or ignorance, may be a significant entry point for critical researchers seeking to make visible, and disrupt, the discourses, practices, and enactments of educational neoliberalism.

Scene One: When Evidence Justifies Privatization
In 1991, I wrote *Framing Dropouts*, a critical ethnographic tale of a school building serving low-income Black and Latin@ youth, most pushed out and rendered "disposable" prior to graduation (1). The book was celebrated in critical education studies and critical race studies but ignored by policy-makers. Two decades later, as the neighbourhood whitened, I learned that Brandeis High School would be closed—deemed a failing school. A complex of four small schools would be resurrected in its place. The gentrifying Upper West Side wanted its own public high school. I pulled *Framing Dropouts* off the shelf to remember the opening:

> It was 1988 when I sat in the back of what I called Comprehensive High School auditorium and cried. Salty tears of joy and rage. Two hundred and fifty young people walked across the stage, with flowers and corsages, cheers and the rapid lights of cameras flickering for the survivors. Mothers, aunts, fathers, siblings, grandparents gathered from the Bronx and Harlem, Puerto Rico and the DR to celebrate their babies graduating high school. (Fine 1991, 1)

My field notes read, "I just want a moment of silence for the 500 missing." In a school of three thousand, barely one-twelfth graduated. Where were the disappeared? If this were a school with middle-class white students, everyone would be outraged; it would be closed. What we tolerate for the poor is unthinkable for elites. At Brandeis, in the 1980s and certainly since, I learned that it was normative for black and brown bodies to drain out of public institutions without diplomas. Few were alarmed by the disposability of a substantial majority of students of colour. Progressives and conservatives may explain the leakage differently—one side argues structural causation (racism, capitalism), while the other blames individuals (poor motivation, inadequate intelligence, and bad mothering are accepted explanations)—but too many agreed on its inevitability (Fabricant and Fine 2012, 102).

Little did I know that, in the late 1980s, when I was knee-deep in ethnographic muck, that mass incarceration was being drip fed into the darkest neighbourhoods of New York state. State coffers were quietly realigning budgets, migrating monies and bodies of colour from schools to prisons. In 1973, the state's prison population was ten thousand; by 1980, it had doubled to twenty thousand. By 1992, it had more than tripled again to almost sixty-two thousand. As I sat in that gymnasium, I did not realize that the state had other bids on their bodies. Only later would I learn that "since 1989, there have been more Blacks entering the prison system for drug offenses each year than there were graduating from SUNY with undergraduate, masters and doctoral degrees—combined" (Gangi et al. 1999, 7).

Almost twenty-five years later, after generations of disinvestment and disproportionate placement of difficult-to-teach, overage, undercredit students into the building, in the midst of a swelling inequality gap in wealth, income, real estate, and human security, the *New York Times* reported that a "crisis" was finally being declared. The solution was to close the school and reopen it for "better" students who live in, and beyond, the district. Echoes of Naomi Klein (2008) on the Upper West Side.

Based on "failing" test scores and graduation rates, Brandeis, like so many other comprehensive high schools serving Black and Latin@ youth in major urban regions of the nation, would be closed. The new building would be a complex of four small schools, three of which would continue to work with low-income Black and Latin@ youth, and one, the new Frank McCourt High School for journalism and writing, would be sponsored by Symphony Space, which enjoys ample support of local parents and community. Ironically, in the name of Frank McCourt—a progressive Irish immigrant writer—the school was being designed, by some, for the newly gentrifying families of the Upper West Side. Frank and Louie (Brandeis) would roll over in their graves if they knew what was being done in their name.

In November of 1910, W. E. B. Du Bois published the first issue of *The Crisis: A Record of the Darker Races*, insisting that a record be kept of the ongoing crisis of "the darker races." Du Bois recognized that crisis, for poor people and people of colour in the United States, had been woven deeply into the fabric of our nation's history; that public schools had served as an institution through which crisis festered and was washed over, structured primarily in ways that reproduce class and racial stratifications (Anyon 1997; Bell 1995; Bowles and Gintis 1997; Delpit 2006; Fine 1991; Kozol 1972; Woodson 2010). Like his colleague Carter Woodson, Du Bois wrote on the searing capillaries through which systemic mis-education of children of colour stains our national history (Woodson 2010). Most significant for our purposes, Du Bois noted that the structural and historic educational cri(s)es of the "darker races" would be routinely ignored until they are attended to for reasons of profit not justice. I heard cries of "crisis" on the Upper West Side, the wise hauntings of Du Bois asked us to be suspect.

Community activists and educators were deeply involved in challenging Brandeis's makeover. Most of the community meetings were cordial and seasoned with public commitments to "diversity." But the slippery discourse of white deservingness was leaking through the doors. "I guess this school will be for 3s and 4s?" asked one parent, referencing high test score signifiers burned into the consciousness and identity of New York City youth. "If we are serious about getting these kinds of students into that building, we'll have to remove the metal detectors," explained another parent, a father of colour. And a woman facilitating the discussion elaborated, "If the other schools want to keep the metal detectors, or need them, we might want to use a different entrance."

Soon, the discursive architecture of separate and unequal was flooding the room, being spoken by white and African American prospective parents. A number of community members spoke: "This school has betrayed central and East Harlem for at least 30 years. It would be a cruel joke to clean it up, invest in transforming the school and then opening it for local elite children. That would, of course, constitute just another betrayal of Black and Brown students in New York." The Department of Education representative explained, "Any child would be welcome to the school...They will submit attendance, grades and test scores and the computer will chose those who are eligible. Then we'll interview." "But how about a preference for the siblings—or the children—of Brandeis' graduates?" someone asked. "No, the building will be open to children city wide, using criteria that are demographically neutral."

Students who satisfy the published criteria (a score of three or four on standardized tests, a writing sample in English, good attendance, and a grade point average of 3.0 in middle school) are eligible to have a parent submit their names into a lottery. The actual conduct of the lottery itself is fair. But all of the preconditions are coated in relative privilege. Test scores in New York are highly correlated with race and class; writing samples in English are often coached by privately paid tutors; regular attendance and GPA are, of course, correlated with stable homes and few family responsibilities that might interfere with education. The most profound imbalance skews the process to favour parents who are savvy, informed, and entitled enough to submit their child's name into a lottery. And therein lies a piece of the makeover, couched in a language of open access and justice, even as the evidence suggests that students in the lottery vastly under-represent the poorest of the poor, English language learners, and students in need of special education. A stunning instance of neoliberal multiculturalism (Melamed 2011), the language of demographic neutrality shrouds economic and cultural inequality and consequent experiences of dispossession.

In neoliberal education wars, "evidence" has been whitewashed as if neutral, escorted in as a sledgehammer of racialized dispossession, camouflaging decades of disinvestment, spraying blame on educators and opening a secret hatch door as young people of colour slide through the cracks into the massive cauldron of the carceral archipelago. Privilege occupies the building, masquerading as innocence, civil rights, and educational progress, arm and arm with the state. And as long as we do not make eye contact with the young people on the corner, we can remain ignorant.

Scene 2: When State Evidence Is Challenged—The Empire Strikes Back
Throughout the United States, and globally, a small but wealthy group of largely white elites advocates audit culture and market logic in an effort to disrupt and privatize public education, undermine labour unions, and smash what they see as a monopoly (Fabricant and Fine 2012). The obvious ones are Republicans, Tea Party members, or libertarians, but equally pernicious are the "liberal Democrats" like Rahm Emanuel, who are presumably dedicated to narrowing the "achievement gap" and supporting "children of colour" without any structural transformation of the political economy. When performing in public, they speak a language of "love" and behave in ways that are "civil." But, returning to Freud, "It is always possible to bind together a considerable number of people in love, so long as there are other people left over to receive the manifestations of their aggressiveness" (Freud 1961, 59).

I take you now to Montclair, New Jersey—my hometown.

Mid-November, I left the YMCA in Montclair, got into my car, checked my messages, and saw an email from a lawyer at CUNY: "When can we talk? We have received a Freedom of Information Act [FOIA] request for your emails. See attached." My stomach dropped as I scrolled down. In some ways I had been waiting for this.

The last year and a half I had been deeply embroiled in a parent-union-educator movement in a small town in New Jersey, long known for progressive education politics, radical attempts at desegregation, and educational innovation. Montclair is a suburban community known to be progressive and racially desegregated. All of the schools are "integrated" by court order, many families are racially integrated, and the community is home to many LGBTQ families. Children grow up with one/two parents who may be mothers/fathers/grandparents/guardians.

Our desegregated schools are organized as magnets and most children take buses. The schools remain fraught (with race and, more so, class gaps), but the town and the schools try to do what most of the country has walked away from. Long recognized as a progressive and integrated community of Black, white, and mixed-race families, we now enjoy a small growing sector of Latin@ and Asian American families. White families range from high middle to upper middle class, and the Black community stretches from extreme poverty to extreme wealth. But when a "direct" train line to New York City was introduced, real estate sticker prices spiked, and a new generation of investment bankers—the ones who like to call themselves socially progressive and economically conservative—moved into town.

Many prominent Obama Democrats, who are well-heeled corporate education reformers in the nation, live here. The architect of Race to the Top; the former president of the Edison Schools, who became commissioner of education for the state and then joined Rupert Murdoch and Joel Klein at AMPLIFY (the digital education division of Rupert Murdoch's News Corp); the innovators behind KIPP (Knowledge Is Power Program) charter schools, to name just a few. We are what well-known blogger Jersey Jazzman calls "Reformyville"—dedicated to high-stakes testing and major investments in technology; hostile to teachers' unions, pensions, and health care; hungry to privatize paraprofessionals and standardize curriculum.

Two years ago, a corporate-reform-minded superintendent was hired, straight from the Eli Broad Leadership Academy, and she quickly moved into gear—dismissive of educators and the union, dedicated to massive amounts of high-stakes testing, bemoaning the achievement gap and slicing most of the supports that would have helped the students who most struggled (except for test prep). In this suburb, she initiated what had become signature neoliberal corporate reforms throughout urban communities.

In the schools, the community, and social media, all hell broke loose (for detailed analysis of the community pushback, and links between Montclair and Newark, see Karp 2015; Blumenreich and Jaffe-Walter 2015). A multiracial coalition of parents and community members, many long-time radicals, joined with educators and the local Education Association, dedicated to asking hard questions about the "evidence" of first failure, and then miraculous

success, at public school board meetings. At first only the parents spoke—
we challenged the PR/"evidence" the district was circulating to justify our
schools as "failures." We challenged the lack of certification and credentials
of top administrators brought in to restructure the district, and then we
demanded invoices and a full accounting of the costs of expanding numbers
of contracts for corporate education, technology, "satisfaction surveys," and
new well-paid "Chiefs" and legal consultants. An anonymous blog popped
up, dedicated to demonizing the African American woman who is president
of the teachers' union, the Black board member who asked hard questions,
the Black town council member who is also a union administrator, the Black
mayor, and a few outspoken parents.

Over time, more and more parents and soon educators mustered the
courage to speak aloud at school board meetings, raising questions about
the swelling legal fees, consultant invoices, and cuts in full-time unionized
labour. Anonymous spoke again—this time in a petition calling for "civility." Not many signatories, but the intent was clear. State violence, particularly when arm and arm with corporate influence, is always made to appear
civil—especially when most deals are cut behind closed doors. As a consequence, and in dialectic relation, democratic protests and demands for deep
accountability are always made to seem uncivil. Dangling the "tragedy of the
achievement gap" before the town—while refusing to address poverty, the
lack of universal public preschool, school funding inequities, or race—the
corporate logic espoused by this administration managed to redirect substantial dollars toward testing, teacher evaluation, public relations, technology, and legal contracts—and away from classrooms, full-time teachers and
aides, and supports for struggling students.

In October 2014, after more than a year of these "reforms," the superintendent announced that the Black–white achievement gap had been
reduced. I, along with a number of other parents from a grassroots group
called Montclair Cares About Schools, raised questions about the "evidence"
they provided—knowing well the distortions that underlay the Texas testing
miracle. I also suggested that the $20,000 merit bonus awarded to the super-
intendent to reward her for narrowing the gap might be placed in escrow
until the data could be confirmed. This was all happening, by the way, while
she and the board were advocating a shift from full-time teacher aides—who
earn $20,000 a year—to contingent, contracted labour.

Within two weeks of our comments at the board, in November 2014, the
anonymous FOIA request arrived, calling for "all emails from and to Michelle
Fine" from a list of what I call the "FOIA 28": three Black elected politicians

in town who have asked questions about the finances and governance of the district; five journalists who have written about educational politics in town; six to eight activist parents; the president of the local Education Association and other trade unionists; a few bloggers; and the superintendent, administrators, and members of the board of education.

In early December, I approached the microphone at the following board of education meeting and addressed the FOIA 28. I explained that I was sorry that so many got "entangled" in this collective witch hunt, which had ghostly vapours of McCarthy's demonization of progressive critics. One of the named bloggers wrote to the CUNY lawyer that s/he considered this an extension of the earlier subpoena; the parents from Montclair were outraged that their personal emails were subject to a Freedom of Information Act request; the journalists were surprised they were not immune. The lawyer for CUNY (CUNY owned the emails; I was just a "witness") asked the person who requested the emails—a.k.a. pseudonym Mark Smith—for a name and address so she could send the requested documents, at an expense of twenty-five cents per page, to which "he" responded, referring to my presentation at the school board:

> The request I made of the University has been publicly show-cased by a representative of the University. While my request is legal, the actions taken but [sic] your University representative has [sic] been disruptive and intimidating. Based on the specific actions witnessed by Dr. Fine, I do not feel safe inspecting the documents at CUNY and if I was to write you a check or provide my address, Dr. Fine would have my name and look to publicly and verbally hurt me in my hometown. While I respect the extra work it may take you and your staff, I would ask that you please consider the special circumstances that were created when Dr. Fine decided to make this a public event. If the University is committed to putting me in an unsafe situation, I will need to hire counsel to address this matter...I was only requesting information which is my right under law. I did not realize it would create such a commotion in my hometown and *it was never my intent for this private request to become a public matter*.

True, his intent was to make *public* education become a *private* matter.

There is much to tell...and I may another time (see Blumenreich and Jaffe-Walter 2015). Suffice it to say, public opinion in our community and nationally rallied against these "anonymous" corporate invaders, the superintendent resigned, the town peaked at a 48 per cent opt-out rate on Common Core/state-mandated exams, and a new healthy and honest board is in place. Meanwhile, CUNY handed over one thousand of my emails, which hang awkwardly on a new "Montclair Kids First" website, dedicated to "quality education," "teacher evaluation," and "responsible taxes." The corporate fight continues to be waged in our neighbouring Newark, New Jersey, where the same reformers hope to create a district that mirrors New Orleans, with upward of 40 per cent charter schools.

While Montclair activists are working in solidarity with parents and educators in Newark, there is also much to be learned about the higher education side of this story. In a short time, I have discovered that a number of public university faculty in the United States who conduct research that challenges corporate interests (and Israel) have been served Freedom of Information Laws (FOILs) or ethics charges, particularly those working on global warming, corporate education reform, Palestinian solidarity, immigration and voting rights reform, Big Pharma, and campaign finance/gerrymandering. The right-wing think tank, American Legislative Exchange Council, seems to be promoting this strategy of FOIA requests against progressive faculty at public universities, exploiting university email as the "portal" to expose and gather intelligence on networks of progressive critics and chill critics in the making. I have learned that administrators vary wildly about how much they simply roll over or defend faculty interests. I have also learned much about how widespread is the fully funded, prefer-to-be-anonymous strategic attempt to silence those in public universities who dare to question the corporate education reform agenda.

Ironic, tragic, or obvious: elite, right-wing, and corporate interests, but also performing as "progressive Democrats" who aim to privatize public education, are exploiting strong public interest legal tools (freedom of information laws, the Open Public Records Act, the Open Performance Review and Appraisal System, even ethics complaints) against public university faculty and everyday community members who dare to challenge corporate spin qua evidence, to induce a sense of surveillance, silencing, and chill.

The Politics of Evidence

Truth be told, I am more than a little nerdy. I love evidence: in stories, statistics, trend lines, embroideries, dance, and various forms of protest. Calls for evidence may best be thought of as an assemblage, as Deleuze and Guattari (1987) would describe, that involves flows of contradictions, divergent motives, and commitments. Civil rights and human rights groups rely on evidence to demonstrate injustice, and insist on evidence to demonstrate commitment to transformation; scientists and lawyers call for evidence, rather than gospel, as the basis of curriculum, public health practices, or contestations in court; activists who display video evidence of police abuse garner a critical tool of documentation.

The difficulty, of course, comes with a series of epistemological and ethics questions that sits at the base of Budd Hall's (see Chapter 6 of this book) and Linda Tuhiwai's (see Chapter 2 of this book) work on participatory policy:

- Who decides what constitutes evidence?
- Who interprets the evidence?
- Who owns the evidence?
- What are the stakes?

Is the context one in which evidence is used for bold liberation and broad-based mobilization, for delicate and deliberate dialogue within a movement, or for public shaming/punishment?[1]

Those of us in public education are living in a moment of punitive accountability. A well-funded, corporate reform strategy seeks to disrupt public school systems and universities, with its eye explicitly on unravelling the influence of teachers' unions, widening the reach of corporate dollars and influence, narrowing and conservatizing the curriculum, reducing reliance on "brick and mortar" schools or full-time (much less tenure track) faculty, and imploding what constitutes "public," whereby empty ideological slogans of *choice* and *freedom* and *flexibility* have been privileged over justice, learning, deep participation, and collective human security/sustainability (as in jobs!).

In systems of punitive accountability, what makes us quite literally sick—as Rosalind Gill attests in Chapter 11 of this book—is an institutional and political culture that invents metrics to justify the swelling of profits/administrative salaries/white privilege; punishes those who have been marginalized; destabilizes labour; demoralizes workers; sets up invidious comparisons and competitions; threatens the spirit and souls of poor and working-class children; dismantles public institutions; and then declares accountability.

The political and embodied consequences of audit culture are everywhere, and damaging. We know, of course, that accumulation—the practices and the subjectivities and discourses of those who are accumulating—is anything but passive. And yet it is difficult, awkward, sometimes even "uncivil," to question the rising piles of profit and the hollowed spaces being dispossessed, especially when our friends, family members, and our own institutions are implicated. But that is our work. We can no longer justify gathering "evidence" of injustice by focusing only on the dis'(sed) contents, the disposables tossed aside, when the walls of privilege are rising higher and higher.

But now is the moment for those of us in the academy to reflect on the ways in which we have, and remain, in contradiction, if not complicit, with audit culture. In education, psychology, and sociology, we have helped to design the metrics that are deployed; we have reified the categories that attach to young bodies (at risk? vulnerable? remedial?). And those of us privileged— by seniority, race, gender—must recognize that the consequences for resistance are unevenly distributed. At the symposium, "Public Engagement and the Politics of Evidence in an Age of Neoliberalism and Audit Culture," it was relatively easy for those of us near retirement to glibly say, "Don't fill out those forms!" And it was harder for younger faculty to admit, "But we must." The stakes for white senior faculty who resist are likely minimal and, yet, Indigenous students or faculty and students and faculty of colour will be seen as irresponsible or "not team players" if they challenge the audit machine.

As we position ourselves to study and contest neoliberal sprawl and audit culture in our own and others' institutions and communities, in times of corporate/elite consolidation and penetration of the public sphere, we are confronted with novel (if historically consistent) configurations of how power operates, penetrates, and punishes; how ideologies and material resources redistribute to anoint merit on historically privileged bodies; how disposability, too, is produced and legitimated by social science; the curious moves of anonymity and the dirty tactics of elites. We can, however, no longer be surprised that the soft skin of privilege is naturalized as "progress" in the resurrection and renaissance of white elite America.

As I noted in the opening of this chapter, higher education is a few years behind the critical consciousness and activism of our colleagues in K–12 schools. In the United States, educators in elementary and secondary schools have endured these relentless regimes of surveillance and punishing metrics; today, they model courageous forms of what Indigenous scholar Gerald Vizenor (2008) calls "survivance": they contest as they labour; they build coalitions among labour, faculty, students, families, and with other public workers eager to sustain a democratic, vibrant commons.

The public is at risk of extinction, contaminated by private dollars and corporate logic. Despair is not an option. In 1982, Audre Lorde wrote,

To refuse to participate in the shaping of our future is to give it up. Do not be misled into passivity either by false security (they don't mean me) or by despair (there's nothing we can do). [Read: higher education, white faculty, senior faculty, elites in the academy, noncontingent academic labour.] Each of us must find our work and do it. Militancy no longer means guns at high noon, if it ever did. It means actively working for change, sometimes in the absence of any surety that change is coming. It means doing the unromantic and tedious work necessary to forge meaningful coalitions, and it means recognizing which coalitions are possible and which coalitions are not. It means knowing that coalition, like unity, means the coming together of whole, self-actualized human beings, focused and believing, not fragmented automatons marching to a prescribed step. It means fighting despair. And in the university, that is certainly no easy task, for each one of you by virtue of your being here will be deluged by opportunities to misname yourselves, to forget who you are, to forget where your real interests lie. Make no mistake, you will be courted; and nothing neutralizes creativity quicker than tokenism, that false sense of security fed by a myth of individual solutions.

Audit culture posits a new challenge to our professional academic sense of autonomy and freedom. In this book, we hear clearly from Marie Battiste, Sandy Grande, Linda Tuhiwai Smith, and Eve Tuck that the historic rhythms of colonial constraint are more familiar to some than others. Those of us for whom oppression is still shocking, and privilege a tradition, would do well to learn from colleagues and allies who know well the long march to freedom and justice. And now the academy is part of the struggle.

Notes

1   Over the past twenty years, those of us at the Public Science Project have been gathering Dispossession Stories: empirical accounts of how public opportunities, institutions, and resources are being demonized, privatized, and redesigned in law, policy, and academic practices that further tip educational advantage in the direction of children of privileged families, while an array of equally expensive public policies—testing, policing, and surveillance—are being unleashed within low-income communities, reinforcing and extending inequality gaps that already characterize urban

America. Across a variety of communities and public sectors, we have been tracking what we call "circuits of dispossession and privilege" (Fine and Ruglis 2009)—how changes in law, policy, and institutional practices on the ground are realigning educational goods once considered "public" toward limited access primarily for the children of elites and a few token, working-class children of colour—what Jodi Melamed (2011) calls "neoliberal multiculturalism." We are interested in the social psychological circuits through which economic and political shifts circulate and find their way under the affective and cognitive skin of parents and youth living in privileged and marginalized communities, all of these shifts represented as good for the city.

References

Anyon, J. 1997. *Ghetto Schooling: A Political Economy of Urban Educational Reform*. New York: Teachers College Press.

Bell, D. A. 1995. "Who's Afraid of Critical Race Theory?" *University of Illinois Law Review* 4: 893–910.

Blumenreich, M., and R. Jaffe-Walter. 2015. "Social Media Illuminates Some Truths about School Reform." *Phi Delta Kappan* 97(1) (September): 25–28.

Bowles, S., and H. Gintis. 1997. *Schooling in Capitalist America: Educational Reform and the Contradictions of Economic Life*. New York: Basic Books.

Deleuze, G., and F. Guattari. 1987. *A Thousand Plateaus*. Minneapolis: University of Minnesota Press.

Delpit, L. 2006. *Other People's Children: Cultural Conflict in the Classroom*. New York: New Press.

Fabricant, M., and M. Fine. 2012. *Charter Schools and the Corporate Makeover of Public Education*. New York: Teachers College Press.

Fine, M. 1991. *Framing Dropouts: Notes on the Politics of an Urban High School*. Albany, NY: SUNY Press.

Fine, M., and J. Ruglis. 2009. "Circuits and Consequences of Dispossession: The Racialized Realignment of the Public Sphere for U.S. Youth." *Transforming Anthropology* 17(1): 20–33.

Freud, S. 1961. *Civilization and Its Discontents*. In *The Standard Edition of the Complete Psychological Works of Sigmund Freud*, vol. XXI (1927–1931). Translated by J. Strachey. New York: Norton. First published 1930.

Gangi, R., et al. 1999. *New York State of Mind? Higher Education vs. Prison Funding in the Empire State, 1988–1998*. Washington, DC: Justice Policy Institute. https://www.academia.edu/23136453/New_York_State_of_Mind_Higher_Education_vs._Prison_Funding_in_the_Empire_State_1988-1998.

Harvey, D. 2007. *A Brief History of Neoliberalism*. New York: Oxford University Press.

Karp, S. 2015. "A Tale of Two Districts: The Long Reach and Deep Pockets of Corporate Reform." *Rethinking Schools* 29(3) (Spring). https://www.rethinkingschools.org/articles/a-tale-of-two-districts.

Klein, N. 2008. *Shock Doctrine*. London: Picador.

Kozol, J. 1972. *Free Schools*. Boston: Houghton Mifflin.

Lorde, A. 1982. "Learning from the 60s." http://www.blackpast.org/1982-audre-lorde-learning-60s.

Luxemburg, R. 2015. *The Accumulation of Capital*. New York: CreateSpace. First published 1913.

Martín-Baró, I. 1994. *Writings for a Liberation Psychology*. Cambridge, MA: Harvard University Press.

Melamed, J. 2011. *Represent and Destroy*. Minneapolis: University of Minnesota Press.

Perez, J. 2015. "CPS Says Dyett to Reopen as Arts School; Hunger Strikers Not Appeased." *Chicago Tribune*, September 4, B2.

Scott, J. 2012. *Two Cheers for Anarchism*. Princeton: Princeton University Press.

Sullivan, S., and N. Tuana. 2007. *Race and Epistemologies of Ignorance*. Albany, NY: SUNY Press.

Vizenor, G. 2008. *Survivance: Narratives of Native Presence*. Lincoln: University of Nebraska Press.

Woodson, C. 2010. *The Mis-Education of the Negro*. New York: CreateSpace. First published 1933.

CHAPTER 6
BEYOND EPISTEMICIDE: KNOWLEDGE DEMOCRACY AND HIGHER EDUCATION

Budd L. Hall

Introduction

I would like to acknowledge that we are meeting on the traditional territory of the Treaty 4 First Nations. Further, I want you to know that I am a settler Canadian of English heritage and that I live and work on the traditional territory of the Coast and Straits Salish First Nations, specifically on the unceded territory of the Lekwungen and Esquimalt peoples. When I acknowledge the traditional territory where I stand now and where I live and work, it is more than a case of protocol or respectful behaviour. I am standing here today as a professor from the University of Victoria as a direct result of my great-grandparents obtaining two hundred acres of Halalt First Nations traditional territory on Vancouver Island through illegal or immoral means in the last quarter of the nineteenth century. Prior to the acquisition of this rich and productive land, my settler ancestors were landless and poor, having travelled from England to Australia, and then to eastern Canada, and finally to Vancouver Island in search of a way to support themselves and their children. Those two hundred acres of Halalt traditional territory transformed my family into the middle class, and all of my great-grandparents' children down to myself have had the opportunity to study and achieve positions of importance in their lives. The taking of that land created poverty among the Halalt First Nations Peoples that persists until today.

I want to share some knowledge stories with you today. I want to speak of past and continuing cultural genocides, linguicides, and epistemicides. And I want to speak about the complicity of the modern university in maintaining unequal knowledge hierarchies. I also want to provide evidence of a possible turning in the world of higher education.

Dispossession and Knowledge

The geographer David Harvey (2004) has elaborated the concept of accumulation through dispossession to explain how capital, the basis of our dominant economic system, began to be accumulated. Dispossessing people of access to their land, he suggests, lies at the heart of early capital accumulation. The story of my family's transformation through the dispossession of the lands of the Halalt First Nations on my island is a perfect example. Harvey draws attention to the processes in fourteenth- to seventeenth-century England, which removed people from their land through what has become known as "enclosures." He tells us of wealthy landowners who used force, and even arms, to transform the traditional open fields and communal pastures into private property for their own profit. A similar process similarly affected the clans of Scotland, and was so widespread that their dispossessions were known as "the clearances." Each of these acts of dispossession left the majority of people without access to land and allowed for wealth to accumulate to those who were now known as private landowners. New categories of people were defined: the landed gentry, the workers in the estates, the landed, and the landless. Lest you think these acts went on unnoticed, let us recall the words of an English rhyme from the period:

> The law condemns the woman or man
> Who steals the goose from off the common
> But leaves the greater felon loose
> Who steals the common from the goose.

A few years ago, I had the opportunity to spend a few days in one of the Oxford colleges, a college that was created at the same time as the enclosures. I entered the college through a low doorway accessible only to students and fellows and their guests. The college was walled in and only accessible through one or two guarded entryways. While I stayed in the college, the linkage between the enclosing of previously common land for private purposes and the creation of walled places for learning became disturbingly apparent. The act of creating Oxford and the other medieval universities was an act of enclosing knowledge, limiting access to knowledge, exerting a form of control over knowledge, and providing a means for a small elite to acquire this knowledge for purposes of leadership of a spiritual nature, a governance nature, or a cultural nature. Those within the walls became knowers; those outside the wall became nonknowers. Knowledge was removed from the land and from the relationships of those sharing the land. The enclosing of the academy dispossessed the vast majority of knowledge keepers, forever relegating their knowledge to witchcraft, tradition, superstition, folkways, or, at best, some form of common sense.

These new academies came into being as well at the time of the rise of European science and, through improvements in navigational aids and the wealth generated by the enclosures and the exploitation of silver and gold from Latin America, the hegemony of mostly white, Eurocentric knowledge spread around the world. Just as colonial political practices carved up the globe in the eighteenth and nineteenth centuries, knowledge, the intellectual energy by which humans operate, became colonized as well. The process of dispossession of other knowledge is a process that Boaventura de Sousa Santos (2007), a Portuguese sociologist, has called *epistemicide*, or the killing of knowledge systems. I will come back to how epistemicide, linguicide, and cultural genocide have been a product of Western modern higher education, but first I want to continue my remarks with some stories about knowledge.

PRIA

In the late 1970s, a young Indian academician by the name of Rajesh Tandon, educated in the elite universities of India and the Unites States, found himself deep in rural Rajasthan working as a researcher with tribal farmers on rural development issues. He found on every issue of rural development he encountered that the unschooled women and men in rural Rajasthan were more knowledgeable than he, not marginally but deeply so. A few years later, when he had the opportunity, he created the nongovernmental research organization that today is known as PRIA, the Society for Participatory Research in Asia, with the aim of supporting the development of grassroots knowledge with the urban and rural poor for social change.

Honey Bee Network
In the late 1980s, in the state of Gujarat in India, a knowledge network was created, dedicated to countering what it noted as a pernicious culture of knowledge asymmetry. Knowledge asymmetry occurs when the people who provide knowledge do not benefit from the gathering and organizing of that knowledge.

> Knowledge [they said] has been extracted, documented without any acknowledgement to the source. The documented knowledge has not been communicated to the knowledge holder for feedback. These practices have not only impoverished the knowledge holders by pushing them further down in the oblivion, but also have hampered the growth of an informal knowledge system, that is robust in nurturing creativity. (SRISTI)

The organizers called their project the Honey Bee Network, based on the metaphor of the honeybee that does two things that scholars often do not do. It collects pollen from the flowers without exploiting or hearing a complaint, and it connects flower to flower through pollination so that, in the end, life itself continues.

Mpambo Afrikan Multiversity
In the late 1990s, a Ugandan intellectual and civil society activist, Paulo Wangoola, returned home to his Kingdom of Busoga after twenty-five years of working in various parts of Africa and abroad to report on the state of the world as he had experienced it. His message to his Elders was this:

> You sent me out, one of the lesser young people of my generation, to gain Western knowledge and to work in the structures and organisations of the Western world. I have been to their universities, have worked with their governments, have created Western style organisations here in Africa and now I have come home to share what I have learned. I have come to tell you that we, the children of Busoga Kingdom, the children of Afrika will never realize our full potential as people in our communities and as contributors to the global treasury of knowledge if we continue to depend wholly on the content and ways of knowledge of the European peoples. Our way forward must be linked to the recovery, replenishment and revitalization of our thousands of years old Indigenous knowledge. (personal communication)

With those words came a decision by Wangoola to withdraw from the Western world's economic structures, to return to a subsistence lifestyle, and to dedicate himself to the creation of a village-based institution of higher education and research that is today known as the Mpambo Afrikan Multiversity, a place for the support of mother-tongue scholars of Afrikan Indigenous Knowledge.

Mpumalanga Traditional Knowledge Commons
Early in the twenty-first century, eighty traditional healers living in Mpumalanga province in South Africa, women and men whose health and medical knowledge has been learned through traditional apprenticeships, created a biocultural knowledge commons for the systematic sharing of their knowledge among each other for purposes of better serving the health needs of the people living in their province. In doing so, they described knowledge as "an outcome of virtuous relationships with the land, the plants and the animals. It is not property to be bought and sold. It is simultaneously cultural and spiritual and its movement and application promotes a kind of virtuous cohesiveness" (Abrell and Bavicatte 2009, 13).

University of Abahlali baseMjondolo
In 2005, in Durban, South Africa, some of the inhabitants of the tin-roofed shacks of the city created a blockade on Kennedy Road to protest the sale of land, originally promised to the poor for house building, to an industrialist for commercial purposes. This movement of those living in these shacks has grown into Abahlali baseMjondolo, the shack dwellers' movement. But what is unique to this social movement is that it has created its own University of Abahlali baseMjondolo, a space for the creation of knowledge about survival, hope, and transformation, where the shack dwellers themselves are the scholars, the professors, and the teachers. They create and share knowledge through song, "live action debates," and discussions, and document the knowledge in a web-based archive (Sefa Dei, Hall, and Goldin Rosenberg 2000).

Languages of the Land
My final story begins with a young Indigenous woman from the Lil'wat First Nation in British Columbia. In the 1960s, she was chosen by her community to work as a research guide for a non-Indigenous linguist who had expressed an interest in working on the development of an alphabet for the St'át'imcets language. She was successful in this challenge and her people have made use of this alphabet since that time.

In 2015, this woman is a leading authority on Indigenous languages in Canada. Her name is Dr. Lorna Williams. She has become the leading scholar of Indigenous language revitalization, but the fate of the language of her community and the fate of most of the Indigenous languages of Canada have not fared well. The impact of colonial domination of Western language traditions has resulted in linguicide, the death or near-death of these carriers of our global cultural heritage.

Knowledge Is the Star

In each of the stories I have just shared with you knowledge is central. Knowledge is the star of each drama. Knowledge is dynamic, active, engaged, and linked to social, political, cultural, or sustainable changes. PRIA's co-constructed knowledge is linked to a variety of social movements in India. Mpambo's mother-tongue scholars are stimulating an unprecedented reawakening of Afrikan spiritual knowledge and sharing in Uganda. The shack dwellers of Durban and beyond have boldly taken the word *university* as their own and turned the knowledge hierarchies upside down in the service of justice for the poor. The Indigenous language champions working with the First Peoples' Cultural Council have staked a claim to epistemological privilege over the Western-trained, non-Indigenous linguists. The healers from South Africa have staked their claims to knowledge superiority, not to settle any epistemological scores with Western science but, in their commitment, to better serve the health needs of their people. These knowledge innovators have all facilitated various means of creating, sharing, and accessing knowledge that is not part of what is often called the Western canon. For a variety of justice, cultural, spiritual, environmental, and health reasons, the application of knowledge from the Western canon in each one of these stories was seen as insufficient. The contexts, conditions, values, uses, and politics of knowledge in each of these stories called for an opening outward of our comfortable assumptions about whose knowledge counts and what the relationship between knowledge and life might be.

The Four Epistemicides of the Long Sixteenth Century

I am grateful to the work of Grosfoguel and Dussel who, in addition to de Sousa Santos, have helped me to understand how the ideas of white men from just a few countries of Italy, France, England, Germany, and the United States came to dominate the world of knowledge (Grosfoguel 2013; Dussel 1993). How and when were the colonial structures of knowledge created? How have we arrived at this point in time when any of us could be parachuted into any university in the world, settled into a social science lecture, and be at home with the authors and ideas being discussed?

To understand that we have to look at what Grosfoguel has called the "Four Genocides/Epistemicides of the Long 16th Century" (2013, 1). It seems the story of dispossessing the people from the ownership of their ideas in the medieval universities, which brought ecclesiastical power to the new universities, was just the start of our knowledge story. Grosfoguel pulls four distinct stories of epistemicide, stories almost always treated as separate historical processes, together. In doing so, we learn in a powerful manner how intellectual colonization has emerged. The first two epistemicides are the conquest of Al-Andalus, being the expulsion of Muslims and Jews from Europe, and the conquest of the Indigenous peoples of the Americas started by the Spanish, continued by the French and the English, and still underway today in the contemporary Western hemisphere. The creation of the slave trade that resulted in millions killed in Africa and at sea and more totally dehumanized by enslavement in the Americas was a third genocidal knowledge conquest. Finally, there is the killing of millions of Indo-European women, mostly through burning at the stake as witches, because of knowledge practices that were not controlled by men. These conquests transformed Europe from being at the periphery of an earlier dominant Islamic centre of intellectual power to taking centre stage. But in a historic irony, Spain and Portugal, the leading military and intellectual powers of the fifteenth century, were shut out of the post-sixteenth-century northern European monopoly of knowledge.

What is important for us to understand is that these four conquests were both military and epistemological/ideological. At the height of the Al-Andalus Empire in Europe, the city of Cordoba had a 500,000-book library. This was at a time when other intellectual centres in Europe would have had libraries of five thousand to ten thousand books. The Spanish burned the library in Cordoba and elsewhere. They destroyed most of the codices in the Mayan, Inca, and Aztec empires as well. Women's knowledge, which was largely oral, was simply silenced, as was the knowledge of Africa. African slaves were portrayed as nonhumans, incapable of Western-style thought. Hegel, for example, in commenting on Africans, says, "Among negroes it is the case that consciousness has not attained even the intuition of any sort of objectivity…the negro is the man as beast (Lectures 218)" (quoted in Dussel 1993, 70). The continued linguicide of Indigenous languages in North America and throughout the world today is evidence that the patterns established through conquest in the sixteenth century is still deeply entrenched in our own minds and most certainly in our higher education institutions.

There are so very many examples of how the Western monopoly of knowledge has distorted our higher education institutions that I could take a look at each and every university in Canada, starting with my own University of Victoria, and carry on for days. But, simply for illustrative purposes, let me share some thoughts from several African scholars about how they see the situation. Lebakeng, Phalane, and Dalindjebo (South Africa); Odora Hoppers (South Africa–Uganda); Wangoola (Uganda); and Ezeanya (Rwanda) have written/worked extensively on the importance of the recovery of the intellectual traditions of the continent. "Institutions of higher education in South Africa were (and still are) copycats whose primary function was (and still is) to serve and promote colonial Western values" (Lebakeng, Phalane, and Dalindjebo 2006, 70). Similarly, Ezeanya adds, "In Africa, the research agenda, curriculum and 'given' conceptual frameworks should be continuously re-examined…with the aim of eschewing all manifestations of new-colonial underpinnings and emphasizing indigenous ideas" (2011, 1).

Ecologies of Knowledge and Cognitive Justice

Boaventura de Sousa Santos has a narrative that begins with his observation that in the realm of knowledge we have created an intellectual abyss, which hinders human progress. Abyssal thinking, he notes, "consists in granting to modern science the monopoly of the universal distinction between true and false to the detriment of…alternative bodies of knowledge" (2007, 47). The global dividing line he is referring to is the one that separates the visible constituents of knowledge and power from those who are invisible. Popular, lay, plebeian, peasant, Indigenous, the knowledge of the disabled themselves, and more cannot be fitted in any of the ways of knowing on "this side of the line." They exist on the other side of the "abyss," the other side of the line. And because of this invisibility, they are beyond truth or falsehood. The "other side of the line" is the realm of beliefs, opinions, and intuitive or subjective understandings that at best may become "objects or raw material for scientific inquiry" (52). De Sousa Santos makes the link between values and aspiration tightly in saying, "Global social injustice is therefore intimately linked to global cognitive injustice. The struggle for global social justice will, therefore, be a struggle for cognitive justice as well" (63).

Shiv Visvanathan (2009) contributes to this discourse expanding the concept of "cognitive justice." He notes that the idea of cognitive justice sensitizes us not only to forms of knowledge but also to the diverse communities of problem solving. What one offers, then, is a democratic imagination with a nonmarket, noncompetitive view of the world, where conversation, reciprocity, and translation create knowledge not as an expert, almost-zero-sum view of the world but as a collaboration of memories, legacies, and heritages; a manifold heuristics of problem solving, where a citizen takes both power and knowledge into his or her own hands.

These forms of knowledge, especially the ideas of complexity, represent new forms of power sharing and problem solving that go beyond the limits of voice and resistance. They are empowering because they transcend the standard cartographies of power and innovation, which are hegemonic. By incorporating the dynamics of knowledge into democracy, we reframe the axiomatics of knowledge based on hospitality, community, nonviolence, humility, and a multiple idea of time, where the citizen as trustee and inventor visualizes and creates a new self-reflexive idea of democracy around actual communities of practice (Visvanathan, 2009).

The problem that arises from the domination of the Western knowledge system is not only that the ways of knowing, the cultures, and the stories of the majority of people of the world are excluded but that, given the Western knowledge narrative that links some forms of knowledge with progress, science, and the future, it looks as though colonialism has disabled the Global North from learning in noncolonial terms. Is the Global North stuck in a rut in histories' path, which does not allow for the existence of histories other than the universal history of the West?

Knowledge Democracy

A discourse of knowledge democracy has been emerging in recent years to help us to understand the relationship of knowledge for a more equitable world for at least two reasons. First, we have found the use of the concepts of the knowledge economy and knowledge society to be wanting from the perspective of justice. Second, we have seen a more general loss of confidence in the capacity of Western, white, male, Eurocentric science to respond to the profound challenges of our times. As Tony Judt (2010, 1) writes in the first sentence of his book, *Ill Fares the Land*, "Something is profoundly wrong with the way we live today."

Knowledge democracy refers to an interrelationship of phenomena. First, it acknowledges the importance of the existence of multiple epistemologies or ways of knowing, such as organic, spiritual, and land-based systems; frameworks arising from our social movements; and the knowledge of the marginalized or excluded everywhere, or what is sometimes referred to as subaltern knowledge. Secondly, it affirms that knowledge is both created and represented in multiple forms, including text, image, numbers, story, music, drama, poetry, ceremony, meditation, and more. Third, and funda-mental to our thinking about knowledge democracy, is understanding that knowledge is a powerful tool for taking action in social movements and else-where to deepen democracy and to struggle for a fairer and healthier world. And, finally, knowledge democracy is about open access for the sharing of knowledge so that everyone who needs knowledge will have access to it. Knowledge democracy is about intentionally linking values of justice, fair-ness, and action to the process of using knowledge.

Knowledge Democracy in Action: Stories of
the Turning in Higher Education?

There are those who say we are in the midst of a great turning. David Korten speaks of such in his book, *The Great Turning: From Empire to Earth Community* (2006). The evidence can be seen in the emergence of the Occupy movement, the Canadian Idle No More movement, the growth of the anti-austerity movements in Europe, as well as the extensive research on inequality from Thomas Piketty (2014), Oxfam (Hardoon 2015), Wilkinson and Pickett (2009), and the International Monetary Fund (Dabla-Norris et al. 2015). And, surprisingly, we have a Pope who has described global capi-talism as the "dung of the devil" and calls for a turn toward a communitarian economy (Reuters 2015). When do we look to the world of higher education for evidence of such a turning?

Marta Gregoric has drawn my attention to the concept of *potencias*, the knowledge-creating power of revolutionary movements of historically subjugated peoples. Potencias can be seen at the heart of self-determining communities engaged in creating new social economies and other means of community development outside the dominant political structures of their locations and times. She gives examples from the Zapatistas in Mexico, the

Caracazo in Venezuela, the Chhattisgarh Liberation Front of 1970 in India, and the *empobrecitos* of Bolivia. The solidarity economies at the centre of these struggles offer concrete ideas about alternatives to global capitalism. She adds, "Scientists or experts for the sake of objectivity and neutrality of our work, we should not and cannot—or will not—exempt ourselves any more" (Gregoric 2015, 164).

It is time for those of us working in higher education to move beyond our already strong ability to critique. Our intellectual task requires reflection and critique. We are so very skilled in those first two stages of intellectual work. But we must now make the move from reflection and criticism to creation. We can create in our own lives in terms of what we choose to read and share with others. We can create in the organization of new types of courses. We can create new research and learning partnerships with community activists and social movements. We may have a chance to create new academic programs. Some of us may create new higher education structures. As we move toward creation, we will find much to draw inspiration from.

Emergence of New Higher Education Narratives

The Barcelona-based network Global University Network for Innovation (GUNi) is related to UNESCO and the UN University. It has produced a series of world reports on higher education. In 2014, it brought out its latest report called *Knowledge, Engagement and Higher Education Contributing to Social Change: World Report on Higher Education 5* (GUNi 2014). What was unique about this report was that it framed the challenges to higher education within the context of deep global issues such as the destruction of the planet, inequality, and violence against women. It called for a new approach to the creation and understanding of knowledge, a turn toward knowledge democracy. This report was launched in thirty-four locations in the world and contained examples of promising practices from seventy nations written by sixty authors. It is the first attempt to create a new global narrative for a higher education based on communitarian values rather than market priorities.

The Multiworld Network, based in India under the leadership of Claude Alvares of India, and with support from Dzulkifli Abdul Razak of Malaysia, is a growing association of people from Asia, Africa, and South America, all joined together in a common objective to restore the diversity of learning that existed from time immemorial. Multiworld welcomes people infected with a similar spirit and conviction to join this enterprise and to fight to restore a world in which many worlds are once again warmly embraced. The issue of "decolonizing" academic curricula and ridding them of Eurocentric biases has occupied centre stage in six international conferences organized by the Multiworld Network, in which scholars from diverse countries located in Asia, Africa, and South America have been involved. The work of this network has received support from the Ministry of Education in Malaysia. *Decolonising the University: The Emerging Quest for Non-European Paradigms* is one of the texts emerging from this active and inspiring network (Alvares and Faruqi 2012).

Decolonization in Established Universities

I suspect there are elements of a knowledge democracy discourse, a decolonizing practice emerging at least in small ways in most of our universities. The fact that the Faculty of Education at the University of Regina has organized an international conference to look at transformative approaches to higher education is a case in point. At the University of Victoria, we have seen a steady growth in efforts to either Indigenize the university or decolonize the university. We have built a First Peoples House in the centre of our Victoria campus. Indigenous community leaders and Indigenous faculty and staff at the university jointly manage this house. We have created the position of director of Indigenous academics and community engagement. But perhaps the most powerful contributions have been in the creation of Indigenous academic programs in law, social work, education, nursing, governance, humanities, Indigenous counselling, and linguistics. The most recent programs that have been created are BA and MA degrees in Indigenous language revitalization. What has gone along with the development of Indigenous academic programming has been a deepening of relations between the University of Victoria and the surrounding Indigenous communities in our part of Vancouver Island.

UNGS

The Universidad Nacional de General Sarmiento (UNGS) is a small-size public university created in 1992 to meet local and regional education needs that were not covered by traditional academic offerings. Its main campus is in Malvinas, Argentina, a locality in the province of Buenos Aires marked by high levels of poverty and other related conditions. Since its inception, the UNGS has facilitated the convergence of research, teaching, and community services to contribute to the socio-economic development of the local communities. The relationship with the local context is a key component of the UNGS identity and has determined its origin, strategic project, institutional design, and ongoing development (UNGS, "Universidad Pública").

In order to promote research partnerships and engagements, the UNGS has established the Community Services Centre to manage, promote, and disseminate local and regional development projects that connect students, faculty members, and a variety of stakeholders (governments, private firms, and civil society organizations) in an institutionalized manner (UNGS, "Centro de Servicios"). This unit integrates the service learning and outreach initiatives presented by UNGS professors that have an impact on key academic functions. Thus, the three principles that structure the institutional identity of the UNGS—research, teaching, and community services—are embodied in the development of training courses and diplomas for non-academic stakeholders, external consulting services, basic and applied research, and local development projects that contribute to the strengthening of science and technology. These community services are offered to achieve two critical goals: (1) to provide solutions to problems identified by civil society actors; (2) to improve the entire process of knowledge production and the existing training and teaching practices within the UNGS.

Creation of Alternative Universities/Social Movement Partnerships

Te Whare Wānanga o Awanuiārangi—Aotearoa is a Māori university headed by Sir Graham Hingangaroa Smith, a distinguished Māori scholar. The mission statement of this visionary institution is as follows:

> We commit ourselves to explore and define the depths of knowledge in Aotearoa, to enable us to re-enrich ourselves, to know whom we are, to know where we came from and to claim our place in the future. We take this journey of discovery, of reclamation of sovereignty, establishing the equality of Māori intellectual tradition alongside the knowledge base of others. Thus, we can stand proudly together with all people of the world. This is in part the dream and vision of Te Whare Wānanga o Awanuiārangi. (Te Whare Wānanga o Awanuiārangi)

Dayalbagh Educational Institute

Associated with the Radhasoami Sect of Hinduism, the Dayalbagh Educational Institute is located in Agra, India, within the heart of a colony of three thousand followers of the Radhasoami faith. The colony provides a space for living together irrespective of caste, creed, and colour, and for the following of a devotional life integrating meditative practices, collective labour in the farm and dairy, use of solar power electricity and cooking, a collective kitchen, rainwater harvesting, and free medical services in both allopathic and Indian systems of medicine. Dayalbagh is a value-based and holistic education institution that combines work-related vocational and crafts teaching with leading-edge scientific programs. It is an institution where the holistic values-based teachings of Radhasoami Hinduism live in respectful harmony with Western scientific knowledge. In Dayalbagh we see an attempt to establish a new order, where women and men live and work in harmony for the service of humanity (Dayalbagh Educational Institute).

COEP

The Committee of Entities in the Struggle against Hunger and for a Full Life (COEP) is a national social mobilization network established in Rio de Janeiro in 1993 to mobilize institutional and public action in support of the popular movement against hunger and poverty. The network's membership now includes more than one thousand member organizations, including public enterprises, nongovernment organizations, private sector firms, and government departments. The COEP was created by a small group of activists led by sociologist Herbert de Souza, known as "Betinho." Together with Luiz Pinguelli Rosa of the Federal University of Rio de Janeiro, and André Spitz of Furnas, the electricity utility, Betinho invited the presidents of the major public entities to discuss their integration into the "Struggle against Hunger and Misery." Soon over thirty enterprises, representing sectors such as banking, energy, telecommunications, health, agriculture, and education, declared their membership.

Each year, the COEP focuses on a specific theme for social development at the national level, aiming for collective impact at the community level throughout Brazil. Currently, major themes throughout the networks are climate change and poverty. An agenda concerned with both preventing and addressing the effects of climate change has been constructed, with the intention of informing dialogue and public policy, as well as implementing specific initiatives (Tremblay, Guthberlet, and Bonatti 2015).

The CUE Movement

The UNESCO Chair in Community-Based Research and Social Responsibility in Higher Education, co-directed by Dr. Rajesh Tandon and myself, has recently published an open-access book on measures taken around the world to strengthen community–university research partnerships (Hall, Tandon, and Tremblay 2015). This book, the result of a global study with survey data, case studies, and analysis, is the product of many contributors from around the world.

Community university engagement (CUE) refers to a combination of practices that are having an impact on many of our higher education institutions, on our own scholars, and on our students. CUE refers to new approaches to the co-construction of knowledge that links community activists to university researchers, and to the engagement of students in community action projects or movements. New structures such as the Institute for Studies and Innovation in Community University Engagement at the University of Victoria, and similar community–university research partnership arrangements in other parts of Canada, Europe, Asia, and Latin America, have much transformative potential. Our students are demanding a new way, a transformative and real-world learning opportunity through CUE, that values community and alternative knowledge. CUE, grounded in principles of community-based research, provides an important space to create how we want to be together—the very practice of listening and understanding our differences is decolonizing the institutions that have long been closed. As my colleague, Dr. Crystal Tremblay, notes,

> Transformation happens, I believe, when you realize your potential and act on it in authentic way[s]. Methods such as CBR [community-based research], PAR [participatory action research] and other CUE approaches often inspire these types of inner discovery, and mutual learning—changing the way we see oneself and each other, and in the end value other knowledge. (personal communication)

Some Questions for Myself

Consider here four critical questions that I continue to ask myself and which inform my own practice as I struggle to be as inclusive as possible in my own thinking, writing, and teaching.

1. How do I decolonize, deracialize, demasculanize, and degender my inherited intellectual spaces?
2. How do I support the opening up of spaces for the flowering of epistemologies, ontologies, theories, methodologies, objects, and questions other than those that have long been hegemonic and that have exercised dominance over (perhaps have even suffocated) intellectual and scholarly thought and writing?
3. How do I contribute to the building of new academic cultures and, more widely, new inclusive institutional cultures that genuinely respect and appreciate difference and diversity—whether class, gender, national, linguistic, religious, sexual orientation, epistemological, or methodological in nature?
4. How do I become a part of creating the new architecture of knowledge that allows co-construction of knowledge between intellectuals in academia and intellectuals located in community settings?

Poets and Idealists

In closing, I draw from the Indian Nobel Prize–winning poet and founder of his own decolonizing university, Rabindranath Tagore. As you read this, take into account that it was written in 1916.

> I know what a risk one runs...in being styled an idealist in these days when the sound that drowns all voices is the noise of the marketplace, and yet...I feel that the sky and the earth and the lyrics of the dawn and the day fall are with the poets and the idealists and not with the marketmen.

Haichq'a

Author's Note

With thanks to Crystal Tremblay, Lorna Williams, Saleem Badat, Paulo Wangoola, Robina Thomas, and Rajesh Tandon for their inspiration.

References

Abrell, E., and K. Bavicatte. 2009. *Imagining a Traditional Knowledge Commons*. Rome, Italy: International Development Law Organization.

Alvares, C., and S. S. Faruqi, eds. 2012. *Decolonising the University: The Emerging Quest for Non-European Paradigms*. Pulau Pinang, Malaysia: University Sains Malaysia Press.

Dabla-Norris, E., K. Kochar, N. Suphaphiphat, F. Ricka, and E. Tsounta. 2015. *Causes and Consequences of Income Inequality: A Global Perspective*. Washington, DC: International Monetary Fund.

Dayalbagh Educational Institute. https://www.dei.ac.in/dei/.

de Sousa Santos, B. 2007. "Beyond Abyssal Thinking: From Global Lines to Ecologies of Knowledge." *Eurozine* 33, June 29, 45–89.

Dussel, E. 1993. "Eurocentrism and Modernity." Introduction to the Frankfurt Lectures. *boundary 2* 20(3): 65–76.

Ezeanya, C. 2011. *Education and Indigenous Knowledge in Africa: Traditional Bonesetting and Orthopaedic Medicine in West Africa*. Washington, DC: Howard University Press.

Gregoric, M. 2015. "The Producing Struggles of Self-Organized Communities— Potencias." Keynote speech delivered at the ESREA conference, June 18, Ljubljana, Slovenia.

Grosfoguel, R. 2013. "The Structure of Knowledge in Westernized Universities: Epistemic Racism/Sexism and the Four Genocides/Epistemicides of the Long 16th Century." *Human Architecture: Journal of the Sociology of Self-Knowledge* 11(1): Article 8. http://scholarworks.umb.edu/humanarchitecture/vol11/iss1/8.

GUNi (Global University Network for Innovation). 2014. *Knowledge, Engagement and Higher Education Contributing to Social Change: World Report on Higher Education 5*. London: Palgrave Macmillan.

Hall, B., R. Tandon, and C. Tremblay, eds. 2015. *Strengthening Community University Research Partnerships*. Victoria and New Delhi, India: University of Victoria Press and PRIA.

Hardoon, D. 2015. *Wealth: Having It All and Wanting More*. Oxford, UK: Oxfam.

Harvey, D. 2004. "The 'New' Imperialism: Accumulation by Dispossession." *Socialist Register* 40: 63–87.

Judt, T. 2010. *Ill Fares the Land*. London: Penguin.

Korten, D. 2006. *The Great Turning: From Empire to Earth Community*. Bloomfield, CT: Kumarian Press.

Lebakeng, J. T., M. M. Phalane, and N. Dalindjebo. 2006. "Epistemicide, Institutional Cultures and the Imperative for the Africanisation of Universities in South Africa." *Alternation* 13(1): 70–87.

Piketty, T. 2014. *Capital in the 21st Century*. Cambridge, MA: Belknap Press.

Reuters. 2015. "Unbridled Capitalism Is the 'Dung of the Devil,' Says Pope Francis." *The Guardian*, July 10. https://www.theguardian.com/world/2015/jul/10/poor-must-change-new-colonialism-of-economic-order-says-pope-francis.

Sefa Dei, G. J., B. L. Hall, and D. Goldin Rosenberg, eds. 2000. *Indigenous Knowledges in Global Contexts: Multiple Readings of Our World*. Toronto: University of Toronto Press.

SRISTI (Society for Research and Initiatives for Sustainable Technologies and Institutions). "Honey Bee Network." http://www.sristi.org/cms/en/our_network.

Tagore, R. 1916. "Nationalism in Japan: A Speech." *The Complete Works of Rabindranath Tagore*. http://bit.ly/2a8ksgt.

Te Whare Wānanga o Awanuiārangi. "Our Vision and Mission." http://www.wananga.ac.nz/about/vision.

Tremblay C., J. Guthberlet, and M. Bonatti. 2015. "Celebrating Community University Research Partnerships: Experiences in Brazil." In *Strengthening Community University Research Partnerships*, edited by B. Hall, R. Tandon, and C. Tremblay. Victoria and New Delhi, India: University of Victoria Press and PRIA.

UNGS (Universidad Nacional de General Sarmiento). "Centro de Servicios." http://www.ungs.edu.ar/ms_centro_servicios/.

———. "Universidad Pública." http://www.ungs.edu.ar/ms_ungs/.

Visvanathan, S. 2009. "The Search for Cognitive Justice." http://bit.ly/3ZwMD2.

Wilkinson, R., and K. Pickett. 2009. *The Spirit Level: Why Equal Societies Almost Always Do Better*. London: Penguin.

CHAPTER 7
WITHIN AND BEYOND NEOLIBERALISM: DOING QUALITATIVE RESEARCH IN THE AFTERWARD

Patti Lather

> Liberalism, late liberalism, and neoliberalism do not exist as things...but rather as actions...They exist insofar as they are evoked to conjure, shape, aggregate, and evaluate a variety of social worlds...A variety of world-making tactics swarms around all of us. We all are in the waiting rooms of history.
> —Elizabeth Povinelli, *Economies of Abandonment*

After what? What posts, post-posts, and neo-posts am I using to situate my remarks on qualitative research in the present moment? What deaths of this and that and (re)turns need to be taken into account?

As a sort of shorthand, in *Getting Lost* (Lather 2007), I listed the various turns in the social sciences, with their attendant citations, as linguistic, structural, critical, deconstructive, rhetorical, cultural, narrative, historical, ethnographic, postmodern, ethical, visual, pragmatic, theological, and policy-driven. Since that 2007 chart, others have emerged, including the material turn (Alaimo, Hekman, and Hames-Garcia 2008); the affective turn

(Clough and Halley 2007; Gregg and Seigworth 2010); the cross-disciplinary love affair with the neopragmatism of the Danish urban planner, Bent Flyvbjerg (2006); and an increased attention to participatory, community-based research, often feminist (Creese and Frisby 2012; Sangtin Writers and Nagar 2006). As well, there have been many announced deaths, perhaps most famously of the subject, of theory, and, quite recently, of the university itself (Lincoln 2011; Evans 2004). The returns include the real, the empirical, and, one of my favourites, objectivity after deconstruction (Melville 1996).

In terms of qualitative research, all of this (re)framing and emerging and dying generates such terms as "positivist qualitative methods" (Schwartz-Shea and Yanow 2002, 457) and "dominant postpositivist" (Mallozzi 2009, 1043), or "conventional interpretive methodology" (St. Pierre 2006, 239) and "plain old ethnography" (Erickson 2009). In earlier work, I tried to capture such movement with layerings of 1.0, 2.0, and 3.0 methodologies. In this schema,[1] QUAL 1.0 is the conventional interpretive inquiry that emerged from the liberal humanism of sociology and cultural anthropology with a fairly untroubled focus on standpoint epistemologies, a humanist subject who has an authentic voice, transparent descriptions of lived experiences, and the generally untroubled belief that better methods and richer descriptions can get closer to the truth.

QUAL 2.0 begins to acknowledge multiple realities and voices, messy texts, reflexivity, dialogue, empowerment, and so on, but remains within the humanist enclosure, grounded in humanist concepts of language, reality, knowledge, power, truth, resistance, and the subject. The field becomes centred, disciplined, regulated, and normalized as qualitative handbooks, textbooks, and journals create "moments" and "designs," and fix the "research process," so it becomes possible *to know it in advance*, for example, to offer a sequence of courses on qualitative inquiry, to teach someone how to "do a phenomenology," to teach someone how to analyze data.

QUAL 3.0 begins to use postmodern theories to open up concepts associated with qualitative inquiry: validity, voice, data, empathy, authenticity, experience, interviewing, the field, reflexivity, clarity, etc. This work is stalled for years when qualitative researchers turn to the defence not just of the methodology but also of the various epistemologies it carries on its back (feminist theories, race theories, class theories, postmodern theories, etc.). The field continues to be structured, and a kind of "interpretive mixed methods" (Howe 2004) enters the picture and begins to be normalized.

QUAL 4.0 is *becoming*, in the Deleuzean sense, as researchers who, weary of a decade of defending qualitative research and eager to get on with their work, again imagine and accomplish an inquiry that might produce different knowledge and produce knowledge differently. This inquiry cannot be tidily described in textbooks or handbooks. There is no methodological instrumentality to be unproblematically learned. In this methodology-to-come, we begin to do it differently, wherever we are in our projects. Here the term "post-qualitative" begins to make a certain kind of sense (St. Pierre 2011).

In what follows, I first sketch efforts to discipline qualitative research via standards and rubrics as a part of neoliberal governmentality at the level of research methods. I will then introduce the concept of post-neoliberalism as a way to imagine escape from such containment. Finally, I will briefly elaborate what post-qualitative might mean and, especially, what it might look like via an exemplar of such practice.

In so doing, I want to go further with what I have been calling "philosophical ethnography" for some time now (Lather 2006). How might we move from what needs to be opposed to what can be imagined out of what is already happening, embedded in the immanence of doing? What opens up if we position alternative methodology as nontotalizable, sometimes fugitive, also aggregate, innumerable, resisting stasis and capture, hierarchy and totality, what Gilles Deleuze might call "a thousand tiny methodologies"?[2]

Discipline and Punish under Conditions of Neoliberalism

The transition from Keynesian liberalism to neoliberalism has set in motion radical principles of limited government. The results include the dismantling of the welfare state, expanded market freedom via efforts to curtail unions and regulatory actions, and privatization and taxation reforms that redistribute the burden of state finance away from the wealthy. Pure market logics push ever deeper into "the tissues of everyday life" (Povinelli 2011, 151). We are, in short, witnesses to a fundamental transformation of the liberal democratic state much tied to the global markets, bio-informatics, and population management of the post-9/11 security state.

Qualitative research is much caught up in such shifts. In education, this is reflected in the efforts of the federal government to dictate "gold-standard" research methods via the "scientific based research" movement (National Research Council 2002) and the consequent pushback. It is helpful to look at other areas of the academy to see how this "disciplining" of qualitative research is about much more than education in terms of meeting such efforts with resistances of various sorts.

In political science, for example, the widely cited efforts of King, Keohane, and Verba (1994) to "help out" qualitative research by offering a "quantitative template" have been countered by Brady and Collier (2004, 15), who call out this "quantitative imperialism" for what it is.

As a further example of pushback, the National Science Foundation's (NSF's) 2004 workshop on qualitative methods has evoked a letter of protest from the International Congress of Qualitative Inquiry regarding the focus on mainstream approaches that marginalizes the proliferation of kinds of qualitative research, in particular, autoethnography, performance ethnography, and critical ethnography (Lather 2013).

A sense of how this has played out in the United States education research scene can be garnered from a comparison of two sets of standards from the American Educational Research Association (AERA) on research reporting. The set of standards for "empirical social science" (AERA 2006) works hard to include more qualitative-friendly criteria within a commitment to transparency of the logic of inquiry. Announcing itself as "not a checklist," a set of structuring binaries—a priori/emergent design, causal inference/ description and meaning, measurement/classification—allows for shared standards until the iterative nature of qualitative work and the necessary role of interpretive commentary demand separate sections for data analysis. Returning to shared standards, generalization is handled in a way that makes space for qualitative work, although conflict of interest and bias are conflated. While undoing some of the constraining effects of the report, *Scientific Research in Education* (SRE), by the National Research Council, the limits of attempting shared standards across the full range of empirical work in education become obvious in comparison with the set of standards for "humanities-oriented research" (AERA 2009).

Such standards made for dissonance, discomfort, and reflexivity; blurred boundaries between the humanities and the social sciences; and room for evocative imagery and narrative. There is space to "depart from the orthodoxies" in demands for transparency and direct refusals of both the movement toward "structured abstracts" and neutrality in favour of research that illuminates, critiques, and evaluates.

This comparison demonstrates that any exploration of the ambiguity, fragmentation, undecidabilities, fluidities, hyper-realities, nonreplicabilities, and incoherencies of a world in process is crowded out in a shared standards approach. Political science is in the midst of figuring this out. The "salutary influence" on qualitative research of "a more complete systematization" of methods, credited to the influence of King, Keohane, and Verba (1994), is much troubled (Brady and Collier 2004). Rather than standardizing qualitative research in the name of providing better evidentiary warrants, such efforts have resulted in a "striking reassertion of qualitative approaches," where shared standards and the fact/value distinction are held in suspicion (Weyland 2005, 392; Steinmetz 2005; Mihic, Engelmann, and Wingrove 2005).

The contest over the science that can provide the evidence for practice and policy pits the recharged positivism of neoliberalism against a qualitative "community" at risk of assimilation and the reduction of qualitative to an instrumentalism that meets the demands of audit culture. To refuse this settlement is to push back in the name of an insistence on the importance of both epistemological and ontological wrestling with governmentality and calling out the unthought in how research-based knowledge is conceptualized and produced.

Escapes

This section makes much of the Spencer Foundation report, issued in September 2009, on the preparation of education researchers, based on lessons learned from Spencer Research Training Grants. It demonstrates, I argue, what it means to think about qualitative research "after" SRE, and, in the following section, "after" neoliberalism.

What is noteworthy about the Spencer Foundation report (2009), in both overt and subtle ways, is the influence of the last decade of protest against the 2002 SRE report. Key terms are acknowledged as matters of dispute (e.g., rigour, value-neutrality, and objectivity are questions, not assumptions) (Spencer Foundation 2009, 99). The "comfortable" navigation of "the complex intellectual, social and educational worlds" (10) is interrupted by calls to "soul-searching," as one follows the debates across, for example, the *Educational Researcher* (22). Grasp of "the epistemological underpinnings" (23) of "warring ideas" (24) is endorsed for all. "Hotly-contested terrain" (26) is both acknowledged and used to warrant a call for producing work "of sufficient quality to withstand critical scrutiny from many directions" (26). Contextual knowledge is posited as key across paradigms (28). In short, rather than a narrowly defined methodological rigour (e.g., control groups), the report endorses "a depth of understanding educational contexts...sensitivity to issues of social justice...and epistemological sophistication" (30). While context is much reduced to classroom culture and less to macro structures and forces, this document is ripe for an analysis of what lies beneath the surface, especially in regard to its contrast with SRE from almost ten years ago.

As someone who frequently whines about the focus on SRE and how it has detracted me from my real interest in feminist research methodology, I was quite heartened by the obvious effect this last ten years of protest has had. Frequent references are made to how the tensions between qualitative and quantitative help one "think deeply" about underlying assumptions (Spencer Foundation 2009, 77). Mindful attendance of "some of the more lively and well-attended" (97) AERA sessions that feature these tensions is endorsed. Even the old chestnut that question determines method is something to be discussed, not assumed (95), and research questions are, finally, seen as evolving (109).

The umbrage taken on the part of qualitative researchers who felt marginalized by calls for a "common language" and "unity of purpose" argues the incommensurability at work in the struggle over science that has to be taken for what it is: power struggles over who gets to set the terms of debate. This is about difference, not sameness, a difference that begins to be acknowledged in this report. Perhaps most exemplary of this is that the much debated six "guiding principles" of the SRE report are elaborated upon in a critical, inclusive manner. Replication and generalizability are, newly, "questionable" (Spencer Foundation 2009, 104), and even the priority of causal knowledge is made a question rather than an assumption (107).

All is not perfect; new positivisms sneak in; for example, the reworking of objectivity as refutability, a rather untroubled idea of triangulation, and the demarcation criteria for science continue to be normative rather than descriptive, more a sort of "who gets to be in the gentleman's club" as opposed to a more science studies approach of "how does it work." The "non-epistemic" of socio-political values is held in place, as is a sort of unacknowledged "context of discovery" versus a "context of verification" distinction.

But ground has been moved. The "objectivity debates" are now acknowledged, and good education researchers are to be trained to be "reflective" and to have well-thought-out positions in the face of such debates (Spencer Foundation 2009, 108). Qualitative research now has "families" with different approaches and debates around "skills-based" versus "theory-based" training (112). The sort of "quantitative imperialism" (Brady and Collier 2004) that so characterized SRE has been shaken and, most encouragingly, seemingly from within the task force itself. The "disciplining" of qualitative research appears to have abated; rather than more "standards," the tables are turned toward the importance of epistemological grounding across paradigms.

Dare I say, the address actually seems more to positivism than previous efforts to foster a sort of "positivist qualitative research" (e.g., National Science Foundation standards for qualitative research documents). While the "disappearance" of less mainstream qualitative research continues— there is no mention of autoethnography, performance ethnography, and critical ethnography—it appears there is room at the table for qualitative research, as long as it behaves itself.

To the extent the Spencer report registers stresses and controversies, I announce no great remaking of old divides. Much work remains to be done, particularly, I would say, on the front of new methodology for new times. To think differently means to work within and beyond the reflexive turn, to problematize inquiry, to redefine objects, to trouble identity and experience and what it means to know and to tell. Most importantly, it means "no methodological a priori" (James Faubion quoted in Marcus 2009, 5). This means that the actual design and practice of the fieldwork of the future are up for grabs. "What is usually thought of as method" (Marcus 2009, 6) shifts to an "arena of metamethod" that is a sort of "running away" from traditional models and an embrace of such new practices as embracing messy conceptual labour; developing metamethodological habits and an ecology of movement within situated inquiry; blending micro and macro in the face of complex objects constituted in systems of networked agencies (Barad 2007); theorizing methodologies of engagement in the "post-theory" era and the "ruins of advocacy"; speaking in different registers, for example, translation into funding structures; seeing incompleteness as a positive norm, as is the focus on reception and attendant revisability, for example, folding reception data into data archives; figuring in new forms of digital communication, for example, blogging as a research tool; and, finally, negotiating the exploding industry of qualitative methods publications.

To break the hold of Cartesian foundations on the research imaginary, there is a performative dimension to mapping new geographies, where to raise doubts about certainties is to contribute to new epistemological ground (Pascale 2011). To take a cultural turn, often to the humanities, is to trouble the holdover of research as a mirroring/objectivism in the naturalizing and systematizing of the social sciences (29). Here, "despite fierce resistance," destabilization has happened as evidenced by the Spencer report.

Perhaps we are caught between two regimes of truth. "To break free of the constraints of positive science" (Rancière 2011, 161), logics have to shift. What does it mean to move beyond the limits of the kinds of change that can be produced within current paradigms in an era crushed by demands for more "evidence-based" research under some "gold standard"? Of course, as many have argued for quite some time, the key is to contest what counts as science, toward something less Cartesian and, perhaps, more Deleuzean. Here the concept of post-neoliberalism may help in shifting the research imaginary.

Post-Neoliberalism?

Post-neoliberalism is a concept derived out of the Great Recession of 2008 and its Ponzi casino economy as a signal of the failure of neoliberalism.[3] If we are, indeed, poised on the edge of the legitimation crisis of neoliberalism, how can we "start to think again" (Brand and Sekler 2009, 62) under conditions of "a post-neoliberalism under construction" (59)? What is "brewing under the surface" (68)?

A group of academics, artists, and activists met at the 2011 Banff Research in Culture seminar to pursue these questions (MacLellan and Talpalaru 2012). After three decades of market deregulation, their interest was in "the affirmative and the positive" in the face of the more typical register of a negative collapse of belief. What can social transformation look like and what new modes of "being-acting-feeling together" might get us there? Focusing particularly on the contributions of art toward the production of new terms of belonging and new relationalities that enact what playwright Tony Kushner (in de Vries 1992) called "non-stupid optimism," such a project interrupts "the notion of neoliberalism's imputed totalization" (Vázquez 2011).

Recent debates on the phenomenon of post-neoliberalism and its playing out, particularly in Latin America (and its relative nonpresence in the United States) also challenge assumptions of totality. As caution to overenthusiasm for its demise, Australian geographer David Harvey (2009) asks if this is *really* an end of neoliberalism and whether this is a crisis or consolidation of capitalism. Vázquez calls out the "boom industry" in denouncements on the part of the academic Left and argues that a neostructuralism is arising, full of participatory rhetoric in the face of discontent "with the uncertainties and social fallout from globalization." Peters (2011) notes the multiple lines of development of neoliberalism and its virulent return and presence as a key element in "the new normal."

From a less cautionary side, Macdonald and Ruckert (2009) refer to post-neoliberalism as an anti-neoliberal shift to the left in the face of the "evident shortcomings in the neoliberal model" (2). Within both continuity and discontinuity with neoliberalism, the interest is in "the range of policy experiments" across the Americas (3). Both a "bad populist" version (à la Hugo Chávez) and a "good social democratic" version are posited, grounded mostly in Latin American efforts to remediate the effects of neoliberalism and deepen democracy. The agenda of the state, policy homogeneity, and deregulation are rejected, and "more socially interventionist and ameliorative forms" of government appear on the horizon, invested in "the emergence of an alternative common sense" to the present commodification of the life world (12).

Neoliberalism needs quantitative reductionism. In the realm of public policy, a kind of "metric mania" disallows what cannot easily be counted (Paulos 2010) in a way that profoundly shapes what counts as science. We have only to look at how federal efforts toward "scientific research in education" have produced a situation where "evidence" is defined very narrowly indeed.

In short, under neoliberalism, we have seen the abuses of the use of scientific authority in the interests of the state. The "problem of science and politics" is deeply embedded in big questions about the ideal of participatory democracy. The free exchange of ideas, claims of scientific neutrality, government by persuasion, democratic deliberation: all are at risk in the face of the increasing suspicion regarding "the problem of expanding and diffusing expertise," where matters of fact are as contestable as anything else. Expertise and its troubling claims to authority are undercutting liberal democracy itself: "expertise is trouble for liberalism" (Turner 2003, 24) and there is increased recognition that the democratic control of science is a messy thing.

Within post-neoliberalism, the move is toward a less imperialist social science, capacious and democratic in its recognition of necessary contingency as the horizon of our intelligibility. This taps into a widespread crisis of legitimacy and authority where, to take Bettie St. Pierre's (2011) advice, we might stop trying so hard to be hard. Instead, we might work to change the terms of the debate we have inherited and contributed to, where we keep moving in order to learn from ruptures, failures, breaks, and refusals. Here, to use the argument of Celine-Marie Pascale in *Cartographies of Knowledge* (2011), we might focus less on issues of interpretation and more on rethinking the very foundations of what counts as science.

The question before us is what it means to think of a science that is accountable to complexity and multiplicity, becoming and difference, the yes that comes from working the stuck places, the beyond that is what haunts us. To do so entails rethinking the theory of the subject in uncertain times.

Subjectivity: What Kind of Subject for What Kind of Science?

The politics of uncertainty holds that an undoing of positivism is essential in reconfiguring governance and economy, sociality and subjectivity, knowledge production and science. As feminist sociologist Patricia Clough (2009) asks in an article on the new empiricism in the *European Journal of Social Theory*, how are ideas of a predictive and usable social science a sort of resonance with neoliberal governance and economy? And, in a Foucauldian vein, what cannot be thought in the terms of that science? What theory of the subject is emerging to help us deal with this question? Clough's is a philosophical intervention into scientific method with which to think politics anew. Such disruption calls for a theory of the subject/agency that attends to how different ontologies feed different politics.

Clough (2009) asserts that critical theories influenced by the "posties" are key in moving us from the unified, conscious, rational subject of humanism (think Paulo Freire) to the post-humanist, split, desiring subject (think Jacques Lacan). Rationality or disciplining or socializing or interpellation are all concepts that have shaped our (humanist, structural) understandings of subjectivity. The "post" move entails a shift from an epistemology of human consciousness to a focus on the limits of our knowing, with an emphasis on an affective turn. Under conditions of conservative neoliberalism, the fluid, post-subject is necessary in moving toward something in excess of meaning, signification, representation, narration, something not containable, something that attends to how affective capacities are modulated and manipulated as quasi-causality. Clough argues this is essential to installing conservative neoliberalism, a kind of indeterminacy haunted by crisis, where populations are put into circulation in order to serve the changing needs of the state. In short, the neoliberal subject is one who conforms to the shifting requirements of global competition and blames themselves if they are not up to the task in a way "responsibilized" out of a market-driven morality (Shamir 2008).

In Rancièrian terms (2004/2000), this is a redistribution of the sensible, a change in common sense to "the order of things" that both sustains neoliberalism and, paradoxically, undermines its economistic ideas of citizenship, workers, and responsible action. Which direction it goes has much to do with the development of a science of indeterminacy, where "the mess is the message" (Collins and Pinch 1993) and the epistemological unconscious is, finally, changed away from its positivism, empiricism, and scientism. "Trained in the ruins of empire," to use David Westbrook's (2008) phrase, such a space might make possible an engaged social science (Lather 2010), where we inherit and invent, each time anew toward the something to come that is already at work, incalculable, pushing past neoliberalism in the development of what Elizabeth St. Pierre (2011) terms "post-qualitative" research.

Being Post-Qualitative in the Neoliberal University

After ten years somewhat lost to fighting governmental incursions into science, the repositivization of the field, and consequent remarginalization of qualitative work, the development of the contemporary scene of education research is taking advantage of the ruins of SBR (standards-based research) to develop new practices. Such practices move us into what Marcus terms "metamethod," which reconceptualizes and experiments with standard practices, moving beyond current scripts and their conventional codifying and disciplining of inquiry. Here is the space of "post-qualitative."

To explore this space, I call upon an exemplar from Australia of the intersection of Western and Aboriginal knowledge systems. Anthropologist Elizabeth Povinelli's (2011) book examines the shift in Australian Aboriginal politics from a state policy based on recognition to one based on neoliberal intervention.

Elizabeth Povinelli, working with Australian Aboriginal peoples across a digital archive, has produced several books.[4] Her *Economies of Abandonment* (2011) tracks the shift in Australian neoliberalism from a politics of cultural recognition and self-determination to what she calls neoliberal "economies of abandonment," dominated by privatization and individualization. She frames a collaborative "augmented reality" project using digital tools as about a "geobiographics" or "positive biopolitics" that refigures markets and difference toward mutual obligation in late liberal governance. Growing out of the land claims struggles of the 1970s, she articulates a move from static animism to "geontologies," where the energy of disrupting Western binaries of organic/inorganic, agency/subjectivity is channelled toward a new animism, a new materialism, a new vitalism toward new possible destinies. Positing a new geological era, the Anthropocene, using GPS technology to focus on the effect of human behaviour on the ecosystem, the project raises such questions as: Does the earth have a metabolism? Can rocks listen? What are the rights of a creek?

It is an analytic purchase on truth that Povinelli wants for her praxis. Against the "necropolitics of colonialism" (Mbembe 2003), she uses the collapse of neoliberalism toward an emplacement of displaced populations that offers the possibility of indwelling otherwise. This is an animism she calls "a queer move toward an environmental ethics based on the return." Mixing cutting-edge technology with an obligation to the totemic imaginary, she seeks to abstract a truth from the interactions between human and space that can give room for new thought. Methodologically, this entails the use of tools, such as GPS and geocoding, to "visibilize" activity on the land so as to learn a "cosmological gaze in cartographic times" in order to see what can be sustained by a people who refuse to be governed by neoliberalism.[5] Most interested in how power is organized in late liberalism, she helps imagine and fund this "Indigenous grassroots project on mixed reality" (Povinelli 2011, 190) that might be socially and economically supportive with an eye toward engaging critically with what is wrought.

This exemplar is in excess of intersectionality in its attention to multi-directionalities, post-human bodies, intra-actional networks, contingency, nonmastery, and incalculables. Taking on issues of messy conceptual labour, difference, Otherness and disparity, and incompleteness as a positive norm, it is beyond tensions between tradition and avant-garde. It is about working the stuck places into which such tensions have gotten us. Critical ideas have become their own orthodoxy in "the reflexive turn" that is its own "best practice" and limit situation. Moving toward glimmers of alternative understandings and practices that give coherence and imaginary to whatever "post-qualitative" might mean, it explores a new culture of method of breaking methodological routine by savouring our critical edges, aporias, and discontents. It troubles visibility and holds up blind spots as productive sites toward "the risk of a new relationality" (Lauren Berlant in Davis and Sarlin 2008). Instead of a voice of masterful, individual authority, it does what Ronell (2010) calls "partnering up with the questioning other" in order to disrupt any settled places in our work.

This is a restorying out of relations tuned "to the ear of the future" of a people to come (Rancière 2009, 55). Instead of papering over difference, Otherness, and disparity, such work reflects/enacts these issues, suggesting further direction and broader possibilities of "being-acting-feeling together" through the production of new terms of belonging (MacLellan and Talpalaru 2012). Clearly, more could be said, but the point is this: method is political and that is a good thing to think with as we explore how much the development of a counterscience "on our own terms" can be community-based, community sustaining, and community serving in ways that might help alter the structures of institutions in more expansive, democratizing ways.

Exemplifying an engaged social science that is between being "in trouble" and "of use" (Childers 2008), it inherits and invents, each time anew toward the something to come that is already at work.

Undergirding my suspicions of efforts to codify and discipline the "beyond" of qualitative work, such an exemplar leaves room for the incalculable, the messy, not knowing, and epistemologies of ruins. Out of an immersion in vitally minor possibilities that work against the forces of homogenization, in Deleuzean terms, this is a molecular vision of the alternative, a plurality of fissions and margins, a system of deviances straining for communicability while protecting its marginality, registering in the local, enacting the future life of difference, and a way to dream and perhaps enact post-qualitative work. The question is: How might we move from what needs to be opposed to what can be imagined out of what is already happening, embedded in an immanence of doing?

Conclusion

In all of this, the institutions of higher education in which we function serve as both harbour and tyrant. What is the cost of the triumph of the mercantilist university? As Jorge Larrosa argues in an essay in a special issue of *Educational Philosophy and Theory* on Jacques Rancière,

> Something is taking its course... We knew the old words but now we are no longer sure they mean anything. And we are not keen to learn new ones: we do not trust them, they are irrelevant to us. Moreover, we are sad and tired. All we feel is rage and impotence. Will we be capable of trying all the verbs once again? Reading, writing, conversing, perhaps thinking. (2010, 703)

What is the university to come, what is its logic, and how is it ruined by what Bill Readings (1997) pointed out some time ago as the "university of excellence" and who could be opposed to that? Larrosa (2010) writes of feeling increasingly tired and "becoming an old grouch" (686), and I have a difficult time separating out the price of toiling in the neoliberal institution and what it means to be retired after forty-plus years of teaching.

In a 2012 AERA paper titled, "Crabby Theory," I write that we are no longer what we once hoped we would be. I do not know if this is generational or a more epochal disappointment. Nietzsche did say most theory arises out of indigestion, so one does not want to assume a certain crabbiness is anything bigger than one's own bile.

But I am crabby. I am crabby about the explosion of higher education administration and its obscene salaries; the scandals around Big Football, sexual and otherwise; the governmental logics of the state, including a middle-management takeover and its measurement mania; and the "combat against stupidity and stultification" that is "a struggle against ourselves" (Larrosa 2010, 689). What does it mean to pay attention to these things, "to be equal to [the something that is happening] and to give it time and space" (694) so we might know how to be and to do within and against it?

Simon Critchley (2010) holds out hope in a view of "teaching as a laboratory for research" (19), if we can break the hold of quality-assurance agencies functioning as the new police force. He uses Foucault to explore the "soul-destroying" (23) elements of how we discipline ourselves to submit to what the state demands. "A culture of depression" has arisen, melancholy in the face of, here comes Habermas, "the colonization of the academic lifeworld" (24), where "no one is to blame, no one is responsible, no one can do anything" (25). Calling himself an "old fart," Critchley turns to Lacan and the erotics of teaching as some force against self-certainty, phallic knowledge, and universities as factories of knowledge production, while telling a story of the end of the university as he has known it.

But I am crabby about this too, inadequate as it is. Can I de-identify with the crabby me who feels the university is no longer a place for the likes of me? Is there any way to go but out and is it such a bad thing to move over for the younger ones? What do we squish by staying "too long" in harness in terms of the kind of post-qualitative projects that are thinkable?

Dominant ideas of qualitative research assume a modernist self, transparent methods, and reflexivity as a "too easy" solution to whatever problems might arise. While the illusion of neat and tidy research has long been troubled, methodological examination tends to set up either-or dynamics in terms of "old school" and "what-comes-next" sorts of practices. Yet, in the complex ecology of qualitative research in the present moment, the task is to move beyond the capture of a narrow scientism where qualitative research is reduced to an instrumentalism that meets the demands of audit culture in inventing practices that do not yet exist.

Every field is heavily fractured and contested around such issues these days. "Deep critical rumblings" abound, with political science being, perhaps, the hottest at present.[6] Shared standards and other such "assimilating moves" (Mihic, Engelmann, and Wingrove 2005, 484) appear to have peaked and maybe even blinked in the face of resistance from post-foundational advocates. Talk of post-neoliberalism is beginning to be heard in some corners of South America and United States art speak. Evidence-based practice seems to be sputtering on its own failure to produce. Even Bill Gates is newly enamoured of stories ("A New Model" 2012).

On the other hand, while countermovements abound, the National Science Foundation continues to spend millions a year on the importance of hypothetico deductive research (Clarke and Primo 2012). The "age of big data" and the "march of quantification" are not going away (Lohr 2012). But the ascendance of reflexive knowledge is a more general pattern (Mihic, Engelmann, and Wingrove 2005), and even "metric mania" is up against its limits as our love affair with numbers is perhaps beginning to run its course in the public imaginary (Kohn 2012).

Structured by relations of difference and ontological troubles, across a variety of angles and different registers, we "imagine forward" (Gaventa 2006) out of troubling a scientificity that claims that objectivity is not political, empiricism is not interpretive, chance can be tamed via mathematization, and progress equals greater control governmentality. In my reading of the tea leaves, what appears to be amassing is a widespread recognition that to do less than a kind of performing forward, an enactment of the "after" of neoliberalism, is to court not just a narrowed science but a narrowed future.

Author's Note

This chapter was originally delivered as the Velma E. Schmidt Endowed Chair Lecture, Coalition for Critical Qualitative Inquiry, at the University of North Texas, in November 2012.

Notes

1   For a more developed schema, see Chapter 4 of Lather (2010).
2   Deleuze is referring to sexualities (Grosz 1993).
3   I wrote about post-neoliberalism in more detail in Lather (2010, 11–14).
4   The archive consists of material from twenty-five years of working with families of her young project members that connects with a local epistemology toward "embodied obligation" (Povinelli 2011, 142).

5   Much of this comes from Povinelli's talk, "Geontologies: Indigenous
     Transmedia and the Anthropocene," at Ohio State University, on October 12,
     2012. Sponsored by Precarity and Social Contract Working Group.
6   The NSF cancelled the August 2013 political science grant cycle due to
     Congressional targeting of the field unless its research benefits either national
     security or economic interests (Mole 2013).

References

Alaimo, S., S. Hekman, and M. Hames-Garcia, eds. 2008. *Material Feminisms*.
     Bloomington: Indiana University Press.
American Educational Research Association (AERA). 2006. "Standards for
     Reporting on Empirical Social Science Research in AERA Publications."
     Educational Researcher 35(6): 35–40.
———. 2009. "Standards for Reporting on Humanities-Oriented Research in AERA
     Publications." *Educational Researcher* 38(6): 481–86.
Barad, K. 2007. *Meeting the University Half-Way: Quantum Physics and the
     Entanglement of Matter and Meaning*. Durham, NC: Duke University Press.
Brady, H., and D. Collier, eds. 2004. *Rethinking Social Inquiry: Diverse Tools, Shared
     Standards*. Lanham, MD: Rowman & Littlefield.
Brand, U., and N. Sekler. 2009. "Struggling between Autonomy and Institutional
     Transformations: Social Movements in Latin America and the Move toward
     Post-Neoliberalism." In *Post-Neoliberalism in the Americas*, edited by L.
     Macdonald and A. Ruckert, 54–70. London: Palgrave.
Childers, S. 2008. "Methodology, Praxis and Autobiography: A Review of *Getting
     Lost*." *Educational Researcher* 37(5): 298–301.
Clarke, K., and D. Primo. 2012. "Overcoming 'Physics Envy.'" *New York Times*,
     March 30. http://www.nytimes.com/2012/04/01/opinion/sunday/the-social-
     sciences-physics-envy.html.
Clough, P. 2009. "The New Empiricism: Affect and Sociological Method." *European
     Journal of Social Theory* 12(1): 43–61.
Clough, P., and J. Halley, eds. 2007. *The Affective Turn: Theorizing the Social*. Durham,
     NC: Duke University Press.
Collins, H. M., and T. Pinch. 1993. *The Golem: What You Should Know about Science*.
     Cambridge, UK: Cambridge University Press.
Creese, G., and W. Frisby, eds. 2012. *Feminist Community Research: Negotiating
     · Contested Relationships*. Vancouver: UBC Press.
Critchley, S. 2010. "What Is the Institutional Form for Thinking?" *differences* 21(1): 19–31.
Davis, H., and P. Sarlin. 2008. "'On the Risk of a New Relationality': An Interview
     with Lauren Berlant and Michael Hardt." *Reviews in Cultural Theory*. http://
     reviewsinculture.com/2012/10/15/on-the-risk-of-a-new-relationality-an-
     interview-with-lauren-berlant-and-michael-hardt/.
de Vries, Hilary. 1992. "A Playwright Spreads His Wings." *Los Angeles Times*, 25
     October.

Erickson, F. 2009. "Affirming Human Dignity in Qualitative Inquiry: Walking the Walk." Keynote address delivered to the Fifth International Congress of Qualitative Inquiry, University of Illinois, May 21.

Evans, M. 2004. *Killing Thinking: The Death of the Universities*. London: Continuum.

Flyvbjerg, B. 2006. "Five Misunderstandings about Case-Study Research." *Qualitative Inquiry* 12(2): 219–45.

Gaventa, J. 2006. "Triumph, Deficit or Contestation: Deepening the 'Deepening Democracy' Debate." Working Paper #264, Citizenship Institute of Development Studies, University of Sussex, UK. http://www.ids.ac.uk/files/dmfile/Wp264.pdf.

Gregg, M., and G. Seigworth, eds. 2010. *The Affect Theory Reader*. Durham, NC: Duke University Press.

Grosz, E. 1993. "Feminism and Rhizomatics." *Topoi* 12(2): 167–79.

Harvey, D. 2009. "Is This Really the End of Neoliberalism?" *Counterpunch*, March 13. https://www.counterpunch.org/2009/03/13/is-this-really-the-end-of-neoliberalism/.

Howe, K. 2004. "A Critique of Experimentalism." *Qualitative Inquiry* 10(1): 42–61.

King, G., R. O. Keohane, and S. Verba. 1994. *Designing Social Inquiry: Scientific Inference in Qualitative Research*. Princeton: Princeton University Press.

Kohn, A. 2012. "Schooling Beyond Measure." *Education Week*, September 19. http://www.edweek.org/ew/articles/2012/09/19/04kohn_ep.h32.html.

Larrosa, J. 2010. "Endgame: Reading, Writing, Talking (and Perhaps Thinking) in a Faculty of Education." *Educational Philosophy and Theory* 42(5–6): 683–703.

Lather, P. 2010. *Engaging Science Policy: From the Side of the Messy*. New York: Peter Lang.

———. 2006. "Foucauldian Scientificity: Rethinking the Nexus of Qualitative Research and Educational Policy Analysis." *International Journal of Qualitative Studies in Education* 19(6): 783–91.

———. 2007. *Getting Lost: Feminist Efforts toward a Double(d) Science*. New York: SUNY Press.

———. 2013. "Methodology-2.1: What Do We Do in the Afterward?" *International Journal of Qualitative Studies in Education* 26(6): 634–45.

Lincoln, Y. 2011. "Critical Qualitative Research and the Corporatized University on a Collision Course: Reimagining Faculty Work and Forms of Resistance." The Velma Schmidt Endowed Chair Lecture, North Texas University.

Lohr, S. 2012. "The Age of Big Data." *New York Times*, February 11. http://www.nytimes.com/2012/02/12/sunday-review/big-datas-impact-in-the-world.html.

Macdonald, L., and A. Ruckert, eds. 2009. *Post-Neoliberalism in the Americas*. London: Palgrave.

MacLellan, M., and M. Talpalaru. 2012. "Remaking the Commons." *Reviews in Cultural Theory* 2(3): 1–6. http://reviewsinculture.com/wp-content/uploads/2015/10/RCT-SP-On-the-Commons.pdf.

Mallozzi, C. 2009. "Voicing the Interview: A Researcher's Exploration on a Platform of Empathy." *Qualitative Inquiry* 15(6): 1042–60.

Marcus, G. 2009. "Notes toward an Ethnographic Memoir of Supervising Graduate Research through Anthropology's Decades of Transformation." In *Fieldwork Is Not What It Used to Be: Learning Anthropology's Method in a Time of Transition*, edited by J. Faubion and G. Marcus, 1–34. Ithaca, NY: Cornell University Press.

Mbembe, A. 2003. "Necropolitics." *Public Culture* 15(1): 11–40.

Melville, S. 1996. "Color Has Not Yet Been Named: Objectivity in Deconstruction." In *Seams: Art as Philosophical Content*, edited by J. Gilbert-Rolfe, 129–46. Amsterdam, the Netherlands: G&B Arts.

Mihic, S., S. G. Engelmann, and E. R. Wingrove. 2005. "Making Sense in and of Political Science: Facts, Values, and 'Real' Numbers." In *The Politics of Method in the Human Sciences: Positivism and Its Epistemological Others*, edited by G. Steinmetz, 470–95. Durham, NC: Duke University Press.

Mole, B. 2013. "NSF Cancels Political Science Grant Cycle." *Nature*, August 2. doi:10.1038/nature.2013.13501.

National Research Council. 2002. *Scientific Research in Education*. Edited by R. Shavelson and L. Towne. Washington, DC: National Academy Press.

National Science Foundation. 2004. *Workshop on Scientific Foundations of Qualitative Research*. https://www.nsf.gov/pubs/2004/nsf04219/nsf04219.pdf.

"A New Model for Doing Good." 2012. *Newsweek*, February 13, 5.

Pascale, C-M. 2011. *Cartographies of Knowledge: Exploring Qualitative Epistemologies*. Los Angeles: Sage.

Paulos, J. A. 2010. "Metric Mania." *New York Times*, May 13. http://www.nytimes.com/2010/05/16/magazine/16FOB-WWLN-t.html.

Peters, M. 2011. *Neoliberalism and After? Education, Social Policy, and the Crisis of Western Capitalism*. New York: Peter Lang.

Povinelli, E. 2011. *Economies of Abandonment: Social Belonging and Endurance in Late Liberalism*. Durham, NC: Duke University Press.

Rancière, J. 2009. *The Emancipated Spectator*. Translated by G. Elliott. London: Verso.

———. 2004/2000. *The Politics of Aesthetics: The Distribution of the Sensible*. Translated by G. Rockhill. London and New York: Continuum.

———. 2011. *The Politics of Literature*. Translated by J. Rose. Cambridge, UK: Polity Press.

Readings, B. 1997. *The University in Ruins*. Cambridge, MA: Harvard University Press.

Ronell, A. 2010. *Fighting Theory*. Urbana: University of Illinois Press.

Sangtin Writers and R. Nagar. 2006. *Playing with Fire: Feminist Thought and Action through Seven Lives in India*. Minneapolis: University of Minnesota Press.

Schwartz-Shea, P., and D. Yanow. 2002. "'Reading' 'Methods' 'Texts': How Research Methods Texts Construct Political Science." *Political Research Quarterly* 55(2): 457–86.

Shamir, R. 2008. "The Age of Responsibilization: On Market-Driven Morality." *Economy and Society* 37(1): 1–19.

Spencer Foundation. 2009. *The Preparation of Aspiring Educational Researchers in the Empirical Qualitative and Quantitative Traditions of Social Science: Methodological*

Rigor, Social and Theoretical Relevance, and More. Report of a Task Force of the Spencer Foundation Educational Research Training Grant Institutions, September. http://floden.wiki.educ.msu.edu/file/view/spencer_task_force_final_final_report%5B1%5D.pdf.

St. Pierre, E. 2011. "Post-Qualitative Research: The Critique and the Coming After." In *The Handbook of Qualitative Research*, 4th ed., edited by N. Denzin and Y. Lincoln, 611–35. Thousand Oaks, CA: Sage.

———. 2006. "Scientifically Based Research in Education: Epistemology and Ethics." *Adult Education Quarterly* 56(4): 239–66.

Steinmetz, G., ed. 2005. *The Politics of Method in the Human Sciences: Positivism and Its Epistemological Others*. Durham, NC: Duke University Press.

Turner, S. P. 2003. *Liberal Democracy 3.0: Civil Society in the Age of Experts*. London: Sage.

Vázquez, E. 2011. "Short-Circuiting the Virtuous Circle." Review of *Latin America Neostructuralism: The Contradictions of Post-Neoliberal Development*, by I. Fernando. *Cultural Theory* 2(1). http://reviewsinculture.com/2011/01/15/short-circuiting-the-virtuous-circle/.

Westbrook, D. 2008. *Navigators of the Contemporary: Why Ethnography Matters*. Chicago: University of Chicago Press.

Weyland, K. 2005. Review of *Rethinking Social Inquiry: Diverse Tools, Shared Standards*, edited by H. Brady and D. Collier. *Perspectives on Politics* 3(2): 392–93.

PART III

THEORIZING THE COLONIAL ACADEMY AND INDIGENOUS KNOWLEDGE

CHAPTER 8

RECONCILING INDIGENOUS KNOWLEDGE IN EDUCATION: PROMISES, POSSIBILITIES, AND IMPERATIVES

Marie Battiste

Introduction

Relatively little is known about Indigenous Knowledges (IK) and their diverse epistemologies, pedagogies, and methodologies in Canadian universities. Editors Archibald, Aquash, Kelly, and Cranmer astutely pointed out in a 2009 special edition of the *Canadian Journal of Native Education* on the theme of Indigenous Knowledges and education that educators have only just begun to conduct research, and develop, implement, and mobilize that research to show "how IK can contribute to and improve education for all learners" (2).

Indigenous peoples represent multiple diversities in their knowledge systems and languages. They live in diverse locations throughout Canada and beyond, from the Far North in the tundra to the eastern and southern coastal regions and the western plains and mountainous regions, in urban areas, and in rural communities. Some communities are isolated in small numbers in remote places, while others in greater numbers are in close proximity to towns and cities. Greatly eroded, their diverse Indigenous languages still exist, through which unique knowledge systems hold many ancestral teachings and skills developed from living on the land, requiring an awareness of the science of ecology and the environment, as well as sustainable economic development through knowledges and creative traditional arts and crafts. The diversity is great, considering the size of Canada, yet when researchers write about Aboriginal peoples of Canada, they are too often characterized as a homogenous whole, without their diversity acknowledged and with little reference to the colonial contexts that have so dramatically changed their situations and their living, learning, and potentials. More importantly, for many Aboriginal researchers educated in Eurocentric institutions is an awareness that the absence of Indigenous Knowledges and teachings prevents the unravelling of racial and colonial myths about Aboriginal people that have damaged Aboriginal knowledge systems and discovering ways to deal with the tragic legacy of assimilation in our histories. As African American poet Audre Lorde (1984) has tried to teach us, "The master's tools will never dismantle the master's house."

As a teacher and educator, my professional and personal journey has been one of discovering how Indigenous students and communities might be enriched by our own deep knowledges and teachings past and present despite our lived experiences of colonization. Today, more than ever, we are aware of how learning and the control of education in exclusive knowledge societies have gone hand in hand with serious inequality, exclusion, and conflict, exemplified in aborted achievements in schools, lack of self-esteem, fragmented identities and self-awareness, and underdeveloped capacities. The European settler societies that developed these systems disregarded IK and its teachings as invalid epistemologies and have used research to examine and appropriate IK for their own purposes. This has led to our continuing distrust of researchers and their disciplines. Disrespect for Indigenous epistemologies and theft of knowledge and its products have alienated Indigenous learners from formal learning and colonial research foundations. This has created a legacy of mistrust between institutions of higher learning and Indigenous peoples, their governance bodies, and their institutions of learning (Battiste and Henderson 2000).

Over the years and in my work with the Aboriginal Learning Knowledge Centre during our brief but intensely researched years with the Canadian Council on Learning, we researchers have found that Indigenous pedagogies and Indigenous content-based curricula are indeed having a positive effect on Indigenous learners (Battiste 2013; Bell 2004; Ireland 2007, 2009;

Little Bear 2009). Less research is available on the impact of Indigenous Knowledge and pedagogies on non-Indigenous learners, as well as how faculty in post-secondary education institutions can orient themselves to a new learning and teaching paradigm.

The last twenty-five years have seen the emergence of an Indigenous peoples' renaissance and self-determining activism. Including Aboriginal and treaty rights as part of the supreme law of the Constitution of Canada in 1982 and the publication of the United Nations global consensus on IK in the *Declaration on the Rights of Indigenous Peoples* in 2007 have begun to change the landscape of education in Canada. In addition, many countries and institutions are asking how IK might be appropriately advanced, included, researched, and shared in authentic and ethical ways so peoples around the globe may benefit from its frameworks, foundations, teachings, and relationships. Indigenous Knowledges in the academy and in the sciences are finding resonance around the globe in such places as New Zealand, Australia, Norway, Hawaii, and Alaska. As the world experiences more resource depletion, the need for more sustainable ways of living and being in the world is driving more researchers and scientists to explore Indigenous peoples' knowledges and ways of knowing for both their sustainable and the profit-driven aspects of knowledge production, inquiry, and research. (See, for example, the UNESCO 1999 publication, *Science for the Twenty-First Century*.)

Indigenous Knowledges have only recently found resonances in policy frameworks of universities and colleges in Canada. The lag in that effort sits squarely on the cognitive, imperialistic, hegemonic foundations of Eurocentric institutions that have controlled what knowledge counts, what gets produced and disseminated in government-funded institutions, what gets researched, and what metrics are used to determine their validity, usefulness, and accessibility. Aboriginal peoples and their knowledges get little attention, support, or uptake. Instead, Eurocentric researchers report on the paucity of life conditions created by the federal government's avoidance of the constitutional rights of Indigenous peoples. This lack creates gaps that support notions of deficiencies and dispositions toward neediness that affirm the myth of racial and cultural inferiority.

As costs increase and the provinces decrease their direct funding to education for various and questionable reasons, universities are increasingly being pressed into a market model to increase their funding opportunities. The pressures of funding priorities lead to a discourse of austerity that creates a top-down model of pressure on faculty and students, and discursive rationalizations of resources and realignment of priorities, while increasing the competition for what are perceived as limited resources. Central to increasing funding is to capture a growing market share of students, region- ally, nationally, and internationally. Student demographics have ushered in new initiatives aimed at increasing numbers of students, and, thus, some argue, "reduc[ing] universities to assembly plants, narrowly defined as working for the market" (Archibald et al. 2009, 3). However, the attempt to attract more Aboriginal students has not led to the university questioning the presumed racial or cultural superiority of Eurocentric knowledge sys- tems for students, either Canadian or Aboriginal.

Indigenization of the universities is a newly generated discourse aimed at increasing the market share, building a stronger competitive framework across Canada, while aiming toward social justice and inclusion. Increasing the number of Aboriginal students in Eurocentric universities is mostly about capturing Canada's fastest-growing demographic—Aboriginal youth. "Between 1996 and 2006, the Aboriginal population in this country increased by 45%, a rate almost six times faster than that of the non-Aboriginal pop- ulation, and Canada is now second only to New Zealand in the proportion of Indigenous people in its population" (Wilson and Battiste 2011, 7). With fewer than 10 per cent of Aboriginal peoples between the ages of twenty-four and sixty-four having a university degree, which is one-third the rate of other Canadians, harnessing the potential of Aboriginal youth through Eurocentric education is viewed as an imperative (AUCC 2011). The harnessing of the potential of Aboriginal youth through education is viewed as a solution to Aboriginal peoples' troubled history, which has prevented them from being full participants in the Canadian economy. While a lack of university educa- tion and high unemployment have been thought to be intractable problems, one should heed the advice offered by Hoppers and Richards when they write,

> In Canada, to encourage Aboriginal students' uptake into uni- versities and colleges, more than 350 initiatives aimed at making a difference, including courses, outreach and financial assistance have been created. Fifty-five universities have physical spaces where First Nations, Métis and Inuit students can gather. Sixty universities have organized special services, including counsel- ling, support and connections to their social and culture activ- ities. Many universities also run successful outreach programs in Aboriginal communities, providing support and mentoring to students. Some universities combine Native studies with other areas of knowledge to create specific programs aimed at serving

the needs of Aboriginal peoples in Canadian society. In the last decade, however, these access and retention initiatives have not generated a significant change in the statistics in Aboriginal graduates (Wilson & Battiste, 2010). The number of Aboriginal people with university degrees increased from 6% in 2001 to 8% in 2006, yet there is a long way to go to catch up to the national 2006 non-Aboriginal average of 23%. (2011, 3)

Considering the growth of the Aboriginal youth population, however, the gap has actually widened between the percentages of Aboriginal and non-Aboriginal people with university degrees. By 2015, the number of Aboriginal students who had graduated from universities had not reached 10 per cent.

Few universities have engaged IK significantly and systematically as a foundation for the education of Aboriginal students. Most Indigenous scholars at the post-secondary level have attempted to build their scholarship on IK amid the systemic bias and prejudice of a basic Eurocentric curriculum that is prevalent, available, researchable, and normalized by the faculty tenure and promotion process. Those persistent scholars butt up against layers of discrimination and systemic barriers as they make their way through the profession. As well, universities are increasingly changing the purpose, production, and dissemination of knowledges to suit more economic interests over human interests, and these contested sites continue to clash in principles, ethics, and desired outcomes with those building on Indigenous Knowledges for human and environmental sustainability. Often Indigenous peoples have contested and resisted these exploitative attempts, as noted in the Idle No More movement, to stop companies from exploitative use of Indigenous lands and resources or in having their knowledges and their resources again used and abused for gain and profits by corporations and governmental interests (Battiste and Henderson 2000).

I want to address universities' approaches to Aboriginal students and the unresolved and contested future of IK in harnessing the potential of Aboriginal students through Indigenizing the universities. While this comes to me as a welcome and crucial step in generating ameliorative action for post-secondary institutions, the approach is drawn mostly from Eurocentric knowledge and the need for Aboriginal students to assimilate into that knowledge system. The cultural additions of universities and colleges are seen, as one Indigenous scholar put it, as a way to lull the Aboriginal student into assimilation (see Chapter 9 of this book)! Indigenization of the universities is about affirming Eurocentric superiority. It is about adding more Aboriginal bodies but ignoring their minds and what they bring with them. Institutional rationalizations and corporate complicities with funding are becoming conventional approaches to address austerity, while the Indigenization of universities for the sake of capacity building conflicts with the mandates and premises and conclusions of many commissions and studies seeking the reform of education. This is especially true for the most recent calls to actions of the Truth and Reconciliation Commission (TRC) (2015) on Indian residential schools (IRS). The report aimed to redress the tragic and silent dark history of Canada's past regarding Aboriginal peoples and has called on the government of Canada, its provinces and territories, its educational institutions, indeed, all Canadians, to reconcile with the colonial and racist history and generate cognitive justice and healing. The report reveals that, for over a century, the central goals of Canada's policy were to eliminate Aboriginal governments, ignore Aboriginal rights, terminate the treaties, and, through a process of forced assimilation through compulsory education, cause Aboriginal peoples to cease to exist as distinct legal, social, cultural, religious, and racial entities in Canada. It declares that the IRS, as well as the day schools system, was a key component of forced assimilation of Indian, Métis, and Inuit students based on the false assumption that European civilization and Christian religions were superior to Aboriginal civilization and spirituality. It notes this cultural genocide policy caused a traumatic loss of IK and languages among the generations of children that were forced to attend the school system.

The TRC's report reveals that the histories of cognitive, epistemic, and spiritual violence and injustice of forced assimilation to Eurocentric knowledge in the education system have never been forgotten by the Aboriginal survivors, even in their imposed silences and emptiness. Unravelling these ignored histories is an unfinished story of the government and churches that were directly responsible for establishing a brutal education system for Aboriginal children based on racist thought and cultural genocide. Victims may be ignored and left behind by Eurocentric education and fade away as nonhistory, but the survivors and their children have been forced to live in dehumanized massive alienation and suffering. The report notes that this legacy has not generated a mutually respectful relationship between Aboriginal and non-Aboriginal peoples.

The TRC's report urges cognitive justice and healing of Aboriginal peoples through a new ameliorative education system as a first principle of Aboriginal education in Canada. This ameliorative education system, premised on a holistic vision of reconciliation, has to be based on the lessons of the past, on the constitutional rights of Aboriginal peoples, on the principles of self-determination, and it must affirm IK. The United Nations Declaration on the Rights of Indigenous Peoples (2007) also emphasizes the need to establish a respectful and healthy relationship among peoples going forward and living together. The TRC defines reconciliation as an ongoing process of establishing and maintaining mutually respectful relationships between Aboriginal and non-Aboriginal peoples in this country that requires the revitalization of Aboriginal culture, languages, spirituality, laws, governance, and way of life. The imperatives of an ameliorative education system involve improving cognitive justice and pluralities to Indigenous Knowledge systems and language rights to achieve equality and equity in funding and dignity, and to achieve healing and reconciliation with Aboriginal peoples. I strongly agree with the TRC and the UN that constitutional reconciliation to the precepts of Aboriginal and treaty rights must be understood, addressed, and implemented in the educational systems throughout Canada, together with clear goals for self-determination and collective good through the resourcing and prioritizing of Indigenous peoples over any perceived market economy.

Indigenous Knowledge in Higher Education

The promise for IK begins with Aboriginal and treaty rights affirmed in the Canadian Constitution in 1982. First Nations (FN) chiefs and leaders negotiated and agreed to enter into nation-to-nation treaties with the sovereigns of Great Britain that would permit European settlers, running from their own oppressive circumstances, to build their own self-determining settlements on FN lands. As Canada was not yet a self-determining nation, the Crown entered into these agreements with First Nations to enable them to access educational and economic benefits, as well as to continue to live according to their knowledge systems, languages, and law. Once these negotiated agreements and treaties were transferred to Canada's government to be implemented through its legislative processes, the settler governments were to provide First Nations with schools and teachers to enable First Nations to benefit from and add to their enriched livelihoods. The funding of these promises was made possible from the federal government's sale of Indian lands and the government's fiduciary management of those funds to build schools, staff them with teachers, and support education and other economic possibilities available to FN (Henderson 1995).

These promises have since been reinterpreted through many self-interested policies and administrations of colonial governments within a growing reign of colonial settler dominance and notions of false superiority, leading to these schools being used for the removal and isolation of Indigenous children, and, ultimately, leading to both cultural assimilation and cultural genocide of Aboriginal students (Sinclair 2015; Battiste 2013, 1986; Schissel and Wotherspoon 2003). The outcome has led to a tsunami of detrimental consequences for Indigenous peoples throughout Canada and beyond that have been researched regularly and revealed in many studies (Ing 2000; Daschuk 2013; Miller 1996; Assembly of First Nations 1988a, 1988b, 1990, 1992) and governmental reports and documents, notably the Hawthorne Report (1967), the five volumes of the report by the Royal Commission on Aboriginal peoples (RCAP) (1996), the Auditor General reports (2004, 2011), the Standing Senate Committee on Aboriginal Peoples (2011), and, more recently, the report of the TRC (2015).

The assimilative government policies and discriminatory practices, the societal assumptions and discourses of Indigenous peoples' presumed inferiority, the racism, and cognitive and physical violence and abuses have been the main themes of Indigenous peoples' tragic testimonies. Such abuses were ushered in through the mechanisms of a fiduciary mismanagement of their resources, the control of their lives through schooling and reserve living, and the lack of ameliorative action after the issues have been revealed— then and now. Indigenous peoples have been denied their Indigenous identities, knowledges, and learning from families and Elders and community members, while being forced to learn in foreign languages about settler colonists' histories, heroes, and successes with varying consequences, including devastating self-loathing and nihilism, internalized oppression, unfulfilling assimilation, and erosion of their own languages and cultures. First Nations, Métis, and Inuit peoples' testimonies have shared painfully but courageously the stories of their stolen childhoods, self-esteem, and shame, and punitive and incompetent teachers and staff in the schools who took from them their families, their language, their joy, and their Elders' teachings. Beyond these, the survivors of the residential school system have shown their tragic emergence through the pain and their capacity for resilience by drawing from their own inner power and the power of their cultural teachings and healing frameworks.

Little can be said for the government of Canada that initially refused to initiate this work but had to be forced into a court settlement with the survivors, which would include the Truth and Reconciliation Commission. Few of the churches shared their documents, and the Catholic Church continues to refuse to turn over to the TRC documents of the residential schools they administered. Likewise, no administrators or teachers have come forward with their testimonies. Rather, it has been only the school "survivors" who have courageously and painfully provided the evidence for the TRC and shaped the recommendations for the TRC report to Canada.

In 1991, the government of Canada established the Royal Commission on Aboriginal Peoples as a commission of inquiry to investigate the evolution of the relationship of Aboriginal peoples with the government of Canada and to propose specific solutions and recommendations to the problems of the past relationship. The Royal Commission's central conclusion in its 1996 report affirms the need for the constitutional guarantees of the rights of Aboriginal peoples of Canada. The commission determined that "the main policy direction, pursued for more than 150 years, first by colonial then by the Canadian governments, has been wrong" (Indigenous and Northern Affairs Canada). The policies of assimilation were based on four dehumanizing (and incorrect) assumptions and ideas about Aboriginal peoples: (1) they were inherently inferior and incapable of governing themselves; (2) Eurocentric colonial authorities knew best how to protect Aboriginal interests and well-being…without regard to inherent and treaty rights; and (3) concepts of development, for individuals or for community, could be defined by non-Aboriginal values alone, including their resource development or environmental exploitation (RCAP 1996, vol. 1, 248).

Canadians have shared a long and sometimes troubled history. Things have happened that are painful to recount and are deplored by the great majority of Canadians. Many of these events were the result of greed or ill will; others were the product of ignorance, misguided intentions, or lack of concern for people already at the edge of Canadian society. The result of this history is evident in the social and economic conditions of Aboriginal communities and in the distrust and betrayal felt by Aboriginal people. A sense of profound injustice and pain was expressed in testimony before the commission. The damage was real and will take time to heal. That history of hurt has to be reckoned with in creating a new relationship (RCAP 1996, vol. 5, 3–4).

In response to the finding of the Royal Commission, the *Statement of Reconciliation* of the government of Canada recognized that policies that sought to assimilate Aboriginal peoples were not the way to build a strong country (Stewart 1998). Instead of an assimilation policy, the Canadian government's Aboriginal Action Plan, in accordance with the Constitution, must "find ways in which Aboriginal people can participate fully in the economic, political, cultural, and social life of Canada in a manner which preserves and enhances the collective identities of Aboriginal communities, and allows them to evolve and flourish in the future" (Stewart 1998).

While then Prime Minister Stephen Harper offered the survivors a government apology in 2008, little political action has occurred since then that would effectively transform the educational systems or effect better conditions for Indigenous peoples. In fact, the situations on reserves have worsened, with people on more reserves living with unpotable water and unhealthy housing and increased suicide rates. A new Liberal government in the fall of 2015 with Prime Minister Justin Trudeau offered Indigenous peoples new hope and aspiration for change at governmental and institutional levels. Federally, the newly named Indigenous and Northern Affairs Canada will have to live up to notable campaign promises of reconciliation with Indigenous peoples, a nation-to-nations relationship, redress for the residential schools, parity in funding for First Nations' schools, and the National Inquiry into Missing and Murdered Indigenous Women and Girls.

As institutions of higher learning ponder how to improve the successes of Aboriginal peoples' education, the rights, the promises, and the possibilities for transformative change hinge on Canada's own acknowledgement of its dark hidden history with Indigenous peoples and redress for the damages of colonial control and mismanagement over the past 150 years. While the promise of IK is real, so will be the resistance already built into the system by the sheer weight of historic racism and hegemonic dominance of Eurocentric knowledge in all of the disciplines of higher education. This structure of knowledge making and meaning making over many periods and generations has created the foundations for cognitive imperialism and injustice that continues to erode Indigenous peoples' identities, languages, livelihood on the land, and their self-determination. The other rising issue is the emergence of a strong neoliberal audit culture; as it gains ascendancy on campuses, institutional dependence on and competition for scarce resources will increasingly be another resisting mechanism for deciding, with its ever-narrowing metrics, what counts as knowledge or does not count as scholarship and on what basis knowledge and research is defended and resourced. The politics of knowledge, and the resourcing of it, will continue to play an important role in the future implementation of IK in and through educational institutions.

Advancing an Ameliorative Agenda of Indigenization

While there have been many systemic resistances and structural difficulties in imagining a transformation of education, a growing sense of hope
among Indigenous peoples and scholars has emerged. The first ray of hope
came from Indigenous peoples themselves. In the last half of the twentieth
century, the resurgence of a first wave of Indigenous scholarship focused
academic interest in locating Indigenous communities' issues and problems
within a colonial framework of hegemony and rethinking solutions to these
issues within Indigenous peoples' own systems of knowing and learning.
The scholars began a movement to restore and renew hope and promise to
current situations that were previously linked directly to colonial relations
embedded in Eurocentrism and racist policy and practice (Cajete 1994; Ing
2000; Smith 1999). They also began to explore the unexamined aspects of
their own knowledge systems, the losses to their Indigenous languages and
stories, and worked to recover the teachings and theories and methodologies
drawn from their unique experience within their spiritual, holistic, commu-
nally activated, land-based, situated knowing (Archibald 2008; Bastien 2004;
Cajete 1994, 1999, 2000, 2015). These and many other scholars have generated new insights, building from Indigenous theory and methodologies,
to a relational ontology with many living and nonhuman entities, thus creating alternative lenses to view and address problems and situations within
Indigenous communities. Community-based action research and activity
have helped to illustrate the value of Indigenous Knowledges in various sectors of social work, health, social justice and jurisprudence, education, art,
the humanities and sciences, and beyond. As well, many Indigenous scholars
have used the concept of decolonizing education as a frame for analyzing the
past and reframing the future of education (Smith 1999; Battiste 2013; Gray
et al. 2013).

Since 1972, when the National Indian Brotherhood issued its policy for
Indian Control of Indian Education, a critical mass of educated Aboriginal
people have taken up certain professions in such fields as social work, education, law, health, medicine, justice, and policing. Primarily, they work in fields
where they have a large influence on social justice and equity programming,
and less on business and the economy, although this area too is beginning
to grow. Many educational institutions have embraced Indigenous content
in their curricula, and a growing literature base has begun to address the
challenges and successes of these changes in programming for Aboriginal
people of Canada.

In 2007, the Association of Canadian Deans of Education formulated with Aboriginal scholars an *Accord on Indigenous Education* that includes the mandate to develop Indigenous principles and goals in their schools of education, preparing teacher candidates for new ways to engage Aboriginal students, communities, and their knowledges and languages. This accord has provided an impetus to the transformation of education agendas across Canada and to a rejection of the status quo and its discourses around "closing the gap" to more enlightened, committed goals for the well-being of Aboriginal peoples. Notably, the accord begins by drawing attention to the recognition of the core Aboriginal and treaty rights embedded in the Constitution of Canada, which sets Aboriginal peoples and their success as a central mandate for Canadian education. It also recognizes the colonial history in which educational institutions and policies have been implicated in the tragic history of Canada's Aboriginal peoples.

The discourse of gaps and deficiencies has another history. Currently, over 1.4 million Aboriginal people have been counted in Canada, representing 4 per cent of the population (62 per cent First Nations, 30 per cent Métis, 5 per cent Inuit), with six out of ten Aboriginal people being under the age of twenty-nine, signalling the largest growing Canadian demographic. By 2017, Aboriginal people aged twenty to twenty-nine years may comprise 30 per cent of the total population in Saskatchewan, 24 per cent in Manitoba, 40 per cent in Yukon, and 58 per cent in the Northwest Territories (Government of Canada 2006 and 2008). These statistics have been of concern to many who suggest that unless Canadian institutions recognize and address undereducation and underemployment among Indigenous populations, the smaller populations of presumably white Canadians in the future will be burdened with a social system of underemployed and undereducated Aboriginal people that they will not be able to afford (Avison 2004).

In 2010, the Council of Ministers of Education of Canada agreed that, with the changing demographics, the provinces' schools needed to change their priorities to include Aboriginal students' success with education. Although they have not agreed upon a common approach or common information gathering, all provinces have agreed to work in their own ways to address educational and employment gaps. Provincial ministries of education are calling for their schools to address the educational "gaps" of Aboriginal students—known more specifically as the variances between outcomes of the Canadian average compared with the Aboriginal average. These gaps are evident in education, employment, health, housing, infant and adult mortality, incarceration, and suicides. As institutions seek to identify ways to improve successes of Aboriginal students in areas such as education and employment, however, the approach has been to focus on individual successes that may help these individuals improve their capacity, skills, and knowledge but has focused little on improving intercultural relations with other students and ignores the situations of poverty, inadequate housing, welfare, and high unemployment on reserves.

In June of 2015, the presidents of Canadian universities convened under the organization of Universities Canada, the former Association of Universities and Colleges Canada, and agreed upon a new agenda involving Indigenous peoples' success in education. On its website, the following statement clearly identifies its position:

> Indigenous peoples face significant barriers to accessing and succeeding in a university education. As a result, far fewer First Nations, Métis and Inuit in Canada have a university degree than non-Indigenous Canadians. This education gap undermines social cohesion and prevents Indigenous peoples from being full participants in the economy.
>
> We ask the federal government to help close Canada's education gap through:
> - Substantial, sustained growth in student support and financial assistance for Indigenous students.
> - New investments to enhance successful institutional programming that serves Indigenous students and communities. (Universities Canada)

Central to its agenda are thirteen core principles to guide its action and shared commitment to enhance educational opportunities for Indigenous students. The website shares this statement about the principles:

> To achieve this goal, the new *Principles on Indigenous Education* recognize the importance of greater indigenization of university curricula and of Indigenous education[al] leadership within the university community, as well as the essential work of creating resources, spaces and approaches that promote dialogue and intercultural engagement between Indigenous and non-Indigenous students. The principles also highlight the need to provide greater exposure and knowledge for non-Indigenous students on the realities, histories, cultures and beliefs of Indigenous people in Canada. (Universities Canada)

The universities' thirteen-point plan for partnerships, inclusiveness, inter-cultural awareness, and more culturally responsive pedagogies aims to build on the individual strengths of students and attract promising students with whom they will work for their success. It should be pointed out that the Indigenizing priorities of the thirteen points represent what most educational institutions with significant populations of Aboriginal students are currently doing (Wilson and Battiste 2011), but innovations that the RCAP and the TRC have asked for are still not identified or embraced. Thus, what might seem to be innovative is actually just more of the same, which has not moved the scales of justice for Aboriginal students very far.

While each principle of Indigenizing is important and needed, there is a significant difference between Universities Canada's priorities and other studies, commissions, and the TRC. Another post-secondary announcement is the 2014 *Indigenous Education Protocol for Colleges and Institutes*, issued by Colleges and Institutes Canada, that called to "respect and recognize that Indigenous people include First Nation, Métis and Inuit people, having distinct cultures, languages, histories and contemporary perspectives." The protocol recognizes that "Indigenous education emanates from the intellectual and cultural traditions of Indigenous peoples in Canada." The signature institutions agree to "implement intellectual and cultural traditions of Indigenous peoples through curriculum and learning approaches relevant to learners and communities," to "establish Indigenous-centred holistic services and learning environments for learner success," and to "build relationships and be accountable to Indigenous communities in support of self-determination through education, training and applied research" (Colleges and Institutes Canada).

In contrast to Universities Canada's principles, the TRC's aims are to improve the relations among all people, to create cognitive justice and healing through ameliorative education, and to improve First Nation, Métis, and Inuit people's abilities and capacities for self-determination at both the collective and individual level. Neither Colleges and Institutes Canada's *Indigenous Education Protocol* nor Universities Canada's principles speak to reconciliation of our colonial histories, or healing from the specific effects of racism in the institutions, or decolonizing the curricula for all students and embracing more holistic Indigenous Knowledges and epistemologies that are rooted in Indigenous languages and place-based experiential learning.

What else is not addressed in Colleges and Institutes Canada's *Indigenous Education Protocol* or Universities Canada's principles is a reconciliation rooted in the educational choices of First Nations parents embedded in

Aboriginal and treaty rights (Henderson 1995). They ignore these constitutional rights as if they do not matter to colleges, institutes, and universities. The Supreme Court of Canada has identified several constitutional purposes of these rights that include determining the historical rights of Aboriginal peoples and giving Aboriginal and treaty rights constitutional force to protect them against legislative powers (*Sparrow* 1990, para. 65); sanctioning challenges to social and economic policy objectives embodied in legislation to the extent that Aboriginal and treaty rights are affected (*Sparrow* 1990, para. 64); and a commitment to recognize, value, protect, and enhance their distinctive cultures (*Powley* 2003, paras. 13, 18). To ensure the continuity of Aboriginal customs and traditions, the Supreme Court has determined that every substantive constitutional right will normally include the incidental constitutional right to teach such a practice, custom, and tradition to a younger generation (*Côté* 2011). Currently, most colleges, institutes, and universities have not acknowledged or attempted to implement these constitutional reforms in the education of Aboriginal peoples. The constitutional framework and court decisions generate an emerging reconciliation of IK and culture in learning and pedagogy that must be translated into policy, practice, and impact in all public forms of education. Constitutional reforms create the context for systemic educational reform to include Indigenous science, humanities, visual arts, and languages, as well as educational philosophy, pedagogy, teacher education, and practice.

To some degree, with the emerging Indigenous renaissance, Aboriginal educators have begun the reconciliation in their academic and social justice activist agendas now growing, empowering Aboriginal people to realize their educational goals and join various professions. However, this is not the responsibility of Aboriginal peoples alone. The federal and the provincial governments must reconcile these constitutional rights to education in each jurisdiction. At present, they have not done so, as evidenced by the lack of negotiation of these constitutional rights across provincial and territorial education systems. Thus, the task is great to sensitize Canadian politicians, policy-makers, and educators to be more responsive and proactive to increase funding, improve curricula, and to displace the continuing failures of Aboriginal peoples in the diverse educational systems across Canada.

The emergence in the Indigenous renaissance saw a first and second wave of Indigenous scholars, leaders, and professionals who were largely educated in Eurocentric universities in Canada. There they developed critical literacies and broad skills that enabled them to question and critique Eurocentric discourses and policies that had left a legacy of systemic discrimination and racism in Canada. Their engagement with scholarship took on a new focus, a new gaze, and an irreversible trend to challenge Eurocentrism, Western privilege and dominance, and settler discourses of difference and deficiency. That movement would change the landscape of Indigenous peoples' experience and raised their testimony in voices of dissent and critique and raised the consciousness of racism, social justice, cognitive imperialism, and human and Indigenous rights. The status of Indigenous Knowledge has been raised among many Indigenous scholars worldwide, and universities no longer are able to defend the Eurocentric empire as the only knowledge system that can assure humanity of its capacity to ensure a quality of life, end poverty and unemployment, and create peace and environmental sustainability.

The very tradition of the university is being subjected to harsh criticism for fostering hierarchal, invidious monoism (Minnich 1990). Women, Indigenous peoples, minorities within nation-states, and others are investing in a new postmodern education built on testimonies, stories, life experience, innovation and technologies, creativity, and fresh imagination to tackle the big problems of the world, rather than drawing on Western traditions and their lessons. A growing body of research, writing, advocacy, and critique into understanding and unpacking the colonial context and its effects on Indigenous peoples has helped fuel a renaissance that questions the assumptions of researchers and findings of research and applied solutions that were drawn from Eurocentric knowledge traditions and methodologies (Smith 1999). Instead, Indigenous scholars like J. Youngblood Henderson, Gregory Cajete, Oscar Kawagley, Graham Hingangaroa Smith, Linda Tuhiwai Smith, Shawn Wilson, Jo-ann Archibald, Taiaiake Alfred, Patricia Monture, and more have helped to build a new and better understanding of Indigenous ontologies, epistemologies, and axiologies from within IK and their languages. These aim to generate an alternative source of solutions for Aboriginal systems of learning, including law, social work, education, physical and mental health, social justice, and economic viability and well-being. In Canada, this first wave of scholars, in their dissemination of knowledge and critique, has mobilized interest among educational institutions to teach treaties and Indigenous Knowledge, and decolonize Eurocentric education. While many institutions are using a discourse of diversity to enlarge this agenda within human rights and social justice, there is still much that needs to be done to help them understand what IK is and how it can be used as a source for strength and motivation not just for Indigenous peoples but also for non-Indigenous peoples as a source of renewing connections to Aboriginal peoples and reconciling the colonial practices of the past and addressing larger issues of humanity and sustainability through holistic relationships. To achieve this larger perspective, the next step required is a reconciliation with Aboriginal peoples' constitutional rights to education, supported by the constitutional power of federal, territorial, and provincial governments to empower treaty education.

The Constitution of Canada articulates the affirmation and the principles of respect for Aboriginal rights and treaties. It is important for educators to be aware of this. This new constitutional framework enables educators to include Indigenous Knowledge and heritage in every curriculum and educational structure. Educators have a responsibility to live up to Canada's reputation as a compassionate and innovative nation that is on the way to becoming a truly just society. We cannot arrive at this truly just society unless we recognize our dependence on Indigenous Knowledge, values, and visions, and unless we renew our investment in holistic and sustainable ways of thinking, communicating, and acting together.

Indigenous Knowledge is protected under the Constitution of Canada in the framework of Aboriginal and treaty rights in section 35. This generates new ways to understand the school ecology of federal, territorial, and provincial education systems and new, inclusive ways of looking at ethics, values, and educational reforms. The convergence of Indigenous Knowledge and constitutional rights also offers Canada and other nations a chance to comprehend another view of humanity as they never have before. It opens the door to understanding Indigenous humanity and its manifestations without paternalism and without condescension. In practical terms, as articulated in the United Nations Working Group's *Guidelines and Principles for the Protection of Indigenous Populations* (Wiessner and Battiste 2000), this means that Aboriginal peoples of Canada must be involved at all stages and in all phases of educational planning so that each nation has an opportunity to rededicate itself to protecting humanity; to redressing the damage and losses suffered by Aboriginal peoples to their languages, cultures, and properties; and to enabling Aboriginal nations and communities to revitalize and sustain their knowledge for their future.

To initiate such a step, politicians, educators, and all Canadians have to first understand how inherent and treaty rights of the Aboriginal peoples in regard to education have reorientated the constitutional framework of education in Canada. Then, educators have to understand the mandatory force of constitutional reconciliation that the Court has created to converge these different constitutional sources of power, creating a complex intersection of interrelated issues that should be addressed in transforming current and future educational outcomes.

The concepts of convergence and consistency establish the framework of constitutional reconciliation as part of the supremacy of the Constitution over federal and provincial laws (section 52[1] of the Constitution Act, 1982). The province marks its jurisdiction over education in section 93 of the Constitution Act, 1867. Pursuant to their own legislation, the provincial governments and their local governments provide funding and oversee formal education in Canada to its citizens, though not to First Nations on reserve, but including First Nations living off reserve and Métis students. Elementary, secondary, and post-secondary education is all within provincial jurisdiction and the ten provincial legislatures and educational departments oversee their institutions and their curricula. Territorial education in the North is under the jurisdiction of Indigenous and Northern Affairs Canada, which funds education for Inuit students.

The constitutional convergence principles apply to provincial constitutional authority over education with Aboriginal and treaty rights involved with education. Provincial powers under section 93 of the Constitution do not give the provinces any original power to deal with constitutional rights of Treaty First Nations and Aboriginal peoples. Recently, however, the Supreme Court of Canada has declared in *Grassy Narrows First Nation* (2014) that both the provinces and Canada are constitutionally responsible for the implementation of the treaty rights within their constitutional powers. This gives the provinces and territories the constitutional obligation to implement the educational provisions of treaties. Moreover, any direct or incidental exercise of educational authority of the provinces or territories under contract with federal authorities has to be consistent with the educational rights contained in Aboriginal and treaty rights in section 35. Under its legitimate constitutional powers, the provincial and territory governments have the ability to take action to preserve, promote, and implement Aboriginal and treaty rights that embody IK in regard to education and the distinct knowledge and distinctive cultures that underpin these rights. Moreover, any provincial legislation, agreement, or policy that negatively affects constitutional rights of Aboriginal people will be judged by the constitutional standards of consistency, honour of the Crown, fiduciary obligations, division of powers, interjurisdictional immunity, paramountcy, and the justification on any infringements on Aboriginal peoples' rights. These judicial interpretations of the Constitution have created the need for constitutional reconciliation and Indigenizing of the curriculum.

The Court has stated that the fundamental objective of the modern law of Aboriginal and treaty rights is to attempt the constitutional reconciliation of

Aboriginal peoples and non-Aboriginal peoples and their respective claims, interests, and ambitions (*Haida Nation* 2004; *Mikisew* 2005). This would include constitutional reconciliation between the federal and provincial governments about the education of Aboriginal peoples.

Toward Constitutional Reconciliation and Cognitive Justice

Differing levels of internal and external self-determination exist in the Constitution of Canada for different people in a shared territory. The various peoples of Canada comprise the differential political sovereign, which generates the institutional form of life and society. As part of the supreme law of Canada, section 52(1) of the Constitution Act, 1982, specifically directs and mandates recognition and affirmation of existing Aboriginal and treaty rights at every level of Canadian society, creating new contexts for the honourable interpretation of governmental responsibility and treaty rights in Canada. However, gaps exist between the constitutional vision and commitment with the institutional commitment and implementation. Most institutional administrations are also unaware of this part of the Constitution and how it applies to the governments' policies and practices and funding in post-secondary institutions.

The Court has developed several approaches as transformative methods to protect Aboriginal peoples, their distinct knowledge systems, legal traditions, and way of life. The subject is crucial, and its importance is daunting. These constitutional principles also inform institutional change and educational reform in Canada. They embody both conceptual and practical arrangements. They should also embody Indigenous Knowledge.

Most politicians and Canadians were (are) taken aback by the constitutional reform and vision, by the differentiated coordinates of political sovereignty, and by its necessary legal and institutional transformations. Superimposing an innovative vision of constitutionalism on Canadian consciousness derived from British colonialism is difficult and complicated, especially since it conflicts with existing knowledge structures, including cognitive themes, scripts, schemas, categories, and stereotypes that ensured all sovereignty and power came from the imperial Crown. That sole power and authority has been consistently challenged and has been powerfully refuted. In more than fifty cases since 1982, the Supreme Court of Canada has begun to generate a truly Canadian legal system based on constitutionalism and legal and epistemic plurality, attempting to create fair processes for a just, honourable government, and trans-systemic convergences and reconciliations of the common law traditions with the Aboriginal legal traditions. The Court's trans-systemic approach to constitutional law developed innovative principles of adjudication that create a unique reorientation of Canadian constitutional jurisprudence.

The Court has determined that the wording of section 35(1) of the Constitution Act, 1982—the recognition and affirmation of existing Aboriginal and treaty rights—provides a trans-systemic constitutional framework that recognizes the fact that First Nations lived on the land in distinctive societies with their own sovereignty, legal orders, practices, traditions, and cultures, which were brought within the protection of the constitutional law of Canada (*Van der Peet* 1996, 31). The Court has held that the phrase "recognized and affirmed" in section 35(1) establishes constitutional supremacy over parliamentary supremacy, and recognizes the ultimate principle of Aboriginal sovereignty upon which asserted British authority was constructed. In establishing this *sui generis* approach (i.e., that it must be understood on its own terms and not on precedent of previous case law) to Aboriginal and treaty rights, the Court sought to displace positivism and the common law and establish honourable government over good government.

Moreover, the Court held that neither the rights of individuals in the Canadian Charter of Rights and Freedoms (Part I of the Constitution Act, 1982) could override Aboriginal and treaty rights (section 25), nor did equality rights preclude ameliorative or remedial law, policy, or programs of the Crown designed to proactively combat discrimination for disadvantaged persons or groups and help Aboriginal peoples improve their situation and process to self-sufficiency (section 15[2]). These constitutional provisions distinguish legislation between Aboriginal and non-Aboriginal people in order to protect interests associated with Aboriginal sovereignty, territory, culture or way of life, or the treaty process or implementation, and ensured that this provision deserves to be shielded from Charter scrutiny to promote substantive equality (*Kapp* 2008; *Corbiere* 1999).

In their efforts to comprehend the deep structure of Aboriginal and treaty rights, and Aboriginal Knowledge and legal traditions, the Canadian courts, including the Supreme Court, have been burdened by the lack of a method to comprehend these constitutional rights of Aboriginal peoples. They have rejected the basic schemes of explanation available in Eurocentrism, an entrenched prejudice among knowledge systems, based on logical analysis and causal explanation. They have developed a *sui generis* approach and a trans-systemic symbiosis of the constitutional framework that is required in the constitutional reconciliation of Aboriginal and treaty rights with the older colonial parts of the Constitution. In these complementary approaches, the courts have validated the distinct knowledge systems and legal tradition of the Aboriginal peoples that inform their constitutional rights. They generate innovative concepts of the honour of the Crown and honourable governance to guide the relationship between constitutional powers and Aboriginal and treaty rights and its development of a trans-systemic symbiosis approach to constitutional convergence and reconciliation of the legal traditions of Aboriginal peoples with Eurocentric traditions.

In considering the promise of IK further, the courts have duly recognized Aboriginal and treaty rights as distinctive processes embedded in Aboriginal peoples' experiences, languages, and knowledges that create a knowledge system that is not Eurocentrically driven. In the case of *R. v. Côté* (2011), the Supreme Court noted that, where Aboriginal rights exist, Indigenous peoples have the right to pass on that knowledge through their generations. These ontologies, epistemologies, and axiologies are distinctively generated among Aboriginal peoples and have their own theories and methodologies generated within them.

In addition, the minimum standards of the global consensus in the United Nations Declaration on the Rights of Indigenous Peoples (2007), which the TRC has viewed as the appropriate framework for a holistic vision of reconciliation that provides the necessary principles, norms, and standards for reconciliation to flourish in twenty-first-century Canada, include:

- Article 37(1): Indigenous peoples have the right to the recognition, observance, and enforcement of treaties and to have States honour and respect such treaties.
- Article 37(2): Nothing in this Declaration may be interpreted as diminishing or eliminating the rights of Indigenous peoples contained in treaties and agreements.
- Article 5: Indigenous peoples' rights to maintenance of their cultural institutions.
- Article 9: Determining their own membership in accordance with their traditions.
- Article 11(1): Practising and revitalizing their cultural traditions and customs.
- Article 11(2): Redress with respect to their cultural, intellectual, religious and spiritual property taken without their free, prior, and informed consent or in violation of their laws, traditions, and customs.

- Article 12: Manifesting, practising, developing, and teaching their spiritual and religious traditions, customs, and ceremonies and maintaining their religious and cultural sites together with repatriation of their human remains.
- Article 14: Culturally appropriate education.
- Article 24: Maintaining their own traditional medicines and health practices.
- Article 13: A focus on Indigenous intangible heritage, stressing that Indigenous peoples have the right to "revitalize, use, develop, and transmit to future generations their histories, languages, oral traditions, philosophies, writing systems, and literatures."
- Article 31: Affirms the right of Indigenous peoples "to maintain, control, protect, and develop their cultural heritage, traditional knowledge, and traditional cultural expressions."

The growing recognition of how these constitutional and global human rights are interrelated has generated the imperative of Indigenization of the Canadian education system. Aboriginal academics and scholars have used these rights, principles, and norms to identify their own communities' theories and methodologies to address problems within the communities and in their relationships with others, and to recover from the personal and collective losses using their language, stories, ceremonies, and land. Moreover, they have declared in many fora that Indigenization requires the establishment of proper principles to mediate between Aboriginal and Eurocentric knowledge systems and to govern the emerging needs to create a nobler and better life for Aboriginal peoples through education. An absence of consensus on the appropriate method may exist within the university community because of the lack of public education and concerted effort. They have encouraged the university community to make substantial efforts to break through the veil of indifference among non-Aboriginal faculty, students, and staff toward Indigenization by increasing public knowledge and awareness of the imperatives of Indigenous Knowledge, culture, and languages and how they contribute to post-secondary education and society.

References

Archibald, J. 2008. *Indigenous Storywork: Educating the Heart, Mind, Body, and Spirit.* Vancouver: UBC Press.

Archibald, J., M. Aquash, V. Kelly, and L. Cranmer, eds. 2009. "Editorial: Indigenous Knowledges and Education (ECE-12)." *Canadian Journal of Native Education* 32(1): 1–5.

Assembly of First Nations. 1988a. *The Aboriginal Language Policy Study*. Ottawa: Assembly of First Nations Education Secretariat.

———. 1988b. *Tradition and Education: Towards a Vision of Our Future*, vol. 1. Ottawa: Assembly of First Nations Education Secretariat.

Assembly of First Nations Education Secretariat Aboriginal Languages Steering Committee. 1990. *Towards Linguistic Justice for First Nations*. Ottawa: Assembly of First Nations Language and Literacy Secretariat.

Assembly of First Nations Language and Literacy Secretariat. 1992. *Towards Rebirth of First Nations Languages*. Ottawa: Assembly of First Nations Language and Literacy Secretariat.

Association of Canadian Deans of Education. 2007. *Accord on Indigenous Education*. https://csse-scee.ca/acde/publications-2/#indigenous.

Association of Universities and Colleges of Canada (AUCC). 2011. *Trends in Higher Education, Volume 1—Enrolment*. Ottawa: AUCC. https://www.univcan.ca/wp-content/uploads/2015/11/trends-vol1-enrolment-june-2011.pdf.

Auditor General of Canada. 2004. *Indian and Northern Affairs Canada: Elementary and Secondary Education*. Report to the House of Commons, Chapter 4. Ottawa: Minister of Public Works and Government Services Canada.

———. 2011. *June Status Report of the Auditor General of Canada. Chapter 4—Programs for First Nations on Reserves*. http://www.oag-bvg.gc.ca/internet/English/parl_oag_201106_04_e_35372.html.

Avison, D. 2004. *A Challenge Worth Meeting: Opportunities for Improving Aboriginal Education Outcomes*. Prepared for the Council of Ministers in Education Canada.

Bastien, B. 2004. *Blackfoot Ways of Knowing: The Worldview of Siksikaitsitapi*. Calgary: University of Calgary Press.

Battiste, M. 2013. *Decolonizing Education: Nourishing the Learning Spirit*. Saskatoon and Vancouver: Purich Publishing and UBC Press.

———. 1986. "Micmac Literacy and Cognitive Assimilation." In *Indian Education in Canada: The Legacy*, edited by J. Barman, Y. Hébert, and D. McCaskill, 23–44. Vancouver: UBC Press.

Battiste, M., and J. Y. Henderson. 2000. *Protecting Indigenous Knowledge and Heritage: A Global Challenge*. Saskatoon and Vancouver: Purich Publishing and UBC Press.

Bell, D. 2004. *Sharing Our Success: Ten Case Studies in Aboriginal Schooling*. Kelowna: Society for the Advancement of Excellence in Education.

Cajete, G. A. 1999. *Ignite the Sparkle: An Indigenous Science Education Curriculum Model*. Skyland, CO: Kivaki Press.

———. 2015. *Indigenous Community: Teachings of the Seventh Fire*. St. Paul, MN: Living Justice Press.

———. 1994. *Look to the Mountain: An Ecology of Indigenous Education*. Skyland, CO: Kivaki Press.

————. 2000. *Native Science: Natural Laws of Interdependence*. Santa Fe, NM: Clearlight Publishers.

Colleges and Institutes Canada. 2014. *Indigenous Education Protocol for Colleges and Institutes*. https://www.collegesinstitutes.ca/policyfocus/indigenous-learners/protocol/.

Council of Ministers of Education, Canada. 2010. *Strengthening Aboriginal Success: Summary Report*. CMEC Summit on Aboriginal Education. Ottawa: CMEC.

Daschuk, J. 2013. *Clearing the Plains: Disease, Politics of Starvation, and the Loss of Aboriginal Life*. Regina: University of Regina Press.

Government of Canada. 2006 and 2008. *Census Canada*. Ottawa: Government of Canada.

Gray, M., J. Coates, M. Yellow Bird, and T. Hetherington. 2013. *Decolonizing Social Work*. Burlington, VT: Ashgate Publishing Company.

Hawthorne, H. B., et al. 1967. *A Survey of the Contemporary Indians of Canada*. Ottawa: Information Canada.

Henderson, J. Y. 1995. "Treaties and Education." In *First Nations Education in Canada: The Circle Unfolds*, edited by M. Battiste and J. Barman, 245–61. Vancouver: UBC Press.

Hoppers, C. O., and H. Richards. 2011. *Rethinking Thinking: Modernity's "Other" and the Transformation of the University*. Pretoria: University of South Africa.

Indigenous and Northern Affairs Canada. "Highlights from the Report of the Royal Commission on Aboriginal Peoples." https://www.aadnc-aandc.gc.ca/eng/1100100014597/1100100014637#chp2.

Ing, R. N. 2000. "Dealing with Shame and Unresolved Trauma: Residential School and Its Impact on the 2nd and 3rd Generation." PhD diss., University of British Columbia.

Ireland, B. 2009. "Moving from the Head to the Heart—'The Indian's Canada problem.'" In *Reclaiming the Learning Spirit: Aboriginal Learners in Education*. Saskatoon: Aboriginal Learning Knowledge Centre, University of Saskatchewan.

————. 2007. *The Power of Place: Integrating St'at'imc Knowledge into Lillooet & Sk'il Mountain School Curriculum & Pedagogy: Literature Review*. Social Planning and Research Council BC.

Little Bear, L. 2009. "Jagged Worldviews Colliding." In *Reclaiming Indigenous Voice and Vision*, edited by M. Battiste, 77–85. Vancouver: UBC Press.

Lorde, A. 1984. "The Master's Tools Will Never Dismantle the Master's House." In *Sister Outsider: Essays and Speeches*, edited by A. Lorde, 110–14. Berkeley, CA: Crossing Press.

Miller, J. 1996. *Shingwauk's Vision: A History of Native Residential School*. Toronto: University of Toronto Press.

Minnich, E. K. 1990. *Transforming Knowledge*. Philadelphia, PA: Temple University Press.

Royal Commission on Aboriginal Peoples (RCAP). 1996. *Report of the Royal Commission on Aboriginal Peoples*. Ottawa: Minister of Supply and Services, Canada.

———. 1996. *Report of the Royal Commission on Aboriginal Peoples.* Vol. 1, *Looking Forward, Looking Back.* Ottawa: Minister of Supply and Services, Canada.

———. 1996. *Report of the Royal Commission on Aboriginal Peoples.* Vol. 5, *Renewal: A Twenty-Year Commitment.* Ottawa: Minister of Supply and Services, Canada.

Schissel, B., and T. Wotherspoon. 2003. *The Legacy of School for Aboriginal People.* New York: Oxford University Press.

Sinclair, M. 2015. "For the Record: Justice Murray Sinclair on Residential Schools." *Maclean's*, June 2. http://www.macleans.ca/politics/for-the-record-justice-murray-sinclair-on-residential-schools/.

Smith, L. T. 1999. *Decolonizing Methodologies: Research and Indigenous Peoples.* London: Zed Books.

Standing Senate Committee on Aboriginal Peoples. 2011. *Reforming First Nations Education: From Crisis to Hope.* Report of the Standing Senate Committee on Aboriginal Peoples. December. https://sencanada.ca/content/sen/committee/411/appa/subsitedec2011/reports-e.htm.

Stewart, J. 1998. "Address by the Honourable Jane Stewart Minister of Indian Affairs and Northern Development on the Occasion of the Unveiling of Gathering Strength—Canada's Aboriginal Action Plan." https://www.aadnc-aandc.gc.ca/eng/1100100015725/1100100015726.

Truth and Reconciliation Commission of Canada (TRC). 2015. *Honouring the Truth, Reconciling for the Future: Summary of the Final Report of the Truth and Reconciliation Commission of Canada.* http://www.trc.ca/websites/trcinstitution/File/2015/Honouring_the_Truth_Reconciling_for_the_Future_July_23_2015.pdf.

UNESCO. 1999. *World Conference on Science for the Twenty-First Century: A New Commitment.* http://unesdoc.unesco.org/images/0012/001207/120706e.pdf.

United Nations. 2007. *Declaration on the Rights of Indigenous Peoples.* https://www.un.org/development/desa/indigenouspeoples/declaration-on-the-rights-of-indigenous-peoples.html.

Universities Canada. 2015. "New Principles on Indigenous Education." http://www.univcan.ca/media-room/media-releases/new-principles-on-indigenous-education/.

Wiessner, S., and M. Battiste. 2000. "The 2000 Revision of the United Nations Draft Principles and Guidelines on the Protection of the Heritage of Indigenous People." *St. Thomas Law Review* 13(1): 383–90.

Wilson, A., and M. Battiste. 2011. *Environmental Scan of Educational Models Supporting Aboriginal Post-Secondary Education.* Prepared for the Commonwealth of Australia as represented by the Department of Education, Employment and Workplace Relations.

Cases

Corbiere v. Canada (Minister of Indian and Northern Affairs), [1999] 2 SCR 203.
Grassy Narrows First Nation v. Ontario (Natural Resources), [2014] 2 SCR 447.

Haida Nation v. British Columbia (Minister of Forests), [2004] 3 SCR 511.
Mikisew Cree First Nation v. Canada (Minister of Canadian Heritage), [2005] 3 SCR 388.
R. v. Côté, [2011] 3 SCR 215.
R. v. Kapp, [2008] 2 SCR 483.
R. v. Powley, [2003] 2 SCR 207.
R. v. Sparrow, [1990] 1 SCR 1075.
R. v. Van der Peet, [1996] 2 SCR 507.

CHAPTER 9

BITING THE UNIVERSITY THAT FEEDS US

Eve Tuck

For many scholars, working inside universities represents an opportunity to leverage university resources on behalf of communities. Other scholars use other ways to reframe university-based labour with regard to promoting social justice. Discarding the notion of academic work as contained in an ivory tower, these scholars emphasize how we can be in service to communities. Yet the settler colonial roots of the academy have been thoroughly documented, and, with neoliberal rationalism guiding administrative decision making, it is not hard to guess at its settler colonial futures. This chapter is part of a longer, perhaps never-concluding, conversation about the futurities the academy can entertain. There are parts of the higher-education project that are too invested in settler colonialism to be rescued. I offer that here as a truism, not something I will necessarily take the space to argue in this chapter. There are parts of academic labour that might be refused in order to generate new possibilities: another truism.

In this chapter, I want to think through the theories of change at work in academic research, and which of those theories of change can connect most meaningfully to decolonization projects undertaken by Indigenous communities. This is to consider research activities that bite the university that feeds us. I use the space of this chapter to move between discussions of the settler colonial roots and imperatives of the university, documenting damage as a prevalent theory of change and other possible theories of change that might shape academic labour. Along the way, I hope to argue again, as is my persistent insistence, that reflecting upon and calibrating our theories of change is a worthwhile activity for researchers, community organizers, communities, collectives, and all of us seeking to influence social change.

In 2010, I made a decision that any time anyone ever asked me to talk or teach or write about neoliberalism, I would talk about settler colonialism instead. Extensive trust in the free market, goals toward no public expenditures, intense focus on the individual, distaste of collective action, workforce-flexible, few state regulations, high tolerance for unemployment, and blaming individuals for their oppression (see Chapter 1 of this book): all of this can be directly linked to the settler colonial structuring of our societies. Settler colonialism is different from other colonial formations that focus on extractions of labour and resources: often, in addition to these extractions, settler colonialism is ultimately about the pursuit of land for settlement. Settler colonialism requires the destruction of Indigenous communities to clear the land for settlement. Through genocide, assimilation, appropriation, and state violence, Indigenous presence is erased. Settler colonial nation-states are founded on Indigenous erasure, both because Indigenous peoples have moral and often legal claims to land but also because Indigeneity is collective. Indigenous collectivity is the context for the hyper-focus on the individual and distaste for collectivity that are so typical of neoliberal and white settler societies. Settler colonialism is relentless but never fully "successful" because of Indigenous survivance (Vizenor 1999). Indigenous communities have always resisted (and theorized) dispossession.

In the United States and other slave estates (Spillers 2003; see Walcott 2003 for a discussion of slavery in Canada), the remaking of land into property was/is accompanied by the remaking of (African) persons into property, into chattel—this can be connected to neoliberalism's ideation of the flexible land-less workforce (Wilderson 2010; Spillers 2003; see Tuck and Yang 2012 for a more full discussion on this). The remaking of Indigenous land and Black bodies into property is necessary for (white) settlement onto other people's land.

Indigenous Erasure, Anti-Blackness, and Universities

In settler colonialism, Indigenous erasure and anti-blackness are endemic. This is why Indigenous trans and cis women in Canada are asking #AmINext?, while organizers in the United States have to remind us again and again to

#SayHerName to bring attention to Black women killed by police, often in custody. Black and brown trans women have been murdered at devastating rates. This violence is all connected, and Indigenous theorizations of settler colonialism and Black theorizations of anti-blackness flay open those networks of connections.

Monique Guishard and I have synthesized several recent projects in which scholars have traced the histories of their academic disciplines, such as anthropology, psychology, bioethics, and education, and the work of these disciplines on behalf of the false logics of emergent settler colonial nation-states (Tuck and Guishard 2013). When we look at the origin stories of many academic disciplines, we see they are entangled with the projects of settler colonialism: justifying the theft of Indigenous land and the demolition of Indigenous life, and establishing racial hierarchies to justify the enslavement of Africans.[1] For example, early anthropology sought to study the Native to confirm societal notions of the depravity of Indigenous cultures and justify the theft of Indigenous land (Wolfe 1999). Early psychology was concerned with proving that the intellects of white people were superior to the intellects of Black people, Indigenous people, and immigrants—some from groups now considered to be white (Tuck and Guishard 2013). When we bring the settler colonial roots of the academy to the forefront, we can also speak realistically about the futurities it can entertain. This history makes apparent that there continue to be some aspects of the academy that are too invested in settler colonialism to be "rescued."

The settler colonial roots of the academy can help us to interpret the stalled attempts that universities in the United States have made in diversifying their faculties. Table 9.1 shows the number of doctoral degrees awarded by universities in the United States from 2011 to 2012 (Gaquin and Dunn 2015). I have highlighted the number within the categories of American Indian/Alaska Native and Native Hawaiian/Pacific Islander because those are the groups at the centre of my own analyses, but the imbalance toward the production of mostly white people with PhDs is evident.

Table 9.2 provides a sense of the number of full-time faculty in degree-granting institutions, by race and Indigeneity (National Center for Education Statistics 2012). In this table, you might pay attention to the percentage of all faculty/faculty at various ranks that are white, Black, Latino/a, Indigenous, or Asian, but please also look at the real numbers. With regard to American Indian/Alaska Native faculty, there were 3,529 working in degree-granting institutions in 2011. This number stops me in my tracks every time. It is no wonder that universities create diversity initiatives that so often result in broadening the definition of diversity to occlude real gains on racial diversity among faculty. It is no wonder that universities create diversity initiatives that are just smoke and mirrors. Universities will never make hiring policies that reduce the number of positions that can go to white candidates. The current numbers schema cannot be interrupted by the placement of affirmative action statements on job positions or by requiring candidates to write diversity statements alone. More intervention is needed to disrupt the forces that keep predominantly white institutions predominantly white.

Those faculty and administrators who point this out are often people of colour and are often explicitly or tacitly punished for suggesting that meaningfully increasing faculty diversity by race requires big moves and big investments. Sara Ahmed's important 2012 book, *On Being Included*, is an extended discussion on this topic, and Ahmed's work more broadly demonstrates the ways in which the person who says there is a problem becomes the problem.

Table 9.1. *U.S. Doctoral Degrees Awarded by Race, Ethnicity, and Gender, 2011–12*

	Number	Distribution by Race/Ethnicity	Percentage of Total Awarded to Women
All	**170,297**	**100%**	**51.4%**
White	100,784	59.2%	51.2%
Black	10,811	6.3%	65.1%
Latino/a	8,490	5.0%	54.4%
Asian	16,261	9.5%	56.7%
American Indian / Alaska Native	846	**0.5%**	54.5%
Native Hawaiian / Pacific Islander	314	**0.3%**	51.9%
2 or more races	1,448	0.9%	55.4%
Race unknown	11,852	7.0%	50.9%
Non-resident student	19,491	11.4%	38.7%

Source: Gaquin and Dunn 2015

Table 9.2. *Full-Time Faculty in Degree-Granting Institutions (U.S.), 2011*

	Total	Professor	Associate Professor	Assistant Professor	Instructor	Lecturer	Other Faculty
Total	**761,619** (100%)	**181,508** (23.8%)	**155,200** (20.4%)	**174,045** (22.9%)	**109,054** (14.3%)	**34,477** (4.5%)	**107,335** (14.1%)
White	563,689 (74.0%)	150,334 (82.8%)	119,371 (76.9%)	118,014 (67.8%)	80,703 (74.0%)	25,823 (74.9%)	69,444 (64.7%)
Black	41,649 (5.5%)	6,517 (3.6%)	8,695 (5.6%)	10,994 (6.3%)	8,600 (7.9%)	1,688 (4.9%)	5,155 (4.8%)
Latino/a (Hispanic)	31,331 (4.1%)	5,180 (2.9%)	6,143 (4.0%)	7,428 (4.3%)	6,906 (6.3%)	1,773 (5.1%)	3,901 (3.6%)
Asian	65,438 (8.6%)	14,425 (7.9%)	14,129 (9.1%)	19,443 (11.2%)	5,449 (5.0%)	2,421 (7.0%)	9,571 (8.9%)
Pacific Islanders	1,449 (0.2%)	221 (0.1%)	280 (0.2%)	379 (0.2%)	359 (0.3%)	35 (0.1%)	175 (0.2%)
American Indian / Alaska Native	3,529 (**0.5%**)	589 (0.3%)	597 (0.4%)	701 (0.4%)	981 (0.9%)	135 (0.4%)	526 (0.5%)
2 or more races	4,121 (0.5%)	656 (0.4%)	804 (0.5%)	1,043 (0.6%)	865 (0.8%)	210 (0.6%)	543 (0.5%)
Race unknown	17,000 (2.2%)	2,202 (1.2%)	2,477 (1.6%)	4,926 (2.8%)	3,263 (3.0%)	849 (2.5%)	3,283 (3.1%)
Non-resident worker	33,413 (4.4%)	1,384 (0.8%)	2,704 (1.7%)	11,117 (6.4%)	1,928 (1.8%)	1,543 (4.5%)	14,737 (13.7%)

Source: National Center for Education Statistics 2012

Hunger Games: Academic Edition

The pressure on Indigenous people and people of colour to get into and stay in the academy is immense—even when it does not seem that great once we are finally in. From the tables above (even though the real numbers may cause us to pause), we can observe that there have been some small gains in increasing the diversity of university faculties over the past decade. However, I think it is crucial to point out that these small gains in faculty of colour have coincided with the increased neoliberalization of the university. Insofar as neoliberalization is motivated by (and experienced by faculty as) the lack of trust of faculty, the coincidence may actually be the rationale: as faculty have become more diverse, we have been surveilled more intensely.

Alongside the politics of evidence, Indigenous scholars and scholars of colour are kept in line through a politics of civility, which came into full view with the firing of Steven Salaita from the University of Illinois at Urbana-Champaign after he critiqued Israel's deadly actions against Palestinians in 2014. In June 2015, a Black woman scholar, Zandria F. Robinson, became the target of trolling on Twitter by racist conservatives who were angered by her posts on the Confederate flag. This led to a false Twitter rumour that Robinson had been subsequently fired by her employer, the University of Memphis, a rumour sparked by the University's own tweet, which read, "Zandria Robinson is no longer employed by the University of Memphis."

Within an hour or so, Dr. Robinson used Twitter to share that she had not been fired but had taken another position at Rhodes College. Rhodes College, in contrast to Robinson's former institution, issued a pitch-perfect statement, a great example of a university having a professor's back, praising her extensive scholarship for bringing "clarity and context to the sound bite world of social media" (quoted in Grollman 2015).

Dr. Robinson then used her blog platform to describe her reasons for leaving the University of Memphis. The entire blog post, titled "Zeezus does the firing 'round hurr," is one of the most important critiques of neoliberal universities I have ever read. She described the professional climate as follows:

> Amongst other things, wages were low, salary compression was high, the gender wage gap was atrocious, and we were expected to produce and do more with much less. In short, we were supposed to research like a Research I, teach like a liberal arts college, and serve like Serena. A new administration came in and threatened us with increased teaching loads and a new funding model that

would pit departments against one another for resources. MA programs, like the one that made me and so many other good students, were seen as a drain on resources unless students were paying out of pocket. Budgets were cut. One time it was seriously suggested that we give up telephones in our offices and talk to students via Skype to save money. It was Hunger Games: Academic Edition. (Robinson 2015)

"Hunger Games: Academic Edition" resonates so strongly with several of my former academic workplaces, especially with regard to treatment of faculty of colour and support for Black studies and Indigenous studies programs. Scholars who study the trends in higher education that have produced these hunger games credit the expansion of administrative staff, the bulging salaries of top-level administrators, and the downloading of state budget crunches onto departments. Yet, to link this to my previous point about universities' simultaneous attempts to diversify, I argue that we need to see the neoliberalization and privatization of the university as an extension of its settler colonial imperatives. Thus, I think it is important to consider these two processes—the remaking of the university into Hunger Games: Academic Edition and the diversification of university faculty as co-constituting processes.

For these reasons, in the remainder of this chapter, I want to think about the labour conditions for Indigenous faculty and faculty of colour alongside what I see as the bigger social science context for some communities—particularly Indigenous, ghettoized, and Orientalized communities—who are overcoded, that is, simultaneously hyper-surveilled and invisibilized/made invisible by the state, by police, and by social science research (Tuck and Yang 2014a; see also Smith 1999; Kelley 1997; Said 1978). Though people have been overstudied, the promised benefits of participating in social science research have been slow to accumulate (Tuck 2009).

Theories of Change in Academic Research

Over the past ten years, I have been asking questions about whether research: Is research really the intervention that is needed? Is research going to make it better or worse? Is the research going to do what we think it will do? If we need it to do something specific, is it still research? Do we really need research, or do we need organizing?

I have also been asking questions about whither research: Why are these the questions that we need to ask in this place? What questions have been asked before, and how satisfying were the answers? What is the history of inquiry in this place? What research crimes have been done here, and what forms of knowing have been dismissed? What questions need to be asked here, even if they cannot be answered through research?

The context of these questions is one in which stories of pain are highly valued in social science research. That is, the research stories that are considered most compelling, considered most authentic in social science research, are stories of pain and humiliation. Reporting on that pain with detailed qualitative data and in people's "real voices" is supposed to yield needed material or political resources; this is the prominent but unreliable theory of change in the academy. Of course, settler colonialism, other colonial configurations, white supremacy, heteropatriarchy, and the pursuit of wealth by some at the expense of others have indeed caused pain in the lives of real people, which deserves scrutiny and exposure. It is important that we put settler state violence under scrutiny—too many Indigenous women are murdered and missing, and too many Black women are killed in police custody. This, of course, is part of the configuration of settler colonialism that requires Indigenous erasure and anti-blackness and containment.

In related writing (Tuck and Yang 2014a), K. Wayne Yang and I presented three axioms of social science research that ground our analysis of the need for refusal to inquiry as invasion. The axioms are:

1. *The subaltern can speak but is only invited to speak her/our pain.* Drawing from bell hooks's (1990) observation that the academy fetishizes stories of the violated, we note that what passes for subaltern "voice" in research is a commodities market for pain narratives: "No need to hear your voice. Only tell me about your pain. I want to know your story" (343).

2. *There are some forms of knowledge that the academy does not deserve.* This axiom is the crux of refusal. The university is not universal; rather, it is a colonial collector of knowledge as another form of territory. There are stories and experiences that already have their own place, and placing them in the academy is removal, not respect.

3. *Research may not be the intervention that is needed.* This axiom challenges the latent theory of change that research—more academic

knowing—will somehow innately contribute to the improvement of
tribes, communities, youth, schools, etc.

Though Yang and I have taken these axioms in other directions in other
writings (2014a; 2014b), in this chapter my reason for bringing them to the
fore is to point to the ways that research relies on unexpressed and often
unconsidered theories of change. I have to note that I am somewhat fixated
on theories of change—many of my writings over the years have tried to
draw attention to the often-overlooked significance of theories of change in
social science research.

Theories of change may be hidden, but they are at work in all social science research, and likely all research. The theory of change, even if implicit,
will have implications for the directions a project takes, how it begins and
where it ends, who a project is responsible to, speaking to, and speaking for.
The theory of change shapes how we think things are known, what counts
as evidence, and what argumentation style will convince those we want to
convince. The ethical stance of a project is operationalized by its theory of
change. A theory of change determines what is considered data, what is considered a finding, and what we share and what we refuse to circulate.

Muscogee scholar Daniel Wildcat (2001) writes that his collaborative
writings with Dakota philosopher Vine Deloria Jr. on power and place were
concerned with the question, "How shall we live?" This question, *how shall
we live?* is the driving question of my concerns with theories of change; the
need for justice will outlast my years, and I have children in this world. I am
a mother, and I need time to bathe my children, to care for them, and help
them grow. My attention to theories of change also intensifies during times
of grief, like when my father died suddenly several years ago, or when a close
mentor of mine passed away. The only way I can talk myself out of grief is
to say to myself that life is long, life is long, even when there is not enough
evidence that it is. *How shall we live?* How shall I spend my time when I am
not bathing my children?

The question of how we shall live becomes even more striking in the face
of almost certain climate-change-driven collapse of some of the human environments around the world. Whether through the rising of water tables, fires
spreading, ice caps melting, air saturated with toxins, and wars waged only for
oil, the question of how we shall live has an urgency in the Anthropocene. As
an aside, this too should be linked to the drive for productivity—universities
are now setting the dual aims of shrinking footprints and increasing (faculty)
productivity, not willing to see how those two goals materially compete.

I am using the words "theory of change" to refer to beliefs or assumptions about how social change happens, is prompted, or is influenced. Much time and human energy is invested in various political activities—but how is it that change really happens? This is a question that communities and individuals may never ask themselves. I am interested in this question for its pedagogical implications, not as a prescriptive. I do not think the point of the question is to find the singular best answer but, instead, to have the conversation, to really have it, together, in all of its mired contestations.

Indigenous intellectuals and post-structuralists assert that change is inevitable, constant, but what is the role of human agency in such accounts of change, or is there no role? In North America, many people believe that social change is achieved through social movements, but what is it about social movements that yields change? What does it mean that social movements take different shapes in different nation-states, comparing the history of social movements in North America to Māori movements in New Zealand, for example? Others emphasize the importance of paradigm shifts and breaks, but, invoking an image of a surfer paddling out, how might one spend her time while waiting for the next set of breaks to accumulate?

Documenting Damage Is a Theory of Change

In some of my earlier work (Tuck 2009), I was intent on developing a critique of damage-centred research. Documenting damage is among the most common theories of change in social science. It is a theory of change that mimics the legal system. It is a teleological theory of change that places the Western world and neoliberal ideology at the finish line of societal evolution. It is a colonial theory of change, because it locates power and control outside of communities and requires them to appeal to the logics of the state to get piecemeal gains (though, ironically, as Signithia Fordham has observed, moral arguments are rarely effective with the neoliberal state or other authorities [personal communication]).

It is a powerful idea to think of all of us as litigators, putting the world on trial, but *does it actually work*? Do the material and political wins come through? And, most importantly, are the meagre wins worth the long-term costs of *thinking of ourselves as damaged* (Tuck 2009)?

When the wins do not come through, researchers focus more intently on the effectiveness of the demonstration (legitimation, validity), but not on the flawed theory of change. *The theory of change is flawed because it is a colonial theory of change that assumes that it is outsiders, not communities, who hold power to make changes.* Further, it assumes that those outsider power people behave as a judge or jury behaves, and can be convinced by strong arguments and evidence to give up power or resources.

Documenting damage as a theory of change pivots on humanizing the oppressed, or providing evidence of humanity in the face and force of oppression. In *Toward a Global Idea of Race*, Denise da Silva (2007) turns the proposition of humanizing upside down. Da Silva explains that the Western subject is entirely conferred through the exercising of power over *affectable* others. The Western subject exercises power over others, and others cannot exercise power over it. Others are affected by the power of the Western subject but cannot exercise power. This produces a dilemma for the Western subject—an anxiety by which affectability is a contagion. The Western subject must make itself separate from the others and their affectability—separate in both time and space. This is Othering and separating a global project of racialization—the co-production of the West, and the subject as located in the West. The Western subject is separated from the Other temporally through the teleology of modernity.

For da Silva, the conferring of human and humanity has been/is always already a *racial* project. To be human is to exercise power over those made Other in this self same process. The human is made universal, and the Other always particular, always teeming, always yearning.

Da Silva observes that this generates two important problems with regard to humanization as a process of liberation. First, the project of liberation is tied to becoming human, which is always constructed as exercising power over others. The second is that the affectable others must presume that by demonstrating their worthiness, they might be recognized as human.

This notion of being human doesn't pop out of nowhere; it is tied to a long-standing ordering of life. Sylvia Wynter asks,

> How are we not to think, after Adam Smith and the Scottish School of the Enlightenment, that all human societies are not teleologically determined with respect to their successive modes of economic production that determine who they are? How are we not to think in terms of an ostensibly universal human history, that itself has been identified as one in which all human societies, without exception, must law-likely move from hunter-gatherer, to pastoral, to agricultural modes of material provisioning, to one based on a manufacturing economy? Therefore,

how are we not to think in the same correlated terms of the teleologically determined hegemony of the bios (i.e., the material) aspect of our being human? (Wynter quoted in McKittrick 2014, 40)

Documenting damage (Tuck 2009) is about demonstrating worthiness to be recognized as human within a framing of humanity that requires the oppression of others. In this construction of power and humanity, power is scarce, there are limited amounts of it, and it is evident only in wielding it above others. This is what I mean when I say that documenting damage relies on colonial understandings of power and change—power is concentrated, scarce, and always external to the colonized.

At the risk of bruising friendships, I also ask that we think fully about theories of change that rely on raising awareness or raising visibility. This theory of change assumes that people are unaware of an injustice or issue or illness or social calamity—and that in making them more aware, we ready them to take appropriate action. It is a theory of pre-change. It assumes that people will generally do the right thing with the right information. It anticipates that the reason for inaction thus far is missing information, or lack of depth of understanding of the significance of need.

Raising awareness is a cousin theory of change to documenting damage—both often rely on circulating narratives and tropes of the mutilated body, the broken spirit, the flooded neighbourhood. Images of destruction compete for dollars on Facebook, to wrench the most sympathy for donations, for charity, for compassion, for hashtag solidarity, for newsworthiness, for value, for mattering. There is no relationship between the evocativeness of the photograph and the amount of the donation that goes to those in need. There is no relationship between the story of loss and the supplies that come.

So much of what we do to compel change relies on raising awareness. *But what if we—as communities, as collectives—were to disbelieve awareness as change? What if we, as Indigenous peoples, as people of colour, as disenfranchised peoples, believed that our own awareness, our own knowing, is enough to make change? What if we did not wait for others to also know but are inspired by our own knowing? What if we hold true that we are the ones who need to know, and not others? What if we believe that we are the ones who can make change, and that others are not more powerful than us to effect change?* These are radical questions that throb at what gets taken for granted as the work of social justice, of organizing, of public scholarship.

In contrast to damage, desire-based research (Tuck 2009) understands power as diffuse, as abundant, as connective and relational. Dakota philosopher Vine Deloria Jr. describes power as the living energy that inhabits and composes the universe. Muscogee scholar Daniel Wildcat, writing about Deloria's philosophies of power, explains that his concept of power is nonquantifiable. "Power is a qualitative dimension shaping our thoughts, desires, habits, and actions that operates to a great extent without us thinking about it" (Deloria and Wildcat 2001, 140). For Deloria, power is amorphous, it takes many forms, it is diffuse, it surrounds us as an atmosphere of influences. "Power is quite literally flowing around and into us" (Deloria and Wildcat 2001, 140).

I read this as having a great deal in common with materialist theories of power and change that come from Gilles Deleuze and Félix Guattari in *A Thousand Plateaus*. The big departure between Deleuze and Guattari and Deloria is that Deloria contends that if we are "properly attentive, power can be used by us" (quoted in Deloria and Wildcat 2001, 140). For Deloria, power is social, it is agentic.

Imagining Other Theories of Change

In this neoliberal, settler, colonial moment, it can be so difficult to imagine other theories of change. It requires a sort of mental yoga to even remember other theories of change. In our book, *Youth Resistance Research and Theories of Change*, Wayne Yang and I (2014c) created a list of other popular theories of change and I can never remember what was on the list. I have to look at the list to remember, because raising awareness and documenting damage figure so prominently in my imagination.

Here is the list we made, but I did have to look back at our book to remember: boycotts, psychotherapy, peace (Nhat Hanh 1989), revenge (Tuck and Ree 2013), anarchy, prayer, doing nothing.

In the remainder of this chapter, I turn to three examples of theories of change that step outside of documenting damage. These are also discussed in my work with Marcia McKenzie (Tuck and McKenzie 2015) as examples of research in which place and land are engaged meaningfully. I see these as compelling theories of compelling change: all three are authored by Indigenous women, all three consider change and land materially, and all three move within Indigenous understandings of power and place. I offer them to contest the colonial theories of change that overdetermine what counts as knowing and action in the social sciences, and to describe closely a selection of theories of change that intend to bring about the rematriation of Indigenous land and life. These are theories of change that can help those of us working in the academy to bite the university that feeds us.

(Re)mapping

The first theory of change is what Seneca scholar Mishuana Goeman has called (re)mapping. (Re)mapping is a Native feminist theory of change that cannot be detached from material land. Its goal is to unsettle imperial and colonial geographies by refuting how those geographies organize land, bodies, and social and political landscapes (Goeman 2013, 3). Recognizing that colonial geographies "enframe" state borders, assert control over state populations, and overdetermine action and contestation, (re)mapping is a refusal of the order by disorder exerted on Indigenous life and land. (Re)mapping is

> the labor Native authors and the communities they write within and about undertake in the simultaneously metaphoric and material capacities of map making, to generate new possibilities. The framing of "re" within parenthesis [sic] connotes the fact that in (re)mapping, Native women employ traditional and new tribal stores as a means of continuation or what Gerald Vizenor aptly calls stories of survivance. (Goeman 2013, 3)

Goeman's scribing of (re)mapping, with its use of parentheses, is deliberate, a pointed way to sidestepping the assumption that the past is pure, or can be brought forth into the present. Goeman's project is to gather together exemplars of how Indigenous women have defined Indigeneity, their communities, and themselves through challenges to colonial spatial order, especially through literary mappings. Goeman does this not to embark upon a (problematic) utopian project of land recovery via "pure ideas of Indigeneity" layered atop of colonial mappings. Even if Indigenous boundaries were materially and legally recognized, Goeman does not believe that this alone would sufficiently unsettle colonialism. Goeman recognizes that some element of a recovery project may be expected of a (re)mapping method:

> Recovery has a certain saliency in Native American studies; it is appealing to people who have been dispossessed materially and culturally. I contend, however, that it is also our responsibility to interrogate our ever-changing Native epistemologies that frame

our understanding of land and our relationships to it and to other peoples. In this vein, (re)mapping is not just about regaining that which was lost and returning to an original and pure point in history, but instead understanding the processes that have defined our current spatialities in order to sustain vibrant Native futures. (2013, 3)

The task is not to recover a static past but to "acknowledge the power of Native epistemologies in defining our moves toward spatial decolonization" (Goeman 2013, 4).

Mapping Place-Worlds and Place-Making
A second compelling theory of compelling change comes from Abenaki author Lisa Brooks. Brooks provides an etymology of an Abenaki word that has roots in words meaning to draw, write, and map (2008, xxi). *Awikhigawôgan* is at the centre of the theory of change that Brooks creates and enacts in her book, *The Common Pot*. This is a method that maps "how Native people in the northeast used writing as an instrument to reclaim lands and reconstruct communities, but also a mapping of the *instrumental* activity of writing, its role in the rememberment of a fragmented world" (Brooks 2008, xxii).

Brooks's employment of "place-worlds" and "place-making" echoes Keith Basso's emphasis that within Indigenous world views, the *where* of events matters as much as the *what* and the consequences of the events themselves. The building of place-worlds is collective, creative, and generative. In building place-worlds, place-making is also a revisionary act, a re-memory act, in which multiple pasts co-mingle and compete for resonance toward multiple futures. Keith Basso writes that building and sharing place-worlds

is not only a means of reviving former times, but also of *revising* them, a means of exploring not merely how things might have been but also how, just possibly, they might have been different from what others have supposed. Augmenting and enhancing conceptions of the past, innovative place-worlds change these conceptions as well. (1996, 6)

In this theory of change, place and land are not abstractions. Brooks spent much time walking the land and paddling the waterways that are featured in her book, sometimes alone, other times with friends with whom she would share and swap place-making stories. "To be clear," Brooks writes, "what I am talking about here is not an abstraction, a theorizing about a conceptual category called 'land,' or 'nature,' but a physical, actual, material relationship to an 'ecosystem present in a definable place'" (2008, xxiv).

The chapters in *The Common Pot* are an elaboration of Brooks's *Awikhigawôgan* theory of change. Each chapter begins with an *awikhigan*, a communicative device of some sort—a map, a photograph (of a shell, a wampum belt or string), a birch bark scroll, a portrait, a letter—which then spills, floods, into the place-world from which it came forth and has most meaning. The chapters in the book do not have a chronological progression but instead progress with regard to what the *awikhigan* seeks to accomplish or communicate, and how this relates to the one before and after it. Brooks calls this a stylistic progression, but what it serves to do is provide a narrative that works much more like space than time. It begins somewhere, not because it happened first but because it helps to make sense of what takes place beside it. It is its own orientation. Brooks even says, "I admit that I mean to plunk readers right in the middle of the territory and provide a map to enable navigation. (If you feel a bit disoriented, that's okay. You'll find your way. Use the maps)" (2008, xi).

Shell Mound Work

In 1999, Chochenyo Ohlone community organizer Corrina Gould co-founded a community organization in Oakland called Indian People Organizing for Change (IPOC). Shell mounds have been mischaracterized by geographic historians as middens—large pre-colonial piles of discarded seashells that have been located throughout the North American continent. The shell mounds found throughout the traditional homeland of Ohlone peoples (the San Francisco Bay Area) are more than heaps of discarded shells; they are the burial grounds of their ancestors.

One of the largest shell mounds was at the site of the proposed Emeryville Mall. It was more than sixty feet high and 350 feet in diameter, so large that it was marked on an 1852 Coast Survey Map. Upon learning about the plans to place a shopping mall on the site, Gould and IPOC petitioned developers to halt their plans and instead create a suitable memorial to Ohlone peoples at the shell mound. The developers refused and went ahead with their plans, digging up hundreds of remains in the process. Many remains were simply hauled off to waste dumps, with no notification to Ohlone peoples ("Transcript & Audio of Corrina Gould"). In particular, they excavated a site where infants and children were buried in order to install movie theatres and a parking garage (Gould 2012).

Every year, IPOC organizes a protest on Black Friday (the day after Thanksgiving in the United States, a big day for shopping) to educate shoppers on their participation in the continued mistreatment of sacred grounds. Soon after, Gould and IPOC also began organizing shell mound walks to educate themselves, other Ohlone, Bay Miwok, and Indigenous peoples, and allies about the shell mounds, their locations, and their continued presence even beneath the asphalt, shopping centres, and condominiums. The first time they did a shell mound walk, they used Nelson's 1909 map of the 425 shell mounds and did a three-week route of 280 miles, from Sogorea Te to San Jose, praying and learning all the way. People from all over the world, who were moved to learn and commemorate the land and the ancestors, joined them. They have completed this walk numerous times, often making different tracings across the land to visit and acknowledge each site. They also now organize shorter walks—perhaps visiting several sites in just one city—to pray and visit the shell mounds now covered by buildings, streets, and parking lots.

This shell mound work is an example of public science, meaning it seeks to be accountable to real people, to tangible relationships, and it disbelieves the permanence of the settler-colonial nation-state.

The List of Theories of Change on My Cellphone
I want theories of change that are not deferments—of time, of place, of responsibility and power. I want us to figure out which parts of the university can be made useful for communities, and to figure out how to dismantle the parts that are not.

Each of the theories of change in the previous section exposes the matrices of settler colonialism but almost as a side project. The main energy is dedicated to providing multiple points of entry, and multiple opportunities to draw meaning, value, and action from the work. These theories of change are anticipatory and proactive (not reactive). They interrupt existing knowledge hierarchies, taking seriously the expertise that is derived of lived experience. They require humility and vulnerability, contestation and creative production. They make space to speak what is otherwise silenced, make transparent that which is otherwise concealed, and make meaningful that which is otherwise forgotten or devalued. There is dignity in the work of creating a space for ourselves, the kind of space that has been systematically denied to us (see also Tuck and Guishard 2013, 20).

A few pages ago, I shared a list of theories of change that I cannot remember. I cannot remember them because remembering other understandings of power and change can be so difficult. I also cannot remember them because they are not *my* theories of change. Lately, I have begun to keep a list of theories of change in my cellphone so I can remember something more meaningful than raising awareness. Something more material than raising consciousness. Something more to the touch than visibility. My list of compelling theories of change: haunting, billboards, visitations, Maroon societies, decolonization, revenge, mattering.

Notes

1   See Tuck and Guishard (2013) for a review of other texts that have told these histories.

References

Ahmed, S. 2012. *On Being Included: Racism and Diversity in Institutional Life.* Durham, NC: Duke University Press.
Basso, K. H. 1996. *Wisdom Sits in Places: Landscape and Language among the Western Apache.* Albuquerque: University of New Mexico Press.
Brooks, L. 2008. *The Common Pot: The Recovery of Native Space in the Northeast.* Minneapolis: University of Minnesota Press.
da Silva, D. F. 2007. *Toward a Global Idea of Race.* Minneapolis: University of Minnesota Press.
Deleuze, G., and F. Guattari. 1988. *A Thousand Plateaus: Capitalism and Schizophrenia.* London: Bloomsbury Publishing.
Deloria Jr., V., and D. R. Wildcat. 2001. *Power and Place: Indian Education in America.* Goldon, CO: Fulcrum Publishing.
Gaquin, D. A., and G. W. Dunn, eds. 2015. *The Almanac of Higher Education 2014–15.* Lanham, MD: Bernan Press.
Goeman, M. 2013. *Mark My Words: Native Women Mapping Our Nations.* Minneapolis: University of Minnesota Press.
Gould, C. 2012. "An Update for Supporters and Friends of Sogorea Te." January 7. http://protectsogoreate.org/2012/update-letter/.
Grollman, E. A. 2015. "Scholars Under Attack." *Inside Higher Education,* July 9. https://www.insidehighered.com/advice/2015/07/09/essay-how-support-scholars-under-attack.
hooks, b. 1990. *Yearning: Race, Gender, and Cultural Politics.* Boston: South End Press.
Kelley, R. 1997. *Yo' Mama's Disfunktiona: Fighting the Cultural Wars in Urban America.* Boston: Beacon Press.

McKittrick, K., ed. 2014. *Sylvia Wynter: On Being Human as Praxis*. Durham, NC: Duke University Press.

National Center for Education Statistics. 2012. *Digest of Education Statistics, 2012*. Washington, DC: National Center for Education Statistics, Institute of Education Sciences, U.S. Department of Education.

Nhat Hanh, T. 1989. *The Moon Bamboo*. Berkeley CA: Parallax Press.

Robinson, Z. F. 2015. "Zeezus Does the Firing 'Round Hurr." *New South Negress* [blog]. http://newsouthnegress.com/zeezusyear/.

Said, E. W. 1978. *Orientalism*. New York: Pantheon Books.

Smith, L. T. 1999. *Decolonizing Methodologies: Research and Indigenous Peoples*. London: Zed Books.

Spillers, H. 2003. *Black and White in Color: Essays on American Literature and Culture*. Chicago: University of Chicago Press.

"Transcript & Audio of Corrina Gould in San Francisco, May 10, 2011." Protect Sogorea Te. http://protectsogoreate.org/2011/corrina-gould-may-10/.

Tuck, E. 2009. "Suspending Damage: A Letter to Communities." *Harvard Educational Review* 75(3): 409–27.

Tuck, E., and C. Ree. 2013. "A Glossary of Haunting." In *Handbook of Autoethnography*, edited by S. Holman Jones, T. E. Adams, and C. Ellis, 639–58. Walnut Creek, CA: Left Coast Press.

Tuck, E., and K. W. Yang. 2012. "Decolonization Is Not a Metaphor." *Decolonization: Indigeneity, Education and Society* 1(1): 1–40.

———. 2014a. "R-Words: Refusing Research." In *Humanizing Research: Decolonizing Qualitative Inquiry with Youth and Communities*, edited by D. Paris and M. T. Winn, 223–48. Los Angeles: Sage Publications.

———. 2014b. "Unbecoming Claims: Pedagogies of Refusal in Qualitative Research." *Qualitative Inquiry* 20: 811–18.

Tuck, E., and K. W. Yang, eds. 2014c. *Youth Resistance Research and Theories of Change*. New York: Routledge.

Tuck, E., and M. Guishard. 2013. "Uncollapsing Ethics: Racialized Sciencism, Settler Coloniality, and an Ethical Framework of Decolonial Participatory Action Research." In *Challenging Status Quo Retrenchment: New Directions in Critical Qualitative Research*, edited by T. M. Kress, C. S. Malott, and B. J. Portfilio, 3–27. Charlotte, NC: Information Age Publishing.

Tuck, E., and M. McKenzie. 2015. "Relational Validity and the 'Where' of Inquiry: Place and Land in Qualitative Research." *Qualitative Inquiry*. doi:10.1177/1077800414563809.

Vizenor, G. R. 1999. *Manifest Manners: Narratives on Postindian Survivance*. Winnipeg: Bison Books.

Walcott, R. 2003. *Black Like Who? Writing Black Canada*. Toronto: Insomniac Press.

Wilderson, F. 2010. *Red, White, and Black: Cinema and the Structure of U.S. Antagonisms*. Durham, NC: Duke University Press.

Wolfe, P. 1999. *Settler Colonialism and the Transformation of Anthropology: The Politics and Poetics of an Ethnographic Event*. New York: Cassell.

CHAPTER 10

REFUSING THE UNIVERSITY

Sandy Grande

What does it mean to refuse a passport—what some consider to be a gift or a right, the freedom of mobility and residency? What does it mean to say no to these things, or to wait until your terms have been met for agreement, for a reversal of recognition, or a conferral of rights? What happens when we refuse what all the (presumably) "sensible" people perceive as good things? What does this refusal do to politics, to sense, to reason? When we add Indigenous peoples to this question, the assumptions and histories that structure what is perceived to be "good" (and utilitarian goods themselves) shift...(refusal) may seem reasoned, sensible, and in fact deeply correct. Indeed, from this perspective, we see that a good is not a good for everyone.

—Audra Simpson, *Mohawk Interruptus*

Can we have...another sense of what is owed that does not presume a nexus of activities like recognition and acknowledgement, payment and gratitude. Can debt "become a principle of elaboration?"

—Stefano Harney and Fred Moten, *The Undercommons*

n September 2015, animated by the murders of Eric Garner, Sandra Bland, Tamir Rice, and others,[1] student protesters at the University of Missouri (re)cast a spotlight on the systemic and structural racism within their institution.[2] In the wake of the Mizzou protests, students at eighty other colleges and universities also took action, issuing demands to their respective administrations. Collectively, these actions registered students' shared refusal to absorb the high cost of institutional racism upon their bodies. Together, the youth of #BlackLivesMatter and #ConcernedStudent1950 led a co-resistance movement that disabused the nation of its post-racial fantasy, exposing the apparatuses of state violence and institutional negligence predicated upon anti-Black racism and white supremacy.

In his incisive essay "Black Study, Black Struggle" (2016), Robin Kelley considers the genealogy of political protest and its relationship to Black studies, reminding us that the incidence of "fires" spreading from street and campus echoes a historical pattern. He writes, "The campus revolts of the 1960s for example, *followed* the Harlem and Watts rebellions, the freedom movement in the South, and the rise of militant organizations in the cities." Beyond this similarity, Kelley's essay focuses on the dissonances between student uprisings then and now. In particular, he marks the tension between "reform and revolution, between desiring to belong and rejecting the university as a cog in the neoliberal order." More specifically, he laments the general thrust of current students' demands to make the university "more hospitable for Black students" (e.g., greater diversity, inclusion, safety, affordability). While, given the current context, he understands why students seek inclusion, recognition, and belonging, he also cautions against "granting the university so much authority." As such, Kelley's essay reads as a kind of radical tough-love letter in which he exhorts student activists to think about what it means, "to seek love from an institution incapable of loving them." Instead, he asks them to think beyond the desire for institutional *recognition* and toward a self-radicalizing project: to *refuse* "the university-as-such." Kelley offers the Mississippi Freedom Schools and Fred Moten and Stefano Harney's (2004) notion of the undercommons as models of this refusal, and for building autonomous and subversive spaces of learning.[3] In essence, he suggests that "reform" of the university is untenable, and that such efforts tacitly, if unintentionally, perpetuate the very racist structures they fight.

One of the most vibrant analytical spaces within critical Indigenous studies concerns theorizations of both *recognition* and *refusal* in relation to Indigenous-state politics.[4] Drawing upon a wide range of theorists (e.g., Franz Fanon, Elizabeth Povinelli, Charles Taylor), scholars of critical Indigenous studies (CIS)[5] critique recognition-based politics, their rootedness in liberal theories of justice, and legitimation of the state as the arbiter of recognition and thus of colonialist relations of domination. In response, CIS scholars, such as Audra Simpson and Glen Coulthard, posit a politics of refusal that not only actively "negates that which negates" Indigenous peoples but, in so doing, functions as an act of Indigenous affirmation. While Kelley does not frame his analysis around the constructs of *recognition* and *refusal* per se, there is common conceptual ground, particularly in the shared rejection of liberal theories of justice that privilege a respect for difference over critiques of power.

The differently structured but shared experience of Black and Indigenous peoples under settler colonialism, particularly as amplified by neoliberalism, urges renewed thinking about the relationship between anti- and decolonial struggles both in and outside the academy. I am particularly interested in examining the promissory relationship between the Black radical tradition and CIS, as both share a commitment to thinking beyond the liberal, capitalist, settler state and the university as one of its primary attendant institutions. In so doing, I am aware of the tensions and antagonisms produced by the specificities of Black and Native experience as produced through the history of white supremacist, settler logics. As noted by Patrick Wolfe (2006), Black and Native peoples have been racialized in ways that reflect their differentiated roles in the formation of society in the United States. Specifically, he argues that since enslaved Blacks augmented settler wealth, they were subject to an *expansive* racial taxonomy, codified in the "one-drop rule," whereby any amount of African ancestry made a person "Black" (i.e., more enslaved peoples = more settler wealth). Indigenous peoples, who impeded settler wealth by obstructing access to land, were instead subjected to a calculus of elimination, whereby increasing degrees of non-Indian blood or ancestry made one less "Indian" (i.e., fewer Indians = more settler wealth).

This originary calculus continues to structure Black and Native experience, producing particularities that reveal the limits and aporias of both settler colonial and race discourses. For instance, while Native peoples are racialized, race is not the primary analytic of Indigenous subjectivity nor is racism the main structure of domination; that would be settler colonialism. Moreover, while issues of Indigeneity are taken up within critical ethnic and American studies, both offer ill-fitting explanatory frameworks for Native peoples who are neither "ethnic" nor "American" but rather members of distinct tribal nations with complicated histories and relationships to citizenship and the nation-state. At the same time, the logic of anti-blackness troubles analyses of settler colonialism, calling into question the Indigenous/settler binary and the indiscriminant folding of the experience of "racial capture and enslavement into the subject position of settler" (Day 2015, 103). That said, current manifestations of anti-blackness also reveal the limits of liberal race discourses, suggesting the need to ground analyses in the broader logics of capital accumulation. The above tensions and intersections demonstrate the need for greater interchange, as well as raise the following questions:

- What kinds of solidarities can be developed among subaltern groups with a shared commitment to working beyond the imperatives of capital and the settler state?
- What are the critical distinctions between sovereignty and social justice projects, which is to say between those shaped by genocide, erasure, and dispossession and those by enslavement, exclusion, and oppression?
- What kinds of generative politics can be developed from the synergies among Black radical notions of abolition/fugitivity/liberation and Indigenous notions of refusal/resurgence/sovereignty?

While the above questions guide this inquiry, I am centrally interested in how they play out on the ground, particularly in the university setting. Specifically, I aim to build and expand upon Kelley's (2016) analysis by bringing it into conversation with critical Indigenous theories, deploying them both as a means of thinking through what it means to work "within, against, and beyond the university-as-such"—to, in effect, *refuse the university*.

To be clear, this analysis turns upon a theorization of the academy as an arm of the settler state—a space where the logics of elimination, capital accumulation, and dispossession are reconstituted—which is distinct from other frameworks that situate and critique the academy as fundamentally neoliberal, racist, Eurocentric, and/or patriarchal. The hope is that such a shift opens up even more possibilities for reimagining relationships to and within the university. Finally, as I write in the immediate context of #BlackLivesMatter and #NoDAPL, I am moved to journey through Kelley's conceptual triumvirate—love, study, struggle—with even greater vigilance for places of refuge, points of co-resistance, and spaces for collective work.

Toward that end, I begin by articulating the particularities of settler colonialism and Native elimination and follow with an examination of liberal theories of justice as the underlying structure of recognition-based politics. Next, I discuss the academy as an arm of the settler state and the ways in which it refracts settler logics and the politics of recognition. In the final section, I examine emergent scholarship on the politics of refusal as a field of possibility for building co-resistance movements between Black radical, critical Indigenous, and other scholars committed to refusing the settler state and its attendant institutions.

The Particularities of Settler Colonialism and Native Elimination

In contrast to other forms of colonialism, "settler colonies were not primarily established to extract surplus value from indigenous labor" but rather premised upon the removal of Indigenous peoples from land as a precondition of settlement (Wolfe 1999, 1). Settlers, moreover, "sought to control space, resources, and people not only by occupying land but also by establishing an exclusionary private property regime and coercive labor systems, including chattel slavery to work the land, extract resources, and build infrastructure" (Glenn 2015, 54). Thus, while white supremacy, patriarchy, neoliberalism, and other technologies of domination may render the contours of settler colonialism more visible (and, in some ways, function as co-constitutive logics), a settler colonial framework represents a particular set of relations, one that originates with the theft of Indigenous land and the "remove to replace" logics that enable that theft (Wolfe 1999, 1). A logic that, in shorthand, Wolfe refers to as one of elimination (Wolfe 2006, 387).

As evidence of ongoing "Native elimination," consider the following: (1) that in this moment of Black Lives Matter, the ongoing police violence against Indigenous peoples (killed at a higher rate than any other group)[6] has been virtually absent from the public discourse; (2) that Rexdale Henry, Sarah Lee Circle Bear, Paul Castaway, Allen Locke, Joy Ann Sherman, Christina Tahhahwah, Myles Roughsurface, and Naverone Christian Landon Woods were all killed by police around the time of the student protests but rarely added to the running list of victims; (3) that in states with large American Indian populations, police target vehicles with license plates that identify the drivers as reservation residents; (4) that in Canada, Indigenous peoples, particularly those who live in the more rural western provinces, suffer higher rates of police stops, profiling, incarceration, sentencing, and killings;[7] and (5) while the plight of missing and murdered Indigenous women in Canada has reached epidemic proportions—estimated at four thousand over the last thirty years—it continues to receive limited attention.[8] As a result, Native peoples across the continent have also taken to the streets, with the #IdleNoMore, #AmINext, and #NativeLivesMatter movements leading the way.

If nothing else, the combined death tolls of Native and Black peoples not only illustrate how, five hundred years after settler invasion, Indians are still being eliminated but also that the "violence of slave-making" is ongoing (Wilderson 2010, 54). They also substantiate the profound insight of Patrick Wolfe's (2006) apothegm that settler colonialism is a *structure* and not an *event* (388). That is, it is not an event "temporally bound by the occurrence of invasion" but rather a "condition of possibility that remains formative while also changing over time," which is to say, a structure (Goldstein 2008, 835). This construction shifts current understanding of ongoing Black death and Native elimination from being anomalous—moments of disruption along an otherwise linear path of racial progress—to being endemic; a congenital feature of a state built upon the "entangled triad structure of settler-native-slave" (Tuck and Yang 2012, 1).

The structures of settler colonialism precipitate distinctive forms and modalities of Indigenous resistance. Struggle, in this context, is organized around *decolonization*—a political project that begins and ends with land and its return. As such, Tuck and Yang argue that struggles for decolonization are not simply distinct from social justice projects but rather are incommensurable. They write, "Decolonization (a verb) and decolonization (a noun) cannot easily be grafted on pre-existing discourses/frameworks, even if they are critical, even if they are anti-racist, even if they are justice frameworks" (Tuck and Yang 2012, 3).[9] According to the authors, the difference between *decolonial* and *critical, anti-racist, justice* frameworks is that the former seeks "a change in the order of the world" while the latter desires reconciliation:[10] the very nature of settler colonialism precludes reconciliation.

While the broader point—that decolonial and anti-racist projects turn upon different analyses of power—is well-taken, the more nuanced elements of each project are occluded by the rather blunt claim of incommensurability. If the aim is to create greater possibilities for co-resistance, it is important to consider the theories of justice underlying each project. More specifically, it is worth questioning whether the noted incommensurability between decolonization and other frameworks is, in part, more fundamentally underwritten by the distinction between liberal theories of justice as recognition and critical Indigenous theories of "justice" as refusal.[11] For example, while

Kelley's framework is decisively "anti-racist," he also critiques the limits of liberal race discourses and the politics of recognition, pointing instead to elements of refusal within the Black radical tradition. All of which suggests the need for closer examination of the relationship among liberal political theories, state formation, and the genealogy of recognition.

Liberal Theories of Justice and the Politics of Recognition

Historically, theories of recognition emerged alongside political processes undertaken in "transitional nation-states" (i.e., those "moving toward democracy" from a state of war), where demands for recognition—by oppressed and minoritized groups to the state—were levied as a means of ushering in that transition (Kymlicka and Bashir 2008, 3). Within this context, (state) recognition assumes many forms (e.g., truth and reconciliation commissions, reparations) that are generally elucidated through liberal discourses of apology, forgiveness, healing, trauma, and memory (6).[12] The overarching claim is that the recognition and affirmation of cultural difference must precede and/or serve as a precondition for establishing relations of equality, freedom, and justice.

More recently, recognition-based politics have surfaced in established democracies such as Australia, Canada, and the United States as increasing demands to reconcile Indigenous claims to nationhood and sovereignty have gained greater traction (Coulthard 2007, 438). This development in Indigenous politics has drawn renewed attention to some of the classic literature on recognition (e.g., Butler 1990; Fraser 1997; Honneth 1992, 1995; Kymlicka 1995; Taylor 1994). Though varied, these works made an important intervention in theories of identity and cultural difference, initiating a shift away from atomistic to dialogical models that underscore the ways in which identity formation does not occur in isolation but rather through complex relations of political recognition (Taylor 1994). In so doing, acts of recognition—of acknowledging and respecting the status, being, and rights of another—became integral to theories of justice. Stated differently, political theories of recognition help to expose the conditions of oppression that arise when individuals are denied the equitable grounds upon which to formulate healthy notions of self as a result of a given society's dominant and exclusionary patterns of interpretation and valuation (Baum 2004, 1073). Taylor, in particular, considers the significant impact of nonrecognition and misrecognition on marginalized peoples and their potential to produce crippling forms of self-hatred. As such, he argues that "due recognition is not just a courtesy we owe people. It is a vital human need" (Taylor 1994, 26).

As policies and politics of recognition have come to increasingly condition Indigenous-state relations, there has been a corollary increase in scholarship examining their impact. Indigenous scholars, in particular, have developed trenchant critiques of recognition and the underlying liberal theories of justice that fail to account for asymmetries of power. Coulthard (2014), for example, argues that while recognition brings much-needed attention to the role of misrecognition in reinforcing colonial domination, the breadth of power at play in colonial systems cannot be transcended through the mere institutionalizing of a liberal regime of mutual recognition. By leaving intact the state's power to serve as the sole arbiter of Indigenous recognition, Coulthard argues that recognition-based politics ultimately reproduce the very configurations of colonial power that Native peoples seek to transcend. Indeed, given that the state emerged through the criminal acts of genocide, land dispossession, and enslavement, and the legal fictions of "discovery" and "terra nullius," its own legitimacy is what should be at stake, not the sovereignty of Indigenous nations.[13]

That said, Coulthard (2014) acknowledges the deep significance of, and "psycho-affective attachment" to, the desire for recognition and the ways in which it is cultivated and internalized. Specifically, he points to Fanon's "painstaking" articulation of the multiple ways in which such feelings of "attachment" are cultivated among the colonized, particularly through the unequal exchange of institutionalized and interpersonal patterns of recognition between the colonial society and the marginalized. Sara Ahmed (2004) similarly theorizes the production of psychic forms of attachment or desire through what she terms the "affective economy,"[14] examining its function in the reconsolidation of the (neoliberal) nation-state. To clarify, the affective economy is one of the central mechanisms by which subjects become "invested emotionally, libidinally, and erotically" in the polity (Agathangelou, Bassichis, and Spira 2008, 122). In the context of Indigenous-state relations, Wolfe writes about "inducements" as a tool of the affective economy by which the desire for recognition has been cultivated. He writes, "From the treaty era onwards Indigenous peoples have been subjected to a recurrent cycle of inducements" extended in the form of allotments, citizenship, and tribal enrolment that have continuously served to entice Native peoples to "consent to their own dispossession" (Wolfe 2013, 259). But people who are held hostage are not simply making "choices"—adaptation while under threat of annihilation is nothing more than a ransom demand. Moreover, when recognition comes in the form of economic gain for individuals, Coulthard (2007) argues that it carries the potential for creating a new (Aboriginal) elite whose "thirst for profit" comes to "outweigh their ancestral obligations" (452).[15] This is how recognition confers elimination.

In the following section, I graft these critiques of the politics of state recognition onto Kelley's analyses of students' desire for institutional recognition. I am particularly interested in the ways in which such demands are also conditioned by and through liberal theories of justice that ultimately sustain relations of institutional oppression. I begin with a brief history of how the academy refracts settler logics and then move to a discussion of how such logics and history continue to be played out, particularly through the affective economy of desire.

The Settler Academy and the Politics of Recognition

Historically, the university functioned as the institutional nexus for the capitalist and religious missions of the settler state, mirroring its history of dispossession, enslavement, exclusion, forced assimilation, and integration. As noted by Craig Wilder (2014), author of *Ebony and Ivy: Race, Slavery, and the Troubled History of America's Universities*, the academy was both a "beneficiary and defender" of the same social and economic forces that "transformed West and Central Africa through the slave trade and devastated indigenous nations in the Americas" (2–3). He writes,

> American colleges were not innocent or passive beneficiaries of conquest and colonial slavery. The European invasion of the Americas and the modern slave trade pulled peoples throughout the Atlantic world into each others' lives, and colleges were among the colonial institutions that braided their histories and rendered their fates dependent and antagonistic. The academy never stood apart from American slavery—in fact it stood beside church and state as the third pillar of a civilization built on bondage. (Wilder 2014, 11)

Across the text, Wilder similarly registers (albeit unevenly) how the academy also never stood apart from the genocide and dispossession of Indigenous peoples, all of which illuminates the university's history as a long-time co-conspirator in perpetuating white supremacy.

Indeed, it was not until the dawn of the Civil Rights Movement that the underlying justification for institutional exclusion and segregation was broadly questioned as incompatible with the norms of liberal democracy. During this time, the university became one of the primary sites of struggle and social transformation. In "Black Study, Black Struggle," Kelley recounts the rich tradition of Black studies advanced through the "mass revolt" of "insurgent intellectuals" committed to the development of "fugitive spaces" not just outside but also in opposition to the Eurocentric university. He cites the works of James Baldwin, Ella Baker, Walter Rodney, Frantz Fanon, Angela Davis, Barbara Smith, C. L. R James, and Cedric Robinson, among others, as the "sources of social critique" that helped to inspire alternative spaces like the Mississippi Freedom Schools. The aim was not simply to offer a broader, more inclusive curriculum but rather to design one that examined power along the axes of race and class, developing "trenchant critiques of materialism" that challenged "the myth that the civil rights movement was just about claiming a place in mainstream society" (Kelley 2016). The desire, as articulated by Kelley, was not for "equal opportunity in a burning house" but, rather, "to build a new house."

But since the settler university can only "remove to replace," it was not long before the revolutionary and redistributive aims of Black radicalism were supplanted by and absorbed within the project of liberal pluralism, substituting the anti-capitalist critique with a politics of recognition as inclusion. So that now, the structures of settler logics render the demands of #ConcernedStudent1950 virtually illegible, except as expressed as the desire for more "intense inclusion" (Kelley 2016). As Kelley argues, while demands for safe spaces, greater diversity, mental health counselling, curricular representation, and renamed campus buildings are hardly inconsequential, they also have the potential to function as inducements, a "promise project" waged on a series of (non)promises made to those who remain outside of and excluded by the university (Agathangelou et al. 2008). Thus, just as recognition-based politics impede Indigenous struggles for decolonization, they also constrain efforts for a more radical vision for Black study and struggle within and against the university. In other words, the settler state has an array of strategies—recognition being one of them—to placate dispossessed people while evading any effort to change the underlying power structure.

Within the context of the liberal academy, discourses of recognition garner wide appeal, as they provide a means for neatly bracketing what are fundamentally complex and ongoing sets of power relations. That is, they mark a definitive endpoint to a history of wrongdoing, as well as a means for moving beyond that history (Corntassel and Holder 2008). Consider, for example, the growing wave of colleges and universities seeking to reconcile their involvement in the slave trade. The University of Alabama (in 2004), the University of Virginia (in 2007), and Emory University (in 2011) have all issued formal apologies. The University of North Carolina at Chapel Hill erected a memorial, Washington and Lee removed all its confederate flags, and the College of William and Mary launched an investigation into its history of complicity. After it came to public light that Georgetown University sold 272 enslaved men, women, and children (the youngest was two months old) in 1838 in order to avoid bankruptcy (sale proceeds are estimated at $3.3 million in today's dollars), university alumni helped launch the "Memory Project," an initiative dedicated to tracing and locating living descendants of those sold. In 2003, Brown University launched one of the most comprehensive projects that included a commissioned three-year study, an acknowledgement, a memorial, and an endowment for Providence city schools. Still, over ten years later, only 7.3 per cent of Brown's student body and 4 per cent of its faculty are African American. And no institution to date has offered reparations.

Despite (or because of?) its failure to restructure material conditions, recognition continues to serve as the dominant framework for addressing the persistence of structural racism. Just as it fails to address the dual structures of settler colonialism, it fails to address the interplay between the affective economy and material conditions of institutional racism. And, thus, as noted by Kelley (2016), student activists now unwittingly participate in their own domination by parroting the discourses of recognition. Indeed, a thematic analysis of student demands issued across seventy institutions shows that 88 per cent demanded either changes to curricula or diversity training (especially for faculty); 87 per cent demanded more support for students of colour (i.e., multicultural centres, residence halls, financial aid, mental health services); 79 per cent demanded greater faculty diversity; and 24 per cent desired apologies and acknowledgments. It is not so much the nature of the demands per se that Kelley takes issue with but rather their framing through the discourse of *personal* trauma and the potential to "slip into" thinking about "ourselves as victims and objects rather than agents" (Kelley 2016). In some instances (e.g., DePaul University, University of Wisconsin, Madison), faculty have formed coalitions with students, registering their own demands for recognition. Faculty grievances generally respond to recent attacks on tenure, the exploitation of contingent faculty, and increasing violations of academic freedom, which disproportionately impact women and faculty of colour.

One of the most recent and widely celebrated texts to narrate both the struggle and political project of women of colour in the academy is *Presumed Incompetent: The Intersections of Race and Class for Women in Academia* (Gutiérrez y Muhs et al. 2012). According to the authors, the central aim of the text is to provide a space for women to "name their wounds in order to heal them," and their collective demand is for future generations of women of colour to enjoy "more fulfilling, respectful and dignified experiences" (Gutiérrez y Muhs et al. 2012, xx). The thirty personal narratives of the contributors each capture the visceral nature of racism and sexism as played out upon their bodies. The importance of putting a face to what often goes unnamed and dismissed cannot be underestimated. The women's stories underscore the effect of non- and misrecognition as not only dehumanizing but also cumulative; as Kelley (2016) notes, "the trauma is real." While these aims are indisputable—everyone deserves respect and dignified experiences at work—the political project seems to end there.

Among the one hundred-plus recommendations made in the final chapter of *Presumed Incompetent*, none call for collective action against the neoliberal capitalist or settler logics that situate women in asymmetric relations of power in the first place. Their main contention is not with the structures and systems of domination that gave rise to the university but rather with women's inability to fully participate in them (and thus have access to the inducements associated with its recognition). This aim is most evident in the following passage:

> The essays in *Presumed Incompetent* point...toward the Third World Feminist recognition that the business of knowledge production, like the production of tea, spices, and bananas, has an imperialist history that it has never shaken. Inventing the postcolonial university is the task of the twenty-first century. We can only hope that this task of decolonizing American academia is completed before the tenure track itself disappears. Otherwise scholars in the next century may confront another ironic example of women finally rising in a profession just as it loses its prestige and social value. (Gutiérrez y Muhs et al. 2012, xx)

Ultimately, the demand for belonging and inclusion—for presumed competence—is mobilized through a politics of recognition that not only legitimates the institution's power over women of colour but also mistakes the formation of an intellectual elite (even if it is an elite of colour) for radical social change. And as Robin Kelley (2016) urges, "The fully racialized social and epistemological architecture upon which the modern university is built cannot be radically transformed by 'simply' adding darker faces, safer spaces, better training, and a curriculum that acknowledges historical and contemporary oppressions." Indeed, the "promise project" extended by such forms of recognition may only serve to domesticate aspirations of liberation.

Academic Refusal and the Possibilities of Co-Resistance

In the broader field of critical theory, the work of Marcuse (2013) is central to theorizations of refusal. His basic argument is that in modern capitalist societies—where worth is equated with the "reproduction of value" and "extraction of profit"—human beings exist only as "an instrumental means" of capital and, thus, "simply to exist, to be, is an act of refusal" (Garland 2013, 376). For Marcuse, refusal should not be confused with "passive withdrawal or retreat" but rather understood as an active instantiation of "a radically different mode-of-being and mode-of-doing" (375). Frank Wilderson (2003) challenges this notion of refusal from the standpoint of Black subjectivity. Specifically, in distinction to what he refers to as the "coherent" subjects of anti-capitalist struggle (e.g., the worker, the immigrant, the woman), Wilderson posits the "incoherence" of Black subjects (i.e., the unwaged slave, the prison slave) as destabilizing, as "the unthought" of historical materialism (2003, 21–22). He writes,

> Black liberation, as a prospect, makes radicalism more danger-ous…not because it raises the specter of an alternative polity (such as socialism or community control of existing resources), but because its condition of possibility and gesture of resistance function as a negative dialectic: a politics of refusal and a refusal to affirm a program of complete disorder. (Wilderson 2003, 26)

Within this context, Black refusal is theorized as "an endless antagonism that cannot be satisfied (via reform or reparation)" (26).

Taking into account the power relations of both capitalism and white supremacy, Indigenous scholars posit refusal as a positive stance that is "less oriented around attaining an affirmative form of recognition…and more about critically revaluating, reconstructing and redeploying culture and tradition in ways that seek to prefigure…a radical alternative to the structural and psycho-affective facets of colonial domination" (Coulthard 2007, 456). In other words, it is both a refusal of the (false) promise of inclusion and other inducements of the settler state and an instantiation of Indigenous peoplehood. In her groundbreaking book, *Mohawk Interruptus: Political Life across the Borders of Settler States* (2014), Audra Simpson theorizes *refusal* as distinct from resistance in that it does not take authority as a given. More specifically, at the heart of the text, she theorizes refusal at the "level of method and representation," exposing the colonialist underpinnings of the "demand to know" as a settler logic. In response, she develops the notion of *ethnographic refusal* as a stance or space for Indigenous subjects to limit access to what is knowable and to being known, articulating how refusal works "in everyday encounters to enunciate repeatedly to ourselves and to outsiders that 'this is who we are, this is who you are, these are my rights'" (Simpson 2007, 73).

Mignolo (2011) and Quijano (1991) similarly take up *refusal* in relation to knowledge formation, asserting Indigenous Knowledge itself as a form of refusal; a space of *epistemic disobedience* that is "delinked" from Western, liberal, capitalist understandings of knowledge as production. Gómez-Barris (2012) theorizes the Mapuche hunger strikes as "extreme bodily performance and political instantiation" of refusal.[16] Understood as expressions of sovereignty, such acts of refusal threaten the settler state, carrying dire if not deadly consequences for Indigenous subjects. As noted by Ferguson (2015), "capitalist settler states prefer resistance" because it can be "negotiated or recognized," but refusal "throws into doubt" the entire system and is thereby more dangerous.

While within the university the consequences of academic refusal are much less dire, they still carry a risk. To refuse inclusion offends institutional authorities offering "the gift" of belonging and, as such, creates conditions of precarity for the refuser. For example, refusal to participate in the politics of respectability that characterizes institutional governance can result in social isolation, administrative retribution, and struggles with self-worth. Similarly, the refusal to comply with the normative structures of tenure and promotion (e.g., emphasizing quantity over quality, privileging single-authored monographs) can and does lead to increased marginalization, exploitation, and job loss.[17] And, in a system where Indigenous scholars comprise less than 1 per cent of the professoriate (see Chapter 9 of this book), such consequences not only bear hardships for individuals but also for whole communities. That said, academic "rewards" and inducements accessed through recognition-based politics can have even deeper consequences, namely, the continuation of settler domination. As Jodi Byrd reminds us, the colonization of Indigenous lands, bodies, and minds will not be ended by "further inclusion or more participation" (2011, xxvi).

The inspirational work of Black radical and Indigenous scholars compels thinking beyond the limits of academic recognition and about the generative spaces of refusal that not only reject settler logics but also foster possibilities of co-resistance. The prospect of coalition re-raises one of the initial animating questions of this chapter: What kinds of solidarities can be developed among peoples with a shared commitment to working beyond the imperatives of capital and the settler state? Clearly, despite the ubiquitous and often overly facile calls for solidarity, building effective coalitions is deeply challenging, even among insurgent scholars. Within this particular context, tensions between Indigenous sovereignty and decolonial projects and anti-racist, social justice projects raise a series of suspicions: whether calls for Indigenous sovereignty somehow elide the a priori condition of blackness (the "unsovereign" subject; see Sexton 2014), whether anti-racist struggles sufficiently account for Indigenous sovereignty as a land-based struggle elucidated outside regimes of property, and whether theorizations of settler colonialism sufficiently account for the forces and structures of white supremacy, racial slavery, and anti-blackness.

Rather than posit such tensions as terminally incommensurable, however, I want to suggest a parallel politics of dialectical co-resistance. When Black peoples can *still* be killed but not murdered, when Indians are *still* made to disappear, when (Indigenous) land and Black bodies are still destroyed and accumulated for settler profit, it is incumbent upon all those who claim a commitment to refusing the white supremacist, capitalist, settler state to do the hard work of building "interconnected movements for decolonization" (Coulthard 2014). The struggle is real. It is both material and psychological, both method and politics, and, thus, must necessarily straddle the both-and coordinates of revolutionary change. In terms of process, this means simultaneously working beyond *resistance* and through the enactment of refusal— as fugitive, abolitionist, and Indigenous sovereign subjects.

Within the context of the university, this means replacing calls for more inclusive and diverse safe spaces *within* the university with the development of a network of sovereign safe houses *outside* the university. Kelley reminds us of the long history of this struggle, recalling the Institute of the Black World at Atlanta University in 1969, the Mississippi Freedom Schools, and the work of Black feminists Patricia Robinson, Donna Middleton, and Patricia Haden as inspirational models. As a contemporary model, he references

Moten and Harney's vision of the undercommons as a space of possibility: a fugitive space wherein the pursuit of knowledge is not perceived as a path toward upward mobility and material wealth but rather as a means toward eradicating oppression in all of its forms (Undercommoning). The ultimate goal, according to Kelley (2016) is to create in the present a future that overthrows the logic of neoliberalism. Scholars within Native studies similarly build upon a long tradition of refusing the university, theorizing from and about sovereignty through land-based models of education. Whereas a fugitive flees and seeks to escape, the Indigenous stands ground or, as Deborah Bird points out, "to get in the way of settler colonization, all the native has to do is stay at home" (quoted in Wolfe 2006, 388). The ultimate goal of Indigenous refusal is Indigenous resurgence; a struggle that includes but is not limited to the return of Indigenous land.

Again, while the aims may be different (and in some sense competing), efforts toward the development of parallel projects of co-resistance are possible through vigilant and sustained engagement. The "common ground" here is not literal but rather conceptual, a corpus of shared ethics and analytics: anti-capitalist, feminist, anti-colonial. Rather than allies, we are accomplices—plotting the death but not murder of the settler university. Toward this end, I offer some additional strategies for refusing the university.

First and foremost, we need to commit to collectivity—to staging a refusal of the individualist promise project of the settler university. This requires that we engage in a radical and ongoing reflexivity about who we are and how we situate ourselves in the world. This includes but is not limited to a *refusal* of the cycle of individualized inducements—particularly, the awards, appointments, and grants that require complicity or allegiance to institutions that continue to oppress and dispossess. It is also a call to refuse the perceived imperative to self-promote, to brand one's work and body. This includes all the personal web pages, incessant Facebook updates, and Twitter feeds featuring our latest accomplishments, publications, grants, rewards, etc., etc. Just. Make. It. Stop. The journey is not about self—which means it is not about promotion and tenure—it is about the disruption and dismantling of those structures and processes that create hierarchies of individual worth and labour.

Second, we must *commit to reciprocity*—the kind that is primarily about being answerable to those communities we claim as our own and those we claim to serve. It is about being answerable to each other and our work. One of the many things lost to the pressures of the publish-or-perish, quantity-over-quality, neoliberal regime is the loss of good critique. We have come to confuse support with sycophantic praise and critical evaluation with personal injury. Through the ethic of reciprocity, we need to remind ourselves that accountability to the collective requires a commitment to engage, extend, trouble, speak back to, and intensify our works and deeds.

Third, we need to *commit to mutuality*, which implies reciprocity but is ultimately more encompassing. It is about the development of social relations not contingent upon the imperatives of capital—that refuses exploitation at the same time it radically asserts connection, particularly to land. Inherent to a land-based ethic is a commitment to slow-ness and to the arc of intergenerational resurgence and transformation. One of the many ways the academy recapitulates colonial logics is through the overvaluing of fast, new, young, and individualist voices and the undervaluing of slow, Elder, and collective ones. And, in such a system, relations and paradigms of connection, mutuality, and collectivity are inevitably undermined. Among other things, this distinction also marks the edges of the binary that colonial logics seek to eliminate: *the difference between subjectivities produced in and through relationship to land and those produced under and through significations of property.*

Toward this end, I have been thinking a lot lately about the formation of a new scholarly collective, one that writes and researches under a nom de guerre—like the Black feminist scholars and activists who wrote under and through the Combahee River Collective, or the more recent collective of scholars and activists publishing as "uncertain commons."[18] If furthering the aims of insurgence and resurgence (and not individual recognition) is indeed what we hold paramount, then perhaps one of the most radical refusals we can authorize is to work together as one; to enact a kind of Zapatismo scholarship and a *balaclava politics*, where the work of the collectivity is intentionally structured to obscure and transcend the single voice, body, and life. Together, we could write in refusal of essentialist and identitarian politics, of individualist inducements, of capitalist imperatives, and other productivist logics of accumulation. This is what love as refusal looks like. It is the un-demand, the un-desire to be either *of* or *in*. It is the radical assertion to be *on*: land. Decolonial love is land.

Notes

1   I feel the necessity to mark the effort to try and keep up with the growing body count of Black men and women killed by police as I wrote and revised this

chapter. As the effort proved increasingly and depressingly futile, I decided to insert the words, "and others."

2 While the most public of the protests commenced on this date, students at the University of Missouri report significant issues with the campus racial climate dating back to 2010, when two white students were arrested for dropping cotton balls in front of the Black Culture Center.

3 As defined by Moten and Harney (2004), the *undercommons* is a fugitive space that is *in* but not *of* the university.

4 Audra Simpson (2016) clarifies "the political" as that which "describes distributions of power, of effective and affective possibility, the imagination of how action will unfold to reach back to that distribution for a re-sort, but also for a push on what should be" (326).

5 The primary concern of CIS is Indigenous resurgence and decolonization. Toward that end, it undertakes (Western) critical theory as a means of "unmapping" the structures, processes, and discourses of settler colonialism while at the same time working to disrupt and redirect the matrix of presuppositions that underlie it (Byrd 2011).

6 According to a Center on Juvenile and Criminal Justice analysis of Centers of Disease Control and Prevention data, Native Americans account for 1.9 per cent of all police killings while they make up only 0.8 per cent of the population. In comparison, African Americans make up 13 per cent of the population and 26 per cent of police killings.

7 In Saskatoon, Saskatchewan, there is also a legacy of "starlight tours" spanning roughly from 1990 to 2010, whereby Saskatoon police officers arrested Aboriginal men, drove them out of the city, and abandoned them. The number of victims dying of hypothermia as a result of these "tours" is unknown.

8 It should be noted that as I was writing this chapter, Canada launched the National Inquiry into Missing and Murdered Indigenous Women and Girls (Government of Canada).

9 It should be noted that the authors do not distinguish between liberal and radical justice projects in their analysis, other than to name both as incommensurable with decolonial projects.

10 Tuck and Yang clarify that reconciliation "is about rescuing settler normalcy, about rescuing a settler future" (2012, 35).

11 It should be noted that "justice" is not an Indigenous construct and that CIS scholars work to intervene in and disrupt "the network of presuppositions" that underpin "political theory, social theory and humanist ethics," which are themselves built upon the forms and discourses of liberal governance (Povinelli 2011, 13).

12 Consider, for example, the truth and reconciliation commissions in South Africa following apartheid and in Chile after the Pinochet regime.

13 Scholar-activists of the Undercommoning project similarly claim that "the university has always been a thief, stealing peoples' labor, time and energy," and, thus, "charge that the university-as-such is a criminal institution" (Undercommoning).

14 Ahmed (2004) argues in "Affective Economies" that "emotions do things" (119). Specifically, the circulation and mobilization of emotions (e.g., desire, pleasure, fear, hate) work to bind subjects with communities. In so doing, they function as a form of capital "produced only as an effect of their circulation" (120).

15 Agathangelou, Bassichis, and Spira (2008) similarly theorize the affective economy as transpiring through what the authors define as an "imperial project of promise and non-promise" (128). A process by which a series of (false) promises are granted to certain subjects that is reliant on another series of (non)promises made to (non)subjects upon whom the entire production is staged (123). For example, with regard to the promise project of gay marriage, they describe how liberal theories of justice manifest through the individual inducement of marriage (that functions as a false promise), and how this affective economy not only sustains material relations of oppression but also serves to domesticate the "gay agenda." They write,

> We...locate the mobilization of highly individualized narratives of bourgeois belonging and ascension within a larger promise project that offers to some the tenuous promise of mobility, freedom, and equality. This strategy is picked up in a privatized, corporatized, and sanitized "gay agenda" that places, for example, gay marriage and penalty-enhancing hate crime laws at the top of its priorities. This also helps us understand the ways in which revolutionary and redistributive yearnings that would challenge the foundations of the U.S. state, capital, and racial relations have been systematically replaced with strategies for individualized incorporation in the U.S. moral and politico-economic order. It has been this promise project that has been crucial in rerouting so much of queer politics and longing from "Stonewall to the suburbs." (123–24)

16 As Gómez-Barris explains,

> In the nexus of settler capitalism, Mapuche hunger strikes have become a dominant form of political expression, and of embodied cultural politics that transform the colonial relationship through collective and self-definition. Contemporary hunger strikes shape and are shaped by a neoliberal landscape that has both deepened and localized indigenous responses. In such locations, the starving body of the hunger striker has become the site of resistance against the modern nation state's continued practices of colonial subjugation...As extreme bodily performance and political instantiation, the Mapuche starving body literally enacts the condition of precariousness, specifying the meanings of social death for indigenous peoples living within a state of permanent war. (2012, 120).

17 According to *The Journal of Blacks in Higher Education*, Blacks make up approximately 5.2 per cent of faculty nationwide in the United States ("Black Faculty").

18 Authors writing under this nom de guerre recently published *Speculate This!* (2013).

References

Agathangelou, A. M., D. Bassichis, and T. L. Spira. 2008. "Intimate Investments: Homonormativity, Global Lockdown, and Seductions of Empire." *Radical History Review* 100: 120–43.

Ahmed, S. 2004. "Affective Economies." *Social Text* 22(2): 117–39.

Baum, B. 2004. "Feminist Politics of Recognition." *Signs* 29(4): 1073–1102.

"Black Faculty at the Nation's Highest-Ranked Colleges and Universities." *The Journal of Blacks in Higher Education.* http://www.jbhe.com/features/48_blackfaculty_colleges-uni.html.

Butler, J. 1990. *Gender Trouble: Feminism and the Subversion of Identity*. New York: Routledge.

Byrd, J. A. 2011. *The Transit of Empire: Indigenous Critiques of Colonialism.* Minneapolis: University of Minnesota Press.

Corntassel, J., and C. Holder. 2008. "Who's Sorry Now? Government Apologies, Truth Commissions, and Indigenous Self-Determination in Australia, Canada, Guatemala, and Peru." *Human Rights Review* 9(4): 465–89.

Coulthard, G. S. 2014. *Red Skin, White Masks: Rejecting the Colonial Politics of Recognition*. Minneapolis: University of Minnesota Press.

———. 2007. "Subjects of Empire: Indigenous Peoples and the 'Politics of Recognition' in Canada." *Contemporary Political Theory* 6(4): 437–60.

Day, I. 2015. "Being or Nothingness: Indigeneity, Antiblackness, and Settler Colonial Critique." *Critical Ethnic Studies* 1(2): 102–21.

Ferguson, K. 2015. "Refusing Settler Colonialism: Simpson's *Mohawk Interruptus*." *Theory & Event* 18(4). *Settler Colonial Studies* [blog], October 25. https://settlercolonialstudies.org/2015/10/25/.

Fraser, N. 1997. *Justice Interruptus: Critical Reflections on the "Postsocialist" Condition*. New York: Routledge.

Garland, C. 2013. "Negating That Which Negates Us." *Radical Philosophy Review* 16(1): 375–85.

Glenn, E. N. 2015. "Settler Colonialism as Structure: A Framework for Comparative Studies of U.S. Race and Gender Formation." *Sociology of Race and Ethnicity* 1(1): 52–72.

Goldstein, A. 2008. "Where the Nation Takes Place: Proprietary Regimes, Antistatism, and U.S. Settler Colonialism." *South Atlantic Quarterly* 107(4): 833–61.

Gómez-Barris, M. 2012. "Mapuche Hunger Acts: Epistemology of the Decolonial." TRANSMODERNITY: *Journal of Peripheral Cultural Production of the Luso-Hispanic World* 1(3): 120–33.

Government of Canada. "National Inquiry into Missing and Murdered Indigenous Women and Girls." http://www.aadnc-aandc.gc.ca/eng/1448633299414/1448633350146.

Gutiérrez y Muhs, G., Y. F. Niemann, C. G. González, and A. P. Harris. 2012. *Presumed Incompetent: The Intersections of Race and Class for Women in Academia*. Logan: Utah University Press.

Harney, S., and F. Moten. 2013. *The Undercommons: Fugitive Planning and Black Study*. New York: Minor Compositions.

Honneth, A. 1992. *The Struggle for Recognition: The Moral Grammar of Social Conflicts*. Cambridge, MA: MIT Press.

———. 1995. *The Struggle for Recognition: The Moral Grammar of Social Conflicts*. Translated by Joel Anderson. Boston: MIT Press.

Kelley, R. D. 2016. "Black Study, Black Struggle." *The Boston Review*. http://bostonreview.net/forum/robin-d-g-kelley-black-study-black-struggle.

Kymlicka, W. 1995. *Multicultural Citizenship: A Liberal Theory of Minority Rights*. New York: Oxford University Press.

Kymlicka, W., and B. Bashir. 2008. *The Politics of Reconciliation in Multicultural Societies*. New York: Oxford University Press.

Marcuse, H. 2013. *One-Dimensional Man: Studies in the Ideology of Advanced Industrial Society*. New York: Routledge. First published 1964.

Mignolo, W. 2011. "Epistemic Disobedience and the Decolonial Option: A Manifesto." TRANSMODERNITY: *Journal of Peripheral Cultural Production of the Luso-Hispanic World* 1(2): 44–67.

Moten, F., and S. Harney. 2004. "The University and the Undercommons: Seven Theses." *Social Text* 22(2): 101–15.

Povinelli, E. 2011. *Economies of Abandonment: Social Belonging and Endurance in Late Liberalism*. Durham, NC: Duke University Press.

Quijano, A. 1991. "Colonialidad y Modernidad/Racionalidad." *Perú Indígena* 13(29): 11–20.

Sexton, J. 2014. "The *Vel* of Slavery: Tracking the Figure of the Unsovereign." *Critical Sociology* 30: 319–34. doi:10.1177/0896920514552535.

Simpson, A. 2016. "Consent's Revenge." *Cultural Anthropology* 31(3): 326–33. doi:10.14506/ca31.3.02.

———. 2014. *Mohawk Interruptus: Political Life across the Borders of Settler States*. Durham, NC: Duke University Press.

———. 2007. "On Ethnographic Refusal: Indigeneity,'Voice' and Colonial Citizenship." *Junctures: The Journal for Thematic Dialogue* 9: 67–81.

Taylor, C. 1994. *Multiculturalism: Examining the Politics of Recognition*. Edited by A. Gutmann. Princeton, NJ: Princeton University Press.

Tuck, E., and K. W. Yang. 2012. "Decolonization Is Not a Metaphor." *Decolonization: Indigeneity, Education & Society* 1(1): 1–40.

uncertain commons. 2013. *Speculate This!* Durham, NC: Duke University Press.

Undercommoning. *Undercommoning: Revolution within, against and beyond the University*. http://undercommoning.org.

Wilder, C. S. 2014. *Ebony and Ivy: Race, Slavery, and the Troubled History of America's Universities*. London: Bloomsbury Publishing.

Wilderson, F. B. 2003. "The Prison Slave as Hegemony's (Silent) Scandal." *Social Justice* 30(2): 18–27.

———. 2010. *Red, White & Black: Cinema and the Structure of U.S. Antagonisms*. Durham, NC: Duke University Press.

Wolfe, P. 2013. "Recuperating Binarism: A Heretical Introduction." *Settler Colonial Studies* 3(3–4): 257–79.

———. 2006. "Settler Colonialism and the Elimination of the Native." *Journal of Genocide Research* 8(4): 387–409.

———. 1999. *Settler Colonialism and the Transformation of Anthropology: The Politics and Poetics of an Ethnographic Event*. London: Cassel.

PART IV

FROM COUNTING OUT, TO COUNTING ON, THE SCHOLARS

CHAPTER 11

BEYOND INDIVIDUALISM: THE PSYCHOSOCIAL LIFE OF THE NEOLIBERAL UNIVERSITY

Rosalind Gill

> The end result of reading this article was—I had to lock my door—I cried…Maybe, if I'm being honest, perhaps I also cried for myself—which surprised me. I wonder if I'm cut out for this game. How can I survive in it? Do I want to do this? Do I want to be part of this? Am I really any good? I hope it moves people to some form of action. It has stirred "something" in me.
>
> —Early-career, male academic, writing to Andrew Sparkes in "Embodiment, Academics, and the Audit Culture"

Introduction

Several years ago I co-edited a book with a dear friend and colleague, Róisín Ryan-Flood. Titled *Secrecy and Silence in the Research Process: Feminist Reflections* (Ryan-Flood and Gill 2010), the book was situated in a long tradition of critical work that sought to interrogate and trouble practices of power in research—in this case, asking about the secrets, the silences, and the erasures that mark research. In her powerful and generous foreword to the collection, Sara Ahmed captured the multiplicity of ways in which secrecy and silence matter:

Sometimes silence can be a tool of oppression; when you are silenced, whether by explicit force or by persuasion, it is not simply that you do not speak but that you are barred from participation in a conversation which nevertheless involves you. Sometimes silence is a strategic response to oppression; one that allows subjects to persist in their own way; one that acknowledges that, under certain circumstances speech might not be empowering, let alone sensible. Sometimes you might speak out to announce a disagreement with what is being said, sometimes not, as to speak can mean to participate in a conversation you don't agree with. Sometimes we might stay silent about some of the findings of our research because we do not have trust in how those findings might be used by other actors...To recognise this contingency as a feminist ethics is to live and work in a state of suspension: we will not always know in advance (though sometimes we might) when it makes sense to be silent and when it does not. (2010b, xvi)

It was with this sense of "not knowing" that I approached my own contribution to the book, an attempt to raise questions and open a dialogue about the "hidden injuries" of neoliberal academia. The conditions in which research is produced, our experiences as "knowledge workers," and our labouring subjectivities—these seemed among the biggest and most systematic silences about research. For all the talk of reflexivity, its parameters often seem to lie at the boundaries of the individual study and not to enquire more widely into the institutional context in which academic work is produced. Yet all around me I saw colleagues and students suffering from "exhaustion, stress, overload, insomnia, shame, anxiety, aggression, hurt, guilt and feelings of out-of-placeness, fraudulence and fear of exposure within the contemporary academy" (Gill 2010, 229). These feelings, these affective, embodied experiences, I argued, had a strange relation to questions of secrecy and silence. They were at once ordinary and everyday, yet, at the same time, they remained deeply silenced in the official and public sites of the academy. They suffused the "spaces between"—corridors, bathrooms, conference coffee breaks—but they were (and perhaps still are) "officially" unrecognized, do not have "proper channels," and rarely make it onto the agendas of departmental meetings or committees or formal records of university life.

What would it mean, I asked, if we were to turn our lens upon our own labour processes, organizational governance, and conditions of production? What kinds of insights could we generate if we were to "think together" literatures about transformations in capitalism, the corporatization of the university, the micro-politics of power, and emerging interests in the "psychic life" of neoliberalism? How might we make links between macro-organization and institutional practices, on one hand, and experiences and affective states on the other, and open up exploration of the ways these may be gendered, racialized, and classed?

Writing the article was an uncomfortable experience. With no claim to science or authority, my "data" were the "unending flow of communications and practices in which we are all enmeshed, often reluctantly: the proliferating emails, the minutes of meetings, the job applications, the peer reviews, the promotion assessments, the drafts of the Research Assessment Exercise narrative, the committee papers, the student feedback forms, even the after-seminar chats" (Gill 2010, 229). The article necessitated personal exposure, including quoting from a rejection letter I had received from a journal, and reflecting upon my own shame, disappointment, and multiple failures to "cope." In doing this, I experienced breaking the "feeling rules" (Hochschild 1979) of the academy. More importantly, it involved great discomfort about privilege—both the privilege of academics generally as an occupational group, and my own particular privilege as a white, tenured academic living in a metropolitan centre. My "check-your-privilege" meter is well honed, and my worry about self-indulgence significant; for those reasons, the article nearly did not get written. Ultimately, I placed discussions of all these dilemmas at the heart of the article: questions about the obligations of a critical, politically engaged scholar; reflections on the way that experiences in the academy are related to structural inequalities and biographies that produce very different degrees of "entitlement"; and a searing critique of precariousness.

Breaking the Silence: Sharing Stories

Like Andrew Sparkes (2007), whose poignant, honest, and painful stories "seeking consideration" prompted the epigraph that opens this chapter, I could not have been prepared for the reaction that greeted my modest attempt to speak out about what I saw and felt. In the eight years since publication, scarcely a week has gone by when I have not received at least two or three emails from people telling me how and why they have been touched by it. Many of these were expressions of gratitude and relief that their writers no longer felt so alone or "the only one who felt like this." My archive of letters and emails now runs to nearly two thousand items of correspondence; a veritable catalogue of tales of toxic experiences within the neoliberal univer-sity that underscore my sense of a deep, affective, and somatic crisis.

I have become, in effect, a particular kind of accidental "vulnerable observer" (Behar 2014), a bearer of witness to collective injuries and strug-gles that are nonetheless always experienced as individual—leaving their traces written on our bodies and psyches. Many of these letters have moved me profoundly. I have tried to respond to each one as I have received it, with care and empathy. I am sure I missed a few on days when my inbox was espe-cially punishing. But more widely I am not sure how to respond to them or to honour the experiences they share. The social scientist in me recognizes they represent a huge "selection bias." More significantly, as a human being, I am not sure how—or indeed whether—it is ethically permissible to report these stories, which have been entrusted to me by strangers—even with all the usual caveats about anonymity and confidentiality that pass for "research ethics" in the corporate university, with its checkboxes and barely concealed concern with brand management, global reputation, and avoidance of litiga-tion, rather than anything I would understand as ethics. Representing others is always and ineluctably a political project, suffused with power relations that are rarely acknowledged (Alcoff 1991; Wilkinson and Kitzinger 1996). For now, I treat the stories as gifts: fragments of letters dance around my head; others haunt me with sadness; I practice the "art of listening" (Back 2007).

These responses represent merely a fraction of the voices that are now debating, arguing, and protesting conditions in the neoliberal university. Seven years on from "Breaking the Silence: The Hidden Injuries of the Neoliberal University" (Gill 2010), there has been an immense shift in dis-cussion and debate about the transformation of universities and life within them. The silence has been broken. As Maria do Mar Pereira (2016) puts it,

> It is no longer a (thinly veiled) secret that in contemporary uni-versities many scholars, both junior and senior, are struggling—struggling to manage their workloads; struggling to keep up with insistent institutional demands to produce more, better and faster; struggling to reconcile professional demands with family responsibilities and personal interests; and struggling to maintain their physical and psychological health and emotional wellbeing. (100)

Central to the new visibility of such concerns has been the huge variety of social media that provide sites for a wide range of commentaries about academia—from critical essays, personal accounts, Tumblr, GIFs, jokes, Twitter feeds, memes, and a number of well-established blogs such as *Chronicles of Higher Education*; *Tenure, She Wrote*; *Academic Diary*; *Hook and Eye*; *The Feminist Wire*; and *Academics Anonymous*. Much informed, critical debate circulates in and between these spaces—and many others—with particular focus on the academic precariat. Compared with the early 2000s, there has also been a significant upsurge of research into academic labour, including—in a European context—major research networks concerned with gender (GARCIA and Gender-Net), and a growing interest in the toxic effects of "new public management" (Lorenz 2012; Shore 2008; Martin 2012). Books, articles, and special issues abound (Back 2016; Collini 2012; Evans 2004; Edu-Factory Collective 2009; Giroux 2002; Readings 1996; Roggero 2011). Activist movements both within and outside traditional trade unions have also flourished, bringing together students, academics, and other workers to protest the privatization of universities, the "enslavement by debt" of students, and promoting new visions of a "public university" (see Halffman and Radder 2015). Alongside demonstrations, strikes and occupations have featured prominently in this activism in Canada, the Netherlands, and the United Kingdom.

Life in the Neoliberal University

In this chapter I will draw together some of the themes of current research and writing on the university, highlighting contemporary concerns about precarious employment, working hours, and surveillance and audit cultures. I want to raise some critical questions, returning to my original interests in the psychic life of neoliberalism—in particular, its individualism. I will make three brief arguments: first, arguing against individualization and calling for a collective struggle and resistance; second, calling for an expanded notion of precariousness that can speak to the multiplicity of ways in which precarity operates in the neoliberal university; and, third, relatedly discussing what I will call "difficult solidarities"—particularly the need to work collectively across differences and to resist the pressures toward competition and division.

Casualization and the Academic Precariat

Q: How many PhDs does it take to change a light bulb?
A: One but 500 applied.

> A: None because changing a light bulb is a job and there are no
> jobs for PhDs currently.
> A: None. The broken bulb has tenure.
> —Taken from Twitter

The energy, creativity, and rage of "contingent" and precarious workers within the academy have been central to the discussion of casualization—and activism around this—in recent years (Adsit et al. 2015; Krause et al. 2008; SIGJ2 Writing Collective 2012; The Res-Sisters 2016). The idea that academics are privileged, with "cushy" tenured positions (and long holidays) has a firm hold in the popular imagination. In reality, precariousness is the "new normal" (Berlant 2011), and one of the defining experiences of academic life. In the UK, the "adjunct" system is not as institutionally ossified as it seems in North America, and there is greater mobility from short-term, temporary positions into more secure ones. Nevertheless, data from the University and College Union (UCU 2016) shows more than 50 per cent of academics are on short-term contracts—some of them "zero hours," that is offering no security or benefits beyond any particular hour being worked, with the possibility of being "dropped" at any time—with considerable vulnerability. This resonates with figures in Australia, Canada, and the United States, where the figure is reported to be as high as 70 per cent (UCU 2016). Only the hospitality industry has a greater number of temporary workers and "casuals." As Ruth Barcan (2013) has noted in the Australian context, "this is an intellectual and social catastrophe masking as flexibility" (114).

The speeding up of this process in the last few years has been devastating—echoing trends in other sectors that have seen the systematic casualization of workforces and the degradation of pay and conditions. This is not a conspiracy—though it can feel like one—but it is a marked and patterned feature of this moment of capitalism and surely needs to be recognized as such. More than 150 years ago, Karl Marx explained how a "reserve army of labour" operated as part of the dynamic of proletarianization. Today, the notion of a *precariat* brings a focus on precariousness to novel understandings of the proletariat—a "class" (if you will) that includes increasing numbers of artists, journalists, doctors, and academics, alongside cleaners, janitors, and others (Mitropoulos 2006; Galetto et al. 2007; Morini 2007; Weeks 2005; Federici 2012; Standing 2011).

As I noted in "Breaking the Silence," the workers most affected by this shift are early-career academics—though the term is really a misnomer since "the designation can now extend for one's whole 'career' given the few opportunities for development or secure employment" (2010, 232). At that time, "teaching fellowships," in which staff were paid only during the teaching semesters, looked grossly exploitative, but now—in a measure of how much worse things have become—they seem to represent relative privilege compared with the reality of "visiting lectureship" or "teaching assistantship" positions in which tens of thousands of hourly paid PhDs and post-docs deliver mass undergraduate teaching with little or no support and few rights. Many are on zero-hours contracts—or do not even have contracts—and often find themselves burdened with tutoring or grading responsibilities that, if costed properly, would work out at a fraction of the minimum wage. I know this from the universities I have worked in. Like many colleagues, I have challenged this repeatedly, but with limited or sometimes no success. For those involved, it represents "hope labour" (Kuehn and Corrigan 2013) par excellence—imagined as a foot in the door, a way of gaining a "proper job." As Valerie Hey (2004) has put it: "we hope that if only we work harder, produce more, publish more, conference more, achieve more, in short 'perform more' that we will eventually get 'there'" (80). If the pay and insecurity are appalling, so too is the lack of care, sometimes bordering on contempt, with which such workers are treated: "disposable staff are opportunistically left dangling with temporary contracts, often with an appeal to their sense of responsibility towards their students" (Halffman and Radder 2015; see also Gill 2014). They, in turn, are under extreme pressure to be "uncomplaining"—to present a pleasing and happy countenance (cf. Hochschild on emotional labour 2003), the production of which could be understood as instantiating a further layer of injury: not only the exploitation itself but also the requirement to self-censor and erase all "bad affect," to keep on smiling and saying "yes" while inside every fibre of your being is screaming "No-o-oo" (for vivid examples, see *Academics Anonymous*).

For younger people trying to gain a place in the academy, all this constitutes part of a matrix of intergenerational inequality that includes (the lack of) access to housing, pension rights, and job security. Even if they achieve the longed-for position, "younger academics are likely to retire 30% worse off than professors today" (Godard 2014, 5). In this sense, things are getting worse, not better, for academics. However, this needs to be read carefully and with political nuance, not merely in terms of some kind of naturalized generational strife.

More, Better, Faster! Academic Time in the Neoliberal University

> Good scholarship requires time: time to think, write, read, research, analyse, edit, and collaborate. High quality instruction and service also require time: time to engage, innovate, experiment, organise, evaluate and inspire.
>
> —Alison Mountz et al., "For Slow Scholarship"

Compared with casualization, it has seemed to be much harder for academics to recognize our punishing workloads as a political issue—rather than simply a private indication that we "can't hack it," are not good enough, or are failing to cope. Finally, we seem to be breaking through these individualized and pathologized responses toward a recognition that workloads constitute a structural political issue that is profoundly harmful to health. Increasing numbers of people report being at "breaking point," completely exhausted, and close to physical and mental collapse. Halffman and Radder (2015), writing about the Netherlands, note terrifying levels of "burn out." In my own conversations with friends and colleagues, I have noticed how metaphors of drowning and suffocation suffuse talk about work: people speak of "going under," they dream about "coming up for air," and routinely report they are "drowning." Such terrifying and violent imagery should surely give cause for concern.

Mike Crang (2007) has argued that time is perhaps the biggest source of dispute, anxiety, and stress in academia, as we are called on to do more with less in an "always on" (Gregg 2009) culture, marked by a constant state of "emergency as rule" (Thrift 2000). As Crang (2007) notes, academics want more time to research, do not have enough time to read, spend too much of their time at work, cannot spend enough time with students, cannot fit their job into the available time, do not have time for anything outside work—children, friends, other activities—and then are subjected to the poisonous myth that they are time-rich and leisured! The harsh reality of long working hours is borne out by study after study. As long ago as 2006, the university trade union used official statistics to calculate that academics were working on average nine extra hours per week. In the UCU's 2016 workload survey, based on more than twelve thousand responses from academics, that figure has increased to an average of 13.4 hours extra per week, with senior academics working significantly longer. Expressed differently, academics are working for free for two extra days per week—that is, *working the equivalent of a seven-day week every week*. The 2016 *University Workplace Survey*, conducted by *Times Higher Education*, has free comments that translate these figures into reality and make for sobering reading:

> "I feel unappreciated—I work 100 hours a week and I'm exhausted."
> "I thought this was my dream job...but the workload is unmanageable."
> "I don't think I can realistically keep this up until retirement without making myself seriously ill from stress." (Grove 2016)

As well as chronic stress, exhaustion, and increasing rates of ill health, there are a myriad of more subtle impacts of this kind of extreme pressure and overwork. In a moving blog post for the *Guardian*'s *Academics Anonymous* site, one lecturer began, "Dear student, I do not have time to mark your essay properly...In an ideal world your work would be read by an enthusiastic engaged professional, but the reality is very very different" (*The Guardian* 2016). Such accounts hint at the huge personal frustrations and disappointments experienced by academics, and the very particular forms of alienation that accompany not simply being stressed but also feeling unable to carry out one's job as one believes it should be done. Many public sector workers— not just academics—experience this at considerable personal psychological cost. It is another hidden injury that does violence to our sense of professionalism and integrity, which can be felt as an attack on the self.

Similarly injurious processes accompany the harsh decline in care, kindness, and compassion in academic workplaces, and the isolation felt by many—vividly conveyed in the hundreds of letters I have received. Again, there are a multiplicity of things that need to be unpacked and explored. They include increasing rates of bullying and harassment, increasing competition, declining experiences of community, and the spiralling sense of not being listened to—not having a voice; more than half of academics report that they feel they cannot get their voices heard within the university (Grove 2016). Academics often provide extraordinary care and support for their students but feel unsupported themselves: "dropped in at the deep end," as many new staff report, left to "sink or swim"; the analogies to drowning once again abound. For more established scholars, the pressures can be different: "I feel like I am the world's mentor and supporter," one friend tells me. "I constantly have colleagues crying on my shoulder, I spend my weekends writing references and commenting on their grant applications and trying to be a good supportive colleague and feminist. But I never get to do any of my own work and there's absolutely nobody to take any care of me. I've never had a f***ing mentor in my life!"

More broadly, as Kathleen Lynch (2010) has argued, these systems produce "care-less" workers. Workloads are so heavy and expectations of productivity are so high, she argues, that they can only be achieved by workers who have no relationships or responsibilities that might constrain their productive capacities. There is a growing literature about motherhood and the academy (Evans and Grant 2008; Meyers 2012; Connelly and Ghodsee 2011), as well as a flourishing self-help and advice sphere that instructs on topics such as "how to ensure that your children do not 'show'" (Mannevuo 2016).

One woman quoted by Mona Mannevuo (2016, 80) suggests that her maternity leave makes her look very bad: "like a criminal record on the CV." Maria do Mar Pereira (2016) argues this pressure also extends to activism—increasingly squeezed out by time and proliferating other demands. In the current context, as Lauren Berlant (2011, 3) puts it, to "have a life" at all increasingly seems like an accomplishment.

Equally pernicious perhaps is the damage done to our ways of relating *within* the academy, where it becomes routine to see compassion vying for space with less generous emotions. Here is a typical scenario: we work in a small department, delivering several undergraduate and postgraduate degrees and already feeling overwhelmed. We get the news that one of our colleagues is unwell and has been "signed off" work by her doctor for three months. People are genuinely sad and upset to hear this. Our lovely colleague is sick. We have been worried about her for a while. But then it hits: all the marking is about to come in, and dissertation anxiety has reached a peak among students. Who is going to take over her methods teaching, her supervisees, and pick up the grading of all those essays? It is nearly the end of the financial year and our head of department informs us there is no money left to pay anyone to help with this. We sigh and a little hard knot of resentment forms. It is not directed against our colleague. Not really. Not yet. But, before long, someone will ask, "Isn't she better yet?" or "Might she be well enough to do some of her marking from home?" And so it begins: the damage to relations of generosity and compassion. Indeed, I was asked to do marking when I was off sick by a colleague whom I like and respect. She is not a bad person, but simply a person operating in a bad system, under impossible pressure, where there is no "slack" and precious few systems for dealing with even routine occurrences such as people getting sick. This is an occupational health disaster, but the care-less-ness is *structural*; it is institutionally produced, and it diminishes us all.

Against "fast academia" (Gill 2010), or, "academia without walls" (Gill 2010; Pereira 2016), there has been a growing interest in "slow academia"—captured in the quote at the start of this section as a way of resisting the temporal logics of neoliberalism. However, some have chosen to interpret this slow movement critically, seeing in it a failure to recognize privilege and an attempt to mystify institutional hierarchy. In a much circulated public letter, Mark Carrigan and Filip Vostal (2016) critique the authors of *The Slow Professor* (Berg and Seeber 2016), calling into question the idea that academics are stressed and arguing that "slow professorship" only makes sense when such decelerating professors can take it for granted that junior associates will accelerate to "pick up the slack." Yet this is to misunderstand the notion of "slow scholarship"—at least in its radical versions—which repeatedly emphasizes that the "slow" in slow scholarship is not just about time but about structures of power and inequality (Martell 2014). A feminist geography collective underlines that "slow scholarship cannot just be about making individual lives better, but must also be about re-making the university" (Mountz et al. 2015).

Surveillance and Quantified Control

> Sometimes the antagonist isn't wielding a gun. In this kind of attack, there is no person or event that can be met head-on with a protest or a strike. There is no explosion, no great conflict, no epic battle. Such is the case with higher education's silent killer: the slow, incremental creep of "audit culture."
> —Spooner, "Higher Education's Silent Killer"

> Punitive accountability is undoing all things public.
> —Chapter 5 of this book

In a wonderful Tumblr animation produced by the Department of Omnishambles, Karl Marx is catapulted forward to the early twenty-first century, and we see him having his "end-of-year assessment" with his department head: "Hi Dr. Marx," says the computer-generated voice, "good to see you":

> Thanks for coming in for this assessment. (Hi.) So, Karl, I really like what you did with, what was it, *Das Kapital*? Great stuff. (Thanks, I aim to please.) In terms of impact points it scored

very highly. Very highly indeed. Great what you did with the whole 20th century and stuff. Those revolutions and whatever. Massive impact there. (Right.) But, obviously, not a peer-reviewed document so I can't count it towards your publications for the REF [Research Excellence Framework] assessment. Er, kind of a problem. (Oh?) I mean a man can't live by impact alone, if you know what I mean, Karl. And, departmentally, I'm sorry to say, you're just not pulling your weight in terms of publications. (What about *The Communist Manifesto*? That had quite a lot of citations.) It falls into the same trap, I'm afraid, Karl. It doesn't help the REF at all. Where is the new work? (Department of Omnishambles)

The video goes on to reveal that the teaching evaluations are not great, and that failure to publish in top journals is letting the department down. Karl Marx is "exposed" as a loser, whose work just does not cut it in the contemporary academy. The Department of Omnishambles brilliantly uses what we might call (following the artist Marcel Duchamp) "found objects" or "ready-made" language from the corporate academy to satirize our current state. In this case, its target is the rapidly proliferating regimes of audit and surveillance in which academics are located. As Roger Burrows (2012) has argued, any individual academic in the UK can now be ranked and measured on more than one hundred different scales and indices that become the "qualculations" (Callon and Law 2005) that measure academics' value and monetize them. These metrics measure our grant income, research "excellence," citation scores, student evaluations, esteem indicators, impact factor, PhD completions, etc., etc. They produce what I have dubbed the "quantified self of neoliberal academia" (Gill 2015). These metrics work with a regime of value that is highly selective and yet seeks to render everything quantifiable. Some have suggested that we count different things—less (I suspect) to support a new proliferation of measures than as a radical thought experiment to disrupt the taken-for-granted reporting of "marketable outputs of a quantifiable nature" (Nussbaum 2010). "What if we counted differently?" Mountz et al. (2015) ask: "Instead of articles published or grants applied for, what if we accounted for thank you notes received, friendships formed, collaborations forged?" Undoing "counting culture," they argue, becomes part of a broader project of decolonizing knowledge. Indeed, "the very failure of our individual strategies of professional advancement and survival is the possibility of our collectively remaking the university" (1244). As Halberstam (2011) has argued, the "queer art of failure" offers subversive possibilities here to over-turn established regimes and to value different things (see also Back 2016).

Yet, importantly, these metrics, this new algorithmic culture, are not simply about "audit"—which suggests a measuring—however partial and problematic—of what is there. Much more perniciously they materialize new ways of doing and being in the academy. An example of "governing at a distance," they take on a life of their own, becoming autonomous actors that do things in the world—generate funding, damage reputations, single out people for redundancies, close down courses. They constitute a central part of the "new managerialism" or "new public management" or "performativity" (Ball 2000). As Stuart Hall has argued, they replace "professional judgment and control by wholesale importation of micro management practices of audit, inspection, monitoring, efficiency and value for money, despite the fact that neither their public role nor the public interest objectives can be adequately reframed in this way" (quoted in Redden 2008, 11). They incite a regime of "document everything, reveal nothing" (Butterwick and Dawson 2005, 55), calling on us to remake ourselves as "calculable rather then memorable" (Ball 2000)—exactly as Marx is rendered in the Omnishambles Tumblr and how he can be judged to be "not pulling his weight," despite having produced work that transformed Western thought.

The psychosocial costs of this are enormous. It produces new structures of feeling in the academy and contributes to our own self-surveillance and monitoring and commodification. Cris Shore argues that "auditing processes are having a corrosive effect on people's sense of professionalism and autonomy" (2008, 292). They produce what Chris Lorenz (2012) dubs "inner immigration," which I understand (through my reading of Frantz Fanon) as a specific form of alienation from oneself, in which the ability to hold a "double consciousness"—in other words, refusing to take on the university's way of seeing you and holding onto a separate/independent sense of one's own worth and value—is both essential, difficult, and agonizingly painful.

We are exhorted to view ourselves through the optic of these metrics that permeate every sphere of our working lives and dictate the worth of everything we do. "How many papers is a baby worth?" asked two feminist geographers (Klocker and Drozdzewski 2012). After an (ahem) pregnant pause, the Higher Education Funding Council of England (HEFCE) delivered its answer: "Each period of maternity leave equates to a reduced output expectation equivalent to one paper across each four year period" (HEFCE quoted in Gill 2014)—in other words, *one*! Sometimes it is hard not to think that one has tumbled down a rabbit hole into a parallel universe, so absurd does it seem that even a baby is "calculable" within our "metric assemblages" (Burrows 2012). The politics of life itself indeed.

More broadly, what is fascinating and disturbing is our growing complicity in these processes as a profession, as well as is the shift from a moment early on in these regimes, in which they were felt as something alien imposed upon academics from the outside, to the situation now, in which these qualculations are treated as meaningful and real (especially by those scoring best in them). I am always surprised when I see that otherwise apparently sane, critical, and smart colleagues have added little statements to the bottom of their emails, informing people how (well) their department scored in the Research Excellence Framework, or where they are located in some league table or other. What makes it even more comical/surreal is that there is now such an abundance of these measures—a new league table is published practically every week, and universities hire armies of consultants and administrators to produce the best possible spin on each one: so your university dropped fifty places in the Global Reputation rankings—oh dear— but, never mind, because its score for employability of graduates in science disciplines ranks in the top ten—definitely one for the website (ka-ching!). Of course, this is a deadly serious business—Shore (2008, 286) aptly notes "the policy of naming and shaming failing institutions has become an annual ritual and humiliation." But surely there is a need to keep some distance, even—dare I say—a level of playfulness that prevents us from suggesting that these indices genuinely represent "quality." I understand the need to try to do "well"—these are the "rules of the game," after all, and, hey, we are academics. But do we really need to suspend *all* critical judgment? There is much to learn, I believe, from anarchists and other activists who explore what it means to be *in and against the state* (see London-Edinburgh Weekend Return Group 1980), who embrace the ambivalence and complexity of that location rather than becoming card-carrying members of a regime of spurious, fabricated, market competition that our combined intelligence—let alone ethical sensibilities—must surely tell us is deeply suspect.

Beyond Individualism: The Psychosocial Life of the Neoliberal University

Contemporary academic capitalism works through affects and languages of love, flexibility and productivity.
—Mona Mannevuo, "Caught in a Bad Romance?"

> We must radically change the way in which we think about our-
> selves and our work.
> —Maria do Mar Pereira, "Struggling within and
> beyond the Performative University"

In this chapter I have discussed some of the emerging debate and critique about working conditions in the neoliberal university. In concluding, I want to interject some different perspectives. They develop from my interest in the affective and psychic life of academia. They do not start from the top— for example, from accounts about the structural transformation of the university that stress corporatization, "massification, marketization and internationalisation" (Barcan 2013)—but begin from the bottom—from the ground up—with experiences of academics as workers.

One of the enduring themes of my research—including my writing about the university—has been to challenge the persistence of individualism as a way of organizing and accounting. This has been evident in long-held interests in the relationship between culture and subjectivity, in my interest in exploring the "mentality" part of "governmentality," and in investigating the psychosocial aspects of neoliberalism and postfeminism. "Breaking the Silence" (Gill 2010) sought not simply to highlight the silenced and difficult aspects of academics' experiences and to render them knowable and speakable (as with the symposium in 2015) but also—crucially—to expose the extent to which these experiences are/were lived through a toxic individualizing discourse. What I have been struck by again and again in conversations with academics is the dominance of an individualistic register—a tendency to account for ordinary experiences in the academy through discourses of excoriating self-blame, privatized guilt, intense anxiety, and shame. Whether it is paralyzing job insecurity that made it impossible to make any kinds of plans for the future, or one-hundred-hour working weeks, academics are more likely to respond in a way that suggests *they* are failing than to express legitimate anger at being placed in such a situation. Time and again, I hear colleagues use languages of self-contempt, recrimination, or self-pathologization to talk about the struggles they experienced. Perfectly reasonable difficulties at dealing with hundreds of emails per day on top of "regular" work are evinced as signs of obsession or compulsion. Rejections (in a system in which nearly everything is rejected) are treated as evidence of shameful failure. Illness signifies an inability to cope and probable confirmation that one is not good enough or tough enough to be there. It was not that these injuries were not *felt*; it was that they were apprehended through a resolutely individualizing discourse that turned upside down the notion of the "personal as political." As Sara Ahmed (2010a) has argued, consciousness-raising is—at least in part—raising consciousness of unhappiness. But there is a need to move beyond what M. E. Luka et al. (2015) call the "documentation of shared misery, frustration, or trauma" (185) to something else—something that can transform these affects into action for change. It requires—as Eve Tuck (see Chapter 9 of this book) has powerfully expressed it—not "raising awareness" but making our experiences knowable in new and—importantly—*more disruptive* ways. As I see it, this involves acts of translation, dialogue, and political interruption.

There are examples of this in many sites—strikes, occupations, acts of solidarity, refusals, campaigns, reimaginings of the university. Indeed, as I write, I am just getting news that the campaign against brutal and coercive performance management at Newcastle University in the UK—the notorious "Raising the Bar"—has been successful, that university management has climbed down and agreed to engage in a more collaborative and bottom-up process for improving research.

But what I am struck by too is how tenacious individualism is—how many of our responses to academia themselves seem to reproduce precisely the individualizing tendencies we need to challenge. We see them in the burgeoning of attempts by university counselling departments and occupational health services to respond to the crisis (that is the new normal) with courses, training sessions, yoga, meditation, and events on time management or "handling difficult people"—and the new program de jour: resilience training. These interventions address alarming levels of stress, unhappiness, precariousness, and overwork through a resolute focus on individual psychological functioning. They systematically reframe our experiences in personal terms so the solution becomes trying to develop your "resilience quotient" (RQ) rather than organizing for change. This is not a conspiracy—and from my experience the professionals who run such courses and programs are caring and sensitive people, genuinely seeking to share resources and strategies—yet it is hard to avoid the conclusion that these are plans for managing the unmanageable and "fingers in the dam" of psychosocial and somatic catastrophe afflicting universities.

Another example is the proliferation of computer and smartphone applications that effectively take these courses and create mobile or online applications. Everything from mindfulness to "getting things done" have been promoted to—and taken up with alacrity by—academics, instilling the idea that it is our *relation* to work that needs to be changed, rather than the *nature* of working conditions themselves. These apps—again frequently perceived as tremendously valuable by colleagues and students—construct a view of academics as "inefficient" and "failing," requiring a suitably upgraded form of subjectivity and a "makeover" of how we work. Self-care can be "warfare," as Sara Ahmed and Audre Lorde both argue, and it can offer a critique of the neoliberal university (Barker 2011). But, when it remains stuck within the confines of cognitive behavioural or neurolinguistic (re)programming interventions, it risks trapping us within the very neoliberal logics that are in need of critique.

In thinking about the grip that individualism has, Ngaire Donaghue and I (Gill and Donaghue 2016) have also observed the agonizing contortions/paralysis that surrounds (relative) privilege and—with that—the apparent difficulty in offering politicized responses to anything other than the issue of casualization. Looking at academic blogs, we noticed that, unlike discussion of the academic precariat, "a striking contrast exists in the ways in which the experiences of tenured (or otherwise securely employed) academics are discussed—the sharp economic, political and ideological analysis shifts to a more personal register, with an orientation away from pressing the case for fundamental structural reform of universities in favour of venting, commiserating and sharing strategies for 'coping'" (Gill and Donaghue 2016, xx). The "luxury" of having a secure job makes writers feel "like a jerk" if they complain about their position, as they know they are "the lucky ones." Embarrassed and ashamed of their privilege, they retreat into what we call "reluctant individualism"—reluctant because these are thoughtful and critical scholars and this is not their usual mode of analysis, but individualism nonetheless because it offers no way of framing the situation beyond strategies for better self-management (being better at saying no, organzing time more effectively, etc.). The self-blame, guilt, and self-contempt that run through these accounts is extraordinarily painful to me—perhaps because it resonates. But, in my view, it produces a seriously impoverished critique (compared to what is needed). Perhaps, unwittingly, it suggests that "the only intelligible and legitimate critique must focus on casualization," thereby "missing so much else within the neoliberal academy that needs interrogation" (Gill and Donaghue 2016, 96).

Going forward, we urgently need a collective consciousness and action to bring about change—as well as new ways of thinking. Here are four concluding thoughts about what we require—at least to consider—in order to challenge the somatic and psychosocial crisis affecting us. First, a much expanded understanding of precarity—one that acknowledges the multiple forms of insecurity, precariousness, and dispossession within the academy—which includes the situations of all but the most privileged of our students as they find themselves effectively indentured by debt in a situation aggravated by unemployment and austerity; the cleaners, security, and catering staff, increasingly employed by subcontractors with dubious records in the carceral system on minimum wage and zero-hours contracts; the ways in which precariousness is entangled with disciplinary marginalizations—especially for scholars working in ethnic and racial studies, women's studies, postcolonial studies, and queer studies (Nash and Owens 2015; Arrigoitia et al. 2015). As well, the devastating rise of ill health as embodied effect of neoliberal regimes within the university must also surely count as a type of existential, ontological precarity, affecting more and more of us.

Second, and related to this, we need much more attention paid to power and difference and recognition of the deep intersectional inequalities that see women, Black and minority ethnic scholars, disabled people, and others represented in disproportionately small numbers, concentrated in precarious positions, paid less, in more junior positions (Bailey and Miller 2015; Leathwood and Read 2012), making up what Diane Reay (2004) dubbed the "lumpenproletariat" of academia. We need to explore the "inequality regimes" in academia: "the inter-related practices, processes, action and meanings that result in and maintain class, gender and race inequalities" (Acker 2006, 443). These operate in large, quantifiable, patterned ways, impacting hiring, pay, and tenure status but also at a finer grain: in the (felt) disparity between women's and men's pastoral care or "emotional labour" (Hochschild 2003) in the workplace; in how admin is shared out—what Tara Brabazon (2015) calls the "housework of academia" (34).

Third, we need to address the affective and psychosocial aspects of life within academia. Of course, it is possible to think about the neoliberal university or the corporate university or academic capitalism in terms of large-scale macro-economic trends—and this is important. But to do only this is to miss so much of what is going on: the way in which these new regimes get inside us, shape our sense of self, produce particular affects and subjectivities (e.g., shame or anxiety), erode collectivity and collaboration, promote competition, and so on. Some of the most exciting work explores these processes and examines the micro-politics of academic life (Gillies and Lucey 2007; Mannevuo 2016; Pereira 2016) in all its complexity.

Finally, we need to develop solidarities that go beyond our own locations. Drawing on the work of Gail Lewis (2009a, 2009b) on "difficult knowledges," I have dubbed these "difficult solidarities," as they require us to move beyond troubling animosities that often play out in terms of age, generation, and tenure status. An example might be seen in the intergenerational hatreds mobilized by comments about "whining adjuncts," in which contingent, precarious scholars are attacked for complaining about current conditions. They find their counterpart in sneering accounts of "quit lit"—a disparaging shorthand for the letters written by established scholars, who publicly—and painfully—resign from secure positions within academia, and in ageist jibes at those with tenure, as if they were a bevy of self-serving "bed-blockers," stubbornly refusing to make space for the young, even after their sell-by dates have long since been exceeded. In these cases, the animosity is, in my view, misdirected—on the one hand, it misrecognizes "the enemy," or at least what is at stake; on the other, it is politically unproductive and unhelpful. Moreover, it cements a way of relating that is the antithesis of the empathetic and generous engagement we need in order to go forward. To a long-time activist like myself, it might cynically be seen as a deliberate attempt to orchestrate division so we fight among ourselves.

We must resist the "neoliberal logics" and "hyper extensions of colonial time" (Shahjahan 2014, 3) that sort individuals into opposing categories and develop new, critical solidarities (Mountz et al. 2015). This will not be easy—for there are real differences—but making dialogues across these and relating with empathy and generosity is our only hope for radical social transformation. As Audre Lorde reminds us, the master's tools will never dismantle the master's house, but feminists in positions of power may be called on to "stand alone, unpopular and sometimes reviled" in order to create "our common cause…a world in which we can *all* flourish" (1984, 114).

Author's Note

I would like to express my warm appreciation to Marc Spooner and James McNinch for inviting me to their symposium on accountability and evidence in the neoliberal university. They created a very special space for discussion and collaboration, and I learned so much from so many people there—especially Michelle Fine, Leigh Patel, Eve Tuck, and Linda Tuhiwai Smith. I would also like to thank Meg-John Barker, Gail Lewis, Christina Scharff, and Shani Orgad for their very helpful comments and conversations while I was writing this chapter.

References

Acker, J. 2006. "Inequality Regimes, Gender, Class, and Race in Organizations." *Gender & Society* 20(4): 441–64.

Adsit, J., et al. 2015. "Affective Activism: Answering Institutional Productions of Precarity in the Corporate University." *Feminist Formations* 27(3): 21–48.

Ahmed, S. 2010a. *The Promise of Happiness*. Durham, NC: Duke University Press.

———. 2010b. "Secrets and Silence in Feminist Research." Foreword to *Secrecy and Silence in the Research Process: Feminist Reflections*, edited by R. Ryan-Flood and R. Gill, xvi–xxi. Abingdon, UK: Routledge.

Alcoff, L. 1991. "The Problem of Speaking for Others." *Cultural Critique* 20: 5–32.

Arrigoitia, M. F., et al. 2015. "Women's Studies and Contingency: Between Exploitation and Resistance." *Feminist Formations* 27(3): 81–113.

Back, L. 2016. *Academic Diary or Why Higher Education Still Matters*. London: Goldsmiths Press.

———. 2007. *The Art of Listening*. London: Berg.

Bailey, M., and S. J. Miller. 2015. "When Margins Become Centred: Black Queer Women in Front and Outside of the Classroom." *Feminist Formations* 27(3): 168–88.

Ball, S. J. 2000. "Performativities and Fabrications in the Education Economy: Towards the Performative Society?" *The Australian Educational Researcher* 27(2): 1–23.

Barcan, R. 2013. *Academic Life and Labour in the New University: Hope and Other Choices*. London: Ashgate.

Barker, M-J. 2011. "Self-Care." https://socialmindfulness.wordpress.com/2011/04/11/self-care/.

Behar, R. 2014. *The Vulnerable Observer: Anthropology That Breaks Your Heart*. Boston: Beacon Press.

Berg, M., and B. Seeber. 2016. *The Slow Professor: Challenging the Culture of Speed in the Academy*. Toronto: University of Toronto Press.

Berlant, L. G. 2011. *Cruel Optimism*. Durham, NC: Duke University Press.

Brabazon, T. 2015. "I Think She's decided to Be a Manager Now: Women, Management and Leadership in the Knowledge Factory." *Journal of Women's Entrepreneurship and Education* 3–4: 28–53.

Burrows, R. 2012. "Living with the H-Index? Metric Assemblages in the Contemporary Academy." *The Sociological Review* 60: 355–72.

Butterwick, S., and J. Dawson. 2005. "Undone Business: Examining the Production of Academic Labour." *Women's Studies International Forum* 28(1): 51–65.

Callon, M., and J. Law. 2005. "On Qualculation, Agency and Otherness." *Society and Space* 23: 717–33.

Carrigan, M., and P. Vostal. 2016. "Against the 'Slow Professor.'" https://markcarrigan.net/2016/04/13/against-the-slow-professor/.

Collini, S. 2012. *What Are Universities For?* London: Penguin.

Connelly, R., and K. Ghodsee. 2011. *Professor Mommy: Finding Work-Family Balance in Academia*. Lanham, MD: Rowman & Littlefield Publishers.

Crang, M. 2007. "Flexible and Fixed Times Working in the Academy." *Environment and Planning A*. 39(3): 509–14.

Department of Omnishambles. "Karl Marx's End-of-Year Departmental Assessment." *YouTube*. https://www.youtube.com/watch?v=of_fxiT-jK4.

Edu-Factory Collective. 2009. *Toward a Global Autonomous University: Cognitive Labor, the Production of Knowledge, and Exodus from the Education Factory*. New York: Autonomedia.

Evans, E., and C. Grant. 2008. *Mama, PhD: Women Write about Motherhood and Academic Life*. New Brunswick, NJ: Rutgers University Press.

Evans, M. 2004. *Killing Thinking: Death of the University*. London: Bloomsbury Publishing.

Federici, S. 2012. *Revolution at Point Zero: Housework, Reproduction, and Feminist Struggle*. Oakland, CA: PM Press.

Galetto, M., et al. 2007. "A Snapshot of Precariousness: Voices, Perspectives, Dialogues." *Feminist Review* 87: 104–12.

Gill, R. 2014. "Academics, Cultural Workers and Critical Labour Studies." *Journal of Cultural Economy* 7(1): 12–30.

———. 2010. "Breaking the Silence: The Hidden Injuries of the Neoliberal University." In *Secrecy and Silence in the Research Process: Feminist Reflections*, edited by R. Ryan-Flood and R. Gill, 228–44. Abingdon, UK: Routledge.

———. 2015. "The Quantified Self of Academia." Paper presented at the "Public Engagement and the Politics of Evidence" conference, University of Regina, Saskatchewan, July 23–25.

Gill, R., and N. Donaghue. 2016. "Resilience, Apps and Reluctant Individualism: Technologies of Self in the Neoliberal Academy." *Women's Studies International Forum* 54: 91–99.

Gillies, V., and H. Lucey, eds. 2007. *Power, Knowledge and the Academy: The Institutional Is Political*. London: Palgrave Macmillan.

Giroux, H. 2002. "The Corporate War against Higher Education." *Workplace* 9. http://ices.library.ubc.ca/index.php/workplace/article/view/184051.

Godard, L. 2014. "Higher Education: A Tale of Two Payslips." *Intergenerational Foundation*. http://www.if.org.uk/archives/5409/higher-education-a-tale-of-two-payslips.

Gregg, M. 2009. "Function Creep: Communication Technologies and Anticipatory Labour in the Information Workplace." *New Media and Society*.

Grove, J. 2016. THE *University Workplace Survey 2016: Results and Analysis*. https://www.timeshighereducation.com/features/university-workplace-survey-2016-results-and-analysis.

The Guardian. *Academics Anonymous* [blog]. https://www.theguardian.com/higher-education-network/series/academics-anonymous.

———. 2016. "Dear student, I just don't have time to mark your essay properly." *Academics Anonymous* [blog], May 20. https://www.theguardian.com/higher-education-network/2016/may/20/dear-student-i-just-dont-have-time-to-mark-your-essay-properly.

Halberstam, J. 2011. *The Queer Art of Failure*. Durham, NC: Duke University Press.

Halffman, W., and H. Radder. 2015. "The Academic Manifesto: From an Occupied to a Public University." *Minerva* 53(2): 165–87.

Hey, V. 2004. "Perverse Pleasures—Identity Work and the Paradoxes of Greedy Institutions." *Journal of International Women's Studies* 5(3): 33–43.

Hochschild, A. R. 1979. "Emotion Work, Feeling Rules, and Social Structure." *American Journal of Sociology* 85(3): 551–75.

———. 2003. *The Managed Heart: Commercialization of Human Feeling*. Berkeley: University of California Press.

Klocker, N., and D. Drozdzewski. 2012. "Survival and Subversion in the Neoliberal University." http://ro.uow.edu.au/smhpapers/1184.

Krause, M., et al. 2008. *The University against Itself: The NYU Strike and the Future of the Academic Workplace*. Philadelphia, PA: Temple University Press.

Kuehn, K., and T. F. Corrigan. 2013. "Hope Labor: The Role of Employment Prospects in Online Social Production." *The Political Economy of Communication* 1(1): 9–25.

Leathwood, C., and B. Read. 2012. *Assessing the Impact of Developments in Research Policy for Research on Higher Education: An Exploratory Study*. https://www.srhe. ac.uk/downloads/Leathwood_Read_Final_Report_16_July_2012.pdf.

Lewis, G. 2009a. "Animating Hatreds: Research Encounters, Organisational Secrets, Emotional Truths." In *Secrecy and Silence in the Research Process: Feminist Reflections*, edited by R. Ryan-Flood and R. Gill, 211–27. Abingdon, UK: Routledge

———. 2009b. "Birthing Racial Difference: Conversations with My Mother and Others." *Studies in the Maternal* 1(1): 1–21.

London-Edinburgh Weekend Return Group. 1980. *In and Against the State*. London: Pluto Press.

Lorde, A. 1984. *Sister Outsider: Essays and Speeches by Audre Lorde*. Trumansburg, NY: The Crossing Press.

Lorenz, C. 2012. "If You're So Smart, Why Are You under Surveillance? Universities, Neoliberalism and New Public Management." *Critical Inquiry* 38: 599–629.

Luka, M. E., et al. 2015. "Scholarship as Cultural Production in the Neoliberal University: Working within and against 'Deliverables.'" *Studies in Social Justice* 9(2): 176–96.

Lynch, K. 2010. "Carelessness: A Hidden Doxa of Higher Education." *Arts and Humanities in Higher Education* 9(1): 54–67.

Mannevuo, M. 2016. "Caught in a Bad Romance? Affective Attachments in Contemporary Academia." In *The Post-Fordist Sexual Contract: Working and Living in Contingency*, edited by L. Adkins and M. Dever, 71–88. Basingstoke, UK: Palgrave Macmillan.

Martell, L. 2014. "The Slow University: Inequality, Power and Alternatives." *Forum Qualitative Sozialforschung/Forum: Qualitative Social Research* 15(3) (September). http://www.qualitative-research.net/index.php/fqs/article/ view/2223/3692.

Martin, R. 2012. *Under New Management: Universities, Administrative Labor and the Professional Turn*. Philadelphia, PA: Temple University Press.

Meyers, M., ed. 2012. *Women in Higher Education*. New York: Hampton Press.

Mitropoulos, A. 2006. "Precari-us?" *Mute* 1(29). http://www.metamute.org/editorial/articles/precari-us.

Morini, C. 2007. "The Feminisation of Labour in Cognitive Capitalism." *Feminist Review* 87: 40–59.

Mountz, A., et al. 2015. "For Slow Scholarship: A Feminist Politics of Resistance through Collective Action in the Neoliberal University." *ACME* 14(4): 1235–59.

Nash, J., and E. Owens. 2015. "Institutional Feelings: Practicing Women's Studies in the Corporate University." *Feminist Formations* 27(3): vii–xi.

Nussbaum, M. 2010. *Not for Profit: Why Democracy Needs the Humanities*. New Brunswick, NJ: Princeton University Press.

Pereira, M. 2016. "Struggling within and beyond the Performative University: Articulating Activism and Work in an 'Academia without Walls.'" *Women's Studies International Forum* 54: 100–10.

Readings, B. 1996. *The University in Ruins*. Cambridge, MA: Harvard University Press.

Reay, D. 2004. "Cultural Capitalists and Academic Habitus: Classed and Gendered Labour in UK Higher Education." *Women's Studies International Forum* 27: 31–39.

Redden, G. 2008. "From RAE to ERA: Research Evaluation at Work in the Corporate University." *Australian Humanities Review* 45. http://www.australianhumanitiesreview.org/archive/Issue-November-2008/redden.html.

The Res-Sisters. 2016. "I'm an Early Career Feminist Academic: Get Me out of Here?" In *Feminist Beginnings: Being an Early Career Feminist Academic in a Changing Academy*, edited by R. Thwaites and A. Godoy-Pressland, 267–84. Basingstoke, UK: Palgrave Macmillan.

Roggero, G. 2011. *The Production of Living Knowledge: The Crisis of the University and the Transformation of Labor in Europe and North America*. Philadelphia, PA: Temple University Press.

Ryan-Flood, R., and R. Gill, eds. 2010. *Secrecy and Silence in the Research Process: Feminist Reflections*. Abingdon, UK: Routledge.

Shahjahan, R. A. 2014. "Being 'Lazy' and Slowing Down: Toward Decolonizing Time, Our Body, and Pedagogy." *Educational Philosophy and Theory* 47(5): 488–501.

Shore, C. 2008. "Audit Culture and Illiberal Governance: Universities and the Culture of Accountability." *Anthropological Theory* 8(3): 278–98.

SIGJ2 Writing Collective. 2012. "What Can We Do? The Challenge of Being New Academics in Neoliberal Universities." *Antipode* 44(4): 1055–58.

Sparkes, A. 2007. "Embodiment, Academics, and the Audit Culture: A Story Seeking Consideration." *Qualitative Research* 7(4): 521–50. doi:10.1177/1468794107082306.

Spooner, M. 2015. "Higher Education's Silent Killer." *Briarpatch Magazine*. https://briarpatchmagazine.com/articles/view/higher-educations-silent-killer.

Standing, G. 2011. *The Precariat: The New Dangerous Class*. London: A & C Black.

Thrift, N. 2000. "Performing Cultures in the New Economy." *Annals of the Association of American Geographers* 90(4): 674–92.

University and College Union (UCU). 2016. *UCU Workload Survey*. https://www.ucu.
org.uk/media/8196/Executive-summary---Workload-is-an-education-issue-
UCU-workload-survey-report-2016/pdf/ucu_workloadsurvey_summary_
jun16.pdf.

Weeks, K. 2005. "The Refusal of Work as Demand and Perspective." In *Resistance
in Practice: The Philosophy of Antonio Negri*, edited by T. S. Murphy and A. K.
Mustapha, 109–35. London: Pluto Press.

Wilkinson, S., and C. Kitzinger, eds. 1996. *Representing the Other: A Feminism &
Psychology Reader*. Thousand Oaks, CA: Sage.

CHAPTER 12

FATAL DISTRACTION: AUDIT CULTURE AND ACCOUNTABILITY IN THE CORPORATE UNIVERSITY

Joel Westheimer

There is a story about a man crossing a border on his bicycle. He has two large bags attached to the bike rack. When he reaches the border control, the agent asks him, "What's in the bags?" "Sand," he replies. Skeptical, the agent searches first one bag, then the other, and finds nothing in them but sand. The agent returns the bags to the man and lets him cross the border. The following day, the same thing happens. The agent asks, "What's in the bags?" "Sand," says the man. The agent again searches the bags and finds nothing but sand and again allows him to cross. This sequence of events is repeated every day for months. Finally, the border agent pulls the man aside. "Look, I've been doing this for many years, and this is driving me crazy. I know you're smuggling something, but I don't know what it is. I'm not going to give you any trouble, but I just need to know: What are you smuggling?" The man looks at the border agent and says, "Bicycles."

As audit culture takes root in higher education, university faculty are finding themselves distracted by endless requests for accountability, data, value-added measures of success, demonstrably patentable products, evidence of public-private partnerships, and forms, forms, and more forms. We resist. We push back against this particular measure over here and argue for a more reasonable one over there. We complain about larger class sizes or arbitrary benchmarks for success or "efficiency." Like the border agent, more and more of us are mired in these fine grains of sand while missing the wholesale theft of bicycles. Except it is not bicycles we stand to lose but fundamental principles of academic life. As we seek cover from the sandstorm born of the winds of audit culture and sift through the resulting wreckage and debris, the forces of neoliberal ideology and the actions of corporatized boards of trustees—who either fail to resist the neoliberal flow or actively promote it—are steadily spiriting away the most important ideals of a university education: the promotion of critical thought, and a commitment to democratic community and the public good.

Every policy recommendation that calls for austerity, public accountability, and greater focus on career preparation serves as distraction from more robustly democratic goals for education. As Yvonna Lincoln's chapter in this book deftly demonstrates, these kinds of neoliberal goals of the past decade have dramatically and broadly rewritten the educational landscape of K–16 education. Pseudo-evidentiary notions of austerity, a widespread cultural obsession with accountability, a reframing of public education as job training, and the concomitant privileging of STEM subject areas over the humanities and social sciences have dominated public and policy discourse on educational goals and means. In the process, the historic role of universities founded on ideals of knowledge and service in the public interest has been challenged. In this chapter, I examine the effects of neoliberal reforms and ask how we might begin to restore higher education's public purpose.

I will focus on five developments (let us call them distractions) stemming from a neoliberal view of education: the foregrounding of budget shortfalls to create a climate of contrived scarcity, which I will call "fictive austerity"; an obsession with accountability; the elimination of critical thinking and a culture of criticism; the weakening of intellectual independence and democratic faculty governance; and the promotion of a meritocracy myth that drives the work of graduate students, and junior and senior faculty alike. Taken together, these distractions draw our collective attention away from the grand heist hidden in plain sight: public understanding of the importance of a liberal democratic education. Private economic and technocratic goals sideline public ones, threatening not only historic ideals of university life but also the future of democratic thinking itself.

I want to underscore that these are not five independent distractions that happen to take place at the same time like an unlucky confluence of events in a perfect storm. Rather, each is systematically entangled with the other four.

The first distraction (*fictive austerity*) lays the groundwork for widespread acceptance of the other four by casting opposition to them as naive, foolish, and unrealistic. The second distraction (*accountability*) follows logically from this climate of scarcity while advancing anti-intellectualism in the guise of educational improvement. The third (*attacks on critical thinking*) and fourth (*hierarchical governance*) erode democratic thinking by curbing the habits of mind and heart that enable democracy to flourish—what John Dewey (1916, 360) called the "associated experience[s]" essential to democratic life. The last (*the meritocracy myth*) attacks the heart of these associated experiences by diminishing the power of the community to nurture collective meaning and worth. I will conclude with possibilities for renewed emphasis on education for the common good.

Fictive Austerity: "I Drank All the Water; We Have to Conserve Water"

I call this first distraction "fictive austerity," not because I think universities do not have financial problems (they do) but because I feel strongly about the need for academics and administrators alike to challenge the inevitability of those problems. To accomplish that goal, I want to start with some recollections of the Occupy Wall Street movement and its relationship to so-called austerity measures.

You may recall the summer of 2011, when the Vancouver-based magazine and activist group *Adbusters* proposed a peaceful occupation of Wall Street to protest the ever-increasing corporate influence on the world's democratic institutions and processes. On September 17, 2011, that occupation began with a few hundred people gathering first in Battery Park in New York City and then moving to the now infamous Zucotti Park, where they formed an encampment (Adbusters 2014; Elliot 2011). By October 15 of that year, global demonstrations had reached 950 cities in eighty-two countries (Sieczkowski 2011). In Madrid, the Occupy protests attracted more than half a million protesters. The claims of insignificance began immediately following the September 17 gathering: they have no agenda; they have no leaders; they have no goals; they lack political affiliation; they are hippies; they are drug users; they are disorganized; they lack organizational skills; they are misinformed; they are bitter; and so on. In fact, these criticisms and claims of insignificance and inefficacy continue among media pundits, politicians, and in the public imagination today (Westheimer 2012).

But Politico reporter Dylan Byers (2011) showed a remarkable transformation that few predicted but that everyone experienced. Byers conducted a LexisNexis search and found that, across major news media, the use of the term "income inequality" surged by more than 500 per cent from ninety-one instances in the week before the Occupy Wall Street protests began to more than five hundred instances in the first week of November 2011. Income inequality had become part of the national and global discourse in a way it had not been in decades. Max Read, writing for Gawker.com, called it "the best sign that Occupy Wall Street is working," adding, "not bad for a group of people who almost fell apart over a bunch of drummers" (Read 2011). In other words, Occupy Wall Street may go down in history—if for nothing else—for the critically important task of making economic justice part of the conversation. The terms "1 per cent" and "99 per cent" are now burned into our vocabulary as an important shorthand for a discourse on economic justice that had previously been confined to only one end of the political spectrum.

There are as many illustrations of what that gap between the 1 per cent and the 99 per cent means as there are Starbucks in Manhattan. But, for illustrative purposes, I will cite one popular one: the seven wealthiest individuals in the world have a net worth of $386.2 billion (Forbes 2016). Units of billions of dollars have become so commonplace in our collective dot-com imagination that these numbers have lost their true meaning. To put these kinds of figures into perspective, imagine those seven wealthiest individuals riding together in a minivan. The combined wealth of the passengers in that minivan is equivalent to the combined gross domestic product (GDP) of seventy-one of the planet's approximately 190 nations (International Monetary Fund 2016; World Bank 2016).[1]

In Canada, where I live, income inequality has been increasing at a faster rate than in the United States (partly, to be sure, because inequality is so much greater to begin with in the United States). Between 1980 and 2009, the wealthiest 20 per cent of Canadians saw household market income increase by 38 per cent, while that of the bottom 20 per cent decreased by 11.4 per cent. Canada's richest 10 per cent now owns 58 per cent of national wealth, while the bottom 50 per cent owns 3 per cent (Conference Board of Canada 2012). In the United States the numbers are more stark. The top 0.1 per cent of American families now owns approximately the same share of wealth as the bottom 90 per cent (Saez and Zucman 2014; Saez 2015). These are, as political economist Gar Alperovitz (2005) observes, "medieval numbers."

Okay, you might be thinking, but what does this have to do with education? Why am I writing about wealth inequality in a chapter about the corporate university? Why should education professionals (since most of us are neither economists nor political scientists) be concerned with any of these numbers? The massive allocation of national and global resources away from the provision of public goods and toward private gain for a select few is a matter of concern for any educator at any level of the system. What does so-called austerity mean against this backdrop? Who should be austere, exactly, and what choices do we have to grapple with budget shortfalls?

Since 2012, I have been the education columnist for CBC Radio's *Ottawa Morning* and *Ontario Today* shows, and a number of times hosts or callers have asked me what, exactly, I would cut from educational programs given that we are in a time of fiscal crisis or austerity. I have tried my best to respond politely, but I always wonder: Who declared this a time of austerity? Did I miss a ministerial, presidential, or divine proclamation?

Since Canada is a tenth of the size of the United States, the savings called for in education are often cited in millions of dollars. Sometimes provincial policy-makers talk in hundreds of thousands—something along the lines of, "We have to cut funding for a student assistance centre that costs $187,000 per year to run." But who designated education and other public services like health as the de facto targets for savings? Here are some facts about Canada (and keep in mind that Canadian tax policies tend to be more progressive and equitable than those in the United States). Currently, in Canada:

- Stock options are taxed at half the rate that Canadians pay on employment income (Government of Canada 2015).
- The corporate tax rate fell below 25 per cent in 2012 and has barely risen since, remaining at about 28 per cent for most provinces (Canada Revenue Agency 2017).
- The highest tax rate in Canada (between 40 per cent and 50 per cent, depending on which province) has long applied to those whose income exceeds $200,000, without any further distinctions above that level. After years of grassroots work by a broad variety of nongovernmental organizations, a 2014 modest tax increase was applied in Ontario to personal incomes over $500,000, raising $300 million for social services (Income Security Advocacy Centre 2017).
- An additional 6 per cent tax on those who make more than $1.8 million per year would raise approximately $5 billion annually; Ontario alone would raise $1.7 billion.

- Restoring a 14 per cent provincial corporate tax would recoup $2 billion annually.
- As Canadian economist and Member of Parliament Erin Weir (2012) noted, "Restoring a corporate capital tax just for banks and adding two percentage points of tax on personal income over half a million dollars would collect a further $1.2 billion annually."

Statistics like these make me question whether this is, indeed, a time of belt-tightening for all or just for the poor and middle class. Why did the Occupy Wall Street movement resonate with so many in the United States and around the world? At the time the Occupy protests spread so widely, 43 per cent of Americans were "liquid assets poor," meaning they lack the money to live for three months if their main source of income were lost (Corporation for Enterprise Development 2013). More than forty-six million Americans were living in poverty and on food stamps. More than seventeen million women lived in poverty. Fourteen million people were unemployed. Over fifty million Americans were uninsured. Another fifty million were underinsured. A Harvard study from a few years earlier (Wilper et al. 2009) showed that forty-five thousand were dying every year because they lacked health insurance. (Although more Americans now have health insurance because of the Affordable Care Act, economic inequality has remained the same or worsened.)

At the same time that these fifty million Americans were uninsured, ExxonMobil's profits rose 35 per cent to a whopping $41.1 billion. That is nearly $5 million in profit every hour, or more than $1,300 every second. Yet Exxon pays a lower effective tax rate than most Americans and refused to pay $92 million in cleanup costs for the Valdez Alaskan oil spill (Leber 2012). Yet, in 2011, Exxon had no problem paying one individual—CEO Rex Tillerson—$29 million in one year's salary and bonuses (Gonzalez 2011). Tillerson's salary rose to $34.9 million the following year. When economic inequality has reached medieval levels, nobody should be asking educators what schools and universities should be cutting in a time of austerity. The questions posed by policy-makers and the mainstream media that ask "What programs of immense public benefit should be cut in this *time of austerity*?" should instead begin with "How should our public revenue systems be adjusted in this time of *radically medieval economic injustice*?"

Underfunding is not a force of nature. It is a policy choice that benefits those at the top of the income curve at the expense of public institutions and programs that benefit everyone. In the United States, Warren Buffett has drawn attention to the need to increase funding for education and for other institutions that benefit the public by pleading with congressional leaders to raise his effective tax rate so it is at least as high as the tax rate paid by his secretary (Buffett 2011). In a similar gesture, the Canadian group, Doctors for Fair Taxation, adopted the motto, "Tax us. Canada's worth it" (Babad 2012; Doctors for Fair Taxation 2014). More than sixty years ago, former United States Supreme Court Justice Louis Brandeis is purported to have warned, "We can have democracy...or we can have great wealth concentrated in the hands of a few, but we can't have both." Democratic institutions are worthy of public support, and public support requires pushing back against fictive austerity.

Accountability

Despite the success of the Occupy Wall Street movement in placing inequality squarely in the national conversation, in K–12 education reform circles, the notion of "inequality" has most often been hijacked by proponents of accountability measures, such as increased standardized testing to mean a gap in test scores only. Moreover, the tests tend to hold schools "accountable" in only two subject areas: math and literacy. Many of the failed policies in K–12 learning are now moving to higher education as well, most visibly in the idea of value-added testing models and narrowing of the curriculum to those courses that lend themselves to such a model.

This does not mean there is no place for assessment in education. Many opponents of a testing-all-the-time curriculum make the need for thoughtful forms of assessment and educational frameworks clear. But No Child Left Behind and Race to the Top legislation and related reforms that call for ever-more-standardized rubrics and frameworks have severely restricted K–12 teachers' abilities to act in a professional capacity and exercise professional judgment on behalf of their students, and I fear the same short-sighted deprofessionalization efforts are now being extended to professors as well.

Finnish educator Pasi Sahlberg (2012) calls the kind of school reform that elevates the pursuit of accountability and standardization above all other educational considerations GERM (Global Education Reform Movement). He describes GERM as follows:

> It is like an epidemic that spreads and infects education systems through a virus. It travels with pundits, media and politicians.

> Education systems borrow policies from others and get infected. As a consequence, schools get ill, teachers don't feel well, and kids learn less. (Sahlberg 2012)

Not only do kids learn less. What they learn also tends to follow prescriptive formulas that match the standardized tests or whatever other "accountability" measure is put in place. In the process, more complex and difficult-to-measure learning outcomes get left behind. Professors of education have become exceedingly familiar with the many critiques of an accountability-driven, test-based curriculum: its enforced uniformity; its bias; its relegation of all but math and literacy to the margins of the school experience. University professors are now becoming familiar with these trends as well. Standardized tests; value-added, merit-based pay schemes; and similar accountability measures settle easily in universities that have moved from a mission of public knowledge and citizenship to a mission of job training and profitable patents.

In K–12 reforms, the narrowed curriculum that comes from a focus on accountability is overlooked by well-meaning stakeholders. Even though parents do not like all the testing, and teachers do not like all the testing, and kids do not like all the testing, the discourse on accountability and quantification of outcomes trumps the discourse on a meaningful quality education. It is a much simpler task to find out whether students know the answers, which can be memorized to fact-based questions, than to hold them accountable for their critical thinking skills, their creativity, or their proclivity for civic engagement. Higher education has been slower to adopt these kinds of constraints, leaving professors with freedom to exercise professional judgment in determining the experiences students have in their classrooms and lecture halls. But, as a corporate approach to educational management gains footholds in pedagogical decision making, professors find themselves increasingly subject to the same kind of reductionist, anti-intellectual thinking that has plagued K–12 teachers for the past decade. Accountability frameworks demand that when we are unable to measure the things we care about, we start to care about only the things we can measure.

The Impact of Neoliberal Reforms on Critical Thinking

As enforced accountability measures facilitate the reduction of education from its public purposes to goals of job training and individual gain, a focus on prescribed knowledge and skills crowds out traditional efforts at developing the capacities for critical thought. Laws in Florida, Oklahoma, Arizona, and other states in the United States seek to dictate the degree to which teachers are allowed to raise classroom discussions that challenge. One of the clearest examples of these trends comes from Florida. In June 2006, the Florida Education Omnibus Bill included language specifying,

> The history of the United States shall be taught as genuine history.…American history shall be viewed as factual, not as constructed, shall be viewed as knowable, teachable, and testable. (Craig 2006; see also Immerwahr 2008)

The bill also went on to require educators to stress the importance of free enterprise to the U.S. economy. Of course, both K–12 teachers and professors of history almost universally regard history as exactly a matter of interpretation; indeed, the competing interpretations are what make history so interesting. Historians and educators alike widely derided the mandated adherence to an official story embodied in the Florida legislation, but the impact of such mandates should not be underestimated. The stated goal of the bill's designers was "to raise historical literacy," with a particular emphasis on the "teaching of facts." For example, the bill requires that only facts be taught when it comes to discussing the "period of discovery" and the early colonies. We could say that Florida became the first state to ban historical interpretation in public schools, thereby effectively outlawing critical thinking. But Florida is not alone. Legislation in Colorado seeks to promote "positive" American history and downplay the legacy of civil disobedience and protest. History, the Colorado board suggested, should promote "patriotism, benefits of the free enterprise system [and] respect for authority" (Glenza 2014; Jacobs 2014). Arizona State Bill 1108 bars teaching practices that "overtly encourage dissent" from "American values," without specifying exactly what dissenting from American values might mean (*Proposed House of Representatives Amendments*).

While examples of curtailment of critical thinking in classroom practice in higher education are increasingly common, it is worth examining universities' new penchant for limiting the research professors conduct to investigations that do not run afoul of funders or that work against the new notion of the university as a place for simple job skills training. The impact of a corporatized university on the pursuit of knowledge in the public interest has been severely compromised. From the mission statement of the University of Toronto:

> Within the unique university context, the most crucial of all
> human rights...are meaningless unless they entail the right to
> raise deeply disturbing questions and provocative challenges
> to the cherished beliefs of society at large and of the university
> itself...It is this human right to radical, critical teaching and
> research with which the University has a duty above all to be
> concerned; for there is no one else, no other institution and no
> other office, in our modern liberal democracy, which is the cus-
> todian of this most precious and vulnerable right of the liberated
> human spirit. (University of Toronto 1992)

This excerpt might be hailed as a shining example of the centrality of university campuses in promoting and preserving critical thinking as the engine of
progress in any democratic society. Except for one thing: institutional leaders at the university who drafted these words do not believe them and do not
abide by them. The University of Toronto is the site of two of the most noto-
riously blatant violations of these principles in the past decade: the well-
publicized cases of the University of Toronto's Nancy Olivieri, who, in the
late 1990s, was sued by the drug company Apotex for going public with data
that cast doubt on an experimental drug; and David Healy, who, in 2000,
had an offer of a clinical directorship and professorship at the University of
Toronto withdrawn after he publicly questioned the safety of the popular
antidepressant Prozac. Both incidents revealed the university's unwilling-
ness to stand up to corporate funders and protect academic freedom and the
integrity of critical inquiry.

Unfortunately, the Olivieri and Healy cases do not stand alone. Over the
years, there have been scores of examples of scientific and social scientific
research essential to public welfare being undermined by private influence
(see Soley 1995; Newson and Buchbinder 1988; Kirp 2004; Turk 2008;
Washburn 2005). The balance of private funding of clinical medical research
in Canada reached majority territory by 2004, when a Canadian Association
of University Teachers (CAUT) report found more than 52 per cent of funding was from corporate sources (Welch et al. 2004). The trend is easiest to
spot and most publicly alarming in the medical sciences, since lives are at
stake. But there is cause for concern as well in the humanities and social
sciences, where publishing inconvenient truths can be discouraged by university administrators.

The harm to the reputation of the university as a reliable source of (especially "scientific") information, untainted by private conflicts of interest, has

been documented extensively. But the ways these changes affect the campus life of faculty and students have been considered far less. As universities turn to business models—becoming certification factories rather than institutions of higher learning—democratic educational ideals are fast becoming obsolete. Consequently, professors find it more difficult in their teaching to foster critical thinking as a necessary underpinning of democratic participation. The "shopping mall" university, where students seek the cheapest and fastest means for obtaining the basic skills and certification they need, is becoming a familiar metaphor and model for university administrators, students, and parents (see, for example, Mattson 2008). Courses not directly related to job training look more and more like useless dust to be eliminated. Meetings among faculty about which program of courses might yield the most robust understanding of a field of study, and of the debates and struggles that field entails, are rapidly being replaced by brainstorming sessions about how to narrow the curriculum to fit into, for example, two weekends, in order to *incentivize* matriculation and increase student enrolment.

The Weakening of Intellectual Independence
and Democratic Faculty Governance

The state of affairs I describe in the previous sections pertains mostly to the emaciated pedagogical and research potential of the newly corporatized university. But, ultimately, what faculty—and especially junior faculty—are being asked to give up is their own intellectual independence. The creeping corporate climate of some university departments and schools can easily lead to the substitution of bureaucratic allegiance, in the form of "budget alignment" or "optimization" in the new parlance, for scholarly inquiry as the cornerstone of academic life. In some cases, the effect on the intellectual life of a department might be plain to see. In some schools and faculties, elected department chairs—who traditionally served terms of a few years and then eagerly returned to their intellectual pursuits within the department—have been replaced by chairs *appointed* by university higher-ups with no, or at best perfunctory, input from department faculty. Some stay in these positions for a decade or more with ever-diminishing interest in, or focus on, scholarly inquiry. In an article titled "Tenure Denied" (Westheimer 2002), where I described more fully my experiences at New York University, I told of a colleague at a Midwestern university whose department chair suggested to the faculty that research questions that the department wanted investigated should be agreed on by a committee (made up of senior faculty and administrators) and posted on a website—and that faculty should align their research with one of those questions. Requiring research to be streamlined according to central criteria (doubtless related to funding opportunities) makes perfect sense if one treats an academic department as a profit centre. But it turns scholarly life into something less than we all hope it to be.

At times, the mere fact that departmental faculty are pursuing an active, diverse, and uncontrolled set of research agendas may be perceived negatively by school administrators. While such departments continue to recruit promising scholars on the basis of their research production, the departmental leadership is caught in a bind. They need such scholars for the department's reputation and grant-getting ability, but, once there, these scholars may pose some threat to the order of business within the department (and to the security of the chair, who has likely already traded the kind of professional security earned from scholarly inquiry and production for the kind won by allegiance and loyalty to university higher-ups).

Appointed chairs can slowly and steadily shift faculty focus from scholarly pursuits that advance a field to those that advance the chair, a possibility especially troubling to junior faculty seeking tenure. Much as external pressures on the corporate university constrain and refocus academic research, so too do internal incentives on the departmental level. As in much of university politics, junior faculty are the most vulnerable. Faculty governance in departments that have remade themselves along corporate culture lines can become little more than a parody of pseudo-democratic (or simply nondemocratic) governance, in which faculty simply (and always) endorse administrative positions. Faculty managers' and department chairs' only convictions are those that do not ruffle administrative feathers of those higher up. And the chill that blankets departments in which power has been centralized results in the further entrenchment of anti-democratic tendencies.

Under these conditions, the university starts to look less like a place of free exchange of ideas and more like a Hobbesian leviathan, a place that boasts, as former State University of New York (SUNY) New Paltz President Roger Bowen warns, "a settled, conforming, obedient citizenry—not dissenters who challenge convention." In these departments, junior faculty either conform or withdraw from departmental life after being tenured. The bottom line is raised to the top. Research that promotes the financial and hierarchical health of the administration is rewarded, while independent scholarly thought is punished. Institutions of higher education become ones of education for hire. Undue administrative influence over research agendas and appointed department chairs, the further erosion of democratic governance, and the hiring of part-time and clinical faculty with no time for scholarly inquiry and little job security are all threats to both critical inquiry and university democracy.

Before moving on to my final point, I want to point out that these conditions are created not only by university administration but also by a complicit faculty who would rather not sacrifice research time to engage in something as time-consuming as democratic governance. In other words, a repressive hierarchy is not required for nondemocratic decision making to flourish. Were university administrators to honour democratic faculty governance fully, would faculty step up to the plate? Under a corporate model of governance, appointed department chairs may stay in their positions for a decade or more. A democratic model, however, would require those deeply engaged in scholarship and research to be willing (or required) to take on leadership positions in administration, in addition to their roles as teacher and scholar. Countering an increasingly hierarchical and corporatized model of university governance requires commitments of time and energy that many faculty members now shun but that a just workplace requires.

The Corporate Benefits of the Meritocracy Myth

One final characteristic of the newly corporatized campus I want to address is the complicity of the professorial (and graduate student) culture. The pervasive culture of increasing individualism results in a story we tell ourselves that goes something like this: "We work in a merit-based system. If I do my job correctly—if I'm a good graduate student or a good professor, and I'm smart and I do my work well—I will be rewarded with a plum teaching assignment, and I will be part of the academic elite and get a job." This is an unfortunate state of affairs for two reasons. The first is economic and concerns the entrenched system of academic labour. The simple reality is that for the majority of disciplines, the claim that the system is merit-based is just not true. There are vastly more qualified, hardworking individuals than there are tenure-track and tenured academic positions for them to fill. At a certain level of proficiency, it becomes the luck of the draw.

But the second cost of an emphasis on individualism in the form of the meritocracy myth might be more insidious. Faculty focused only on individualized measures of professional success miss out on the collective action that has an extensive history in democratic societies and that has sustained and driven countless scholars, artists, scientists, and activists: working together toward a common end. Merit-based rewards encourage faculty to work behind office doors, estranged from colleagues. As my colleague Marc Bousquet (2008) points out in his book, *How the University Works*, believing in the fantasy of merit results in a great loss to everyone, including those dubbed meritorious.

The corporate university, on the other hand, advances and benefits from the illusion that each of us will attain rock star status in the academy. Some readers might recall the episode of the television show *The West Wing* (2001), when fictional President Jed Bartlet explains why Americans seem to vote against their own interests by protecting a tax system that benefits only the super rich. "It doesn't matter if most voters don't benefit," he explains. "They all believe that someday they will. That's the problem with the American dream. It makes everyone concerned for the day they're going to be rich." And so it goes for the star system in the academy. The more graduate students and professors believe that their hopes for professional satisfaction lie in superstar recognition for their individual work rather than in collective meaning making and action, the easier it is for democratic life in the university to be compromised.

Rebuilding Education's Public Purpose

The insidious genius of neoliberalism as an ideology is that it enlists notions of freedom, autonomy, and self-determination in the service of control, dependence, and top-down bureaucracy. Distraction from the core goals of neoliberal reform has come in the form of multiple strategies explored in this chapter. It has, therefore, become increasingly difficult for faculty, administrators, students, and public officials even to talk about the public role of universities in a democratic society. This was not always the case. Universities in Canada, as elsewhere, were founded on ideals of knowledge and service *in the public interest*. Universities had a noble mission—if not always fulfilled—to create knowledge and foster learning that would serve the public good and contribute to social welfare. Academic workers at all levels and of all kinds need to fight to regain this central mission. What is the role of the university in fostering civic leadership, civic engagement, and social cohesion? How can education reinvigorate democratic participation? How can colleges and universities strengthen our communities and our connections to one another?

I sometimes ask my education students to consider how schools in a democratic society should differ from those in a totalitarian nation. It seems plausible that a good lesson in chemistry or a foreign language might seem equally at home in many parts of the world. Every nation wants its educational institutions to prepare students for active participation in the workforce. So what would be different about teaching and learning in a Canadian or American classroom than in a classroom in a country governed by a one-ruling-party dictatorship? Most of us would like to believe that schools in democratic nations would foster the skills and dispositions needed to participate fully in democratic life; namely, the ability to think critically and carefully about social policies, cultural assumptions, and, especially, relations of power. Many schoolteachers and university professors, however, are concerned that students are learning more about how to please authority and secure a job than how to develop democratic convictions and stand up for them.

There are many powerful ways to teach young adults to think critically about social policy issues, participate in authentic debate over matters of importance, and understand that people of good will can have different opinions. Indeed, democratic progress depends on these differences. If universities hope to strengthen democratic society, they must resist the potentially fatal attraction of a curricular and research focus on skills training, workforce preparation, and the commercialization of knowledge to the benefit of private industry. They must instead participate in the rebuilding of a public purpose for education. The first step toward that goal is to reject easy assumptions about the need for austerity and accountability and to focus instead on the central role colleges and universities play in strengthening democratic community for all.

Note

1   According to Forbes (2016), the wealthiest seven individuals in the world are as follows (all in U.S. dollars):
1. Bill Gates (U.S.): $75.0 billion
2. Amancio Ortega (Spain): $67.0 billion
3. Warren Buffett (U.S.): $60.8 billion
4. Carlos Slim Helú (Mexico): $50.1 billion
5. Jeff Bezos (U.S.): $45.2 billion
6. Mark Zuckerberg (U.S.): $44.6 billion
7. Larry Ellison (U.S.): $43.6 billion

If you count the top ten wealthiest instead of seven, their total net worth is more than $505 billion. In addition to the seven billionaires noted above, the list would include Michael Bloomberg ($40 billion), Charles Koch ($39.6 billion), and Charles's brother David Koch ($39.6 billion).

References

Adbusters. 2014. "Occupy Wall Street Archives." http://www.adbusters.org/category/action/occupywallstreet/.

Alperovitz, G. 2005. *America beyond Capitalism: Reclaiming Our Wealth, Our Liberty and Our Democracy*. Hoboken, NJ: John Wiley & Sons.

Babad, M. 2012. "Tax Us More, Doctors Urge (Are the Lawyers Listening?)" *The Globe and Mail*, March 22. http://www.theglobeandmail.com/report-on-business/top-business-stories/tax-us-more-doctors-urge-are-the-lawyers-listening/article536305/.

Bousquet, M. 2008. *How the University Works: Higher Education and the Low-Wage Nation*. New York: New York University Press.

Bowen, R. "The New Battle between Political and Academic Cultures." *Chronicle of Higher Education*, June 22, 2001. B14–15.

Buffett, W. 2011. "Stop Coddling the Super-Rich." *New York Times*, August 14. http://www.nytimes.com/2011/08/15/opinion/stop-coddling-the-super-rich.html.

Byers, D. 2011. "Occupy Wall Street Is Winning." Politico. *On Media* [blog], November 11. http://www.politico.com/blogs/media/2011/11/occupy-wall-street-is-winning-040753.

Canada Revenue Agency. 2017. *Corporation Tax Rates—Canada*. http://www.canada.ca/en/revenue-agency/services/tax/businesses/topics/corporations/corporation-tax-rates.html.

Conference Board of Canada. 2012. *World Income Inequality: How Canada Performs*. Ottawa: Conference Board of Canada. http://www.conferenceboard.ca/hcp/hot-topics/worldinequality.aspx.

Corporation for Enterprise Development. 2013. *Taking the First Step: Six Ways to Start Building Financial Security and Opportunity at the Local Level*. Washington, DC: Corporation for Enterprise Development.

Craig, B. 2006. "History Defined in Florida Legislature." *Perspectives on History*, September. American Historical Association. https://www.historians.org/publications-and-directories/perspectives-on-history/september-2006/history-defined-in-florida-legislature.

Dewey, J. 1916. *Democracy and Education*. New York: Macmillan.

Doctors for Fair Taxation. 2014. http://www.doctorsforfairtaxation.ca.

Elliot, J. 2011. "The Origins of Occupy Wall Street Explained." *Salon*, October 4. http://www.salon.com/2011/10/04/adbusters_occupy_wall_st/.

Forbes. 2016. "The World's Billionaires." *Forbes*, March 1. http://www.forbes.com/billionaires.

Glenza, J. 2014. "Colorado Teachers Stage Mass Sick-Out to Protest U.S. History Curriculum Changes." *The Guardian*, September 30. http://www.theguardian. com/education/2014/sep/29/colorado-teachers-us-history-sickout-protest-contracts-jefferson.

Gonzalez, A. 2011. "Exxon CEO Had $29 Million in 2010 Compensation." *The Wall Street Journal*, April 13. http://www.wsj.com/articles/SB10001424052748703 7301045762608838926556622.

Government of Canada. 2015. *Update of Economic and Fiscal Projections 2015*. Department of Finance. http://www.budget.gc.ca/efp-peb/2015/pub/toc-tdm-en.html.

Immerwahr, D. 2008. "The Fact/Narrative Distinction and Student Examinations in History." *The History Teacher* 41(2): 199–206.

Income Security Advocacy Centre. 2017. http://incomesecurity.org/publications/ provincial-budgets/Ontario-Budget-2017-ISAC-pre-budget-submission.docx.

International Monetary Fund. 2016. "World Economic Outlook Database." http:// www.imf.org/external/pubs/ft/weo/2016/01/weodata/index.aspx.

Jacobs, P. 2014. "Colorado High School Students Are Protesting a Proposed Curriculum They Say Censors U.S. History." *Business Insider*, September 26. http://www. businessinsider.com/colorado-students-protest-curriculum-changes-2014-9.

Kirp, D. L. 2004. *Shakespeare, Einstein, and the Bottom Line: The Marketing of Higher Education*. Cambridge, MA: Harvard University Press.

Leber, R. 2012. "ExxonMobil Made $41.1 Billion in 2011, but Pays Estimated 17.6 Percent Tax Rate." *ThinkProgress*, January 31. https://thinkprogress.org/ exxonmobil-made-41-1-billion-in-2011-but-pays-estimated-17-6-percent-tax-rate-befa7eb1ee5#.k3qovbhke.

Mattson, K. 2008. "The Right's War on Academe and the Politics of Truth." In *Universities at Risk: How Politics, Special Interests and Corporatization Threaten Academic Integrity*, edited by J. Turk, 225–37. Toronto: James Lorimer and Company.

Newson J., and H. Buchbinder. 1988. *The University Means Business*. Aurora, ON: Garamond Press.

Proposed House of Representatives Amendments to Arizona S.B. 1108. https://www. azleg.gov/legtext/48leg/2r/proposed/h.1108rp2.doc.htm.

Read, M. 2011. "The Best Sign That Occupy Wall Street Is Working." *Gawker*, November 12. http://gawker.com/5858927/the-best-sign-that-occupy-wall-street-is-working.

Saez, E. 2015. "Striking It Richer: The Evolution of Top Incomes in the United States (Updated with 2015 Preliminary Estimates)." https://eml.berkeley. edu/~saez/saez-UStopincomes-2015.pdf.

Saez, E., and G. Zucman. 2014. "Wealth Inequality in the United States since 1913: Evidence from Capitalized Income Tax Data." Working Paper 20625. Cambridge, MA: National Bureau of Economic Research. http://www.nber.org/ papers/w20625.

Sahlberg, P. 2012. "How GERM Is Infecting Schools around the World." *The Washington Post*, June 29. http://www.washingtonpost.com/blogs/answer-sheet/post/how-germ-is-infecting-schools-around-the-world/2012/06/29/gjqavelzaw_blog.html.

Sieczkowski, C. 2011. "Occupy Wall Street: 10 Things to Know, One Month Later." *International Business Times*, October 18. http://www.ibtimes.com/occupy-wall-street-10-things-know-one-month-later-324238.

Soley, L. C. 1995. *Leasing the Ivory Tower: The Corporate Takeover of Academia.* Cambridge, MA: South End Press.

Turk, J., ed. 2008. *Universities at Risk: How Politics, Special Interests and Corporatization Threaten Academic Integrity.* Toronto: James Lorimer and Company.

University of Toronto. 1992. *Mission and Purpose.* Approved by Governing Council, October 15. https://www.utoronto.ca/about-u-of-t/mission.

Washburn, J. 2005. *University, Inc.: The Corporate Corruption of Higher Education.* New York: Basic Books.

Weir, E. 2012. "Debunking Drummond." *Behind the Numbers* [blog], February 27. http://behindthenumbers.ca/2012/02/27/debunking-drummond/.

Welch, P., et al. 2004. *Defending Medicine: Clinical Faculty and Academic Freedom.* https://www.caut.ca/docs/default-source/reports/defendingmedicine6ac83bf1c6ef6d389810ff00005eecd3.pdf?sfvrsn=2.

The West Wing. Season 3, episode 3, "Ways and Means." Originally aired October 24, 2001, on NBC.

Westheimer, J. 2012. "Inequality and the Implications of Occupy Wall Street for Educators." Paper presented at the Annual Conference of the American Educational Research Association, Vancouver, British Columbia.

———. 2002. "Tenure Denied: Anti-Unionism and Anti-Intellectualism in the Academy." *Social Text* 73 20(4): 47–64.

Wilper, A., et al. 2009. "Health Insurance and Mortality in U.S. Adults." *American Journal of Public Health* 99(12): 2289–95.

World Bank. 2016. "World Bank Open Data." http://data.worldbank.org/data-catalog/GDP-ranking-table.

CHAPTER 13

PUBLIC SCHOLARSHIP AND FACULTY AGENCY: RETHINKING "TEACHING, SCHOLARSHIP, AND SERVICE"

Christopher Meyers

The traditional university is under siege. As my co-authors' chapters attest, the range of threats is wide and deep: from massive open online courses, to right-wing critics, to legislative and accrediting bodies' demands for greater accountability, to widespread funding cuts, even program eliminations, to an increasing insistence that scholars provide quantitative evidence of the value of their research. Any one of these is a serious concern; taken together, one sees that the clamour for radical transformation represents a loud, pervasive, and deeply troubling commodification of the academy.

The humanities have suffered the brunt of these critiques. It is easier, after all, for a researcher in, say, petroleum engineering to convince a skeptic of the academy that their work is worthy than it is for a metaphysician. One response from humanities scholars has been to reinforce their relevance via a "public" turn, using their historical and cultural insights and critical thinking skills to provide vital assistance in the development of essential social policies and the achievement of a high quality of life (see Imagining America).

At the same time, some humanities faculty simply reject the notion that they should *have* to justify their worth; theirs are, after all, among the oldest and most central of intellectual disciplines. While I also bemoan the short-sightedness, even irrationality, of some critics, I recognize that, for the foreseeable future at least, the loudest and most powerful voices in the conversation will continue to demand such justification. Responding to those voices is thus a good *defensive* reason for engaging in public scholarship.

There are also, though, excellent *positive* reasons for the turn. Taking just one example: the last several decades of the practical ethics movement attest to the tremendous contribution philosophers can make in the public sphere.[1] Philosophers such as Jürgen Habermas, the prolific writer of scholarly texts, along with newspaper columns and essays; Amy Goodman, host and executive producer of *Democracy Now!*; and Michael Sandel, the Harvard professor who speaks widely and is the author of a central text in public philosophy (2006)—among many others doing important work at the local level (see Public Philosophy Network)—are skilled at analyzing and evaluating a wide array of real-world problems, at discerning the salient elements in those problems, and at getting at the conceptual and theoretical concerns that are often at their root. In short, done well, such work helps people *make sense* of the world and its problems, from which there is a greater likelihood of achieving viable resolutions.

Such work is also good for *us*—as philosophers, scholars, teachers, and people. First, it pulls us out of our heads, forcing us to see the relationship between theoretical and conceptual thought experiments and practical, often life-altering, issues; second, it improves our teaching by allowing us to bring realistic examples into the classroom; and, third, it shifts our focus away from the often petty politics of the university and toward things that *matter*. In short, we *should* be doing public philosophy, or at least some of us should—those with the interest and aptitude, especially the communication skills, and the willingness to sacrifice other rewarding professional development. Done well, the work helps others, it helps protect philosophy's place in the university, and it helps us become better teacher-scholars.

While those benefits are often recognized and highly valued by our peers, even the most accomplished public philosophy is rarely counted for anything more than "service" in tenure and promotion evaluations; in other words, it is largely dismissed. People doing public philosophy routinely describe the difficulties they face in being expected to do it *and* meet the customary publication standards required by their respective institutions. This is a particular burden for junior faculty: demanding that they meet standard publication requirements *and* undertake a rich agenda of public philosophy is unrealistic and unjust. Most are wise enough to see the writing on the wall and to accordingly delay their engagement in public work until post-tenure—sometimes with corresponding detriment to their most productive faculty development.

There are undoubtedly good reasons for delay: much of public work requires a seasoned view of real-world cases and problems as well as successful development of key community-based relationships, of the sort that normally emerge only over time. Furthermore, publishing, with the associated layers of peer review, serves to establish scholarly credibility.

At the same time, however, waiting *too* long makes it all the more difficult to establish the necessary community relationships and to hone the verbal and writing skills that are better suited to public engagement. The academy needs to find a way to encourage publishing *and* public work (for those interested in and suited to it), and the best mechanisms we have for doing this are first, through retention and promotion criteria and evaluations, and, second, through the provision of resources (e.g., release time and research funding), historically granted only to traditional scholarship.

In what follows, I will argue for a reconceptualization of the standard triad of "teaching/scholarship/service," urging instead a more holistic criterion: "excellent teacher-scholars," with such excellence achievable through a variety of means, including, but not restricted to, classroom teaching, refereed publications, campus committee work, and engaged public scholarship.

In addition to providing a more just system for public scholars and to encouraging their participation, there is an important secondary benefit, one directly responsive to the overriding concerns expressed throughout this book: taking charge of tenure and promotion criteria reminds faculty of just how much agency they retain, even in the face of those threats. As much as people like Wisconsin governor and one-time Republican presidential candidate Scott Walker might wish otherwise (see devtob 2015), the academy is still largely a self-regulating profession whose members thereby have real power. They have substantial autonomy over the curriculum and even more over who gets to be a member of the club: *they* define the criteria for retention, tenure, and promotion, and *they* determine who has met them.

I am not suggesting, of course, that this power is unlimited or that it is as robust as it was even a decade ago. External bodies are using an array of tools to reduce that power, ranging from attempted bans on specific areas of study,[2] to reduced funding,[3] to an insistence on quantitative, "value-added" assessment of faculty work.[4] Campus administrators also have in-house mechanisms for rewarding favoured work and punishing its contrary, including release time, research funds, graduate student support, and cash grants.[5]

All these inroads into faculty power make it all the more important that they express control where they still can, and retention and promotion criteria are among the more important places to do this, with the added benefit of encouraging public scholarship and treating the faculty who undertake it more justly.

The Value of Public Philosophy

Everything in this discussion so far assumes there is important and assessable academic value to at least some of the work done in public philosophy.[6] But is not the fact that we have so much trouble categorizing it—Is it scholarship? Teaching? Service? All of the above? None of the above?—clear evidence that it is and should be marginalized? Part of the problem here is that most of our colleagues really do not understand the work we do, or how intellectually and philosophically demanding it can be. Let me describe a typical consulting case.

In my role as ethicist for a local hospital, I was discussing a dying patient with his treating team. The family was in denial over how serious his condition was, so the team was pondering whether to declare that additional treatment, beyond palliative, was medically ineffective and cruel to the patient. This declaration would have (arguably) given the team sufficient legal and ethical grounds for making a unilateral decision to put him on comfort care. Many skilful and loving, but ultimately futile, attempts were undertaken in the hope of bringing the family to a point of acceptance. The case was causing some considerable grief to the treating team, especially the bedside nurses, and, of course, the costs involved were significant. I was asked how best to ethically proceed.

Such cases are exceedingly complex, given the unique mix of legal, ethical, religious, emotional, medical, and economic complications attached to each. Being able to be an effective counsel in such cases requires specialized reasoning skills, a strong knowledge of the ethical considerations underlying the various options, the ability to skilfully communicate, an appreciation for institutional politics and power dynamics, and at the very least a strong familiarity with the array of legal, religious, emotional, medical, and economic elements.

When one is engaged in this work, one is clearly *doing philosophy* in much the same way I am doing philosophy as I write this chapter—carefully thinking through problems and seeking the best, reasoned solutions. One is also *teaching*—part of the goal in these consultations is to educate the staff so they do not need to rely upon the ethicist. And one is clearly providing a *service*—the work is often done pro bono, as a way of giving back to the community and as part of the historical service commitment attached to being a professional. So where, exactly, should this activity be categorized when, say, putting together a promotion file? Picking any one of the standard categories would be, at best, arbitrary; the work fits into all somewhat but none completely.

Altogether Artificial Lines

Finding a way to appropriately credit public philosophy is a good but probably not sufficient reason to revise a decades-old model of faculty evaluation: there are just not enough folks doing such work to justify the messiness of revision. It is no surprise that many colleagues with whom I have discussed this proposal have rejected it, usually with an "if it ain't broke…" reaction.

But I contend the current system *is* broken, or at least so flawed as to warrant the messiness, and not just because it cannot adequately address public activities. First, the categories create artificial and not rationally sustainable, but nonetheless hard and fast, lines. Many campuses, for example, fight over whether to count academically rigorous and well-reviewed, if ultimately unsuccessful, grant applications as service or scholarship (or not at all). Similar disagreements exist over how to credit one's role as a reviewer for a top-notch journal (given the scholarly respect that position infers, along with the intellectual engagement such reviews entail), or how to count the publication of a lower-division textbook (teaching or scholarship?), or a multi-authored paper.

Even the seemingly straightforward category of "service" is highly problematic. How should we compare membership on (and maybe only occasional attendance at) a routine campus committee versus serving on the university-wide tenure and promotion review board? Or being a nonpaid ethics consultant for area hospitals? The workload attached to the latter examples dwarfs that of the first, as does the level of intellectual, even scholarly, engagement. And, yet, in typical reviews, one just submits a list and reviewers check to make sure it is long enough (with occasional accolades for the truly dedicated campus citizen).

The work that best highlighted the problem for me was serving for six years as the chair of our campus's "Faculty Rights" team, representing colleagues in their contractual disputes with administration. The often extraordinarily labour- and time-intensive work was also very demanding intellectually (e.g., attempting to interpret vague contractual language or case precedents), ethically challenging (e.g., trying to sort out competing justice claims or institutionally grounded norms), and it frequently called for exactly the kinds of mediation skills I regularly employ in my role as a clinical ethics consultant. Some of the cases, in fact, required considerably more philosophical and intellectual acumen than some of my publications. Furthermore, I frequently took what I learned from the process into the classroom, for example when discussing the adversarial system of law. And, of course, I was fulfilling a vital service to my colleagues and to the university.

Into which box should such work be placed? For a recent post-tenure review, I put it under service, in largest part because I was already a topped-out full professor and did not need credit in any of the areas. If I had a junior colleague doing it, necessarily at the expense of having the time to do other more traditional scholarship, I would fight hard to have it be a major contri-bution to her tenure or promotion—not because it unmistakably qualified as scholarship or teaching, but because it revealed her to be *a vital member of the academy*, a real *teacher-scholar*. Now, granted, many faculty serve in similar positions in a more or less pro forma way, hardly meeting the level of philosophical or intellectual engagement I am describing here. This, though, only serves to reinforce the importance of a *holistic* and *qualitative* evalua-tion of all one's professional activities.

At least as problematic, the categories contribute to a "teaching to the test" mentality: What is the minimum percentage of positive student evaluations needed for tenure? How many journal articles and how high does the jour-nal's ranking have to be? Is serving on one committee a year sufficient? While quantitative criteria can provide peace of mind to junior colleagues, since they know they cannot be denied tenure or promotion if they've met them,[7] they can also motivate complacency: "I've met the criteria, now I can relax."

The exhortation I regularly give junior faculty is that I am looking for col-leagues who keep striving to be better teachers, who engage in research, and who endeavour to improve the campus environment because that is *who they are*. Their *identity* is largely defined through these activities. They enjoy the work and cannot imagine not doing it. They do not do it because it is nec-essary for tenure and promotion but because they are teacher-scholars who do good philosophy, expressing their best talents through writing, teaching, engaging, and/or philosophical consulting.

A key challenge here is to convince all our colleagues—departmental, university-wide, and administrative—that public engagement is import-ant, even fundamental, to what we should be doing as academicians. And it makes good sense why it is such a challenge—public philosophy just is not a natural fit within the traditional academic model, or at least not given the ways in which we categorize scholarship and service. The problem, though, is not with the public work but with the *model*. Rather than seeking to fit into artificial boxes, our goal should seek to be and to promote excellent teacher-scholars, with an expansive understanding of the kinds of activities that contribute to that status.

Quantification and Peer Review

How, though, does this recommendation for a holistic and qualitative evaluative model fit with an academic world where numerical data are increasingly the coin of the realm? My first response is: "It doesn't and hallelujah!" That is, the very question reveals the fundamental inadequacy of quantification: so much of what we do—inspiring students, changing peoples' way of thinking about the world and their place in it, helping to make someone's final days or hours more peaceful—cannot be captured in an Excel spreadsheet. But, just as we have to recognize the need to justify philosophy's place in the modern university, so also must we acknowledge that numbers are, in fact, the currency. Like it or not, we have to engage this method of evaluating our work and it should be easy enough to do so, even if the resulting information is only partial and misleading: How many consults did one perform this year? How many hospital policies or op-ed pieces did one write? How many people attended workshops, panels, or lectures, and what was their feedback to them? How many students are participating in programs, what did they learn, and what was their review of them?

A final, and probably the most telling, problem is effective peer review. While there are various ways of obtaining external assessment of public work (e.g., soliciting blind letters of evaluation from associated nonacademic professionals like physicians, hospital administrators, and community leaders), the process generally will not be as rigorous as that obtained via the standard reviews achieved through publication. These constraints are why I will argue that even the most accomplished public philosopher must also establish her philosophical acumen via publishing.

However, once those credentials *are* established, public philosophy, done well, should be accepted as being as important, as rigorous, and as meaningful as publications. To see why this is the case, it is helpful to do a meta-analysis of the value of traditional research and then see how public philosophy satisfies all the same considerations, in many cases even more effectively.

Research and Scholarship as Vital to the University's Mission

It is surprising just how little thought academics give to the purpose and importance of scholarship. We do it *because that is what academics do*, as we learned from our mentors, who learned from theirs—all reinforced in tenure and promotion reviews.

Scholarship is undoubtedly vital to a university's mission, which I characterize as *educating, advancing ideas, creating an intellectual environment*, and *bettering the lives of others*. Scholarship is what distinguishes universities from trade schools and community colleges, where the teaching and service may be first-rate but where scholarship is optional and, generally speaking, the exception. University scholarship is a source of knowledge creation and, maybe even more importantly, of the enhancement of a campus's intellectual culture. Specifically, here are seven basic goods it promotes:

1. Successful scholarship provides evidence of a faculty member's engagement with and knowledge of ideas, problems, and solutions in her field. It also shows that one has the relevant expertise, as judged by one's peers.

2. It shows one has the intellectual skill set and communication abilities needed to address and extend the scholarly conversation in new and fruitful directions.

3. Good scholarship promotes an active and engaged campus intellectual climate. The difference between campuses with a flourishing intellectual culture and those without is palpable: faculty are sharing ideas with one another and with students; guest speakers are common; grants are bringing extra money; and people are hosting and attending conferences, with the associated scholarly invigoration.

4. Successful scholarship makes us better teachers and mentors (and vice versa) (Kaplan 2007). This mutually reinforcing overlap affirms, in fact, the forced artificiality and inadequacy of the categories: questions that arise in teaching often lead to new scholarship, which returns to inform teaching, and then is used to assist other faculty in their work.

5. Prestige in the academic world is largely attached to scholarship. One makes a name for oneself, one's department, and one's university through the number and quality of publications, with the latter assessed principally by the prestige of the journal or publishing house.

6. Good research is committed to seeking out truth, to making better sense of the world, human relations, and abstract ideas. Such truth-seeking produces a range of pragmatic benefits, often well beyond those one would predict. It also has intrinsic value—it is simply a good thing to distinguish truth from falsehood, regardless of the discipline.

7. New research often results in discoveries that translate into improvements in people's daily lives—everything from antibiotics, to sewage disposal and clean water systems, to smartphones. Such innovations also include better interpretive models or conceptual and theoretical tools that help make sense of problems in a range of real-world contexts.

Research and scholarship, in short, are profoundly important to what academics *do* and *are*; research and scholarship enhance how and where academics work and enhance the communities in which they live.

Well, *some* research and scholarship does this. Some is garbage, written merely to meet a tenure or promotion quota, published in an obscure journal and read by fifteen people; hence, again, the need to move beyond the discrete categories and toward holistic and *qualitative* evaluations.

The "garbage" comment also, of course, applies to public philosophy. Most faculty are not trained to focus their philosophical tools *outward*, or at least outward beyond the classroom; nor are they trained in mediation and consensus building or in the use of accessible language and style—often exactly to the contrary! I am talking about a subset of philosophers who should engage in public work, people with the inclination to pursue it conscientiously enough to acquire those skills and to give up other career-enhancing opportunities. When done well, however, public work satisfies those seven values at least as effectively as many, even most, publications.

Comparing Traditional Scholarship to Public Philosophy

To show that public work satisfies the seven values of research and scholarship, let me return to an analysis of the clinical ethics case consultation, described above, viewed through those values.

1. Evidence of Engagement with, and Knowledge of, Ideas, Problems, and Solutions
One dare not participate in clinical ethics consultations without a rich knowledge base including, but not limited to, the ethical principles or norms

relevant to the specific case; the medical facts; institutional and professional standards, politics, and culture; legal and economic implications; and the particulars of family dynamics. One dare not because their absence could have dire consequences in consultations that typically include life and death ramifications.

2. An Intellectual Skill Set and Communication Abilities

As the case shows, successful public philosophers must be quick on their feet, able to discern and evaluate complicated facts and personalities, and skilled at sorting through the noise to get at the most important considerations. They then must translate their usual philosophy-speak of abstractions and concepts into accessible language that genuinely helps others—often others with deep emotional investment—to find their way to consensus.

3. Creating an Intellectually Vibrant Campus Climate

Much of the work of public philosophers takes place outside the academy and the results are not normally tangible in the same way a book or offprint is. This is why it is so important to regularly educate others about what they do—through colloquia, in department meetings, and via any resulting publications. More directly, though, many of those engaged in public philosophy are also those most inclined to organize campus programs—speakers, workshops, and panels—thereby helping to foster a rich and diverse intellectual climate.

4. Better Teaching

There is nothing like a real-world case to elucidate core philosophical concepts. What better way to show, for example, what is at stake when someone is treated as a mere means than via a clinical ethics case in which family members are forcing a loved one to continue life-sustaining treatment so as to meet *their* emotional or economic needs? Such examples enrich and enliven in ways that even the best-written material cannot touch.

5. Prestige in the Academic World

Prestige is undoubtedly attached to publications. Even the best-known public philosophers—people like Peter Singer and Jürgen Habermas—gained their reputation mainly through publications. While there are wonderful opportunities for career development and acclaim within public work, for example, through organizations like the Association for Practical and Professional Ethics, the Society for Applied Philosophy, and the American

Society for Bioethics and Humanities, even there, admittedly, prestige is generally associated with one's success as a published scholar, rather than with the actual public work.

But, for establishing a *nonacademic* reputation, the public work is far more important. If one is able to provide real assistance in real people's daily struggles with ethical issues, if one motivates community conversations via lectures, panels, and workshops, or generates material improvements in social justice, there can be considerable resulting prestige—for the individual, her program, and her university. This also often results in financial support for these and related activities.[8]

6. Truth Seeking

One of the most important lessons to come from the public philosophy movement, particularly as exemplified in practical ethics, has been a reconsideration of ethics theory and its "application" to real-world problems. The top-down model that dominated the early "applied ethics" movement—"applied" precisely because the belief was that one needed only to take a good theory and apply it to problems—has been largely replaced by models that stress a bottom-up approach, in which contextual contingencies are the driving factors in decision making. Does this mean practical philosophers have discovered a truth about the nature of ethics decision making and its relationship to ethics theory? It is much too early to draw that conclusion, but that this approach has become so dominant in the field certainly speaks to *something* truthful.

Furthermore, there are a number of initiatives looking for better, more truthful solutions to social problems,[9] and each discovers new truths about the nature of practical ethics—what approaches succeed in what environments, how to alter institutional and political structures to prevent recurrence of common problems, and how to better incorporate ethics theory and conceptual analysis into these contexts.

7. Making the World a Better Place

The very raison d'être of public philosophy is activist; at its core, it is committed to improving the world and people's lives. And, when done well, it assuredly achieves this: it directly improves the lives of others by, for example, helping motivate systems to ease poverty, creating greater social responsibility in business practices, pushing for more ethical journalism, and easing someone's passage into death.

From all this emerges my conclusion: public philosophy is on aggregate *at least* as successful at accomplishing the values associated with good scholarship and should be afforded comparable worth in tenure and promotion reviews. That said, such worth will not occur within the current system of evaluation and its discrete categories: public philosophy is just not (traditional) scholarship; nor is it (classroom) teaching; nor is it (campus) service. It is all of those and none of those. What it *is*, however, is the sort of work that is at the core of what it means to be a successful teacher-scholar.

Another way of thinking about the connection is by realizing that in both cases one is *doing philosophy*. When we write, we do philosophy, through the written word, and when we teach, we do it through oral presentation and stagecraft. By the same token, when we are engaged in meaningful public work, we are doing philosophy by evaluating problems through conceptual and logical analysis and seeking resolution to those problems via reasoned and ethical examination. And we often do so in at least as rich and sophisticated a way as when we are writing and classroom teaching. The audience may be different and the style more accessible, but the same skill sets and reasoning method are at work.

Tenure and Promotion Criteria

How, then, do we translate all this into actual tenure and promotion criteria? If evaluation of faculty was always sufficiently rational, motivated by the goal of mentoring faculty into becoming effective, valuable, and valued members of the academic community—while also recognizing that some will not achieve that and must be dismissed—then the only needed criterion would be: "We seek to advance excellent teacher-scholars, the determination of which will be made by one's peers." The reality, however, is that reviews are often marred by personal hostilities, jealousies, and injustices. Thus, the criteria have to be sufficiently explicit and detailed to produce just outcomes.

Here are my proposed criteria, rooted in the mission of the university provided above. The goal is simple: to help develop, tenure, and promote faculty who reveal their standing as excellent teacher-scholars via the following four standards.

Educating

The academy has considerable experience with, and good tools for, evaluating success in classroom teaching, many of which could also be used if a candidate wished to show success in community education (e.g., participant evaluations, review of teaching materials, and peer visitations). Different programs will give higher priority to different aspects of teaching (e.g., student perceptions versus grade reports versus the quality of classroom materials) and evaluations should correspondingly reflect those variations.

Advancing Ideas

Academics advance ideas, first, by acquiring a sufficient understanding of existing ones and, second, by intellectually rigorous suggestions for improvement. The best mechanism for evaluating success here is through external peer review, typically as part of the standard research and publication process. While flawed, this system provides the best means for getting beyond bias, whether personal or intellectual.

But disciplinary research is not the only place where such advancement is important: faculty who come up with new teaching methods, or who motivate innovative programmatic designs and alignments, or who devise more effective shared governance procedures should have such important work recognized. They have directly contributed to the structural conditions that allow a campus to achieve its mission. Similarly, faculty who use their expertise to assist community agencies or organizations achieve their goals should be recognized for how that work contributes to the academic mission. Evaluation processes must describe what counts as success in those areas and devise methods for quantitatively and qualitatively evaluating the achievements. This could include having community partners write letters describing how it made a difference in their particular program.

Because, however, the academy is still developing these standards and processes, publication remains, for now at least, the best mechanism for obtaining seemingly objective evaluations. Criteria for tenure should therefore include some minimum publishing requirement, which could be buttressed by public work. For example, our department criteria require at least two peer-reviewed publications for tenure, *or* one plus a range of other add-ons, including important and externally assessed public philosophy. And, rather than trying to define in abstraction what types of public work count, we ask the candidate to make that case in his/her narrative, with particular emphasis on describing its intellectual and philosophical rigour.

Creating an Intellectual Environment

Intellectual environments are established through, among other means, departmental and university colloquia; hosted panels representing a range of disciplines and, where feasible, community experts; sponsoring research and travel for engaged faculty; major lectures featuring renowned scholars or nationally recognized experts; and providing mentorship to colleagues and students in the development of their research and teaching agendas. All this work can be evaluated by having candidates provide a description of their activities, with an explanation of their respective contributions. Such explanations would move past the all-too-common, and largely meaningless, practice of simply listing committee memberships. It would also more highly credit mentoring of students and colleagues—a value to which we often give lip service but generally ignore in evaluations.

Bettering Others' Lives

This criterion is at once the most difficult to assess and at the same time among the more important of academic goals. We certainly improve our students' lives through traditional classroom teaching and mentoring: we teach them worthwhile content and skills; we teach them to be more engaged and critical thinkers; we teach them to be citizen-participants; and we teach them successful life habits. But, beyond subjective and anecdotal feedback, we have no good means for measuring those impacts. We hopefully also improve our immediate colleagues' lives through good mentorship and guidance, with similar difficulties in assessment.

Judging the impact of public work is similarly complicated, but in some instances the effects are even more immediate and direct—for example, improving patients' and families' experiences in the dying process, working with communities to increase democratic participation, and creating new structures for addressing poverty. Candidates who wished to emphasize this aspect of their work would be expected to detail those impacts and their contributions, including, where appropriate, external evaluation. For other types of public work, where the impacts are not as immediately discernible, candidates could provide their subjective and impressionistic sense of the difference they made in others' lives, with, where appropriate, external confirmation.

Last, a point about traditional service, mainly serving on campus committees. If the primary goal of tenure and promotion evaluations is to determine someone's philosophical acumen, such service is generally irrelevant. What it does reveal is whether the candidate is a *good citizen*, someone who helps with the grunt work of university life. Good citizens make for good colleagues, though they may or may not also be good philosophers.

Successful achievement of these four standards, I suggest, shows one to be an accomplished teacher-scholar, as revealed via *all* the candidate's traditional and nontraditional but mission-enhancing activities. It also thereby encourages faculty, where appropriate, to expand their intellectual activities into the public realm, thereby benefitting the community, university, and faculty member alike. It also reinforces the professional, self-regulating status of the professoriate, and, in so doing, reinforces the considerable agency we retain, even in the face of the types of threats discussed above and elsewhere in this book.

Author's Note

Large sections of this chapter are taken from Meyers (2014). I am grateful to the journal, *Essays in Philosophy*, and its editors, David Boersema and Jack Weinstein, for permission to use this material. I am also grateful to Hugh LaFollette and Rob Negrini for their helpful comments on peer review. Finally, I am indebted to Marc Spooner and James McNinch for organizing the conference that led to this book and for their excellent stewardship of the conversation.

Notes

1   I focus on philosophy, given that, as my home discipline, it is the one with which I am most familiar. As other contributors to this book reveal, important public work is, of course, being done through a wide array of disciplines.
2   See, for example, Arizona's ban on ethnic studies (*HuffPost*), and the Texas legislature's attack on, of all things, *critical thinking* (Strauss 2012).
3   See, for example, Walker's threatened cuts to Wisconsin's highly respected university system (Rivard 2015), and Florida Governor Rick Scott's proposal to charge humanities students higher fees (Griswold 2013).
4   See, for example, the 204-page accreditation manual produced by the Accrediting Commission for Schools, Western Association of Schools and Colleges.
5   As our campus was gearing up for its last accreditation visit, in the midst of the recession, the administration was handing out extensive release time and cash grants to faculty who assisted with the self-study and quantitative assessment processes—all at a time when the campus was otherwise taking major funding cuts that resulted in layoffs, furloughs, significantly reduced course offerings, and an almost complete cessation of funding for research.
6   I define *public philosophy* as any work performed by trained philosophers, in which the intended audience is other than (or in addition to) one's disciplinary colleagues or college students. The range is thus quite broad—from clinical ethics to community activism to writing op-ed columns (for examples, see Public Philosophy Network).

7   And, admittedly, quantitative criteria often prove decisive in grievances.

8   Our campus's ethics centre, for example, is both the campus's most active source for intellectual programs and largely funded through private support (see Kegley Institute of Ethics).

9   See, for example, the Occupy Philosophy Affinity Group (Public Philosophy Network); Holding Media Accountable, a program within the Center for Journalism Ethics at the University of Wisconsin-Madison; and the Bioethics Network.

References

Accrediting Commission for Schools, Western Association of Schools and Colleges. http://www.acswasc.org/schools/public-california/.

Bioethics Network. http://www.bioethics.net.

Democracy Now! https://www.democracynow.org.

devtob. 2015. "Scott Walker Hates Public Higher Education for Two Reasons." *Daily KOS*, January 28. http://www.dailykos.com/story/2015/01/29/1360814/-Scott-Walker-hates-public-higher-education-for-two-reasons.

Griswold, A. 2013. "Majoring in the Humanities Might Soon Cost You More in Florida." *Forbes*, January 18. http://www.forbes.com/sites/alisongriswold/2013/01/18/majoring-in-the-humanities-might-soon-cost-you-more-in-florida/.

HuffPost. "Arizona Ethnic Studies Ban." https://www.huffingtonpost.com/topic/arizona-ethnic-studies-ban.

Imagining America. "Imagining America: Artists and Scholars in Public Life." Mission Statement. http://imaginingamerica.org/about/our-mission/.

Kaplan, T. R. 2007. "Combining Research and Teaching." *The Economics Network*. http://www.economicsnetwork.ac.uk/showcase/kaplan_research.

Kegley Institute of Ethics at California State University Bakersfield. http://www.csub.edu/kie.

Meyers, C. 2014. "Public Philosophy and Tenure/Promotion: Rethinking 'Teaching, Scholarship and Service.'" *Essays in Philosophy* 15(1): 58–76.

Public Philosophy Network. http://publicphilosophynetwork.ning.com/.

———. Occupy Philosophy Affinity Group. http://publicphilosophynetwork.ning.com/group/occupy-philosophy.

Rivard, R. 2015. "Deep Cuts in Wisconsin." *Inside Higher Ed*, January 28, https://www.insidehighered.com/news/2015/01/28/wisconsin-looks-cut-higher-ed-300m-tries-give-something-return.

Sandel, M. J. 2006. *Public Philosophy*. Cambridge, MA: Harvard University Press.

Strauss, V. 2012. "Texas GOP Rejects 'Critical Thinking' Skills. Really." *The Washington Post*, July 9. http://www.washingtonpost.com/blogs/answer-sheet/post/texas-gop-rejects-critical-thinking-skills-really/2012/07/08/gJQAHNpFXW_blog.html.

University of Wisconsin-Madison. Holding Media Accountable. Center for Journalism Ethics. School of Journalism and Mass Communication. http://ethics.journalism.wisc.edu/resources/holding-media-accountable/.

THE DEFENESTRATION OF DEMOCRACY

Peter McLaren

> *Victory was won through gusts of optimism mixed with white-knuckled rage and weapons-grade vitriol. It swept through the white picket fences and onto the porches of America's heartland like a chilly fall breeze teasing a candle flame inside a jack-o'-lantern. Suddenly, its smiling rictus began to resemble the chestburster from* Alien, *a horrific countenance with a row of pointy, glittering, gold-capped teeth. Ill winds began to blow. Something wicked this way came. Its skin was shellacked orange and had matching coloured hair (now apparently dyed white). It announced itself in a bellicose populist voice. And it spoke chaos. A* ban nigheachain *was seen standing atop the steps of the Lincoln Memorial keening for the nation. She was last seen at the reflecting pool, which gleamed red as she began washing the blood from the clothes of all those who were about to die as a result of actions to be taken by the new administration. And the numbers, they were legion. The grass on all the country's golf courses suddenly turned brown.*

This book is going into publication just one year after Donald Trump became the forty-fifth president of the United States. Not surprisingly, events of world-historical importance are happening very quickly. By the time the book is launched at national and international venues, it is unclear how many more disastrous decisions and corporate giveaways will have been made and horrors countenanced by the new White House administration and whether or not the Doomsday Clock will have already struck midnight.

The United States was shaken out of electoral somnolence, as more Trump supporters than expected crawled out of the woodwork to vote, fomenting a whitelash of extraordinary proportions. They came from former railroad towns where the Rust Belt meets Appalachia, from dirt poor white neighbourhoods adjacent to petrochemical processing refineries, where parents grew tired of their children coughing up blood-flecked, blackened phlegm. To get to the polling stations, they passed through ghost towns in rural Tennessee, where shuttered general stores and demolished dime-a-dance halls held nothing but empty memories of earlier generations. They came from neighbourhoods in Iowa where plants were no longer producing tower cranes and had laid off thousands of workers. Supporters of the Orange Leviathan included spindle-shanked retirees in eastern Kentucky, living behind the eight ball on straw mattresses in abandoned horse trailers, angry at the immigrants passing them by on the ladder. Even those laid-off coal plant workers, forced down railroad tracks with their bindlesticks flung over their shoulders, fighting graybacks and a disposable future with nothing left but a ten-dollar bill hidden in the heel of their boot, wore Trump's trademark red cap, emblazoned with the now famous phrase, "Make America Great Again" (Trump had blamed environmental regulation for the loss of coal mining jobs, without mentioning the country's pivot to the exploitation of another fossil fuel, natural gas, that can be an even worse generator of greenhouse gas than coal). Hapless young vagrants and itinerant workers huddled in abandoned coal-loading stations, shooting up OxyContin (known locally as "hillbilly heroin"), with nothing left but to "Catch the Westbound" (as the saying went during the Great Depression), were all behind Trump, even if they were too stoned to cast their ballots. With medically uninsured arthritic knees and aching kidneys, the labouring poor embedded in capital's extractive essence—immiseration and privation—marched to the beat of nationalism, bemoaning the appearance of brown faces in the industrial yards and agricultural fields that spoke a language they could not understand.

They trekked through the dirt roads of Beaufort County, South Carolina, and Duplin County to the north, past acres of pasture-raised Berkshire pigs. They travelled to where they had last registered to vote, even if it meant a trip across the North Georgia mountains, through Clayton and Dillard, all the way to Chattanooga. Truckers for Trump drove their eighteen-wheelers through the low country of Louisiana, gator teeth swinging from the rearview windows, so they could put the man in the red cap into office.

For those who were experiencing city life, you did not have to be on the rocks, or live on the nickel in penthouses made out of cardboard strewn through the streets of skid row, "with cupped hands round the tin can," as John Hartford or Glen Campbell might put it, in order to be a Trump supporter. Although generally risk-averse, many in the wage-labour-rich-class, including socially registered suburban dwellers who loathed plebian sociabilities and were often unforgiving of the errors of their own employees, pushed for a Trump win, hoping that a further deregulation of the business world might bring them some fast cash, at least enough to stoke their meagre retirement savings before the system eventually fell apart like it did in 2008. Some folks were just looking for a good luck charm in the man with the Midas touch, without anticipating that Trump's economic plan would raise taxes on eight million low- and middle-class families while providing massive tax breaks for the rich. It is no secret, especially in the hinterlands of the unemployed, that the Internet and its burgeoning platforms of automation are poised to cut half of U.S. jobs in the very near future. All of these Trump supporters, both the bedraggled and bon vivant, were feeling trapped in Palookaville with Trump their only hope for reaching Xanadu as they followed "the Donald" like a mesmerized Sonny Malone running after a roller-skating Terpsichore played by Olivia Newton-John. After all, Trump could sing a good populist tune, and it was music to the ears of those down on their luck and fearful of being left behind. Perhaps, on the wings of a foul-mouthed billionaire playboy, factory ghost towns could be replaced by Vegas versions of Fourier's phalanstères.

For many of those hooked on drugs, it was too late to enjoy a Trump victory, or to see what kind of health care program Trump would put in place of Obamacare. In Stark County, Ohio, people down on their luck shoot up meth mixed with carfentanil, an animal tranquilizer that is normally used on elephants and tigers, and is one hundred times more powerful than fentanyl (Siemaszko 2017). There are so many overdose fatalities that the coroner's office in Canton has to borrow a twenty-foot-long, cold storage, mass casualty trailer, known as the "death trailer," normally used for victims of airplane disasters, since its morgue facility in the county jail complex on Atlantic Boulevard, which holds about a dozen bodies, cannot deal with the body count. The coroners in Ashtabula, Cuyahoga, and Summit County have to do the same thing—call in the death trailers. In Montgomery County, to the south, the coroner calls local funeral home directors for help (Siemaszko 2017).

Perry Anderson (2017) captures the political ramifications of the election when he writes that, in the United States, issues of national identity, neoliberal austerity, capitalism, and fear of immigration provided the

> conditions in which a U.S. Republican presidential candidate of unprecedented background and temperament—abhorrent to mainstream bipartisan opinion, with no attempt to conform to accepted codes of civil or political conduct, and disliked by many of his actual voters—could appeal to enough disregarded white rust-belt workers to win the election. As in Britain, desperation outweighed apprehension in deindustrialised proletarian regions. There too, much more rawly and openly, in a country with a deeper history of native racism, immigrants were denounced and barriers, physical as well as procedural, demanded. Above all, empire was not a distant memory of the past but a vivid attribute of the present and natural claim on the future, yet it had been cast aside by those in power in the name of a globalization that meant ruin for ordinary people and humiliation for their country. Donald Trump's slogan was "Make America Great Again"—prosperous in discarding the fetishes of free movement of goods and labour, and victorious in ignoring the trammels and pieties of multilateralism: he was not wrong to proclaim that his triumph was Brexit writ large. It was a much more spectacular revolt, since it was not confined to a single— for most people, symbolic—issue, and was devoid of any establishment respectability or editorial blessing.

The irony was not lost on much of the nation that the candidate who was ridiculed for his small hands and seeming in need of a gris-gris bag full of Johnny Jump Up (or at least some high-grade Viagra) turned out to be the most politically potent candidate of all. Much of the Trump win can be chalked up to a vitriolic reaction to what is perceived as Washington's elite and politically correct liberal establishment, a refusal to be disintoxicated from the hatred of the first Black president of the United States, threats of immiseration, and the fear of a white minority race. The latter is a phenomenon that many right-wing movements refer to as "demographic winter," a white supremacist interpretation of the world's falling birth rate, or "birth dearth." This particular group of nativist "dearthers," alarmed by the declining Caucasian population in the United States, blames gays and lesbians, environmentalists, population control advocates, supporters of birth control, and common law couples who refuse to be legally married and even married heterosexual couples who fail to have sufficiently larger numbers of white children for what they see as the demise of the white race—including what they perceive as their racially defined experiences of dispossession as white people who have been passed over by the politically correct multiculturalists in Washington—all of which they understand to be contributing to the impending death of Western civilization. And they warn that Muslim families are reproducing faster than Christian families.

But there are other reasons why working-class whites especially would vote for a candidate and party that have traditionally not served the poor as well as the Democratic Party. The reason: the white working class resents the poor. And they resent as much or perhaps more those middle-class liberals who try to help the poor by pressuring the government to assist them. Many working-class whites appreciate government benefits but only when they are directly tied to work, such as Social Security payments and Medicare. But they resent welfare and Medicaid, food stamps, housing assistance, and payments to the poor or unemployed (Porter 2017). Working-class voters resent "the poor and urban liberal elites who can express enormous sympathy for the disenfranchised while ignoring the struggle of the white working class" (Porter 2017). There is little or no outrage shown among working-class whites when anti-poverty programs are cut to pay for tax cuts because they do not benefit from the social safety net. Eduardo Porter supports his argument by citing a book by Joan C. Williams, *White Working Class: Overcoming Class Cluelessness in America*:

> Ms. Williams, a professor at the University of California Hastings College of the Law, writes that these struggling workers resent not only the poor beneficiaries of the government's largess but also the liberal policy makers who seem to believe that only the poor are deserving of help. And they bristle at the perceived condescension of a liberal elite that seems to blame them for their failure to acquire the necessary skills to rise to the professional class. By contrast, they see themselves as hard-working citizens who struggle to make ends meet, only to be left out of many of the government programs their taxes pay for....."All they see is their stressed-out daily lives, and they resent subsidies and sympathy available to the poor," Professor Williams wrote. (Porter 2017)

And, of course, there is also racial mistrust. According to Porter (2017),

> Racial mistrust is never far from the surface: Only 13 percent of non-Hispanic whites draw benefits from means-tested programs, according to the Census Bureau analysis, compared with 42 percent of African-Americans and 36 percent of Hispanics. So while most beneficiaries of welfare programs are white, many working-class whites perceive them as schemes to hand their tax dollars to minorities.

It is not hard to see how "Mr. Trump's agenda serves both race and class resentment" (Porter 2017). And when we look at how the repeal and replacement of the Affordable Care Act (Obamacare) by the Trump administration (as presently envisioned) will likely force millions to abandon any hope of being able to afford health insurance, we wonder how working-class voters, who overwhelmingly cast their ballots for Trump, will react. Will those voters, say, from West Virginia's McDowell County, which has high rates of chronic illnesses and the shortest life expectancy in the United States, regret how they cast their ballots? Or will their loathing of liberal elites and "politically correct" left-wing radicals take precedence in their minds and offer them sufficient consolation that they made the right decision to vote for Trump?

Mississippi lawmakers have just advanced a proposal to add the firing squad, electrocution, and the gas chamber as execution methods—known as House Bill 638—in the event that a court blocks the use of lethal injection drugs. Republican House Judiciary B Committee Chairman Andy Gipson described this as a response to "liberal, left-wing radicals" (The Associated Press 2017). This could be good news for capitalism's "reserve army of labor," which Marx used to refer to the unemployed or underemployed in a capitalist economy, since, thanks to the school-to-prison pipeline designed for African Americans, there will always be plenty of jobs in the prison industrial complex, which is likely to be expanded under the unabashed corporatism of a Trump presidency, and I am sure there will be a need for expert marksmen should firing squads come back into fashion.

A relentless stream of controversial events coming from the White House have made headlines since Trump took office and the post-truth presidency began to take shape. But that is hardly surprising considering previous behaviour from Trump, the candidate who called for violence against those who were protesting during his rallies, who mocked a disabled reporter, and who was exposed when a 2005 tape surfaced of Trump bragging that his celebrity status allowed him to grab women sexually:

> "I've gotta use some Tic Tacs, just in case I start kissing her," Trump is heard to say on the tape, which the Washington Post released on Friday. "You know I'm automatically attracted to beautiful—I just start kissing them. It's like a magnet. Just kiss. I don't even wait...And when you're a star they let you do it. You can do anything...Grab them by the pussy. You can do anything." (Redden 2016)

And yet Trump had the audacity to post an incendiary claim on Twitter that accused former President Barack Obama of soiling the "very sacred election process" by allegedly tapping the phones in Trump Tower: "How low has President Obama gone to tapp [sic] my phones during the very sacred election process" (Moran 2017). Yes, President Trump, you certainly treated the election process as a very sacred event. Indeed, it is difficult to be surprised by any remarks made by Trump, who has learned to manage news cycles effectively by using his Twitter account to distract attention from controversies surrounding his administration.

The moment Donald Trump was sworn in as president of the United States, the LGBTQ, climate change, health care, and civil liberties pages disappeared from the White House website. Trump and Republican lawmakers, infected by a ghastly actuarialism, are planning the radical overhaul of the U.S. health care system, beginning with the repeal of the Affordable Care Act. This means shutting the doors on millions of Americans in need of health insurance. They also have their eyes on trimming benefits from Medicaid, Medicare, and dismantling the basic system of employer-sponsored health insurance. Senate majority leader Mitch McConnell silenced Senator Elizabeth Warren during a Senate hearing for reading a letter by Coretta Scott King, the widow of Martin Luther King Jr., written thirty years ago opposing the nomination of Jeff Sessions for a federal judgeship (Warren was a strong opponent of Sessions's nomination for attorney general). Sessions had been accused, early in his career, of a shamefully soft investigation of a lynching of a Black man by two members of the Ku Klux Klan. Thanks to a Trump victory, he is now the U.S. attorney general, who is promising to be tough on crime and to "pull back" from monitoring police misconduct because it has negatively affected police morale. He also criticized Department of Justice reports on civil rights violations by police in places like Ferguson, Missouri, and Chicago as "anecdotal," even while admitting he had not read any of the reports. Trump has tried to push through legislation that would bar any non-U.S. citizen from Iraq, Syria, Sudan, Libya, Somalia, or Yemen from entering the United States, and that would even prohibit green card and visa holders from these countries from returning to the United States for ninety days. That battle is still underway. And the deportation forces of the U.S. Immigration and Customs Enforcement have begun their ugly purge, while his architects are busy designing Trump's "great, great wall." And Trump's National Security Advisor Michael Flynn has already resigned for lying about his communications with Russian intelligence personnel, followed by Attorney General Jeff Sessions recusing himself from overseeing possible probes of "Russiagate," the Trump election campaign's communications with Russian officials and its possible connections to the Russian hacking of the U.S. election.

Those private prison companies that invested hundreds of thousands of dollars in Trump's presidential campaign saw their payoff recently when Jeff Sessions announced the reversal of the Obama administration's directive to reduce the Justice Department's use of private prisons. I wonder how many lawmakers in Arizona are going to consider changing the category of misdemeanour into that of a felony for some crimes in order to keep those prisons at maximum capacity. During the crack cocaine epidemic in the 1980s, the Ronald Reagan administration promoted the use of private prisons. According to McGlothlin (2016), "Arizona leads all other states in deals crafted for the private prison industry by guaranteeing 90 to 100 percent of prison beds will be filled in all six state-level private prison facilities." The problem is that private prison companies have a guarantee occupancy clause, issuing contracts that force states to pay to fill a certain percentage of prison beds regardless of how many felons are incarcerated, "which ensures profits and revenues but at the cost of taxpayers" (McGlothlin 2016). According to McGlothlin (2016),

> Arizona trumps all states' inmates quotas with three private prison facilities requiring 100 percent occupancy. Critics argue that this provides incentives to keep prison beds full, running counter to many states' trend of reducing prison populations, sentencing lengths and corrections spending.

In other words, the more incarceration, the higher the profits for the prison companies, and they often cut costs (such as education and addiction treatment programs) and increase revenue to ensure they meet their profit margin.

On the topic of education, Trump has proven extremely consequential should we seriously consider his demands, especially in light of the Betsy DeVos appointment—the abolishment of the Department of Education, working with the American Legion to enforce the Pledge of Allegiance in schools, routinely saluting the flag, and teaching American patriotism and celebrating the great historical accomplishments of the United States: "We will stop apologizing for America, and we will start celebrating America.... We will be united by our common cultures, values, and principles, becoming one American nation, one country under the one constitution, saluting one American flag—always saluting" (Provance 2016).

Audible in these demands is a call for the enforced docility of young Americans through erasing any viable possibility of developing a protagonistic agency by means of education. Trump further laments that "our public schools have grown up in a competition-free zone, surrounded by a very high union wall" and berates Democrats for taking "a strong stand against school choice" ("Donald Trump on Education"). Listeners are given cause to wonder: Will there be patriotism monitors in *Starship Troopers* combat attire, complete with M3 mobile infantry helmets patrolling the hallways? Will there be school suspensions for, say, students accurately linking the wholesale butchering of Native peoples by the United States cavalry to government-sponsored genocide during the U.S. Indian Wars that began in 1775 and did not officially end until 1924? Will students be taught to revere General Custer (as opposed to Crazy Horse or Sitting Bull) and those killed under his imperial command by eviscerating important historical context that could put into perspective the inhumanity and full measure of human depravity and pathology associated with the white settler state in its historical engagement with Native peoples? Will the portentously myopic understanding of the history of genocide of Native peoples in the United States be even more truncated out of existence than it is today? Will behaviour deemed impious toward our elected officials be rewarded with expulsion? Will the man in the Oval Office who exclaimed, "I love the poorly educated!" turn schools into patriotic boot camps, whose disciplinary codes and canonical particulars have been lifted from the film *Full Metal Jacket*?

Trump appointed Betsy DeVos, a wealthy, conservative, and Christian champion of the billion-dollar charter school industry.[1] Vice-President Mike Pence broke a tie vote on the DeVos nomination and handed over our children's futures to a businesswoman who plans to radically defund public education. Steve King of Iowa recently introduced HR 610, The School Choice Act, a bill designed to eliminate the Elementary and Secondary Education Act of 1965, which was instated as part of Lyndon B. Johnson's "War on Poverty," and representatives from Maryland, Texas, and Arizona have joined the proposed purge. According to Cimarusti (2017), HR 610 will use federal funds

> to create "block grants" to be used to "distribute a portion of funds to parents who elect to enroll their child in a private school or to home-school their child." It would also roll back nutritional standards for free lunches for poor children.

Cimarusti (2017) described a recent meeting between DeVos and Trump and ten teachers and parents who had been invited to discuss education priorities for the Trump administration, which includes his signature reform initiative of providing vouchers for private and religious schools and rendering public schools powerless and poor:

> Of the ten attendees, one was a public school teacher and one was a principal of a public school that specializes in special education. There was one public school parent who also had children in private school. The rest of the group were homeschoolers, charter school parents or private school representatives. During the meeting, Trump praised what he referred to as a "Nevada charter school" that he had visited. The school is actually a religious school which regularly excludes students with disabilities.

A video is available that shows children pledging allegiance to the Bible as Mr. Trump approvingly looks on ("Exclusive: Donald Trump Visits School").

Teachers at Westminster High School in Carroll County, Washington, were recently ordered to remove diversity posters they had put up around their school that depicted Latina, Muslim, and Black women. Artist Shepard Fairey, who received instant fame for his "Hope" posters featuring President Barack Obama in 2008, designed the posters. One of the posters reads, "We the people are greater than fear" (Liebelson 2017). At first, the teachers were accused of being anti-Trump by the administration but, after removing the posters, were allowed to put them up again. But then the administration stipulated that "the posters could be seen as political" and that they can only be put up in their classrooms if they are part of the formally sanctioned curriculum and both sides of any political issue are represented (Liebelson 2017). The next time some educational "expert" tells you that teaching is supposed to be—or could be—neutral, do not believe them, not even for a New York minute! Only 4 per cent of Carroll County's school system identifies as minority. Is anyone surprised? Steven Johnson, the county's assistant superintendent for instruction, likens the diversity poster to the Confederate battle flag:

> The Confederate flag in and of itself has no image of slavery or hatred or oppression, but it's symbolic of that....These posters have absolutely no mention of Trump or any other political issue—it's the symbolism of what they were representing. They were carried in these protests. (Liebelson 2017)

The concealed hypothesis that underlies such positions is the proposition that acts of praising diversity and inclusion are somehow independent from the idea of national security. The logic seems to suggest that posters praising diversity and inclusion must be counterbalanced by something that supposedly represents an opposite meaning—Trump's war on undocumented immigrants. What has become of the profession of teaching when we cannot display racial and ethnic diversity on the walls of our classrooms? Diversity, inclusion, and the welcoming of immigrants are supposedly one of the pillars upon which the United States was built. The logic itself is repressive, not neutral. But it teaches us something. It teaches us that another pillar of U.S. culture is the ritual scapegoating of immigrants. A democratic system that procures an advantage to all immigrants is a system that procures an advantage for us all. The Trump administration, by contrast, exhibits a *bellum omnium contra omnes*—the war of all against all—position, where unwelcoming immigrants procures an advantage of security to the population that has forgotten its own immigrant roots.

Forgetting our roots is one of the consequences of banning books. Just months after Trump won the election, a bill was introduced in the Arkansas state legislature by Representative Kim Hendren—HB1834—that attempts to prohibit public schools in the state from assigning books or other material authored by the late author and historian, Howard Zinn, arguably the most important U.S. historian on the Left. The bill prohibits any of Zinn's works written between the years 1959 and 2010 to be used in public schools or open-enrolled public charter schools. In 2013, former Indiana Republican Governor Mitch Daniels attempted to remove all of Zinn's work from classrooms throughout Indiana. Daniels is now president of Purdue University.

Recently, DeVos issued a statement about historically Black colleges and universities (HBCUs): that these institutions were "real pioneers when it comes to school choice" (Allen 2017). This only displayed DeVos's egregious ignorance about the historical context surrounding the creation of historically Black institutions of higher learning. Some interpreted her statement as applauding the Jim Crow segregated education system for giving Black students "more options" (Allen 2017). Morehouse President John Wilson Jr. responded to DeVos, calling HBCUs an example of "school choice" as follows:

> "HBCUs were not created because the 4 million newly freed blacks were unhappy with the choices they had. They were created because they had no choices at all," he said. "[I]f one does not understand the crippling and extended horrors of slavery, then how can one really understand the subsequent history and struggle of African Americans, or the current necessities and imperatives that grow out of that history and struggle?" (Finley 2017)

Alan Singer (2017) reports that stock value for private, for-profit "colleges" has soared since the election of Donald Trump and his race to dismantle federal regulations. These predatory educational institutions, which Singer (2017) notes "have been ripping-off the government and victimizing the poor, veterans, and evangelicals," have been experiencing increased windfalls:

> Strayer's is up 35 percent, Grand Canyon almost 30 percent, and DeVry, which agreed to pay a hundred million dollars in debt relief and cash payments to settle a federal lawsuit for fraudulent advertising last December, more than 40 percent.

These colleges describe themselves in a language reserved for Disney imagineers working on a new installation to make Fantasyland even more fantastic, masquerading under the guise of a legitimate educational institution, but in reality are little more than dream factories intended to make their investors and managers wealthy. They aggressively market themselves to the military, "enrolling them in online programs while they are still on active duty" (Singer 2017). Military personnel use their GI Bill benefits to pay for their education, and, according to a 2014 Senate report, "eight for-profit college companies received about a fourth of all GI Bill benefit educational dollars," and the cost of these institutions is approximately double that of public colleges (Singer 2017).

Trump has asked Jerry Falwell Jr., president of Liberty University, to head a task force that will explore further ways to deregulate American higher education. Singer (2017) reminds us that Trump University "closed in 2010 and agreed to pay $25 million in damages to settle a lawsuit by former students who charged they were defrauded when promised they would learn the secrets of Trump's real estate success." Many of these for-profit colleges, such as Corinthian Colleges, inflate their job placement rate for graduates. Corinthian, which filed for bankruptcy, was fined $30 million by the federal Department of Education. According to Singer (2017), Falwell has made it clear that "his goal was eliminating Obama administration initiates to 'give colleges and their accrediting agencies more leeway in governing their affairs,' which would allow companies like Trump, ITT, and Corinthian to rip-off a new generation of unsuspecting students, many U.S. military veterans, and American taxpayers who insure student loans." Singer's (2017) description of Liberty University should send chills down the spine of those interested in protecting public education from academic predation:

> Falwell and his Liberty University would directly benefit if federal regulation was reduced or suspended. While it is primarily known as a mid-sized residential evangelical Christian college located in Lynchburg, Virginia, it also operates an enormous profit-making online program enrolling 65,000 students. This program generated almost $600 million in revenue in 2013. It is the second largest online "college" in the United States. Most of the tuition dollars for Liberty's online students comes from financial aid programs operated by the federal government's Department of Education, approximately $350 million in 2015. Because it is technically a church-related non-profit institution, Liberty pays no taxes on its earnings. Falwell himself earns over $900,000 a year for managing the business. His so-called college "teaches" students that the Earth is only a few thousand years old and that dinosaurs lived at the same time as people and encourages them to get concealed hand-gun permits so they can protect the country and their college against Islamic terrorists.

But is there a payoff for the graduates? Not according to Singer (2017), who reports,

> A big part of the problem is that after receiving their quality Liberty education over 40 percent of Liberty graduates earn

less than $25,000 per year when they finish college. Earnings-wise, a Liberty degree is worth about the same amount as a high school diploma.

The most dangerous Trump appointment of all was, in my estimation, that of Steve Bannon, the now terminated assistant to the president and chief strategist in the Donald Trump administration—and the West Wing's former resident apocalypticist—and formerly the executive chair of the alt-Right Breitbart News, who has openly admitted to admiring Dick Cheney, Darth Vader, and Satan (Stahl 2016). Bannon brought to the White House a ghoulishly cultic and gangrenous *Gemeinschaft*, and, given his white nationalism, it would be difficult to fault anyone for harbouring lurking suspicions that he set up a Lebensborn clinic somewhere in the bowels of the White House, a place where Trump's new master race can begin their breeding rituals on behalf of the biotruth of the new white ethnostate: whiteness is the closest you can get to godliness. Time to get out the measuring tape and check the pedigree of those Aryan-shaped craniums.

Bannon is a Catholic, and a perplexing Catholic at that. During a talk at a Vatican conference on poverty and wealth creation hosted by the Dignitatis Humanae Institute, Bannon surprisingly expressed disdain for various forms of capitalism he had identified. Bannon referenced four types of capitalism: state-sponsored capitalism, which he equates with Russia and China; "crony" capitalism, which he links to an establishment, neoliberal corporatism that acts against the interests of an open, free market; "the Ayn Rand or the Objectivist School of libertarian capitalism" that treats people solely as economic commodities (which he falsely attributes to Marxism, which is arrayed precisely *against* the commodification of human beings); and, finally, "enlightened" capitalism, grounded in the morality of Judeo-Christian belief and the value systems of Western culture (Feder 2016). Of these four versions of capitalism, all must be rejected except for the latter, "enlightened capitalism," championed by Bannon.

Bannon vociferously decries the forces of secularization and seeks to embark on a Holy War against Islam. I am against crony capitalism and neoliberal capitalism, and I certainly understand the dangerous limitations of state capitalism (originally identified by Marxist humanist Raya Dunayevskaya). And as a Catholic myself, I certainly appreciate Christian belief and value systems. But I also know how dangerously they can be interpreted and employed, especially against those who have already been victimized by society and the state. Bannon, however, seems to self-righteously release the irrational forces of hate as a form of sacred violence embodied in a new type of Anglo-American nationalism driven by a superannuated Christology. There is something about him that echoes a longing for the Nietzschean superman, and there is something Heideggerian about Bannon that recognizes that humanity's foundations are built upon sacred violence. The problem is not in the recognition of violence at the heart of civilization but Heidegger's moral response: he chooses to endorse this condition rather than oppose it. To oppose, in other words, the need to scapegoat and sacrifice the victim in order to solidify the culture. It would serve Bannon's Catholicism well if he were to read the work of René Girard and Gil Bailie on the founding role of mimetic victimage (Bailie 1995; Girard 1979).

One of Bannon's primary goals is to deconstruct the "administrative state," but his attempts at doing so are being undermined by what some critics have called the "deep state," a type of shadow government, about which Dwight Eisenhower warned the American people. Eisenhower referred to the deep state as the "military industrial complex," but it has extended its tentacles far and wide since Eisenhower's time. While Nancy Reagan relied upon her White House astrologer (from 1981 to 1988) to advise her husband in personal and political matters while they occupied the White House, Bannon is another kettle of fish entirely. Bannon religiously follows the pseudo-scientific interpretations of discredited amateur historians William Strauss and Neil Howe, who believe we are at the tail end of a historical cycle of American history,[2] during which time a hero/leader known as the Grey Champion, a messianic strongman figure, will emerge and prevent the United States and Judeo-Christian and Western civilization from destruction. If Trump agrees with Bannon's world view (and he certainly appears to have Trump's ear), and if Trump himself believes he is the Grey Champion (knowing Trump, that would not be very difficult to imagine), the Trump presidency could be on its way toward eventuating an apocalyptic and omnicidal battle with the forces of "radical Islam" and China. In 2016, Bannon made this comment to Reagan biographer Lee Edwards: "We're going to war in the South China Seas in the next five to 10 years, aren't we?" (Blumenthal 2017a). Although an impertinent isolationist, Bannon appears to possess enough influence to persuade Trump to engage in a march through history as ideologically ruthless and unrepentant as Sherman's "March to the Sea," the Nazi blitzkrieg bombing of Poland, or, more recently, the "shock and awe" tactics of General Schwarzkopf during the U.S. invasion of Iraq. The actions by which Trump has hollowed out his life until there was nothing left but a red tie and some expensive hair tint have caused him to take up residence in one of the more fashionable ethical subdivisions (where your neighbour happens to be the Father of Lies). They have also made him gravely susceptible to conspiracy addicts like Bannon and less likely to respond to cries of dereliction from those families bestirred by a system of brutal austerity capitalism who have suffered a dramatic loss of income since the Great Recession, while watching the earnings of the higher-income families rise.

Bannon has repeatedly referred to a racist French novel from the 1970s, *The Camp of the Saints*, by Jean Raspail, to explain his world view. The book—once praised by William F. Buckley Jr.—describes the takeover of France and the West by so-called Third World immigrants, leading to the destruction of Western civilization. Consider these anti-immigrant remarks Bannon has made over the past several years:

> "It's been almost a Camp of the Saints-type invasion into Central and then Western and Northern Europe," he said in October 2015.
> "The whole thing in Europe is all about immigration," he said in January 2016. "It's a global issue today—this kind of global Camp of the Saints."
> "It's not a migration," he said later than January. "It's really an invasion. I call it the Camp of the Saints."
> "When we first started talking about this a year ago," he said in April 2016, "we called it the Camp of the Saints....I mean, this is Camp of the Saints, isn't it?" (Blumenthal 2017b)

Of course, Steve Bannon is not the only Republican politician that is a fan of *The Camp of the Saints*. Iowa Representative Steve King concluded a radio interview in March 2017, recommending to listeners that they read *The Camp of the Saints* (Massie 2017). On the same program, he also responded to reports that whites would become a majority-minority demographic in the United States by 2044 by predicting that Blacks and Hispanics "will be fighting each other" before overtaking whites in the U.S. population (Massie 2017). Only a day earlier, he tweeted, "We can't restore our civilization with somebody else's babies," a comment that was praised by white nationalist and former KKK grand wizard, David Duke, and condemned as "racist" by civil rights icon, Representative John Lewis (Massie 2017). King exhorted white Americans to invest in "our stock, our country, our culture, our civilization," arguing that "we need to have enough babies to replace ourselves" (Massie 2017). That sounds like it came right out of the Bannon playbook.

In 2013, Bannon praised former Senator Joe McCarthy, of "McCarthyism" fame, and compared communist infiltration of America during the Cold War to a "dramatic influence campaign" by the Muslim Brotherhood in today's Washington, DC (Massie and Kaczynski 2017). He notes that there is only one difference separating those two forms of infiltration. According to Bannon,

> It's the banks, it's the investment banks, it's the hedge funds, it's the private equity funds, it's the law firms, it's the power establishment, in the United States, [that are] inextricably linked with the cash coming out of the Middle East....There are voices there of rationality that are being mocked and derided every day and the reason that the establishment looks the other way and the Bush apparatus looks the other way is because there's so much cash, there are so many petro-dollars being funneled back to this town. (Massie and Kaczynski 2017)

As influential as Bannon appears to be in peddling his extreme views, he's no match for the "deep state." According to Gary Olson (2017), the deep state is

> a hybrid network of structures within which actual power resides. It includes the military-industrial complex, Wall Street, hordes of private contractors whose sole client is the government, national security agencies, select (not all) members of the State, Defense, CIA, Homeland Security, a few key members of the Congressional Defense and Intelligence Committees, and so on. Except for a handful of Congresspersons, Deep State members have not been elected and are accountable to no one. They profoundly influence virtually every domestic and foreign matter of consequence. D. J. Hopkins, another close student of this phenomenon, notes that "the system served by the Deep State is not the United States of America, i.e., the country most Americans believe they live in; the system it serves is globalized Capitalism." And they do so regardless of which party is nominally in control. Lofgren takes pains to point out that the Deep State is *not* a coven of diabolical conspirators. It has evolved over several decades to become the antithesis of democracy.

The deep state is set against the economic nationalism of Bannon, and its goal is to ensure that the United States remains the major consolidating force in the growth of the transnational capitalist class. In addition, the deep state will profit mightily from a new Cold War with Russia, especially the Pentagon and its arms dealers, and Trump and Bannon are not to be trusted; they may even "unwittingly expose their 'marionette theater' of contrived democracy" (Olson 2017). It is too early to tell how this drama between the deep state and Bannon will play out.

Another extremely dangerous Trump appointee was Sebastian Lukacs Gorka, also now terminated, a Hungarian immigrant and former deputy assistant to the president. A former national security affairs editor for the alt-Right news agency, Breitbart, Gorka has been a guest on the *Secure Freedom* radio show hosted by Frank Gaffney Jr., a fringe figure who touts the view that Islam and the West represent a fundamental clash of civilizations, and that we are currently at war with a global jihadist movement that interprets certain Koranic passages to support its acts of terror.

Until recently, Gorka himself was a fringe figure but now has found a place in the Trump administration, warmongering and bashing what he calls "Islamic laws of war" and arguing that the Koran's violent passages are the cause for terrorism (Jaffe 2017). He has also made the claim that President Obama's withdrawal of troops from Iraq is to blame for the rise of ISIS and that Trump's attacks on radical Islamic terrorism will have no impact on ISIS recruitment.

According to Kurt Eichenwald (2016), right-wing extremists are a greater threat to the United States than ISIS. He writes that, since 2002, right-wing militants

> have killed more people in the United States than jihadis have. In that time, according to New America, a Washington think tank, Islamists launched nine attacks that murdered 45, while the right-wing extremists struck 18 times, leaving 48 dead. These Americans thrive on hate and conspiracy theories, many fed to them by politicians and commentators who blithely blather about government concentration camps and impending martial law and plans to seize guns and other dystopian gibberish, apparently unaware there are people listening who don't know it's all lies. These extremists turn to violence—against minorities, non-Christians, abortion providers, government officials— in what they believe is a fight to save America. And that potential for violence is escalating every day.

Is it so surprising that Trump is downplaying right-wing terrorism from white supremacists at the same time as emphasizing the threat from what he calls "radical Islamic extremism"? Boehlert (2017) writes,

> Coming in the wake of Trump's controversial decision to sign an executive order temporarily barring individuals from seven majority-Muslim countries from entering the United States, Reuters this week reported that the Trump administration would direct a government-run program called Countering Violent Extremism to change its name to Countering Islamic Extremism or Countering Radical Islamic Extremism. In doing so, the program "would no longer target groups such as white supremacists who have also carried out bombings and shootings in the United States." (The FBI and the Justice Department will still track hate crimes and prosecute homegrown terrorists.) Downgrading the scrutiny given to right-wing radicals has long been a goal of conservative media in America. Now Trump is moving to turn that desire into policy.

The unbridled love showered on Trump by his (really a faux-populism) oleaginous surrogates and followers, who have illicitly consecrated him as the chosen saviour of the country, gushes in direct proportion to Trump's repellent hyperbolic populism and disdain for undocumented immigrants. With the enlivened faces of Trump's venerators shining like Christmas tinsel, they crane their necks at Trump rallies like a possessed Linda Blair in *The Exorcist* in order to catch a glimpse of their ruddy white redeemer as he ascends the stage, arms pumping in patriotic ribaldry. A chilling spectacle of righteous vengeance begins to unfold as Trump begins his attack on the media, which could become the dry tinder for his eventual downfall. His loyal base screech and holler, "lock her up!" (referring to Hillary Clinton) as the social contagion at Trump rallies often turns pathological, leading to violence against protestors. Yet, for his adversaries, Trump's hectoring, haranguing, and impertinent tone have been as suffocating as an hourglass corset with whalebone stays and has famously served as his signature marker (along with his red cap) since the beginning of his campaign. His endless bantering about the destruction visited upon his country by the guardians of political correctness, his pseudo-explanations of what he perceives as the enforced egalitarianism of the Left, his plans for a deportation task force to expel undocumented immigrants, and his paranoid accounting for the vulnerability of the United

States to terrorist attacks have been perceived by many as an incentive to violence, likening Trump to an impertinent catechist of the alt-Right. His podium delivery, with its onrush of acrimony, his exhortations to division and hatred, and his spiteful descriptions of Mexicans, Muslims, women, and the disabled, is as cheap as saloon and dance hall makeup. The hucksterish face of patriotism he wears in front of rapturous crowds is slathered in steady spurts of bile and smeared over the television screens that rarely seem absent of his grim visage for very long. What draws his base together is not something they all share but something they all lack—an incapability of rapprochement between justice and compassion.

The reason that an individual as odious as Trump has been able to insinuate himself so seamlessly and ineluctably into the political system in such a short time is because he *represents* the white supremacist/capitalist/patriarchal unconscious unchained. No matter how fashionable his apostasy, no ideologue of the ilk of a Donald Trump has the ability to free us from the current political system. There will be no apocalyptic fulfillment from the likes of Trump, despite his own media-minded hucksterism and steady pronouncements by the long list of hierophantic agents from Fox News (mostly retired generals, talk show hosts, or scandal-ridden politicians). Despite his irrepressible need for media attention and tweet attacks on Republican backsliders, he remains locked in a parochialism and defensive obstinacy that works to get him through the day. Mainstream ideologues on the Right or the Left are capable only of moulding us more snugly into whatever form is taken by the political ideology of the day, such as today's current incarnation of neoliberalism. And this is equally as true for Hillary Clinton, the cosmopolitan darling of the Dom Pérignon liberals whose speeches are commendably cleansed of Trump-style toxicity and to whom immigrants appear decidedly less craven and pitiable. To her credit, she has skilfully succeeded in anathematizing Trump as a white supremacist in an Italian silk suit. This is not to discount the fact that most of Trump's supporters are not (as often assumed) from the white working class—although there are many workers who have pledged him their unyielding allegiance—but from higher-income earners in the petty-bourgeois class (Hudis 2016). Racial and ethnic animosity, the fear of empowered Blacks, feminists, and gays and lesbians, and resentment of social change is in no way limited to working-class, disenfranchised whites.

Whether the capitalist system seems rudderless, oarless, and without sail, or orchestrated by a baleful cabal of bankers in the death clutch of the Illuminati, weary-eyed from devouring library shelves of well-thumbed alchemical texts, we need to examine the capitalist system itself to uncover its internal relations (see Allman, McLaren, and Rikowski 2003). Whether the face of capitalism is Clinton swaddled in her $12,000 Armani jacket, or a churlish Trump flaunting his $5,000 Brioni suit fashioned for today's corporate overman, or even a naked, penitent hermit navel-gazing atop a state capital flagpole, we need to remember that any face of the capitalist system is only a face and is meant to distract us from the systemic workings of that system. The educational system is no exception.

The very places where you might expect to find some exemption from this madness—public universities—have become the most vulnerable. For example, Marc Spooner (2015, 5) describes university life as festering in the belly of an "audit culture," where the fabled philosophical struggle for determining what constitutes "the good life" is now disturbingly "mak[ing] its appearance in the banal metrics of a standardized bookkeeping program." The businessification, corporatization, and politically domesticating aspects of the neoliberal university have precipitated schismatic ranks who have withdrawn their submission to search for the meaning of truth and justice in favour of settling for the demands of the corporate bottom line. Such tarnished faith in the ancient idea of *paideia* has been compounded by an even more vicious blasphemy: the ascendency of the idea that universities, in order to survive, must function mainly as entrepreneurial workshops that educate new cadres of the ruling class while providing some compensation to those who are anguishing to join their ranks. After all, over the next twenty-five years, 47 per cent of existing jobs will be automated out of existence (Hudis 2016), and I am not optimistic that the technological revolution will find a way to replace them. People of colour who are disproportionately thrust out of any participation in the neoliberal economy face the prospect of complete dehumanization once they are out of work; whites who are pushed out of employment in a white supremacist society desperately cling to their identity as white people as some compensation for their dehumanization. And those who choose to resist, such as the warriors of Black Lives Matter or Idle No More, are branded as terrorists and face being dragged into social compliance by the long arm of the surveillance state. Clearly, the idea of socialist revolution has disappeared from the cultural patrimony of our post-enlightenment intellectual establishment, although it is possible that, given enough time, young people attracted to the Sanders campaign could build a movement strong enough one day to force the establishment's hand.

One of the most discouraging and incontrovertible truths of today is that dead labour continues to dominate living labour. The dual character of labour, according to Marx, drives the logic of capital. Abstract labour is created through the instrumentality of socially necessary labour time, so that the value of a commodity is not based on the actual amount of labour it takes to produce it but on the average amount of time that is necessary to produce it on a world market, so that the relative proportion of living to dead labour (capital) progressively declines in today's system of wage labour, in which profit (value) augmented by investment in labour-saving devices creates greater profits in less time (Hudis 2016).

Abstract labour is indifferent to the needs of the worker in the sense that there is no finite limit to the drive to obey the imperatives of socially necessary labour time as workers are forced to produce more in a shorter amount of time, a situation that leads inexorably to the exploitation of natural resources, which, contrary to the infinite magnitude of value production, are necessarily finite (Hudis 2016). Do we think universities can escape this logic, especially at a time when the wage form of capital has been extended to hundreds of millions of people worldwide as capitalism colonizes the entire lifeworld of the planet? And when capitalism has reached the point of a conditioned universality, leaving the vast population of the planet ensepulchred within a neofeudal capitalist state? Marc Lamont Hill (2016, 173) writes,

> When the only real money is being made on property rather than from hourly and salaried income, what solidarity does the capitalist have with the wage earner? When cheap foreign workers and technological advancements lead to sustained or even greater productivity, what reason is there to care about the worker who has been abandoned by it all?

The social universe in which we live—which has been constituted by a hyper-globalized system whose aim is not to generate material wealth or to satisfy use-value but rather to augment exchange value—is becoming increasingly unbraided; social bonds that were once part of the common storehouse of humanization are fraying as the subjectivity of workers is becoming effaced to the point of total elimination. Capitalism's inbuilt instability—its most recent incarnation manifested in the stillborn recovery of 2008—will intensify dramatically over the next several decades, as climate disaster, rising unemployment, stagnating living standards, increasing personal surveillance of the poor and powerless, and the squandering of natural resources and life-threatening pollution transform our global habitat such that it resembles a future crisis-ridden world not unlike contemporary dystopian landscapes, such as those found in films such as *Elysium*.

Trump's attacks on China's economic policies could lead to tensions within the global economy that could lead to war. William Robinson (2017) and others have written extensively on how the capitalist system "faces a structural crisis of extreme inequality and overaccumulation, as well as a political crisis of legitimacy and an ecological crisis of sustainability." Marxist and progressive educators have been writing about this crisis for decades. But Robinson (2017) notes another aspect to this crisis that could very well lead to "world conflagration," and this has to do with the "disjuncture between a globalizing economy and a nation-state system of political authority" that "threatens to undermine the system's ability to manage the crisis." And this disjuncture, notes Robinson, is at the heart of Trump's attacks on China's economic policies. Today's global economy has fully integrated numerous countries and power blocs such as BRICS (Brazil, Russia, India, China, South Africa) and other countries in the Global South. Just think for a moment of the myriad of ways in which the global economy is dependent upon China, especially in relation to its role in subcontracting and outsourcing and the role its market continues to play in keeping capitalism afloat. Not only does it remain "the workshop of the world" but it leads the way in foreign direct investment. As Robinson (2017) points out, "Between 1991 and 2003, China's foreign direct investment increased 10-fold, and then increased 13.7 times from 2004 to 2013, from $45 billion to $613 billion." Robinson (2017) is essentially correct when he argues that we need "more balanced transnational state institutions that reflect the new realities of a multipolar and interdependent global capitalist system that could deescalate mounting international tensions and the threat of war," and ideally this would lead to a more "interventionist capitalist state."

At the same time, Robinson harbours no illusions that this is enough. We need mass social movements and a massive redistribution downward of wealth and power. But, absent such a revolution from below, it is clear we need more effective transnational state apparatuses of governance to resolve the disjuncture between a globalizing economy and a nation-state–based system of political authority. For example, Robinson (2017) notes, "The World Economic Forum has called for new forms of global corporate rule, including a proposal to remake the United Nations system into a hybrid corporate-government entity run by TNC [transnational corporate] executives in 'partnership' with governments." China is ahead of the United States in this regard, since

> Chinese capitalism has not followed the neo-liberal route to
> global capitalist integration. The state retains a key role in the

financial system, in regulating private capital, and in planning. This allows it to develop 21st century infrastructure and to guide capital accumulation into aims broader than that of immediate profit making, something that Western capitalist states cannot accomplish due to the rollback of public sectors, privatization, and deregulation. (Robinson 2017)

When Trump attacks China, how seriously is he taking into account the fact that global capitalism is in severe crisis? To what extent does he have a critical understanding of China's role in the global economy? Is he, for instance, considering the fact that foreign direct investment between the United States and China has increased exponentially over the past several decades? According to Robinson (2017), in 2015, "more than 1,300 U.S.-based companies had investments of $228 billion in China, while Chinese companies invested $64 billion in the United States, up from close to zero just ten years earlier, and held $153 billion in assets." Is Trump factoring in the reality that "the largest foreign holder of U.S. debt is China, which owns more than $1.24 trillion in bills, notes, and bonds or about 30 percent of the over $4 trillion in Treasury bills, notes, and bonds held by foreign countries," and that "China owns about 10 percent of publicly held U.S. debt" (Robinson 2017)? Robinson (2017) also points out that "deficit spending and debt-driven consumption has made the United States in recent decades the 'market of last resort,' helping to stave off greater stagnation and even collapse of the global economy by absorbing Chinese and world economic output." What would happen if China decided to withdraw billions of dollars in its investments in multiple industries in the United States? If the United States starts sabre-rattling with China, the entire world economy could be in peril, and the world would be at risk of nuclear annihilation.

The embattled stance of the academy to the crisis of capitalist overproduction has been to defend the privatization of the public sphere. This is no more evident than in attempts by universities to market themselves as a brand—that is, as a total experience. This could mean anything from living in a dorm that resembles a five-star hotel, to having the best fraternity and sorority houses in town, to having a group of Nobel laureates on faculty, to being connected to a student body that collectively shares certain religious and/or humanitarian beliefs.

A wide range of critical pedagogies over the last several decades has spiked the educational landscape, and even critical pedagogy itself has become a brand. While many of these "social justice" brands consist of domesticated, denuded, and flatlined versions of Freirean pedagogy, others reflect a stead-fast allegiance to Freire's important work, remaining loyal to critical peda-gogy's historical aim: to critique and transform asymmetrical relations of power and privilege that constitute and are constituted by the surrounding milieu of the classroom; the school; the local, regional, and national aspects of the culture; and the institutional and economic arrangements of society. By "institutional and economic arrangements of society," I am referring to those systems of mediation that negatively impact the academic success of students, that rob counterfactual values of any cognitive validity, and, equally as important, rob students of their ability to think critically and to develop the kind of protagonist agency and predilection for the weak and powerless of human history necessary for a social revolution.

The germinating insight of critical pedagogy is that experience consists of actions in and on the world that can be mediated by critical reflection and thus become protagonistic in shaping the world in the interests of creating a better humanity. Critical consciousness can lead to an ethical obligation to end the needless suffering of the oppressed. It is perhaps more the case that an ethical obligation to assist the oppressed can lead to critical consciousness—since ethics should precede epistemology in the praxis of serving in a community, and not above it. Truth does not begin as a minor infraction against the cold machines of capitalist power with their exacerbated unleashing of deception and promise of universal salvation through the god of commerce, or as an impious indiscretion at a banquet table regaled in splendour for the rich, but as a rasping shout from the barricades! We must denounce social injustice in order to announce the coming of social justice. This is what Paulo Freire taught us in his charter document on critical pedagogy, *Pedagogy of the Oppressed*.

Drawing on research by Michael Burawoy, Spooner (2015) describes the university as a site where a scholar's worth is organized in a system domi-nated by public management technologies and accountancy practices under-lain by a technocratic rationality and measured by restricting academic accomplishments to narrow and retrograde performance indicators and tab-ulating them by means of simple algorithms on a spreadsheet that includes such categories as peer-reviewed publications, journal impact rankings, and research grants. Researchers who collaborate in engaged public scholarship and community-based projects with the intention of contributing to the betterment of the commons are often, according to Spooner, marginalized, depersonalized, and driven to the sidelines, seriously jeopardizing their prospects for tenure. Remaining relentless catechizers while intervening in the lives of the oppressed is considered less legitimate within the neoliberal academy than, say, documenting the theories and epistemological risks inherent in unspecified research protocols. In other words, the neoliberal academy and its clerisy wedded to the establishment of official channels and the principles of the new managerialism as rule creators, rule enforcers, and moral entrepreneurs trained for appropriate decisional responses have brutally cleaved dialectical engagement in two, deracinating its hermeneutical potential by focusing only on one half of what constitutes the dialectic of critical consciousness; such a brutal sundering of the potential for critical analysis is accomplished by validating theory as a discrete entity that should stand on its own, as somehow existing in antiseptic isolation from its dialectical companion: practice. This move not only prohibits any real critical and transformative engagement—any authentic praxis—to emerge from collaboration with living and breathing human beings but actually promotes a radical disjuncture with everyday life. Critical theorists are considered crackpot philosophical sectaries entangled in occult casuistries. This is the very opposite of how a university should function.

The "adjunctification" of universities—a major symptom of the corporatization of the university—and the fear of collective bargaining among administrations in public universities have intensified in recent years, threatening to fracture faculty-student relationships as adjunct graduate student workers attempt to unionize, sometimes against the recommendations of faculty. Yet Marley-Vincent Lindsey (2016) writes,

> The truth is that graduate student unions have little to do with most faculty-student relationships; they instead threaten the very structure of power within bloated administrations that have restructured academic programs and services at personal gain.

He also notes,

> Regardless of how we feel about it, survival in the academy has become a corporate exercise. Instead of looking at unions as the antithesis of academic life, we should consider them an assertion of the authority of those of us who carry out the labor that makes higher education possible. All of us will be better for it.

The question of unions becomes increasingly important as current estimates of nontenured faculty in U.S. universities are between 50 and 70 per cent, an increase of 30 per cent since 1975.

While blatant hate propaganda is not hard to find throughout college campuses in the United States, there has been a recent spike in more subtle versions of white supremacist discourse in sayings such as "Protect your heritage," "Let's become great again," "Our future belongs to us," "White people, do something," and "Serve your people" (Ganim, Welch, and Meyersohn 2017). Recently, the Southern Poverty Law Center, an organization that monitors hate crimes across the country, released its annual report on extremism.

> The report says the number of groups across the country increased in 2016 to 917, up from 892 in 2015. In 2011, SPLC [Southern Poverty Law Center] recorded 1,018 active organizations, the highest tally it found in more than 30 years of tracking hate groups. That number had fallen to 784 in 2014. The largest jump last year occurred in the number of anti-Muslim hate groups, which tripled from 34 in 2015 to 101.The report singled out Donald Trump's pledge to bar Muslims from entering the country, his harsh language around immigration from Mexico, his appearance on conspiracy-theorist Alex Jones's radio program, and his engagement with white nationalists on Twitter as key moments that encouraged extremist groups during the campaign. (Ganim, Welch, and Meyersohn 2017)

White nationalism has received a boost from Trump's presidential election campaign and from his first month in office, as efforts have been made by right-wing groups to normalize the idea that the United States is a country that has always belonged to Europeans and is under threat of being taken away from them by non-white immigrants. According to a recent CNN report, the message of these hate groups is making progress because of the way nationalism is being packaged as "identitarian":

> "They're racist, but they have fancy new packaging," said Brian Levin, director for the Center of Hate and Extremism at Cal State San Bernardino. "They learn to downplay the swastikas and get a thesaurus, so instead of white supremacy they use words like identitarian. It's just a repackaged version of white nationalism."
> "Trump's run for office electrified the radical right, which saw in him a champion of the idea that America is fundamentally a white man's country," wrote Mark Potok, a senior fellow at the SPLC. "Several new and energetic groups appeared last year that

were almost entirely focused on Trump and seemed to live off his candidacy." "The country saw a resurgence of white nationalism that imperils the racial progress we've made, along with the rise of a president whose policies reflect the values of white nationalists," Potok noted.

The White House did not respond to a request for comment. (Ganim, Welch, and Meyersohn 2017)

Today, the leafletting at campuses by white supremacists has received a linguistic facelift, but the message is still the same. They regard the "diversity" emphasis on campuses throughout the country as a cult designed to shut out white people from their inherited right to live in dominion over other races present on this country's soil. This kind of message is at risk of becoming normalized, as students radicalized by this hate set up "watch lists" designed to purge campuses of pro-multiculturalist professors who they claim are anti-American.

If we want to understand how fascism takes hold of educational institutions, a good example would be the recent purge of academics and teachers from universities and high schools and elementary schools in Turkey after a failed coup attempt on July 15, 2016, that the Turkish President Recep Tayyip Erdoğan blamed on a religious group led by the cleric Fethullah Gülen. So far, 28,163 schoolteachers and 4,811 academics have been dismissed from their positions. Many educators have been publicly ridiculed and harassed, including friends and colleagues of mine. According to Eda Erdener (2017),

Professor Bülent Ari, a member of the supervisory board of the Council of Higher Education, or YÖK, recently said: "The growing number of educated people has exasperated me...We need an ignorant generation for the future of the country. Those who have harmed the country are those who have been well educated. Those who will save this country are people who have not even graduated from primary school. We trust them for the new Turkey." This was not an ironic comment. Will our students be taught by those with similar views?

Professor Ari's statement reminds me of the attitude of the famous American journalist and political commentator, Walter Lippmann, who described the vast array of ordinary Americans unworthy of thinking and planning in a democracy as the "bewildered herd." Erdener (2017) also reports,

During peaceful protest against this action, professors were beaten and dragged along the ground by police officers. The police officers, who are around 20 years old and whose education background is unknown, not only physically beat academics—including veteran professors—but humiliated them.

On a visit to Ankara, Turkey, to support critical educators in 2011, I was tear-gassed, trampled upon, and chased through the streets by riot police. Fortunately, I was spotted by a waiter who dragged me into his restaurant, where I was hidden for several hours until the riot police left the area. This was not my first international experience with riot police and clearly it represented fascism in the making, and it is not out of the question that similar conditions could obtain here in the United States, especially under a Trump administration where the president works in witless complicity with the ideas of a Bannon or a Gorka, such that anyone critical of the current administration (such as the so-called fake news mainstream media outlets cited recently by Trump, CNN, ABC, NBC, CBS) could be labelled "an enemy of the American people."

This attitude reminds me of the year 2006, when I was placed on the top of a list of dangerous UCLA professors known as the "dirty thirty," where the right-wing group orchestrating the attack (with the backing of some Republican Party funders) offered to pay students $100 to audiotape our lectures and $50 for their lecture notes. That was the year the FBI was investigating university libraries to see who was checking out what was considered subversive literature.

Speaking of "fake news," Julian Assange recently reported that he was happy about fake news, claiming it represents the direct opposition of the unvarnished and pristine releases by WikiLeaks. Contrasting WikiLeaks with "fake news," Assange asserts that by "uncovering government and corporate conduct," WikiLeaks is "not just another damn story, it's not just another damn journalist putting their damn byline, advertising themselves and their position on another damn story" (Reilly 2017). Assange argues that because newspapers publish nothing more than "weaponised text that is designed to affect a person just like you," written by journalists that act as little more than "opportunistic snipers," he is more than happy with the advent of "fake news," which he believes makes a stronger case for WikiLeaks. He argues that WikiLeaks deals in "pre-weaponized information" that, unlike "fake news," can be wholly trusted. However, the question remains, how do organizations like WikiLeaks—what Assange calls a "rebel library of Alexandria"—choose to release their information? That is why there is still much controversy surrounding a WikiLeaks publication—just a month prior to Election Day—of thousands of hacked emails allegedly from Clinton campaign chairman, John Podesta, including full transcripts of Clinton's controversial speeches to Goldman Sachs and other Wall Street firms. It released those transcripts less than a month before Election Day. Does the careful timing of WikiLeaks' releases not transform its information into weapons-grade material? Not according to WikiLeaks. Staff members at WikiLeaks have described their editorial policy as follows:

> We have an editorial policy to publish only information that we have validated as true and that is important to the political, diplomatic or historical....We believe in transparency for the powerful and privacy for the rest. We publish in full in an uncensored and uncensorable fashion...We are not risk-averse and will continue to publish fearlessly. (Collins 2016)

Assange does admit, however, that WikiLeaks is in the business of scandal making when he remarks, "But the library has to be marketed. And so the scandal-generation business, which we're also in—I view that as a kind of marketing effort for what is much more substantial, which is our archive" (Reilly 2017). We must keep in mind that Julian Assange has come under increasing scrutiny for his correspondence with Trump's election team officials and that Trump, Assange, (Nigel) Farage, and Bannon have been accused of being clandestinely linked together like some confusing, unorientable Möbius band.

If WikiLeaks brands itself as pre-weaponized, anti-fake news, what exactly is meant by the term "fake news"? Clearly, the Trump administration's casuistry about the existence of "alternative facts" has attacked the very credibility of what it means for something to be true, reducing all facts to opinions. The Trump administration has been caught solemnly sanctioning ignorance and making delusion the basis of cultural literacy by rejiggering facts to suit its own base, eviscerating the veridical basis of the facts themselves and reducing them to opinions. This makes "hearsay" into an irrepressible cultural force, eroding the very principles of rational deliberation. This has weighty implications for our cultural commons. When rational argumentation collapses, any opinion that enflames the mind can thus be treated as an "alternative fact" and can influence young people to order their lives around judgmental relativism, releasing their pent-up rage by allying themselves with subcultures of hate, such as white nationalist movements and their fervent incantations surrounding the defence of the white race. Dylann Roof is but one example. While it may be true that what was once held as an incontrovertible and immutable fact—such as the notion that the earth is flat—has over time been proven to be false, there are some facts that can be proven by relatively simple means, such as whether the crowd size at Trump's inauguration was larger than the crowd that was present for Obama's inauguration, or whether thousands of Massachusetts residents travelled to New Hampshire to vote illegally for Hillary Clinton. Or whether children die from asthma resulting from air pollution, or from drinking water laced with contaminants dumped by coal-fired factories.

Sabrina Tavernise (2016) of the *New York Times* defines "fake news" as follows: "Narrowly defined, 'fake news' means a made-up story with an intention to deceive, often geared toward getting clicks." Andrew Selepak (2017), a professor of telecommunications at the University of Florida who provides resources for educators in becoming more critically literate about fake news, expands the definition:

> Fake news can be hoax websites like *The Onion*. Fake news can come from "news outlets" like RT *News*, the first Russian 24/7 English-language news channel formerly known as "Russian Today" and produces stories with approval from the Russian Government. Fake news can be supermarket tabloids like *The Globe*. Fake news can be blogs and websites that look like news sites but are opinion sites created to disseminate one side of a story under the appearance of truth—these sites can lean Right or Left. Fake news can be purposely fictitious disinformation created to deceive an audience for political or financial gain, or for the hollow satisfaction of misinforming readers.
>
> Some say fake news can even be pundit and political talk shows that present one side of a story rather than the full truth such as *Rush Limbaugh* or the *Ed Schultz Show*.
>
> Perhaps most significantly, fake news can be a tweet, a post, or a meme that is shared on the Internet, and becomes accepted as true by those who don't investigate the story further before sharing it with others and thus perpetuating the cycle of fake news.
>
> Fake news sites and some social media accounts deliberately publish hoaxes, propaganda, and disinformation to drive web traffic promoted through social media either to generate ad revenue as a form of clickbait or to spread disinformation.

There are some basic and common sense questions that need to be raised when confronting possible "fake news" and "alternative facts." First and foremost, we need to interrogate our own biases and those of our friends, our colleagues, and our family, and understand the ideological frameworks that have shaped and currently shape our thinking and cause us to select certain information over others. We need to acquire the tools of critical media literacy. For instance, is it still meaningful today to repeat Annette Michelson's (1979) adage, that in the age of advertising, "You are the end product delivered en masse to the advertiser" (quoted in Malmgren 2017)? Or do we need to revise that adage in light of today's digital communications and say that your *data* is the end production rather than yourself (Malmgren 2017)? Are we, in other words, learning to labour for free in the service of Big Data? There are other more technical questions that come to the fore: How does learning on screens differ from learning on paper? In other words, how do they differ in fashioning the reflective self? How do they differ in the production of knowledge from audio-visual media? With the rise of e-books and the death of print media, how does this affect the structures of mediation that inform our ideologically coded selves, especially when the process of reading from computer screens and tablets involves hyperlinks, complicated layouts, and touch screen involvement? How do specific technological developments affect memory, recall, and perception, from the days in which we used to store our artificial memory as stacks of newspaper clippings? How is cognitive capitalism affecting the way we learn and perform our identities in today's cybercultures and other cultural offshoots created by digital technologies? How will digital culture affect the recomposition of the working class? In a recent article in the *New York Times Magazine*, Barbara Ehrenreich (2017) offers a good description of today's working class:

> Now when politicians invoke "the working class," they are likely to gesture, anachronistically, to an abandoned factory. They might more accurately use a hospital or a fast-food restaurant as a prop. The new working class contains many of the traditional blue-collar occupations—truck driver, electrician, plumber—but by and large its members are more likely to wield mops than hammers, and bedpans rather than trowels. Demographically, too, the working class has evolved from the heavily white male grouping that used to assemble at my house in the 1980s; black and Hispanic people have long been a big, if unacknowledged, part of the working class, and now it's more female and contains

many more immigrants as well. If the stereotype of the old working class was a man in a hard hat, the new one is better represented as a woman chanting, "El pueblo unido jamás será vencido!" (The people united will never be defeated!)

If Ehrenreich's description of the working class is accurate, how will today's shift to "cognitive capitalism" contribute to the well-being of its members? First, we must get a grasp of what is meant by this term. Mike Peters (in press) explains:

> Cognitive capitalism is now a huge new development that has grown rapidly concerning the cultural-cognitive sectors of high-tech, finance, media, education, and the cultural industries characterized by digital technologies and associated with the "knowledge economy," the "learning economy," "post-Fordism" and the increasing flexibility of labor markets. The hypothesis of cognitive capitalism (CC) suggests we are entering a third phase of capitalism, following mercantile and industrial phases, where the accumulation is centered on immaterial assets. CC emphasizes the accumulation of immaterial information-based assets protected through the global regime of intellectual property rights to ensure the conditions for a digital scalability that appropriates and profits from the information commons allowing the creation of surplus value from monopolistic rents. Digital reading, along with digital learning, is absolutely core to the knowledge economy—these skills are its necessary points of entry. Labor flexibilization ensures 24/7 Net activity that is put in the service of a new kind of reading. This is not meditative or immersive reading for the pleasure of the text. Rather, it is a kind of pervasive industriousness attuned to forms of *networking* and brain activity that requires continuous training, skills and attention. The connection here between digital knowledge economy, neuroscience, and the psychology of learning is very close as labor processes are moved from traditional hierarchical Tayloristic forms to new network forms that exploit relational, affective and cognitive faculties.

"Cognitive capitalism" is a term being frequently used in today's academy, and it is linked to the concept of the knowledge economy. In this new era of job flexibilization and the knowledge economy, we are told that we constantly need to upgrade our skills as jobs are replaced by those that require more sophisticated retraining programs in digital technology. But rather than using the term "knowledge economy," would it not be easier and perhaps even more accurate to use the term, "low-wage economy"? Barbara Ehrenreich (2017) writes,

> The other popular solution to the crisis of the working class was job retraining. If ours is a "knowledge economy"—which sounds so much better than a "low-wage economy"—unemployed workers would just have to get their game on and upgrade to more useful skills. President Obama promoted job retraining, as did Hillary Clinton as a presidential candidate, along with many Republicans. The problem was that no one was sure what to train people in; computer skills were in vogue in the '90s, welding has gone in and out of style and careers in the still-growing health sector are supposed to be the best bets now. Nor is there any clear measure of the effectiveness of existing retraining programs. In 2011, the Government Accountability Office found the federal government supporting 47 job-training projects as of 2009, of which only five had been evaluated in the previous five years. Paul Ryan has repeatedly praised a program in his hometown, Janesville, Wis., but a 2012 ProPublica study found that laid-off people who went through it were less likely to find jobs than those who did not.

Part of Trump's appeal was to promise to bring back the very same jobs the working class had lost, rather than being retrained, as Clinton had suggested, and this was by far the more popular option. Again, Ehrenreich (2017) writes,

> No matter how good the retraining program, the idea that people should be endlessly malleable and ready to recreate themselves to accommodate every change in the job market is probably not realistic and certainly not respectful of existing skills. In the early '90s, I had dinner at a Pizza Hut with a laid-off miner in Butte, Mont. (actually, there are no other kinds of miners in Butte). He was in his 50s, and he chuckled when he told me that he was being advised to get a degree in nursing. I couldn't help laughing too—not at the gender incongruity but at the notion

that a man whose tools had been a pickax and dynamite should now so radically change his relation to the world. No wonder that when blue-collar workers were given the choice between job retraining, as proffered by Clinton, and somehow, miraculously, bringing their old jobs back, as proposed by Trump, they went for the latter.

If the old jobs are not coming back, there is a better way to address the current crisis of capitalism. Raise the minimum wage! Create a living wage! Ehrenreich (2017) is right on the mark:

> The old jobs aren't coming back, but there is another way to address the crisis brought about by deindustrialization: Pay all workers better. The big labor innovation of the 21st century has been campaigns seeking to raise local or state minimum wages. Activists have succeeded in passing living-wage laws in more than a hundred counties and municipalities since 1994 by appealing to a simple sense of justice: Why should someone work full time, year-round, and not make enough to pay for rent and other basics? Surveys found large majorities favoring an increase in the minimum wage; college students, church members and unions rallied to local campaigns. Unions started taking on formerly neglected constituencies like janitors, home health aides and day laborers. And where the unions have faltered, entirely new kinds of organizations sprang up: associations sometimes backed by unions and sometimes by philanthropic foundations—Our Walmart, the National Domestic Workers Alliance and the Restaurant Opportunities Centers United.

The answer to all of these questions begins, in my view, with an ethical commitment. Any critical pedagogy worth its salt begins with practice born out of a moral commitment to take down all suffering human beings from the cross (McLaren 2015). Following in the tradition of liberation theology and Catholic social teaching, I refer to this as a preferential obligation that we have to our brothers and sisters who share this planet with us yet who continue to suffer under dehumanizing conditions. Some advocates of critical pedagogy have maintained that critical consciousness must be achieved before one is able to make the necessary decisions in working with oppressed groups. However, critical consciousness is not a precondition for acting in and on the world in a transformative manner; it is not a stipulation that must hold in all situations before working with oppressed groups in various capacities and circumstances. Far from serving as a precondition for doing transformative work with communities, critical consciousness is the outcome of working ethically in theoretically informed ways with communities (both virtual and real), both inside and outside of university settings. Years ago, it was Paulo Freire and Chavista activists in Venezuela who taught me the importance of orthopraxis over orthodoxy, that is, the necessity of understanding praxis as the foundation and bellwether of theory. In this instance, crystal theoretical clarity is not necessary before we engage in an active living commitment to the poorest and most marginalized in society. We must live our politics in fidelity with our obligation to help marginalized and oppressed communities before we can arrive at a correct or orthodox understanding of critical theory. That does not mean that theoretical understanding is unimportant. Far from it. Being informed by relevant critical theories admittedly is very crucial in social justice education as these theories can help to refine and fine-tune concrete practices of intervening in the world rather than simply positioning us as passive observers trained only to transpose reality onto a factory foreman's ledger and judge it on the basis of inputs and outputs. But to restrict our theories to or value them mainly for their sumptuous appearance in high-status journals is to reduce the role of the educator to that of an academic.

We are not solely academics—we are teacher activists who persist in our work on behalf of others; we have chosen our profession in order to transform the world through activities bounded by the principles, ethical imperatives, and practices of social justice. Unfortunately, many academics are not concerned if their roles as educators reproduce the very objects of their criticism. On the other hand, those who view their work in the academy more as a political project than an academic career and who fight to redeem the human subject in its totality by struggling for its liberation from capital and the antagonisms entangled with it—racism, sexism, homophobia, and the asymmetrical relations of privilege wrought by the coloniality of power—face the consequences of working in academic environments that find such work either increasingly irrelevant or annoyingly unhinged from their corporate mission.

Social science researchers do not escape the mystifying sway of the big "isms"—capitalism, imperialism, militarism, consumerism, pharmaceuticalism, utilitarianism, nationalism, white supremacism—that underlay our cognitive plutocracy in a common Western belief system known as materialism. Many educational researchers are free-range materialists who share the view that everything in the world supervenes on the physical. And while materialism is not a bad thing in itself (my own Marxist analysis is framed by historical materialist research), often its adherents are unable to give due discernment to, and thereby invalidate and diminish, the cosmovisions and world views of non-Western colonized peoples, even on occasion pouring ridicule on them. I am not endorsing here a type of educational docetism based on coteries congealed around an affinity for a certain subject matter. I am merely highlighting the perils of fetishizing that which can be so intractably trapped within a carnal envelope that its adherents remain irrepressibly uncharitable to anyone who does not view the world as a set of unassailable physical facts. Their position would make more sense to researchers whose chosen scientific heartland is the laboratory and who can be found labouring under a poster of the periodic table and collecting data with nitrile gloves, Erlenmeyer and volumetric flasks, Bunsen burners, graduated cylinders, and with maybe a Jacob's Ladder thrown in to impress onlookers. But educational researchers do not sediment their habits on computer screens, they work with and among people—often with populations who hail from different continents with different belief systems. We cannot remain so ontologically closed-minded, instrumental, and calculative that our philosophical doctrines get in the way of our praxis. Reason skids on slippery ideas by banishing feuding facts. Remaining open-minded and using culturally responsive approaches in our research cannot be overemphasized.

Another pressing task for critical educators is to encourage colleagues to challenge what is too often perceived among mainstream researchers as proscribed domains of discourse (such as participatory action research) and to agitate on behalf of their students, as well as other groups. Too often educational researchers refuse to take an adversarial stance against capitalism, racism, sexism, and homophobia, and likewise are not comfortable making a generic ethical commitment to the oppressed in their own work, hiding behind the "false solemnity" of what they regard as "real science" and citing the principled evasion commonly known as "scientific objectivity" as their defence.

Many students facing higher tuition rates and dismal prospects for decent employment are sometimes less likely to want a critical education that more deeply nests them in oppositional environments. On many occasions, what they seek is a more pragmatic and instrumental return on their investment—a job with a secure future. This is not to say that students are less likely to join groups that foment opposition to the neoliberal state, as the Sanders campaign (modelled less on Marx's concept of socialism than a watered-down version of European social democracy) tellingly brought to light, but that universities have now been so insinuated into the neoliberal corporatocracy and business models of leadership, with their increasing demands for a politics of economic austerity and debt generation, that they are now naturalized as part of the subsector of the economy. After all, economic inequality and insecurity are endemic to capitalism, and the embourgeoisement of the academy teaches its students that a university degree is perceived as one of the few remaining chances for economic advancement. The focus for too many of our students becomes getting prepared for the capitalist world rather than viewing university life as an opportunity to be part of the struggle to bring an alternative social universe into being.

Dissident Knowledge in Higher Education, edited by Marc Spooner and James McNinch, is unsparing in the way it reveals how the university system has become fully insinuated into the world ecology of human capital (Moore 2015a, 2015b), into the logic of neoliberal economics administered by means of a market metric macrophysics of power and set of governing tactics that submits everything in its path to a process of monetization and that simultaneously transforms everything and everyone within our social universe to a commodity form (Brown 2015). It accomplishes this task by avoiding false optimism and engendering a belief in the power of solidarity and struggle. Few books exist today that bring together such a powerful array of critical voices.

Dissident Knowledge in Higher Education includes an extraordinary group of scholar activists, some of the most highly acclaimed cultural workers worldwide who have over the decades provided pathfinding studies that have made possible and helped to legitimize the field of critical pedagogy and critical research methodology. Others are younger scholar activists who are beginning to lead the field with iconoclastic work driven by the imperatives of social justice and liberation. All of the contributors have produced profound ethnographic, philosophical, and theoretical work that has shattered—and continues to shatter—the boundaries of educational research. It is not surprising that the chapters are fearless in their approach, rigorous in their argumentation, and driven by a relentless search for justice. Questions pertaining to Indigeneity and Indigenous Knowledges, including cognitive democracy, epistemicide, the coloniality of power, the politics of accountability, and resistance within and to the neoliberal academy are all shown to be implicated in the development of the broad underpinnings of an encompassing revolutionary critical pedagogy.

We need to address these questions urgently. Especially since recent research indicates that young people born between 1980 and 1994 are more polarized politically than Generation Xers and Baby Boomers, with Millennials more likely identifying as conservatives, compared to the 1980s (Howard 2016). In fact, 23 per cent of Millennials are identified as leaning to the far right (Howard 2016). We need to understand better how universities shape and are shaped by disciplinary regimes of power and privilege that often overshadow their critical role. Here I am referring to courses, programs, faculty hires, and tenure decisions that include criteria such as race, class, gender, disability, and LGBTQ issues. But we should also be concerned with how universities in our society contribute to the social reproduction of capitalism, with its entangled antagonisms such as racism, sexism, patriarchy, homophobia, white privilege, and the colonial imperatives of the white settler state. We need to ask: What is the source of our responsibility as public pedagogues and activists who reject the consumer model of education and, who, as agents and agitators of social change, view our role as cultural workers carrying out our decolonizing projects in spaces both inside and outside the university? How can we better understand the role played by universities in the production, circulation, and consumption of cognitive and informational capitalism? How is academic labour and productivity assessed in a setting where digital education and communication technologies are blurring the distinction between students' and professors' professional and personal lives in our "always on" culture? You cannot shut culture out, after all. It is always already there like an arthritic knee. What role do universities play today in advancing and legitimizing capitalist development? What role do they play in strengthening the military industrial complex and the development of cyber technologies used to control information, in creating ideological submission for the masses to particular political and cultural views, or in supporting research by biotech companies committed to creating weapons technologies used to increase the "kill ratio" of our military? How are faculty and students engaged in or prevented from making decisions about how university financial investments are made? Are decisions about student tuition costs and admissions arrived at collectively? How is value produced in the process of academic labour and how does this affect both permanent and adjunct faculty, as well as graduate assistants? How is freedom of speech protected in a world where social media is obliterating the distinction between public and private lives? These are only a few of the crucial questions that must be raised.

These questions are especially relevant at a time when inglorious documentaries, videos, books, and screeds of all stripes have gobsmacked even those on the Left who have come to expect the most ludicrous conspiracy theories emanating from the Right. For the last twenty years, right-wing conspiracy theorists have been building their case against the Frankfurt School theorists, and this has resulted in a plethora of wing nuts peddling the lunacy of arch conservative ideologues who have gained the attention of the Tea Party and other groups, including white nationalists, libertarian Christian Reconstructionists, members of the Christian Coalition, the Free Congress Foundation, and neo-Nazi groups such as Stormfront. They maintain that blame for the cultural degradation and corruption of the United States can be placed at the feet of the Institute for Social Research, initially housed at the Goethe University in Frankfurt and relocated to Columbia University in New York during the rise of Hitler in 1935. Its illustrious members and associates include Theodor Adorno, Walter Benjamin, Max Horkheimer, Leo Löwenthal, Erich Fromm, and Herbert Marcuse. Peddlers of this crackpot theory include Michael Minnicino, Paul Weyrich, Pat Buchanan, Roger Kimball, and others. They maintain that these "cultural Marxists" (who, unsurprisingly, they are fond of mentioning are all Jewish) set out to destroy the cultural and moral fabric of U.S. society. But it is the fringe writings of William S. Lind, in particular, that have had the most chilling effect. In 2011, Lind's writings inspired Norwegian neo-Nazi mass murderer Anders Behring Breivik to slaughter seventy-seven fellow Norwegians and injure 319 more. Lind and his ilk blame the Frankfurt School theorists for a litany of crimes, including the deindustrialization of America's cities, neoliberal free trade policies, affirmative action, immigration, sexual liberation, gay marriage, multiculturalism, political correctness, the welfare state, and the privileging of the concerns of African Americans, feminists, and homosexuals over those of white citizens. Anyone familiar with critical pedagogy knows that the writings of the Frankfurt School are foundational to its theoretical framework. So, following the logic of Lind and that of his followers, critical educators are de facto promoting the destruction of the very fabric of U.S. society and culture. This gives new meaning to comments made by right-wing pundits such as Donald Trump and Steve Bannon, who are notorious for berating political correctness and feminism and for their toxic disdain toward African American groups such as Black Lives Matter. How will the university be able to counter these egregious theories that, if left unchecked, will only promote the proliferation of hate groups and the mass targeting of the leftist intellectuals?

I was fortunate to be a participant in the extraordinary symposium that gave birth to this book, an international event organized by Marc Spooner and James McNinch. How Marc was able to succeed in bringing such a large and diverse group of scholar activists together under one roof was a question that percolated through the conference. Clearly, the consensus among the participants was that Marc is gifted with an ability to assemble communities of teachers and learners and to make change happen. Marc and James have together produced a text whose intellectual sediment will remain for generations to explore and use as a foundation for new forms of educational activism. This book is a testament to all of the participants' intrepid and unrelenting attempts to make a better world.

All of the contributors to this book emphasize the importance of solidarity and a commitment to those who needlessly suffer—the popular majorities—and I am confident that readers will join them in attempting to tear out by the roots the sources of their suffering. The suffering of the poor can never be the social price for capitalist "progress," and, hence, we refuse to foreclose the future for the few but struggle to make the future for the many. Although we need not craft for critical pedagogy too flattering an unction, since critical pedagogy has always faced situations where agitation for social justice requires pitched battles with those in a much stronger position to adorn and enlighten future generations with the world-rectifying philosophy of capitalism, cunningly devised to discredit all alternatives to the value form of labour. Such battles imperil teachers who refuse to remain diffident and who are vulnerable to school and university officials. Yet we must continue to fight fascism and immiseration capitalism, since our position follows from the facts of economic inequality and civil rights injustices, refuses to remain politically neutral yet at the same time retains a commitment to remaining scientifically impartial in our research.

Part of the success of the Left has been in protesting existing regimes by speaking truth to power, yet part of its failure has been stopping short of promoting robust debate in the public square regarding the development of a viable idea of what might constitute the best alternative to capitalism (Hudis 2016). Without such a debate, we make the further degradation and exploitation of the oppressed all the easier and leave the argument in the hands of the educational patriciate. As part of the ranks of revolutionary educators, we are therefore committed to work in dialogical engagement with subaltern groups—not through polemics and rhetorical efforts alone— but rather in solidarity with other movements and activists to help develop a viable understanding of what a universe outside of the value form of capitalist production might look like and, in so doing, undertake purposive action in and on the world. I find the insights of Marx on the critique of political economy and the struggle for socialism to be indispensable in this task, as well as the work being done by Indigenous scholars in the context of Las Americas, the Caribbean, Australasia, Southeast Asia, and elsewhere.

Readers may find their own inspiration from other sources. The point is that we are in this struggle together, and together we will move into a future with, to paraphrase Antonio Gramsci, a continued pessimism of the intellect and optimism of the will.

The unedifying spectacle of neoliberal capitalism, into whose orbit the entire world is being drawn, is one that exhibits less and less empathy for its victims. Today's imprimatur for moral rectitude is the clenched white fist raised to a stiff salute, accompanied by a rousing rendition of "Tomorrow Belongs to Me" from the film *Cabaret*. Truth is suffered to exist in this populist climate only to the extent that it profits the rich and the powerful. Truth is truth only if it services the lordship of the ruling class. The moral gavel wielded like a tar brush and with impunity by the authoritarian populists and demagogues of the world against the very concept of democracy has solemnly sanctioned violence against immigrants, refugees, people of colour, and the most vulnerable among us. As part of the brutal delights of authoritarianism, it has turned them into scapegoats, propagating deception and sending chills throughout the bloodstained chambers of social justice. This book serves as a critical bulwark to such insanity, a recrudescent demand for civil rights, and a pedagogical revelation to be absorbed not only in order to reclaim the future but to remind all the yesterdays of the past that we are forever bound by memory and by hope. We, the people, are determined to follow the arc of social dreaming and its careening course toward liberation, and to build the infrastructure for living in a social universe free from the fetters of capitalism's value form, where our labour is freely associated and our creativity and humanity is nourished by love and compassion. This is a profound truth indeed. The future of humanity turns upon it. As democracy in the hands of those who would usurp our freedoms circles the drain, we shall renew our commitment to fight the power that is flushing our liberties into oblivion.

I would like to end with a reflection on past history. Following the success of the March on Washington and the passing of the Civil Rights and Voting Rights Acts, Martin Luther King and other members of the Southern Christian Leadership Conference (SCLC) announced the Poor People's Campaign in Atlanta, Georgia, on December 4, 1967. After the assassination of Dr. Martin Luther King on April 4, 1968, the Poor People's Campaign, now led by Ralph Abernathy, constructed a makeshift encampment or shantytown, known as Resurrection City, on the National Mall between the Lincoln

Memorial and the Washington Monument, to the south of the Lincoln Memorial Reflecting Pool. With permits from the National Park Service, Resurrection City housed three thousand participants from poor communities all over the country. Over fifty multiracial organizations participated in the planning, and nine regional caravans were launched to bring the participants—Black, white, Native American, and Latino—to Washington from May 14 until June 24, 1968: the "Eastern Caravan," the "Appalachia Trail," the "Southern Caravan," the "Midwest Caravan," the "Indian Trail," the "San Francisco Caravan," the "Western Caravan," the "Mule Train," and the "Freedom Train" (Cave and Eveleigh 2017).

A pan-racial coalition of the poor, the aggrieved, and the oppressed suddenly took charge of fifteen sprawling acres of West Potomac Park, running across the reflecting pool to the base of the Lincoln Memorial (Cave and Eveleigh 2017). Corky Gonzales and Myles Horton were there, holding workshops near the acrid stench of burning oil drums heaped with refuse. With guitars and banjos in hand, Pete Seeger, Peter, Paul and Mary, and Jimmy "burn baby burn" Collier helped improvise singalongs and square dances to revive the collectivist spirit dampened by twenty-eight (out of forty-two) days of rain, dismal days plagued by mud and pooling water, sometimes hip-deep, that shifted the soggy ground under the plywood-frame tents creatively festooned with political slogans such as "Soul Power," "Indian Power," "Chicano Power," and "Power to the People." Henry Crow Dog, an Oglala Sioux medicine man from the Rosebud Indian Reservation in South Dakota, was there and challenged Seeger and Collier when they sang "This Land Is Your Land" on the grounds that the land belonged to Native Americans—it was his land (Kaufman 2011, 203). The poorest of the Appalachian whites were given shoes and jackets by their Chicano and Puerto Rican counterparts. Scattered among Resurrection City's 650 flywood and plastic-sheeting huts, you could find a lean-to city hall (and its SCLC mayor, Jesse Jackson), a medical tent, dining facilities, a "Poor People's University," a nursery, a cultural centre, and an internal police force. But there were only a couple of showers for the entire camp. Plastic snow fencing separated the inhabitants of Resurrection City from the crowds outside. Military intelligence and FBI agents posed as reporters and wiretapped the campaign, and were accused by Ralph Abernathy of fomenting violence inside the encampment.

And while history has often recorded Resurrection City to have been a strategic failure marred by racial tensions, poor leadership, and insufficient planning, the real source of the failure of Resurrection City is best captured by Robert Chase (1998), who writes,

The failure of the Poor People's Campaign extended beyond questions of leadership and tactics. Ultimately, the PPC failed because the traditional constituency of the Civil Rights movement—the white, middle-class, liberals—was repulsed by the goals of the campaign itself. Bringing the poor together as a racial amalgamation of similar interests and goals heightened the issue of class in America and, consequently, Americans came to view the Civil Rights movement as an instrument questioning the legitimacy of America's economic system and its capitalistic "way of life."

The inhabitants of Resurrection City were systematically tear-gassed on June 24, 1968, and the shantytown was demolished by bulldozers that entered from 17th Street after most of the residents, many vomiting and choking from the tear gas, had been chased out. As the Civil Disturbance Squad ran final sweeps of the encampment, arresting those who had refused to leave, songs of human freedom rang out.

I propose that we set up a Resurrection City outside the grounds of Mar-a-Lago, Trump's Winter White House, and that the caravans streaming in from across the country carry with them the wishes and prayers of all those who are suffering today under the brutality of everyday life in capitalist America.

Notes

1   As a point of interest, DeVos is also the sister of Erik Prince, founder of the infamous private military company that made international headlines in September 2007 after its operatives gunned down seventeen Iraqi civilians, including a nine-year-old boy in Baghdad's Nisour Square (Risen 2014).
2   These are predictable four-part cycles, the latest of which Strauss and Howe refer to as the Fourth Turning. These cycles are based on a series of generational archetypes—the Artists, the Prophets, the Nomads, and the Heroes.

References

Allen, K. 2017. "Betsy DeVos Statement on Black Colleges Sparks Uproar." *ABC News*, February 28. http://abcnews.go.com/US/betsy-devos-statement-black-colleges-sparks-uproar/story?id=45796029.

Allman, P., P. McLaren, and G. Rikowski. 2003. "After the Box People: The Labour-Capital Relation as Class Constitution and Its Consequences for Marxist

Educational Theory and Human Resistance." In *Yesterday's Dreams: International and Critical Perspectives on Education and Social Class*, edited by J. Freeman-Moir and A. Scott, 135–65. Christchurch, New Zealand: Canterbury University Press.

Anderson, P. 2017. "Why the System Will Still Win." *Le Monde Diplomatique*, March. http://mondediplo.com/2017/03/02brexit.

The Associated Press. 2017. "Mississippi Mulls Including Firing Squads as a Method of Execution for Death Row Inmates." *National Post*, February 9. http://nationalpost.com/news/world/mississippi-mulls-including-firing-squads-as-a-method-of-execution-for-death-row-inmates.

Bailie, G. 1995. *Violence Unveiled: Humanity at the Crossroads*. New York: The Crossroad Publishing Company.

Blumenthal, P. 2017a. "Steve Bannon Believes the Apocalypse Is Coming and War Is Inevitable." *Huffington Post*, February 8. http://www.huffingtonpost.com/entry/steve-bannon-apocalypse_us_5898f02ee4b040613138a951?.

———. 2017b. "This Stunningly Racist French Novel Is How Steve Bannon Explains the World." *Huffington Post*, March 4. http://www.huffingtonpost.com/entry/steve-bannon-camp-of-the-saints-immigration_us_58b75206e4b0284854b3dc03?.

Boehlert, E. 2017. "Exciting the Right Wing, Trump Downplays Threat of Right-Wing Terror: Neo-Nazis Celebrate: 'Donald Trump Is Setting Us Free.'" *Media Matters for America*, February 3. http://mediamatters.org/blog/2017/02/03/exciting-right-wing-trump-downplays-threat-right-wing-terror/215226.

Brown, W. 2015. "What Exactly Is Neoliberalism? Wendy Brown Interviewed by Timothy Shenk." *Dissent Magazine*. https://www.dissentmagazine.org/blog/booked-3-what-exactly-is-neoliberalism-wendy-brown-undoing-the-demos.

Cave, D., and D. Eveleigh. 2017. "In 1968, a 'Resurrection City' of Tents, Erected to Fight Poverty." *New York Times*, February 18. https://www.nytimes.com/2017/02/18/us/martin-luther-king-resurrection-city.html?_r=0.

Chase, R. T. 1998. "Class Resurrection: The Poor People's Campaign of 1968 and Resurrection City." *Essays in History* 40. http://www.essaysinhistory.com/articles/2012/116.

Cimarusti, D. 2017. "The Trump/DeVos Privatization Agenda Begins to Take Shape." *The Network for Public Education*, January 16. http://networkforpubliceducation.org/2017/02/8851/.

Collins, T. 2016. "Wikileaks Grilled on Trump, Assange in Rowdy Reddit AMA." *C/Net*, November 11. https://www.cnet.com/au/news/wikileaks-reddit-ask-me-anything-ama-donald-trump-hillary-clinton/.

"Donald Trump on Education." On the Issues: Every Political Leader on Every Issue. http://www.ontheissues.org/2016/Donald_Trump_Education.htm.

Ehrenreich, B. 2017. "Divisions of Labor." *New York Times Magazine*, February 23. https://www.nytimes.com/2017/02/23/magazine/american-working-class-future.html?hp&action=click&pgtype=Homepage&clickSource=story-heading&module=photo-spot-region&region=top-news&wt.nav=top-news.

Eichenwald, K. 2016. "Right-Wing Extremists Are a Bigger Threat to America than ISIS." *Newsweek*, February 4. http://www.newsweek.com/2016/02/12/right-wing-extremists-militants-bigger-threat-america-isis-jihadists-422743.html.

Erdener, E. 2017. "Descent into Ignorance as Critical Voices Are Silenced." *University World News*, February 19. http://www.universityworldnews.com/article.php?story=20170215135033614.

"Exclusive: Donald Trump Visits School in Las Vegas, Nevada." *YouTube*. https://www.youtube.com/watch?v=pzOqoLtheuE.

Feder, J. L. 2016. "This Is How Steve Bannon Sees the Entire World." *BuzzFeed News*, November 16. https://www.buzzfeed.com/lesterfeder/this-is-how-steve-bannon-sees-the-entire-world?utm_term=.oh7Q9dbxW&wpisrc=nl_daily202&wpmm=1#.usL98kvA3.

Finley, T. 2017. "Moorehouse College President Says Visit with Trump Was 'Troubling.'" *Huffington Post*, March 3. http://www.huffingtonpost.com/entry/morehouse-college-president-says-visit-with-trump-was-troubling_us_58b98807e4b05cfof3ffe7a8?mr1g9fvrfuzzg2e29&.

Freire, P. 1970. *Pedagogy of the Oppressed*. London: Penguin.

Ganim, S., C. Welch, and N. Meyersohn. 2017. "'A Resurgence of White Nationalism': Hate Groups Spiked in 2016." *CNN News*, February 15. http://www.cnn.com/2017/02/15/politics/hate-groups-spiked-in-2016/index.html.

Girard, R. 1979. *Violence and the Sacred*. Translated by Patrick Gregory. Baltimore, MD: Johns Hopkins University Press.

Hill, M. L. 2016. *Nobody: Casualties of America's War on the Vulnerable, from Ferguson to Flint and Beyond*. New York: Atria Books.

Howard, J. 2016. "Millennials More Conservative than You May Think." *CNN*, September 2. http://www.cnn.com/2016/09/07/health/millennials-conservative-generations/index.html.

Hudis, P. 2016. "Marxist-Humanist Tasks and Perspectives for Transcending Capitalism." *Report to 2016 Convention of International Marxist-Humanist Organization*.

Jaffe, G. 2017. "For a Trump Advisor, an Odyssey from the Fringes of Washington to the Center of Power." *The Washington Post*, February 20. https://www.washingtonpost.com/world/national-security/for-a-trump-adviser-an-odyssey-from-the-fringes-of-washington-to-the-center-of-power/2017/02/20/0a326260-f2cb-11e6-b9c9-e83fce42fb61_story.html?hpid=hp_hp-more-top-stories_gorka-0831pm%3Ahomepage%2Fstory&utm_term=.b58e33e7f4c8.

Kaufman, W. 2011. *Woody Guthrie: American Radical*. Chicago: University of Illinois Press.

Liebelson, D. 2017. "School Asks Teachers to Take Down Pro-Diversity Posters, Saying They're 'Anti-Trump.'" *The Huffington Post*, February 21. http://www.huffingtonpost.com/entry/school-pro-diversity-posters-trump_us_58ac87b9e4b0e784faa21446?.

Lindsey, M-V. 2016. "How Unions Change Universities." *Jacobin*, September 1. https://www.jacobinmag.com/2016/09/nlrb-graduate-workers-unions-universities-administration/.

Malmgren, E. 2017. "Big Data's Hidden Labor." *Jacobin*, March 14. https://www.jacobinmag.com/2017/03/big-data-smartphones-google-amazon-facebook-surveillance-tech/.

Massie, C. 2017. "Steve King: Blacks and Hispanics 'Will Be Fighting Each Other' before Overtaking Whites in Population." *CNN News*, March 14. http://www.cnn.com/2017/03/14/politics/kfile-steve-king-prediction/index.html.

Massie, C., and A. Kaczynski. 2017. "Steve Bannon in 2013: Joseph McCarthy Was Right in Crusade against Communist Infiltration." *CNN News*, March 6. http://www.cnn.com/2017/03/06/politics/kfile-bannon-mccarthy/index.html.

McGlothlin, D. 2016. "Arizona Tops in Guaranteeing Private Prisons New Customers." *Justice Policy Institute*. http://www.justicepolicy.org/news/10144.

McLaren, P. 2015. *Pedagogy of Insurrection: From Resurrection to Revolution*. New York: Peter Lang.

Michelson, A. 1979. "The Films of Richard Serra: An Interview." *October* 1(10): 68–104.

Moore, J. W. 2015a. *Capitalism in the Web of Life: Ecology and the Accumulation of Capital*. New York: Verso.

———. 2015b. "Jason Moore Interviewed by Kamil Ahsan." *Viewpoint Magazine*, September 28. https://viewpointmag.com/2015/09/28/capitalism-in-the-web-of-life-an-interview-with-jason-moore/.

Moran, L. 2017. "Donald Trump Claims Barack Obama Ordered Wire Tap on Trump Tower before Election." *The Huffington Post*, March 4. http://www.huffingtonpost.com/entry/donald-trump-twitter-barack-obama-tapped_us_58baadf7e4b0b9989417e736.

Olson, G. 2017. "The Deep State versus President Trump." *Common Dreams*, March 5. http://www.commondreams.org/views/2017/03/05/deep-state-vs-president-trump.

Peters, M. (in press). "Digital Reading: From the Reflective Self to the Social Machine." In *The Digital University: A Dialogue and Manifesto*, edited by Mike Peters and Petar Jandric. New York: Peter Lang.

Porter, E. 2017. "Trump Budget Proposal Reflects Working-Class Resentment of the Poor." *New York Times*, March 7. https://www.nytimes.com/2017/03/07/business/economy/trump-budget-entitlements-working-class.html?hp&action=click&pgtype=Homepage&clickSource=story-heading&module=photo-spot-region&region=top-news&wt.nav=top-news&_r=0.

Provance, J. 2016. "Trump Says He Would Require Schools to Teach Patriotism." *Pittsburgh Post-Gazette*, September 1. http://www.post-gazette.com/early-returns/ernational/2016/09/01/Donald-Trump-says-he-would-require-schools-to-teach-patriotism/stories/201609010204.

Redden, M. 2016. "Trump Backers Claim Grabbing Women's Genitals Is Not Sexual Assault." *The Guardian*, October 10. https://www.theguardian.com/us-news/2016/oct/10/sexual-assault-definition-trump-comments.

Reilly, C. 2017. "WikiLeaks Is 'Very Happy' about Fake News: Julian Assange." *C/Net*. https://www.cnet.com/news/julian-assange-wikileaks-very-happy-about-fake-news-election-clinton-podesta-emails/.

Risen, J. 2014. "Before Shooting in Iraq, a Warning on Blackwater." *New York Times*, June 29. https://www.nytimes.com/2014/06/30/us/before-shooting-in-iraq-warning-on-blackwater.html.

Robinson, W. I. 2017. "China and Trumpism: The Political Contradictions of Global Capitalism." *Links: International Journal of Socialist Renewal*, February 14. http://links.org.au/trump-china-global-capitalism.

Selepak, A. 2017. "Teaching Aid for Educators on 'Fake News' and Alternative Facts." *UFSocial*, January 30. http://ufsocial.jou.ufl.edu/2017/01/teaching-aid-educators-fake-news-alternative-facts/.

Siemaszko, C. 2017. "Too Many Bodies in Ohio Morgue, So Coroner Gets Death Trailer." *NBC News*, March 14. http://www.nbcnews.com/news/us-news/too-many-bodies-ohio-morgue-so-coroner-gets-death-trailer-n733446.

Singer, A. 2017. "Trump Unleashes Predator 'Schools' on Vets and Evangelicals." *Huffington Post*, March 3. http://www.huffingtonpost.com/entry/58b7fc29e4b0e9d19b926573.

Spooner, M. 2015. "Higher Education's Silent Killer." *Briarpatch Magazine* 44(5) (September–October): 4–7. http://briarpatchmagazine.com/articles/view/higher-educations-silent-killer.

Stahl, J. 2016. "Steve Bannon Compares Himself Favorably to 'Dick Cheney, Darth Vader, Satan.'" *The Slatest*, November 18. http://www.slate.com/blogs/the_slatest/2016/11/18/steve_bannon_compares_himself_favorably_to_dick_cheney_darth_vader_satan.html.

Tavernise, S. 2016. "As Fake News Spreads Lies, More Readers Shrug at the Truth." *New York Times*, December 7. https://www.nytimes.com/2016/12/06/us/fake-news-partisan-republican-democrat.html?_r=0.

CONTRIBUTORS

Marie Battiste is a Mi'kmaw educator, a member of the Potlotek First Nation, and a professor in the Department of Educational Foundations at the University of Saskatchewan. With graduate degrees from Harvard and Stanford, she is an elected Fellow of the Royal Society of Canada, acknowledged for her work in Indigenous Knowledge and decolonizing pedagogies that has opened new areas of research and inquiry in Canada and beyond. She is a widely published author, including *Visioning a Mi'kmaw Humanities: Indigenizing the Academy*; *Living Treaties: Narrating Mi'kmaw Treaty Relations*; *Decolonizing Education: Nourishing the Learning Spirit*; and *Protecting Indigenous Knowledge and Heritage: A Global Challenge*, co-authored with J. Youngblood Henderson.

Noam Chomsky was born in Philadelphia, Pennsylvania, on December 7, 1928. He studied linguistics, mathematics, and philosophy at the University of Pennsylvania. In 1955, he received his PhD from the University of Pennsylvania. He has taught at Massachusetts Institute of Technology, where he has been Institute Professor (emeritus) in the Department of Linguistics and Philosophy for the past fifty years and Laureate Professor of Linguistics and Agnese Nelms Haury Chair in the Program in Environment and Social Justice at the University of Arizona. His work is widely credited with having revolutionized the field of modern linguistics. He is the author of numerous best-selling political works, which have been translated into scores of languages worldwide. Among his most recent books are *Hegemony or Survival*,

Failed States, *Hopes and Prospects*, and *Masters of Mankind*. Haymarket Books has recently published twelve of his classic works in new editions. His latest books are *What Kind of Creatures Are We?* and *Who Rules the World?*

Norman K. Denzin is Distinguished Professor of Communications, College of Communications Scholar, and Research Professor of Communications, Sociology, and Humanities at the University of Illinois, Urbana-Champaign. He is the author or editor of more than two dozen books, including *Performance Autoethnography*, *The Qualitative Manifesto*, *Qualitative Inquiry Under Fire*, *Searching for Yellowstone*, *Reading Race*, *Interpretive Ethnography*, *The Cinematic Society: The Voyeur's Gaze*, and *The Alcoholic Self*, and, with Yvonna S. Lincoln, editor of five editions of the *Handbook of Qualitative Research*, and founding director of the International Congress of Qualitative Inquiry.

Michelle Fine is Distinguished Professor of Critical Social Psychology, Women's Studies, and Urban Education at the Graduate Center, City University of New York (CUNY). A highly influential educator and activist, her work addresses questions of social injustice that sit at the intersection of public policy and social research, particularly with respect to youth in schools and criminal justice. She has authored, co-authored, or edited more than twenty books, seventy chapters in key national and international volumes, and eighty journal articles. Her most recent book, with Michael Fabricant, is *The Changing Politics of Education: Privatization and the Dispossessed Lives Left Behind*. Recently, she has been intensely involved with MCAS—Montclair Cares About Schools—an activist group of parents in New Jersey working with educators and labour and civil rights groups in a struggle over corporate reform and testing in a racially integrated suburban school district.

Rosalind Gill is Professor of Social and Cultural Analysis at City, University of London. She has an interdisciplinary background in sociology, social psychology, gender studies, and media and cultural studies. Her research looks critically at media, digital culture, and labour, with a particular interest in power, inequality, and the psychic life of neoliberalism. She is the author or editor of numerous books, including *Gender and the Media*; *Secrecy and Silence in the Research Process*, with Róisín Ryan-Flood; and *New Femininities: Postfeminism, Neoliberalism and Subjectivity*, with Christina Scharff. Her newest books are *Aesthetic Labour: Rethinking Beauty Politics in Neoliberalism*, co-edited with Ana Elias and Christina Scharff, and the monograph, *Mediated Intimacy: Sex Advice in Media Culture* (with Meg-John Barker and Laura Harvey).

Sandy Grande (Quechua) is a professor of education, as well as the director of the Center for the Critical Study of Race and Ethnicity (CCSRE) at Connecticut College. Her research interfaces critical Indigenous theories with the concerns of education. Her highly acclaimed book, *Red Pedagogy: Native American Social and Political Thought*, was recently published in a tenth-anniversary edition in 2015. She has also published several book chapters and articles, including "Accumulation of the Primitive: The Limits of Liberalism and the Politics of Occupy Wall Street," in *Settler Colonial Studies*; "Confessions of a Full-Time Indian," in the *Journal of Curriculum and Pedagogy*; "American Indian Geographies of Identity and Power: At the Crossroads of Indigena and Mestizaje," in the *Harvard Educational Review*; and "Red-ing the Word, Red-ing the World," in Paulo Freire's *Intellectual Roots: Toward Historicity in Praxis*. In addition to her scholarly work, she has provided eldercare for her parents and remains the primary caretaker for her ninety-year-old father.

Budd L. Hall is co-chair of the UNESCO Chair in Community-Based Research and Social Responsibility in Higher Education and a professor of community development in the School of Public Administration at the University of Victoria. He was the founding director of the University of Victoria Office of Community-Based Research and is a Senior Fellow at the Centre for Global Studies at the University of Victoria. Former dean of the Faculty of Education at the University of Victoria, he served as the chair of the Adult Education Department at the University of Toronto from 1995 to 2001 and as secretary-general of the International Council for Adult Education. He has worked in Nigeria, Tanzania, Venezuela, Brazil, Chile, Germany, Thailand, Yemen, Uganda, England, and the United States. He has done both theoretical and practical work for almost forty years in various aspects of community-based adult education and learning and participatory research.

Patti Lather is an emerita professor in the School of Educational Studies at Ohio State University. She is the author of five books: *Getting Smart: Feminist Research and Pedagogy With/in the Postmodern*; *Troubling the Angels: Women Living with HIV/AIDS*, co-authored with Chris Smithies; *Getting Lost: Feminist Efforts toward a Double(d) Science*; *Engaging Science Policy: From the Side of the Messy*; and *(Post)Critical Methodologies: The Science Possible After the Critiques: The Selected Works of Patti Lather*. She was the recipient of a 1989 Fulbright to New Zealand. She is a 2009 inductee of the AERA Fellows and a 2010 recipient of the AERA Division B Lifetime Achievement Award.

Zeus Leonardo is Professor of Education and the Critical Theory Designated Emphasis at the University of California, Berkeley. He is an AERA Fellow and vice president of AERA's Division G. He has served on the editorial board of over a dozen journals, including *Educational Researcher* and *AERJ*, as well as the co-editor of *Review of Educational Research* and the associate editor for North America of *Race Ethnicity & Education*. He was a visiting professor at the University of Colorado and University of Washington, where he was the acting director of the Center for Multicultural Education. He has authored or edited several books, such as *Race Frameworks*, and journal articles and book chapters involving critical engagement with race and class stratification, democratic schooling, and theoretical studies of ideological formation. He has received recognitions, including the AERA R. Freeman Butts endowed lecture, the Barbara Powell Speaker Series lecture at the University of Regina, and the Derrick Bell Legacy Award from the Critical Race Studies in Education Association. In addition to the United States, he has delivered keynotes in England, Sweden, Canada, and Australia.

Yvonna S. Lincoln is the Ruth Harrington Chair of Educational Leadership and Distinguished Professor of Higher Education at Texas A&M University. She is the co-editor of the journal *Qualitative Inquiry*, and of the first, second, third, fourth, and now fifth editions of the *SAGE Handbook of Qualitative Research*, and the *Handbook of Critical and Indigenous Methodologies*. As well, she is the co-author, editor, or co-editor of more than a half-dozen other books, and more than one hundred chapters and journal articles on aspects of higher education or qualitative research methods and methodologies. Her research interests include development of qualitative methods and methodologies, and the impact of neoliberalism, globalization, and corporatization on Western higher education.

Peter McLaren is Distinguished Professor in Critical Studies, Donna Ford Attallah College of Educational Studies, at Chapman University. He has authored and edited approximately fifty books. His writings have been translated into over thirty languages. He is the recipient of lifetime achievement awards from the Pedagogy and Theater of the Oppressed, Inc., Miami University of Ohio, the Central New York Peace Studies Consortium, Division B of the American Educational Research Association, and the Faculty of Education, University of Regina, Saskatchewan. He is also the recipient of the Paulo Freire Distinguished Scholar Award, presented by the American Educational Research Association, and the Defence of the Rights of Indigenous Peoples Award (Cheran, Michoacan, Mexico), commemorating the second anniversary of the defence of the forests. He also received the Outstanding Educator of America Award for 2013 from the Association of Educators of Latin America and the Caribbean.

James McNinch is an emeritus professor and the former dean of the Faculty of Education at the University of Regina. He previously served as the director of the university's Teaching and Learning Centre and prior to that was director of the Gabriel Dumont Institute, the post-secondary institution of the Métis peoples of Saskatchewan. His research has focused on gender and sexual diversity, racism and white privilege, and the social construction of masculinity. He was instrumental in bringing Camp fYrefly, an annual leadership and resiliency experience for queer youth, to Saskatchewan ten years ago. This has expanded into fYrefly in Schools—programs and in-service for schools to raise LGBTQ2 awareness, identify the impacts of homophobic/transphobic bullying, and to empower students and teachers to challenge discrimination and become effective allies through effective policy, practice, and curricular changes. He views the unrelenting managerialism in higher education today, exemplified in a pervasive and mean-spirited audit culture masquerading as accountability, as a real threat to genuine and critical engagement in teaching and learning and research and scholarship.

Christopher Meyers is emeritus professor of philosophy and emeritus director of the Kegley Institute of Ethics at California State University, Bakersfield. He is also adjunct faculty for the Department of Medicine at Kern Medical and an ethics consultant for several other area hospitals. The author of three books and some four dozen articles, he is also the associate editor for *Journal of Media Ethics* and provides ethics consulting and education for a wide range of professions and businesses.

Linda Tuhiwai Smith is Professor of Māori and Indigenous Studies at the University of Waikato, New Zealand. She is from Ngāti Awa and Ngāti Porou *iwi* (nations). Linda has previously been the Pro Vice Chancellor Māori and Dean of the School of Māori and Pacific Studies at the University of Waikato. She has been Chair of the Social Sciences Panel of the Marsden Fund, Chair of the Māori Health Committee, Chair of Te Aratake Wānanga for the Ministry of Culture and Heritage, member of the Health Research Council, member of the Constitutional Advisory Commission and is currently a member of the Māori Economic Development Advisory Board. Linda has many distinctions, including the Companion to the New Zealand Order of Merit and the Prime Minister's Lifetime Achievement Award for Education, and she is a Fellow of the Royal Society of New Zealand.

Marc Spooner is a professor in the Faculty of Education at the University of Regina. He specializes in qualitative and participatory action research at the intersections of theory and action on the ground. His interests include homelessness and poverty; audit culture and the effects of neoliberalization and corporatization on higher education; and social justice, activism, and participatory democracy. He has published in many venues, including peer-reviewed journals, book chapters, government reports, and a wide variety of popularizations. Together with colleagues at the University of Regina, he also co-hosts a popular education series that takes place in pubs—not on campus—entitled Talkin' about School and Society. He is oftentimes a social/political commentator who can be followed on Twitter here: @drmarcspooner.

Eve Tuck (Unangax) is an associate professor of critical race and Indigenous studies in the Department of Social Justice Education at the Ontario Institute for Studies in Education, University of Toronto, and Canada Research Chair in Indigenous Methodologies with Youth and Communities. She writes on urban education policy, settler colonialism, and Indigenous studies in education. She is co-editor of *Critical Ethnic Studies*; co-editor of *Indigenous and Decolonizing Studies in Education*, a new book series by Routledge; and co-creator of the Land Relationships Super Collective, all with K. Wayne Yang. She is the producer of the podcast, *The Henceforward*, on Indigenous and Black life on Turtle Island.

Joel Westheimer is University Research Chair in Democracy and Education at the University of Ottawa and education columnist for CBC Radio's *Ottawa Morning* and *Ontario Today*. His newest, critically acclaimed book is *What Kind of Citizen: Educating Our Children for the Common Good*. In 2002, the *New York Times* ran the headline, "Labor Board Rules That N.Y.U. Denied Tenure to Union Backer." Westheimer was the union backer. He is currently directing (with John Rogers, UCLA) The Inequality Project, investigating what schools in North America are teaching about economic inequality. He tweets his biweekly CBC Radio broadcasts at @joelwestheimer.

INDEX

Olson, Gary, 269
On Being Included (Ahmed), 152
ordoliberalism, 11
Orwell, George: on tyranny, xxxi
Oxford university colleges, 85–6

Paine, Thomas, 17
Pascale, Celine-Marie, 110
Pedagogy of the Oppressed (Freire), 277
Pence, Mike, 261
Pereira, Maria do Mar, 196, 202, 207
Peters, Mike, 285
Pickett, K., 93
Pihama, Leonie, 28
Piketty, Thomas, 93
place-worlds, 163
Podesta, John, 282
politics of evidence, 41–2, 50, 65, 78–81
Pōmare, Eru, 35
Poor People's Campaign, 296
Poor People's Campaign in Atlanta, 294–5
Porter, Eduardo, 257, 258
post-neoliberalism, 109–10, 116
potencias, concept of, 93
Potok, Mark, 279
Povinelli, Elizabeth, 102, 112–13
Presumed Incompetent: The Intersections of Race and Class for Women in Academia, 179
privilege: circuits of, 82; reproduction of, 69
promise and non-promise projects, 186n15
promotion and tenure, 12–14, 209, 240, 246–9, 278
publication industry: cost of production, 14; open-access movement, 14–15
public education: corporatization and privatization of, 67–8, 74; current developments in, 218; fundamental goals of, 218; politics of evidence in struggle for, 78–81; *See also* higher education
public philosophy: benefits for academy, 236, 240–1; categorization of, 238–9; definition of, 249n6; publication standards, 236; *vs.* traditional

scholarship, 243–6; value of, 238–9, 243–5
public schools *See* K-12 schools

Qualitative Inquiry (journal), 47
qualitative research: assessment of, 104–5; disciplining of, 104, 107–8; dominant ideas of, 115; evolution of, 103–4, 115–16; methodology, 103, 113; objectivity debates, 107; shared standards, 105–6
Quijano, A., 181

Radder, H., 200
Raspail, Jean, 268
Readings, Bill, 114
Reagan, Nancy, 267
Reay, Diane, 210
recognition: construct of, 169, 170; critiques of, 175; desire for, 175, 176; forms of, 174, 176; liberal academy and discourses of, 177–8; political theories of, 174–5
recognition-based politics, 174, 175
reconciliation, 185n10
refusal: Indigenous scholars on, 180–1; knowledge formation and, 181; Marcuse's work on theory of, 180; notion of, 168, 169, 170; *vs.* resistance, 181; to self-promotion, 183; *See also* Black refusal
refusing the university, 171, 183–4
research: community-based, 98; corporate funding of, 57; culturally responsible approaches in, 289; decolonizing, 32; desire-based, 161; ethically accepted, 48; funding for clinical medical, 226; importance for the academy, 242–3; infrastructure, 29–30, 31; legitimization of, 48–9; measurement of impact of, 21, 25–7, 28, 38, 49–50; mixed-methods of, 44; new forms of, 27; normative ideologies about, 21–2; paradigm wars, 52; post-qualitative, 112–14; practices of power in, 193; in pre-neoliberal university, 22; problem of quality of, 243;